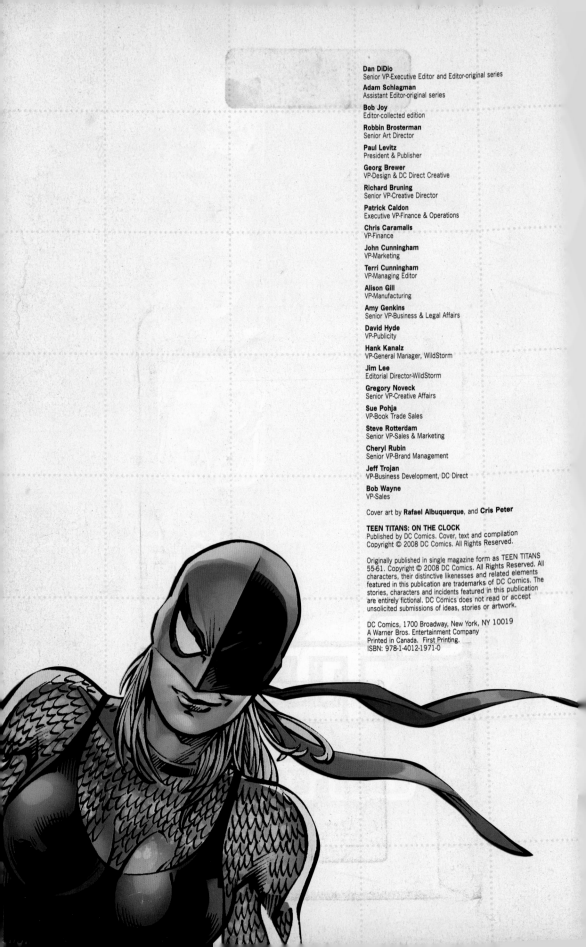

Dan DiDio
Senior VP-Executive Editor and Editor-original series

Adam Schlagman
Assistant Editor-original series

Bob Joy
Editor-collected edition

Robbin Brosterman
Senior Art Director

Paul Levitz
President & Publisher

Georg Brewer
VP-Design & DC Direct Creative

Richard Bruning
Senior VP-Creative Director

Patrick Caldon
Executive VP-Finance & Operations

Chris Caramalis
VP-Finance

John Cunningham
VP-Marketing

Terri Cunningham
VP-Managing Editor

Alison Gill
VP-Manufacturing

Amy Genkins
Senior VP-Business & Legal Affairs

David Hyde
VP-Publicity

Hank Kanalz
VP-General Manager, WildStorm

Jim Lee
Editorial Director-WildStorm

Gregory Noveck
Senior VP-Creative Affairs

Sue Pohja
VP-Book Trade Sales

Steve Rotterdam
Senior VP-Sales & Marketing

Cheryl Rubin
Senior VP-Brand Management

Jeff Trojan
VP-Business Development, DC Direct

Bob Wayne
VP-Sales

Cover art by **Rafael Albuquerque**, and **Cris Peter**

TEEN TITANS: ON THE CLOCK
Published by DC Comics. Cover, text and compilation

DC Comics, 1700 Broadway, New York, NY 10019
A Warner Bros. Entertainment Company
Printed in Canada. First Printing.
ISBN: 978-1-4012-1971-0

Teen Titans

On The Clock

Sean McKeever Writer

Jamal Igle
Eddy Barrows
Carlos Rodriguez
Pencillers

Ruy José
Jimmy Palmiotti

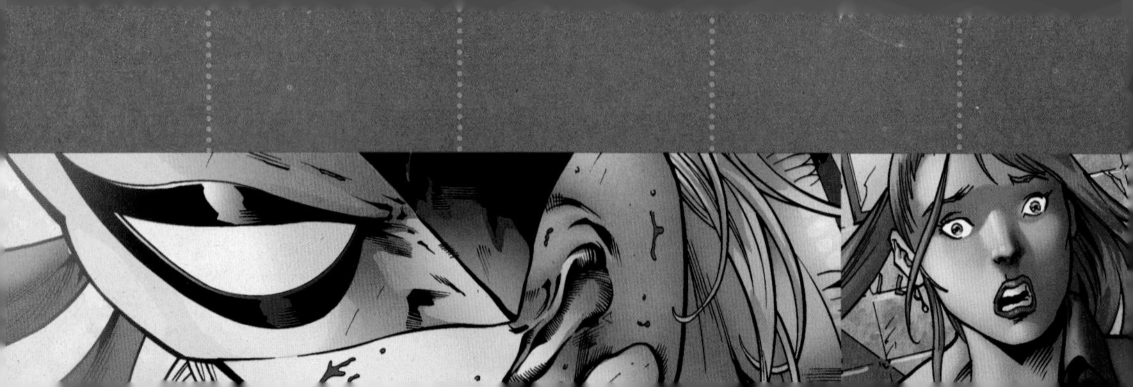

TEEN TITANS 55 - Eddy Barrows, Rob Hunter and Rod Reis

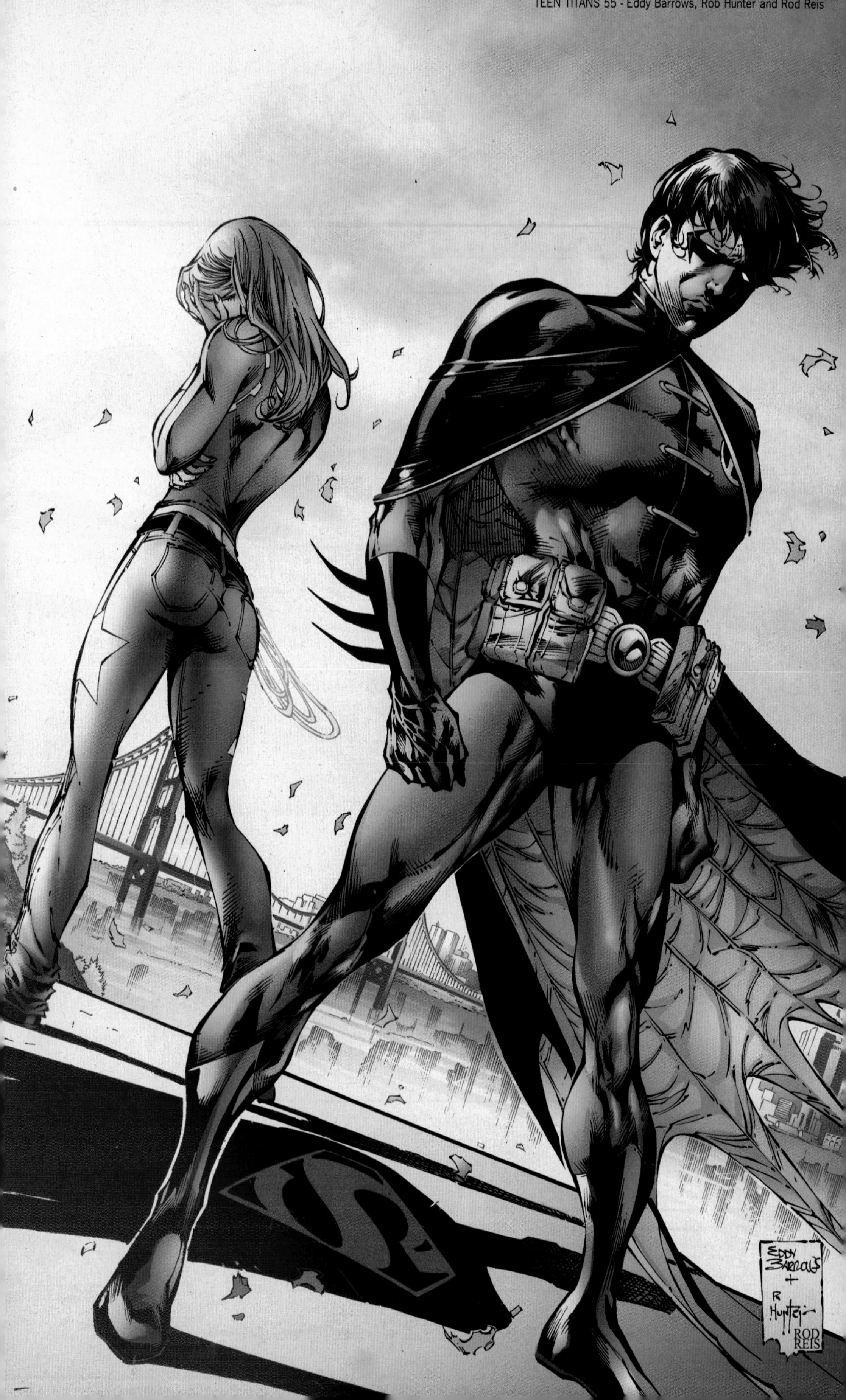
EDDY BARROWS +
R HUNTER
ROD REIS

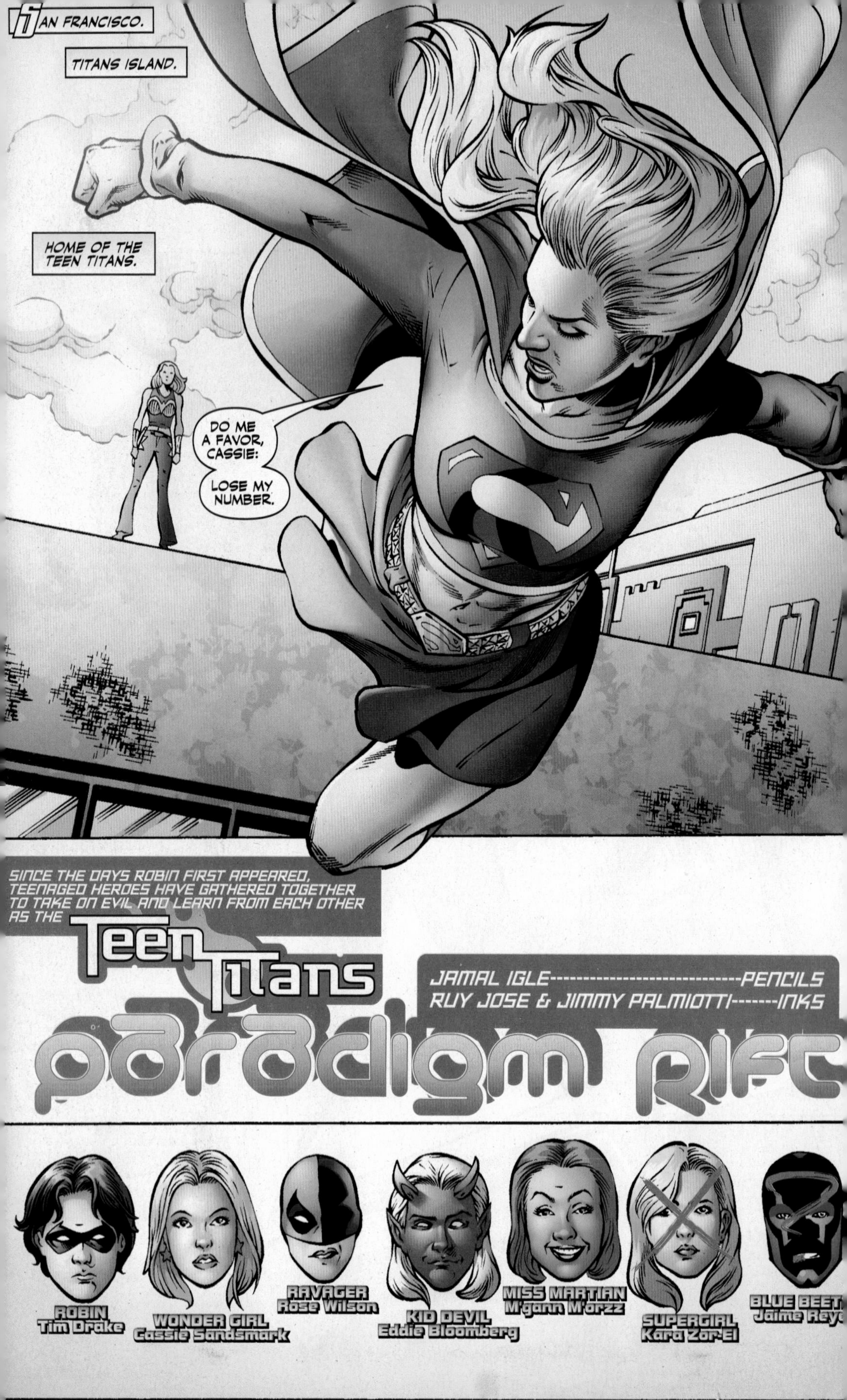
SAN FRANCISCO.
TITANS ISLAND.
HOME OF THE TEEN TITANS.
DO ME A FAVOR, CASSIE:
LOSE MY NUMBER.
SINCE THE DAYS ROBIN FIRST APPEARED, TEENAGED HEROES HAVE GATHERED TOGETHER TO TAKE ON EVIL AND LEARN FROM EACH OTHER AS THE
Teen Titans
JAMAL IGLE------------------------------PENCILS
RUY JOSE & JIMMY PALMIOTTI-------INKS
paradigm rift
ROBIN Tim Drake
WONDER GIRL Cassie Sandsmark
RAVAGER Rose Wilson
KID DEVIL Eddie Bloomberg
MISS MARTIAN M'gann M'orzz
SUPERGIRL Kara Zor-El
BLUE BEET Jaime Rey

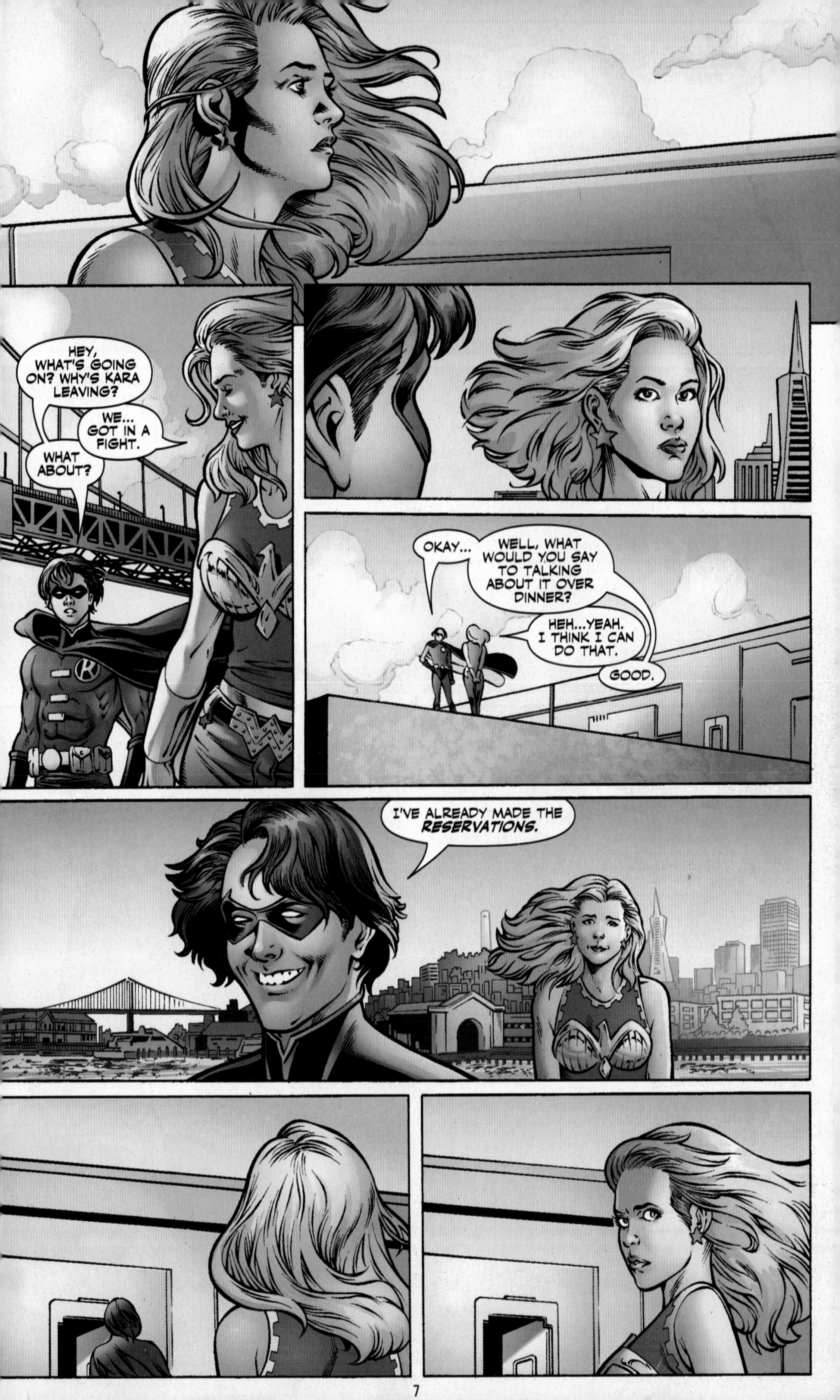

HEY, WHAT'S GOING ON? WHY'S KARA LEAVING?
WE... GOT IN A FIGHT.
WHAT ABOUT?
OKAY...
WELL, WHAT WOULD YOU SAY TO TALKING ABOUT IT OVER DINNER?
HEH...YEAH. I THINK I CAN DO THAT.
GOOD.
I'VE ALREADY MADE THE *RESERVATIONS.*

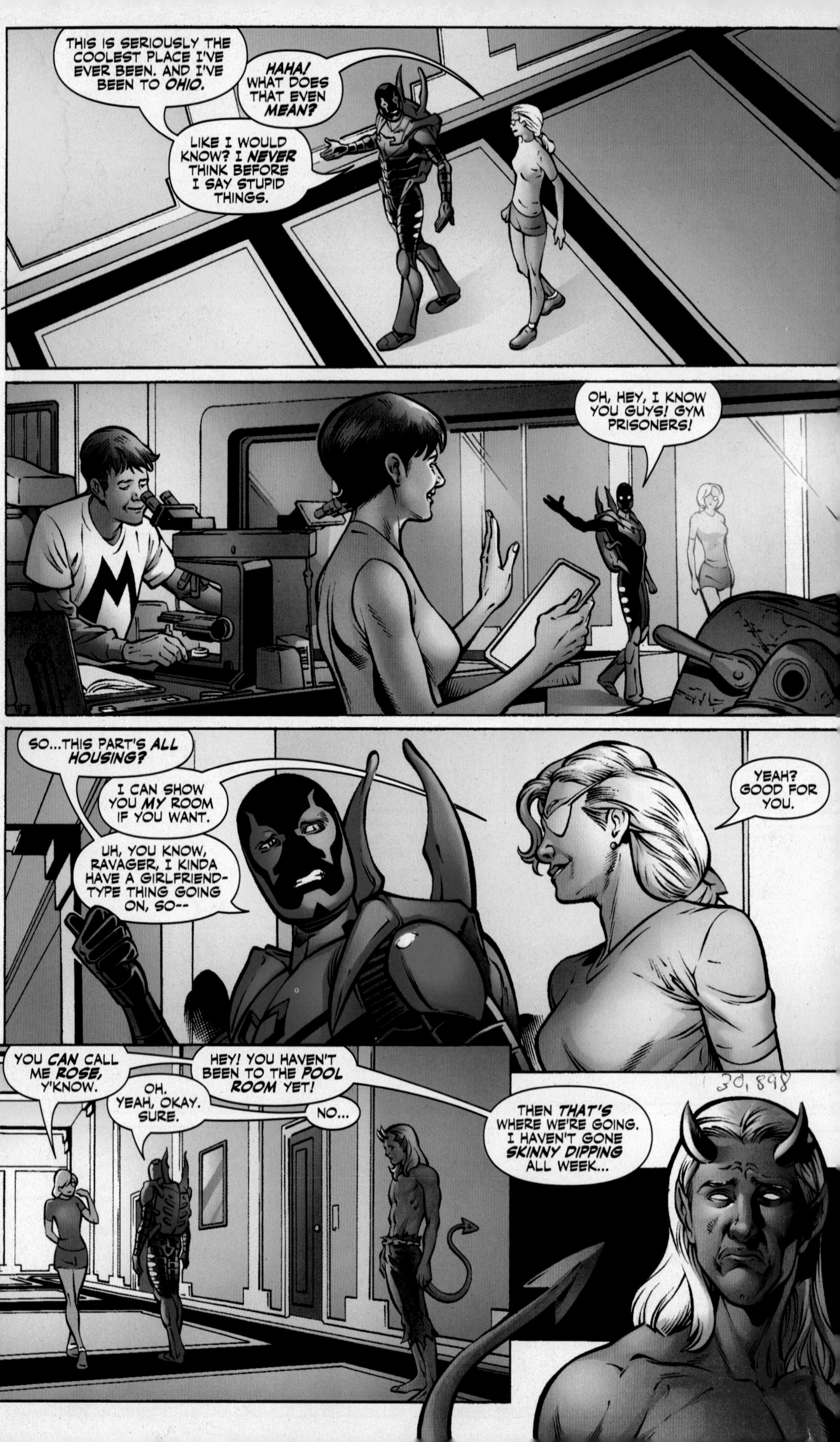
THIS IS SERIOUSLY THE COOLEST PLACE I'VE EVER BEEN. AND I'VE BEEN TO OHIO.
HAHA! WHAT DOES THAT EVEN MEAN?
LIKE I WOULD KNOW? I NEVER THINK BEFORE I SAY STUPID THINGS.
OH, HEY, I KNOW YOU GUYS! GYM PRISONERS!
SO...THIS PART'S ALL HOUSING?
I CAN SHOW YOU MY ROOM IF YOU WANT.
UH, YOU KNOW, RAVAGER, I KINDA HAVE A GIRLFRIEND-TYPE THING GOING ON, SO--
YEAH? GOOD FOR YOU.
YOU CAN CALL ME ROSE, Y'KNOW.
OH. YEAH, OKAY. SURE.
HEY! YOU HAVEN'T BEEN TO THE POOL ROOM YET!
NO...
THEN THAT'S WHERE WE'RE GOING. I HAVEN'T GONE SKINNY DIPPING ALL WEEK...

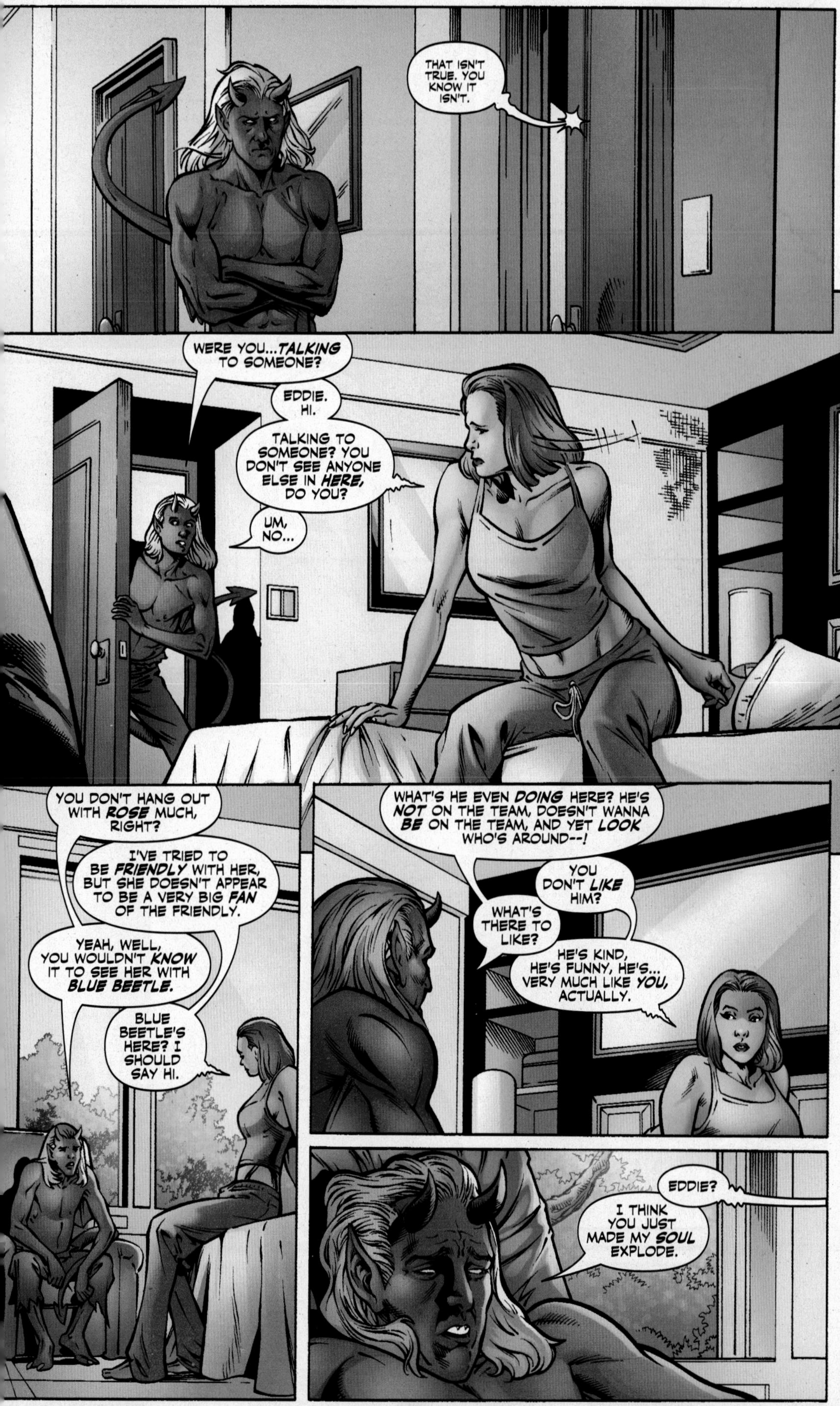

THAT ISN'T TRUE. YOU KNOW IT ISN'T.
WERE YOU...TALKING TO SOMEONE?
EDDIE. HI.
TALKING TO SOMEONE? YOU DON'T SEE ANYONE ELSE IN HERE, DO YOU?
UM, NO...
YOU DON'T HANG OUT WITH ROSE MUCH, RIGHT?
I'VE TRIED TO BE FRIENDLY WITH HER, BUT SHE DOESN'T APPEAR TO BE A VERY BIG FAN OF THE FRIENDLY.
YEAH, WELL, YOU WOULDN'T KNOW IT TO SEE HER WITH BLUE BEETLE.
BLUE BEETLE'S HERE? I SHOULD SAY HI.
WHAT'S HE EVEN DOING HERE? HE'S NOT ON THE TEAM, DOESN'T WANNA BE ON THE TEAM, AND YET LOOK WHO'S AROUND--!
YOU DON'T LIKE HIM?
WHAT'S THERE TO LIKE?
HE'S KIND, HE'S FUNNY, HE'S... VERY MUCH LIKE YOU, ACTUALLY.
EDDIE?
I THINK YOU JUST MADE MY SOUL EXPLODE.

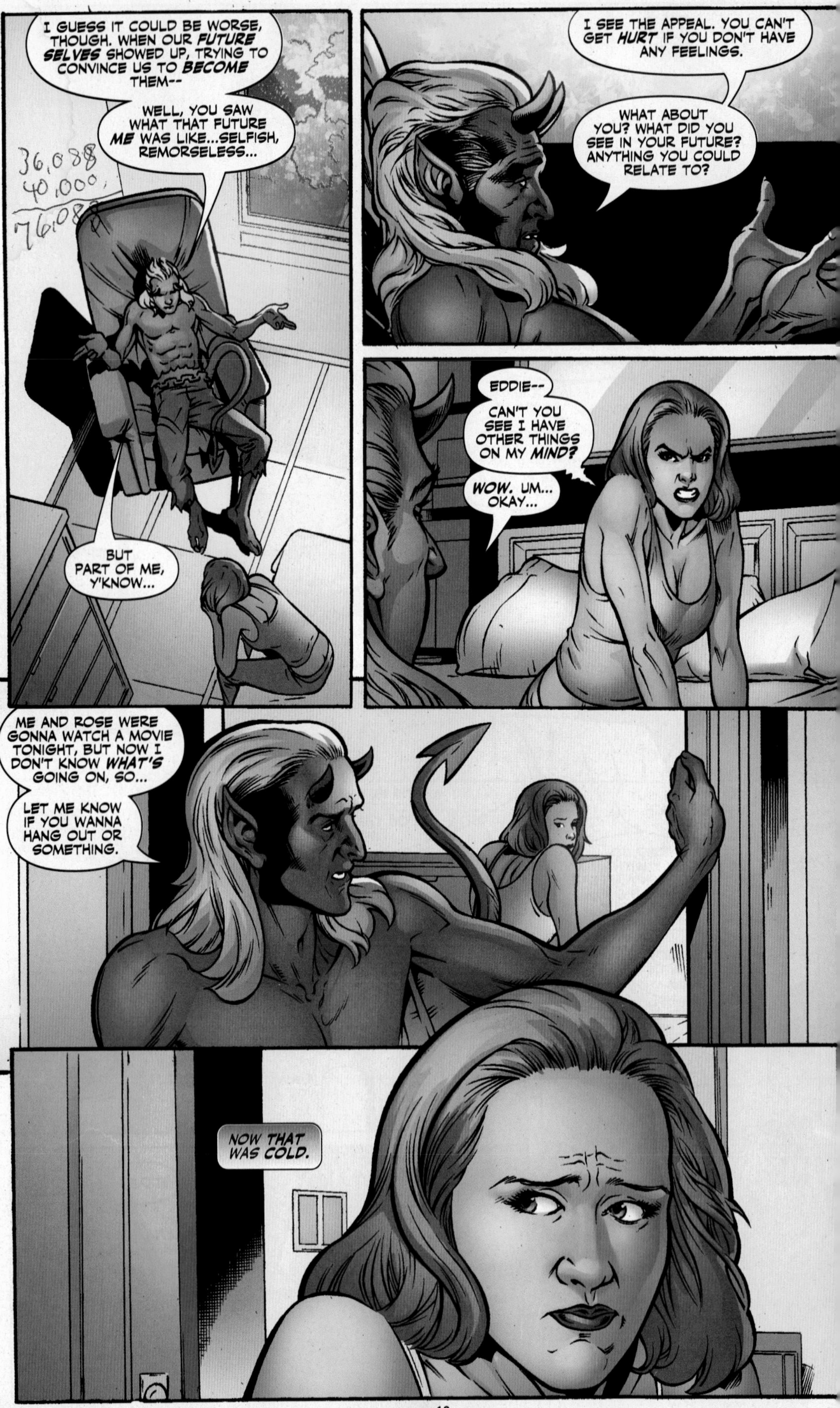
I GUESS IT COULD BE WORSE, THOUGH. WHEN OUR FUTURE SELVES SHOWED UP, TRYING TO CONVINCE US TO BECOME THEM--
WELL, YOU SAW WHAT THAT FUTURE ME WAS LIKE...SELFISH, REMORSELESS...
BUT PART OF ME, Y'KNOW...
I SEE THE APPEAL. YOU CAN'T GET HURT IF YOU DON'T HAVE ANY FEELINGS.
WHAT ABOUT YOU? WHAT DID YOU SEE IN YOUR FUTURE? ANYTHING YOU COULD RELATE TO?
EDDIE--
CAN'T YOU SEE I HAVE OTHER THINGS ON MY MIND?
WOW. UM... OKAY...
ME AND ROSE WERE GONNA WATCH A MOVIE TONIGHT, BUT NOW I DON'T KNOW WHAT'S GOING ON, SO...
LET ME KNOW IF YOU WANNA HANG OUT OR SOMETHING.
NOW THAT WAS COLD.

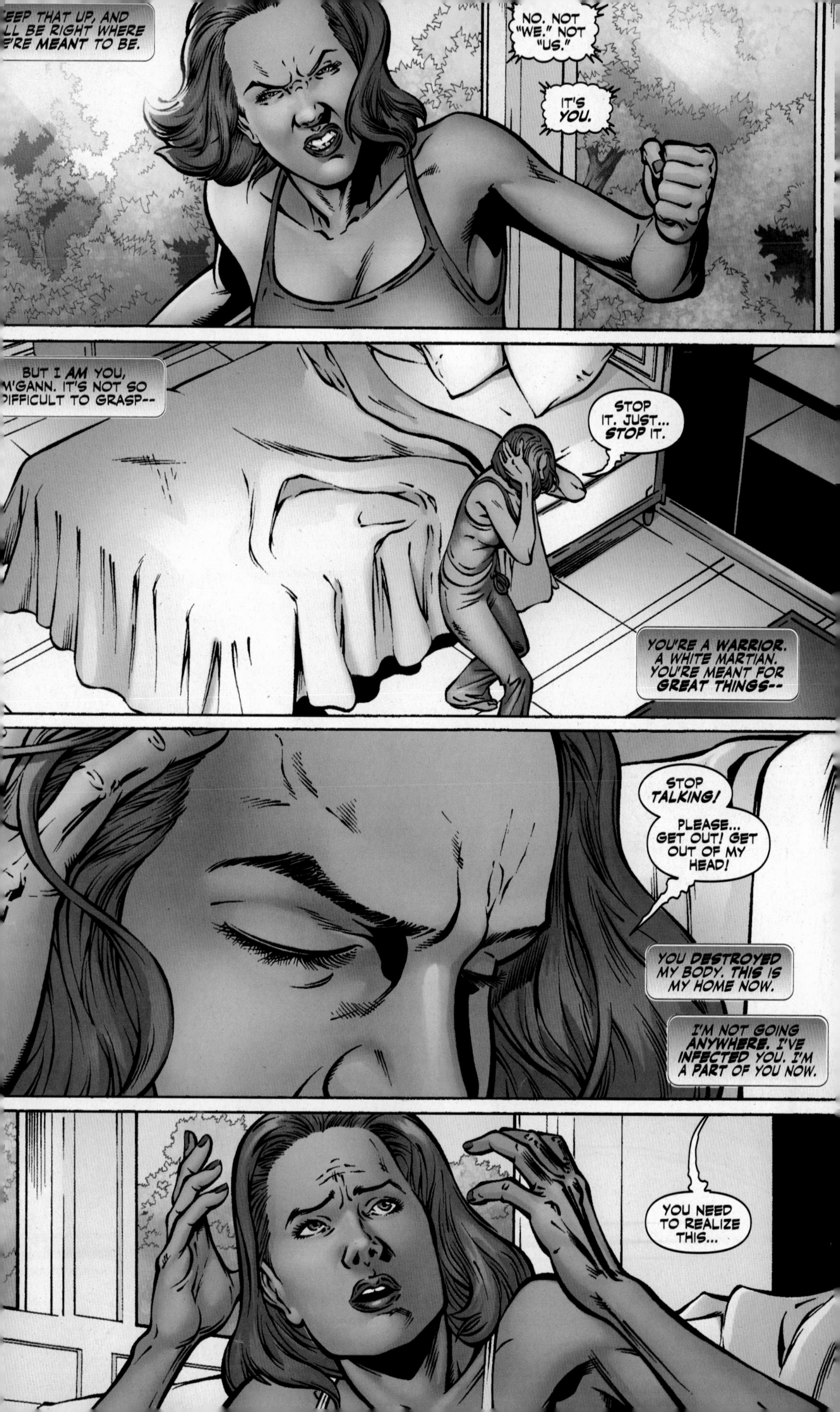
EEP THAT UP, AND
LL BE RIGHT WHERE
'RE MEANT TO BE.
NO. NOT "WE." NOT "US."
IT'S YOU.
BUT I AM YOU, M'GANN. IT'S NOT SO DIFFICULT TO GRASP--
STOP IT. JUST... STOP IT.
YOU'RE A WARRIOR. A WHITE MARTIAN. YOU'RE MEANT FOR GREAT THINGS--
STOP TALKING!
PLEASE... GET OUT! GET OUT OF MY HEAD!
YOU DESTROYED MY BODY. THIS IS MY HOME NOW.
I'M NOT GOING ANYWHERE. I'VE INFECTED YOU. I'M A PART OF YOU NOW.
YOU NEED TO REALIZE THIS...

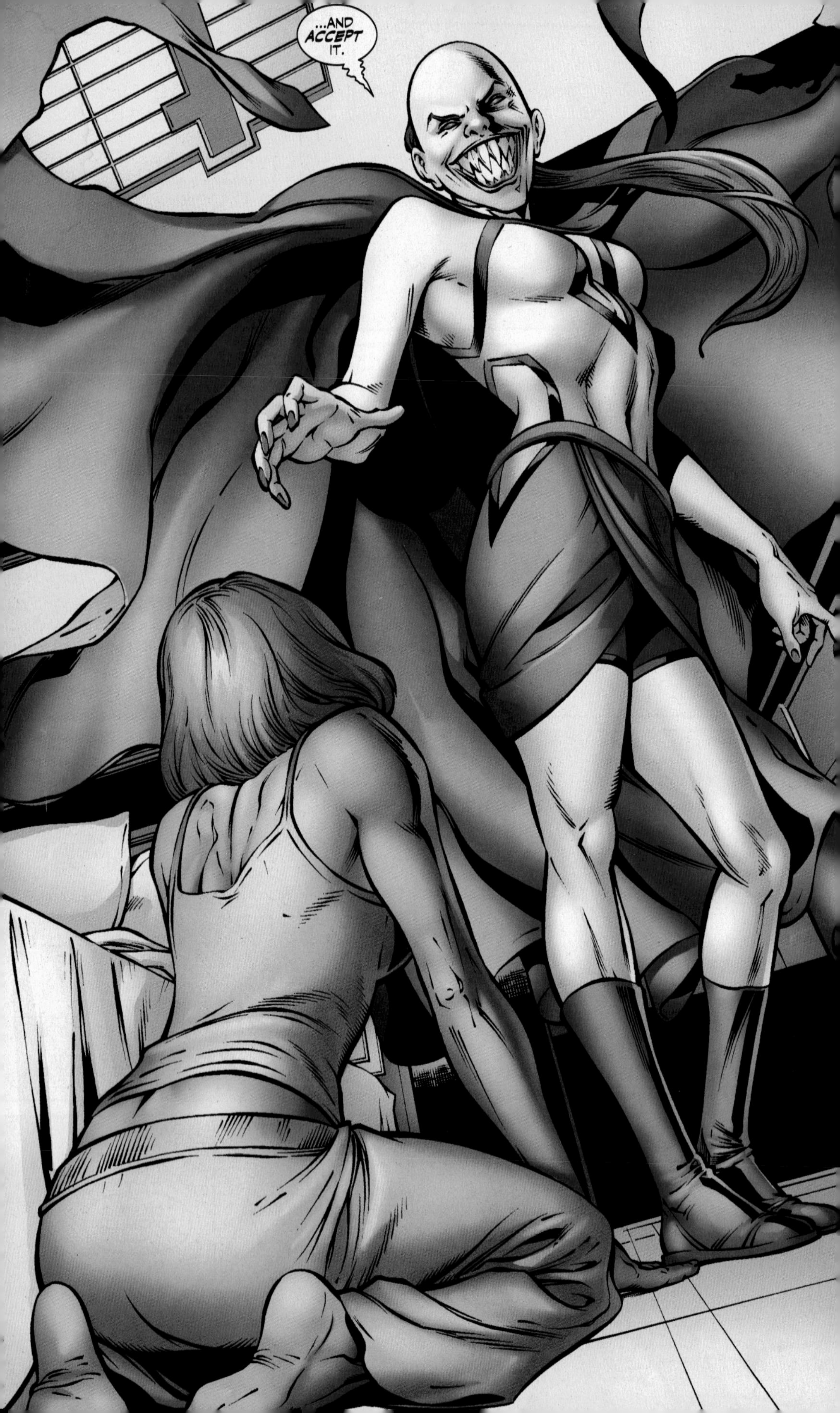
...AND ACCEPT IT.

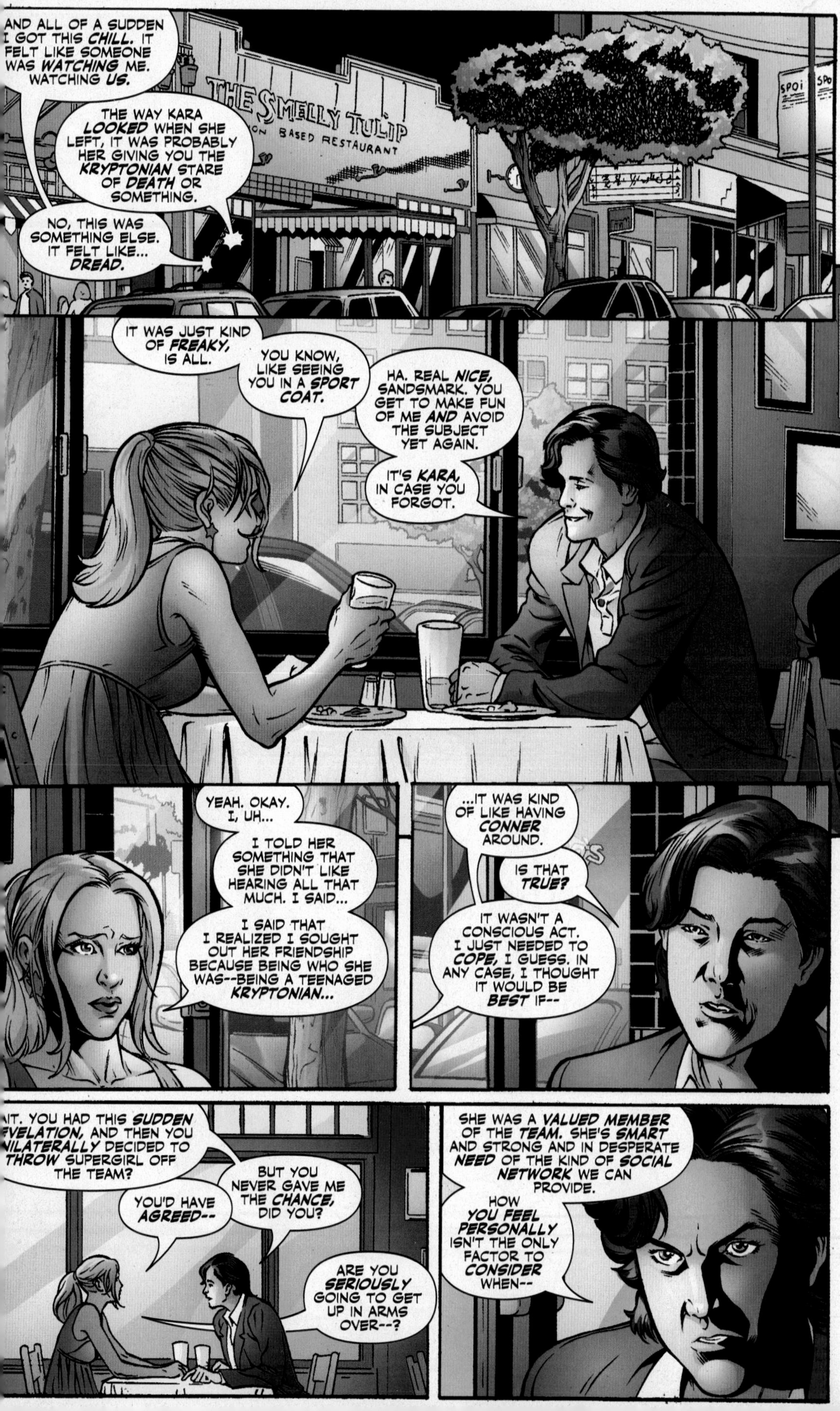
AND ALL OF A SUDDEN I GOT THIS CHILL. IT FELT LIKE SOMEONE WAS WATCHING ME. WATCHING US.
THE WAY KARA LOOKED WHEN SHE LEFT, IT WAS PROBABLY HER GIVING YOU THE KRYPTONIAN STARE OF DEATH OR SOMETHING.
NO, THIS WAS SOMETHING ELSE. IT FELT LIKE... DREAD.
THE SMELLY TULIP
BASED RESTAURANT
IT WAS JUST KIND OF FREAKY, IS ALL.
YOU KNOW, LIKE SEEING YOU IN A SPORT COAT.
HA. REAL NICE, SANDSMARK. YOU GET TO MAKE FUN OF ME AND AVOID THE SUBJECT YET AGAIN.
IT'S KARA, IN CASE YOU FORGOT.
YEAH. OKAY. I, UH...
I TOLD HER SOMETHING THAT SHE DIDN'T LIKE HEARING ALL THAT MUCH. I SAID...
I SAID THAT I REALIZED I SOUGHT OUT HER FRIENDSHIP BECAUSE BEING WHO SHE WAS--BEING A TEENAGED KRYPTONIAN...
...IT WAS KIND OF LIKE HAVING CONNER AROUND.
IS THAT TRUE?
IT WASN'T A CONSCIOUS ACT. I JUST NEEDED TO COPE, I GUESS. IN ANY CASE, I THOUGHT IT WOULD BE BEST IF--
AIT. YOU HAD THIS SUDDEN EVELATION, AND THEN YOU NILATERALLY DECIDED TO THROW SUPERGIRL OFF THE TEAM?
YOU'D HAVE AGREED--
BUT YOU NEVER GAVE ME THE CHANCE, DID YOU?
ARE YOU SERIOUSLY GOING TO GET UP IN ARMS OVER--?
SHE WAS A VALUED MEMBER OF THE TEAM. SHE'S SMART AND STRONG AND IN DESPERATE NEED OF THE KIND OF SOCIAL NETWORK WE CAN PROVIDE.
HOW YOU FEEL PERSONALLY ISN'T THE ONLY FACTOR TO CONSIDER WHEN--

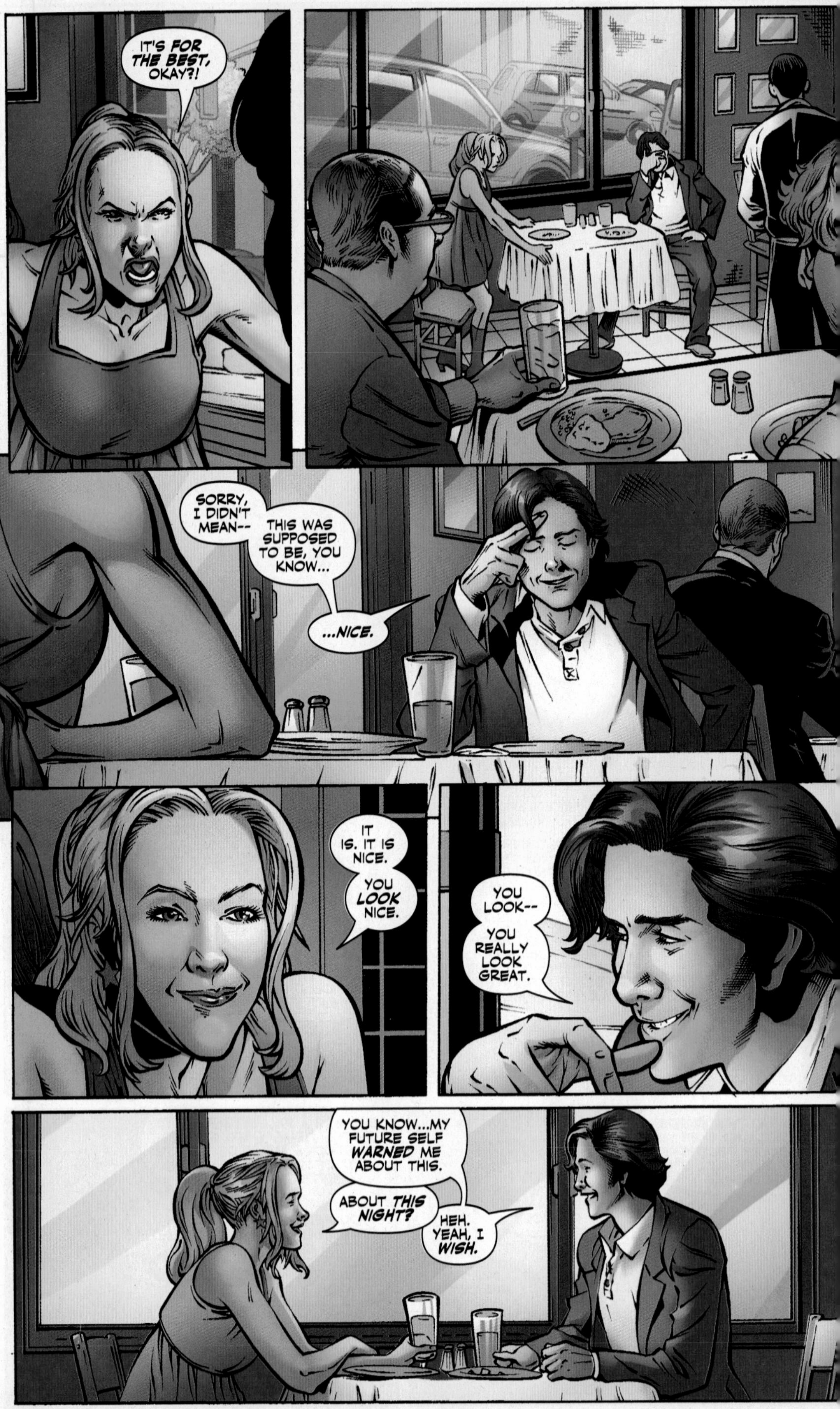
IT'S FOR THE BEST, OKAY?!
SORRY, I DIDN'T MEAN--
THIS WAS SUPPOSED TO BE, YOU KNOW...
...NICE.
IT IS. IT IS NICE.
YOU LOOK NICE.
YOU LOOK--
YOU REALLY LOOK GREAT.
YOU KNOW...MY FUTURE SELF WARNED ME ABOUT THIS.
ABOUT THIS NIGHT?
HEH. YEAH, I WISH.

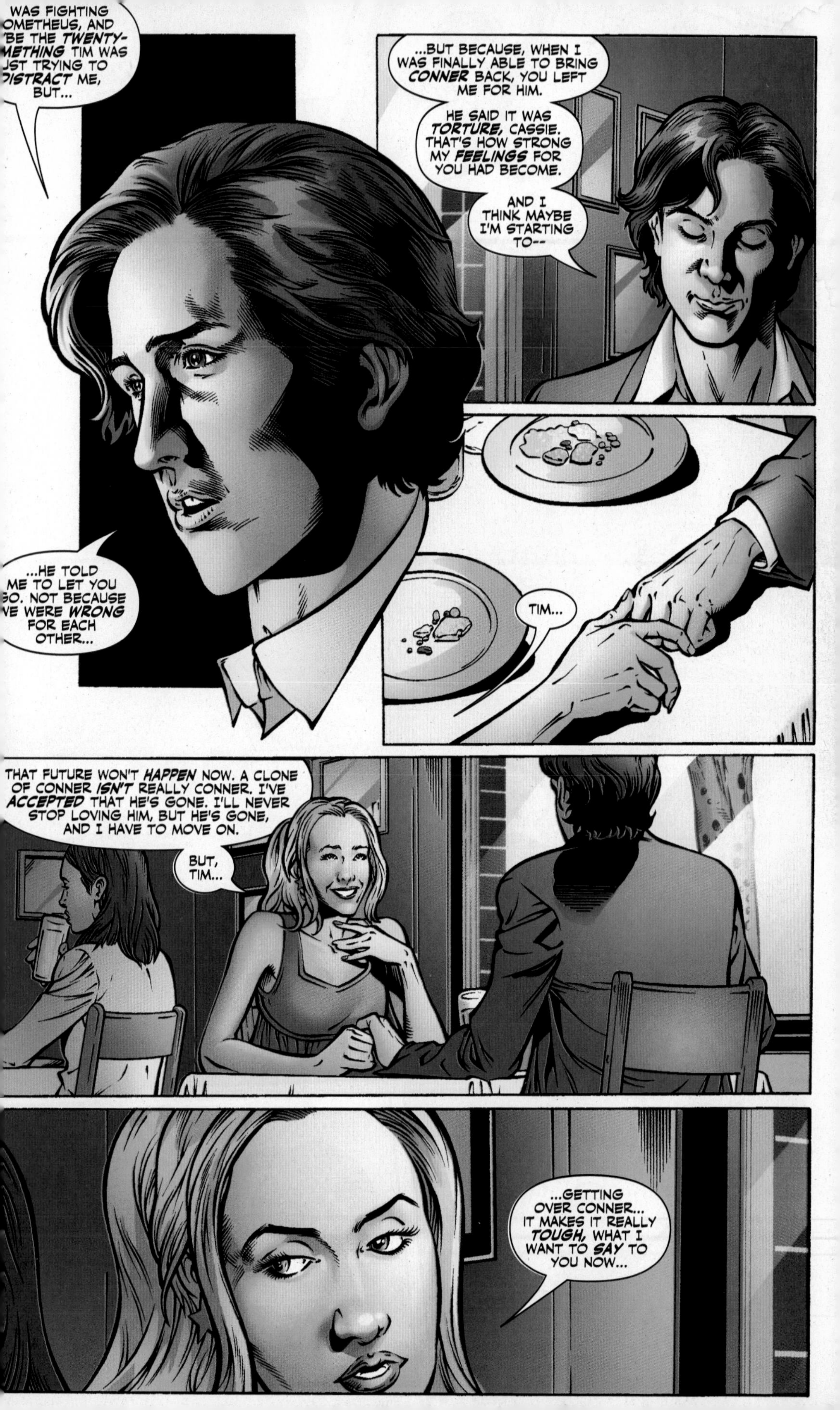
WAS FIGHTING
OMETHEUS, AND
BE THE TWENTY-
METHING TIM WAS
JST TRYING TO
DISTRACT ME,
BUT...
...BUT BECAUSE, WHEN I WAS FINALLY ABLE TO BRING CONNER BACK, YOU LEFT ME FOR HIM.
HE SAID IT WAS TORTURE, CASSIE. THAT'S HOW STRONG MY FEELINGS FOR YOU HAD BECOME.
AND I THINK MAYBE I'M STARTING TO--
...HE TOLD ME TO LET YOU GO. NOT BECAUSE VE WERE WRONG FOR EACH OTHER...
TIM...
THAT FUTURE WON'T HAPPEN NOW. A CLONE OF CONNER ISN'T REALLY CONNER. I'VE ACCEPTED THAT HE'S GONE. I'LL NEVER STOP LOVING HIM, BUT HE'S GONE, AND I HAVE TO MOVE ON.
BUT, TIM...
...GETTING OVER CONNER... IT MAKES IT REALLY TOUGH, WHAT I WANT TO SAY TO YOU NOW...

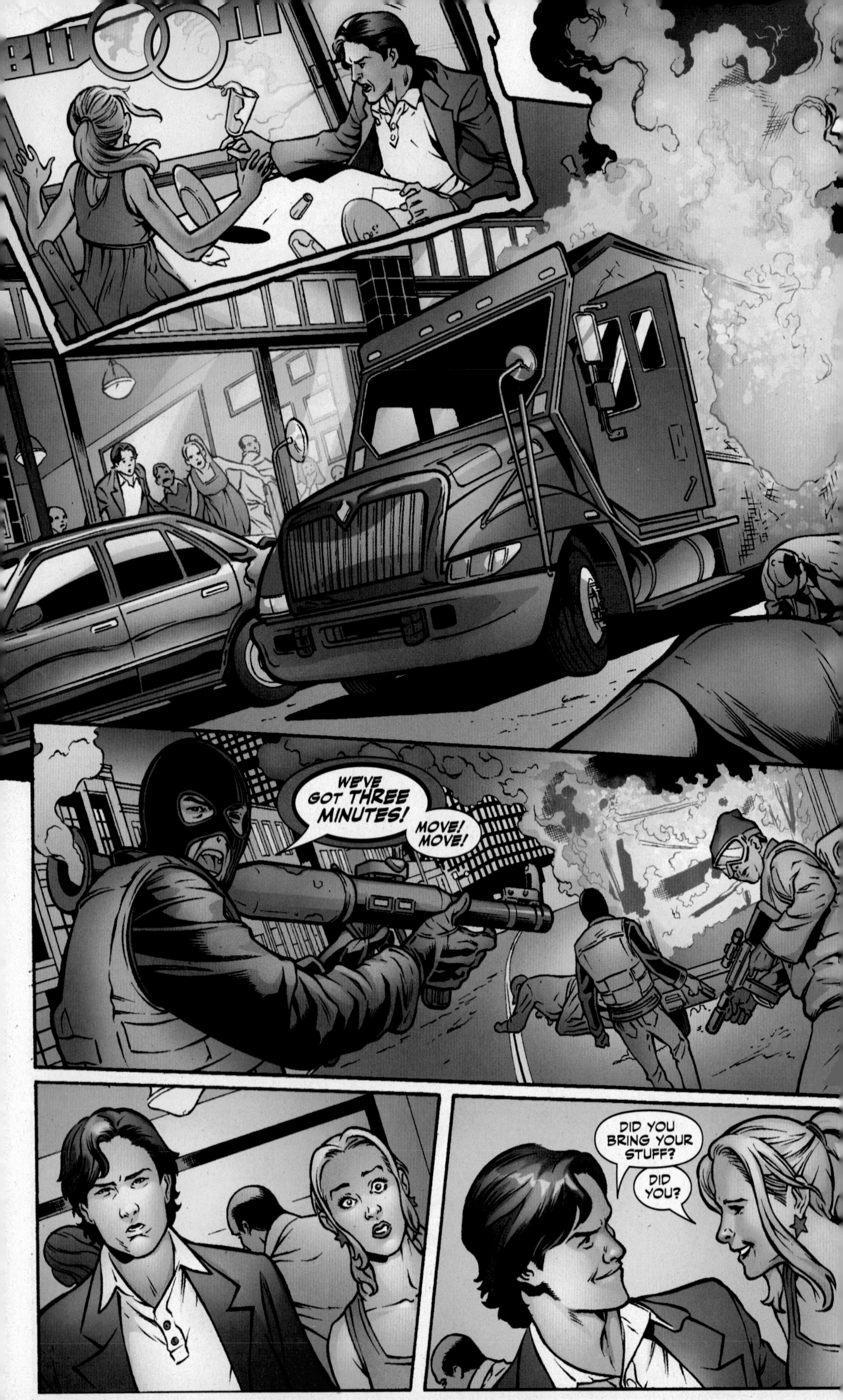
BWOOM!!
WE'VE GOT THREE MINUTES!
MOVE! MOVE!
DID YOU BRING YOUR STUFF?
DID YOU?

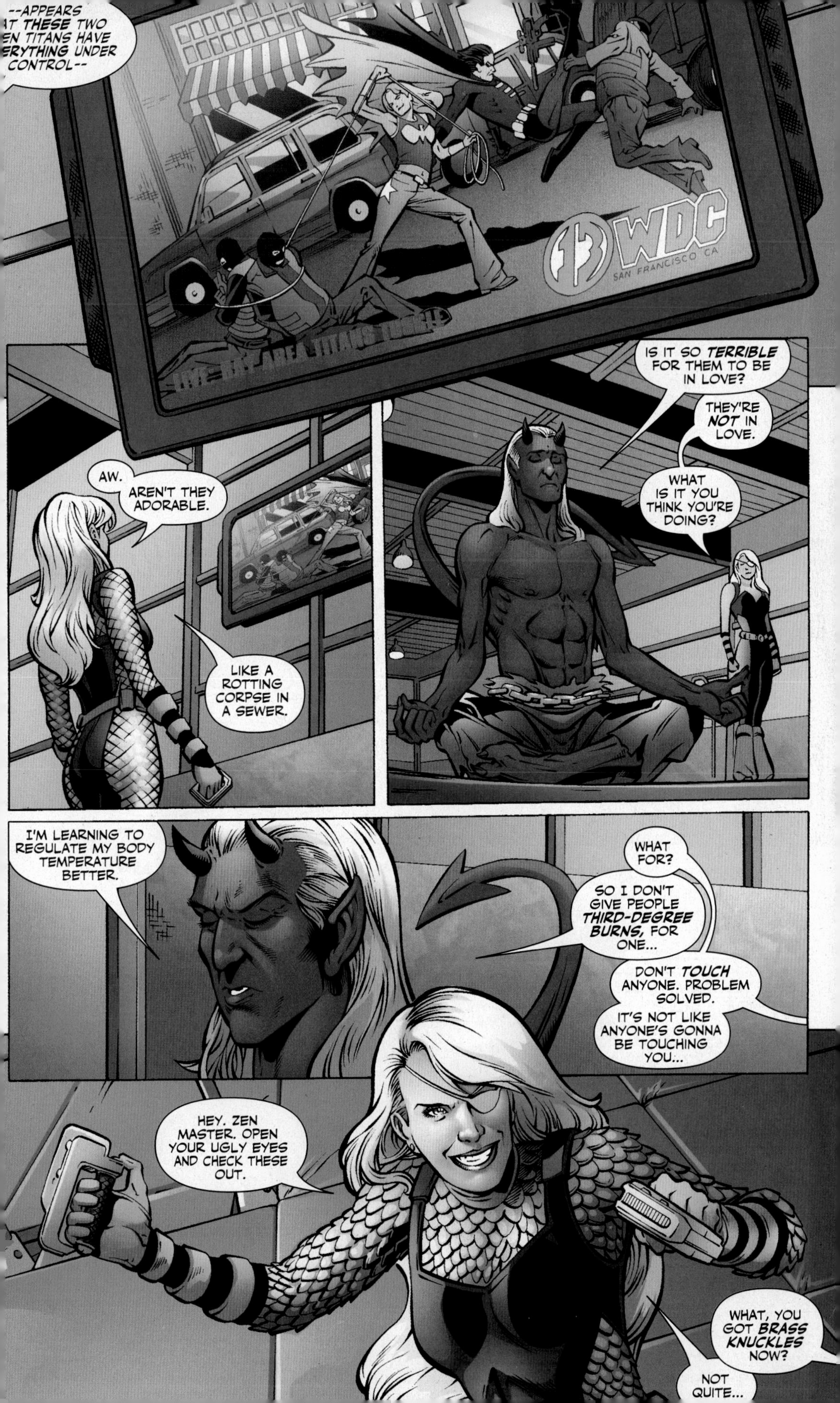
--APPEARS
AT THESE TWO
EN TITANS HAVE
ERYTHING UNDER
CONTROL--
WDC
SAN FRANCISCO CA
AW.
AREN'T THEY ADORABLE.
LIKE A ROTTING CORPSE IN A SEWER.
IS IT SO TERRIBLE FOR THEM TO BE IN LOVE?
THEY'RE NOT IN LOVE.
WHAT IS IT YOU THINK YOU'RE DOING?
I'M LEARNING TO REGULATE MY BODY TEMPERATURE BETTER.
WHAT FOR?
SO I DON'T GIVE PEOPLE THIRD-DEGREE BURNS, FOR ONE...
DON'T TOUCH ANYONE. PROBLEM SOLVED.
IT'S NOT LIKE ANYONE'S GONNA BE TOUCHING YOU...
HEY. ZEN MASTER. OPEN YOUR UGLY EYES AND CHECK THESE OUT.
WHAT, YOU GOT BRASS KNUCKLES NOW?
NOT QUITE...

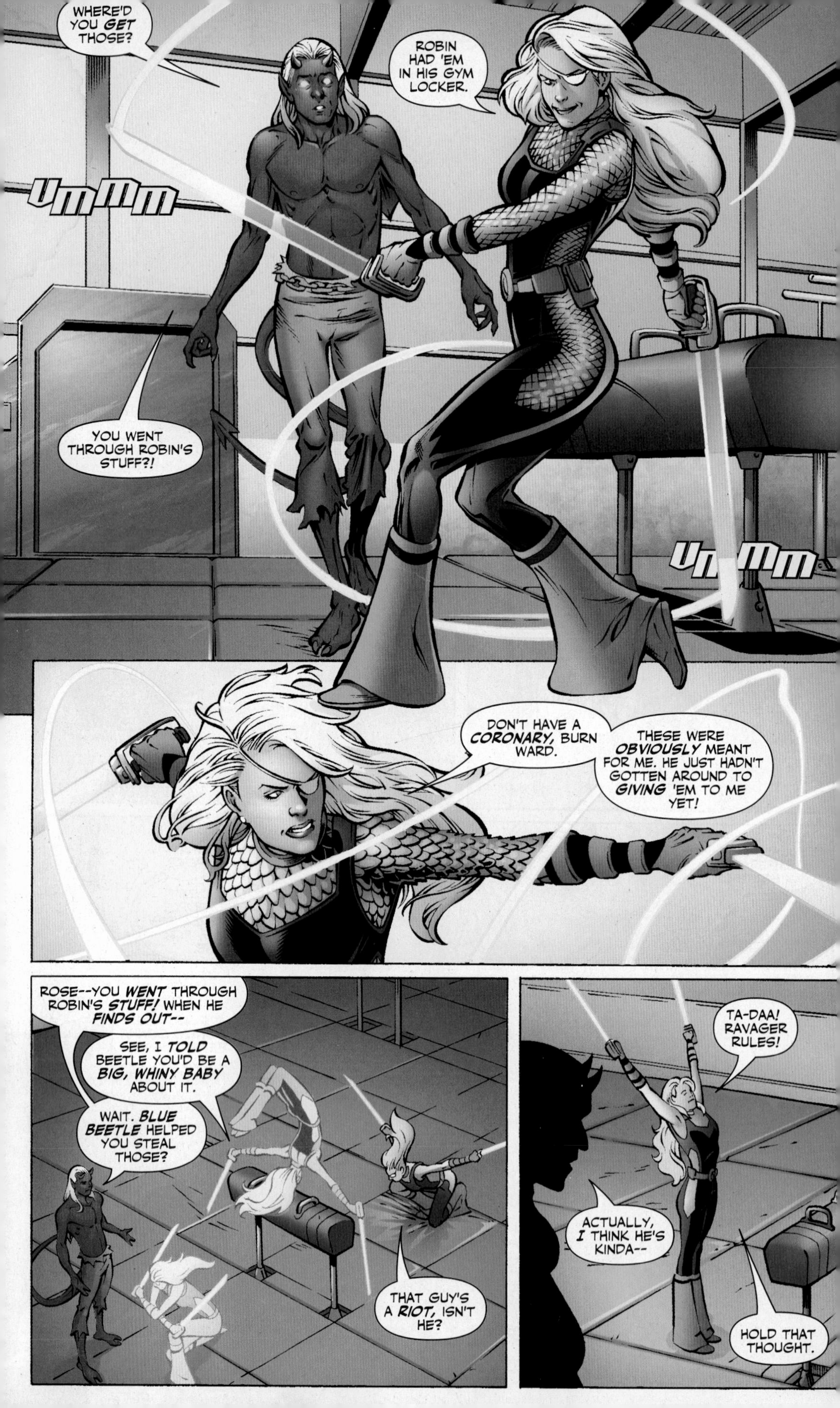
WHERE'D YOU *GET* THOSE?
ROBIN HAD 'EM IN HIS GYM LOCKER.
VMMM
YOU WENT THROUGH ROBIN'S STUFF?!
VMMM
DON'T HAVE A *CORONARY,* BURN WARD.
THESE WERE *OBVIOUSLY* MEANT FOR ME. HE JUST HADN'T GOTTEN AROUND TO *GIVING* 'EM TO ME YET!
ROSE--YOU *WENT* THROUGH ROBIN'S *STUFF!* WHEN HE *FINDS OUT--*
SEE, I *TOLD* BEETLE YOU'D BE A *BIG, WHINY BABY* ABOUT IT.
WAIT. *BLUE BEETLE* HELPED YOU STEAL THOSE?
THAT GUY'S A *RIOT,* ISN'T HE?
TA-DAA! RAVAGER RULES!
ACTUALLY, *I* THINK HE'S KINDA--
HOLD THAT THOUGHT.

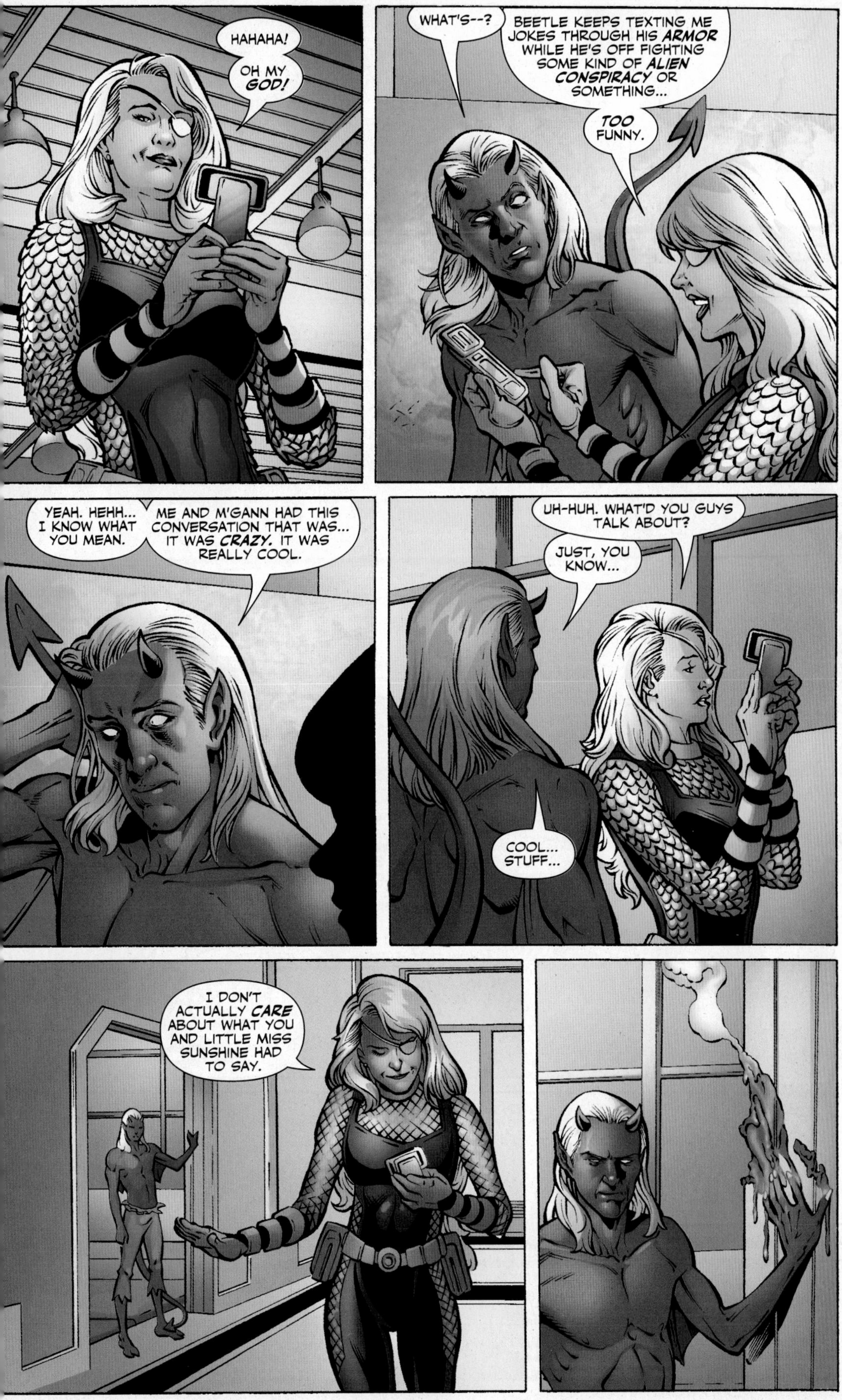
HAHAHA!
OH MY GOD!
WHAT'S--?
BEETLE KEEPS TEXTING ME JOKES THROUGH HIS ARMOR WHILE HE'S OFF FIGHTING SOME KIND OF ALIEN CONSPIRACY OR SOMETHING...
TOO FUNNY.
YEAH. HEHH... I KNOW WHAT YOU MEAN.
ME AND M'GANN HAD THIS CONVERSATION THAT WAS... IT WAS CRAZY. IT WAS REALLY COOL.
UH-HUH. WHAT'D YOU GUYS TALK ABOUT?
JUST, YOU KNOW...
COOL... STUFF...
I DON'T ACTUALLY CARE ABOUT WHAT YOU AND LITTLE MISS SUNSHINE HAD TO SAY.

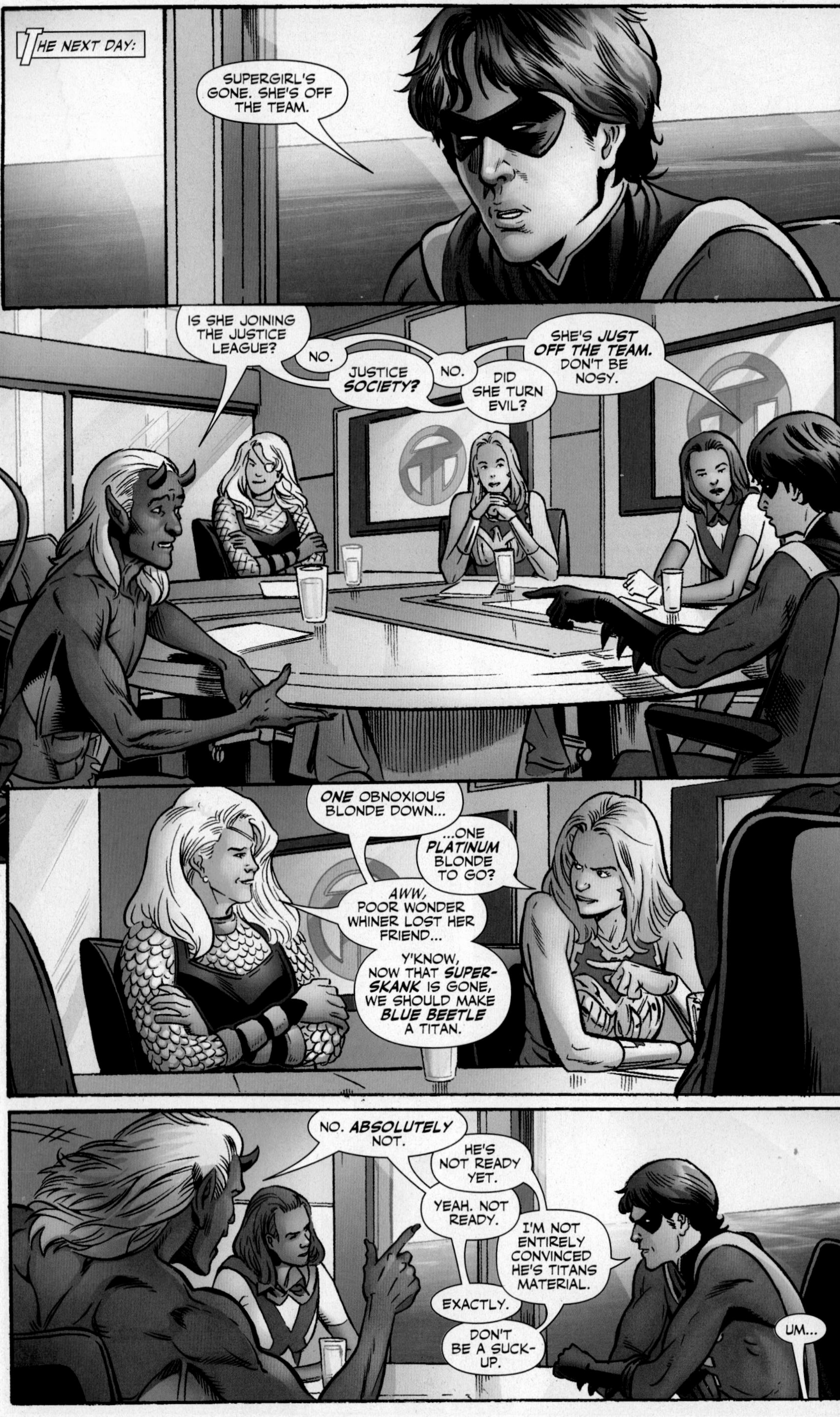
THE NEXT DAY:
SUPERGIRL'S GONE. SHE'S OFF THE TEAM.
IS SHE JOINING THE JUSTICE LEAGUE?
NO.
JUSTICE SOCIETY?
NO.
DID SHE TURN EVIL?
SHE'S JUST OFF THE TEAM. DON'T BE NOSY.
ONE OBNOXIOUS BLONDE DOWN...
...ONE PLATINUM BLONDE TO GO?
AWW, POOR WONDER WHINER LOST HER FRIEND...
Y'KNOW, NOW THAT SUPER-SKANK IS GONE, WE SHOULD MAKE BLUE BEETLE A TITAN.
NO. ABSOLUTELY NOT.
HE'S NOT READY YET.
YEAH. NOT READY.
I'M NOT ENTIRELY CONVINCED HE'S TITANS MATERIAL.
EXACTLY.
DON'T BE A SUCK-UP.
UM...

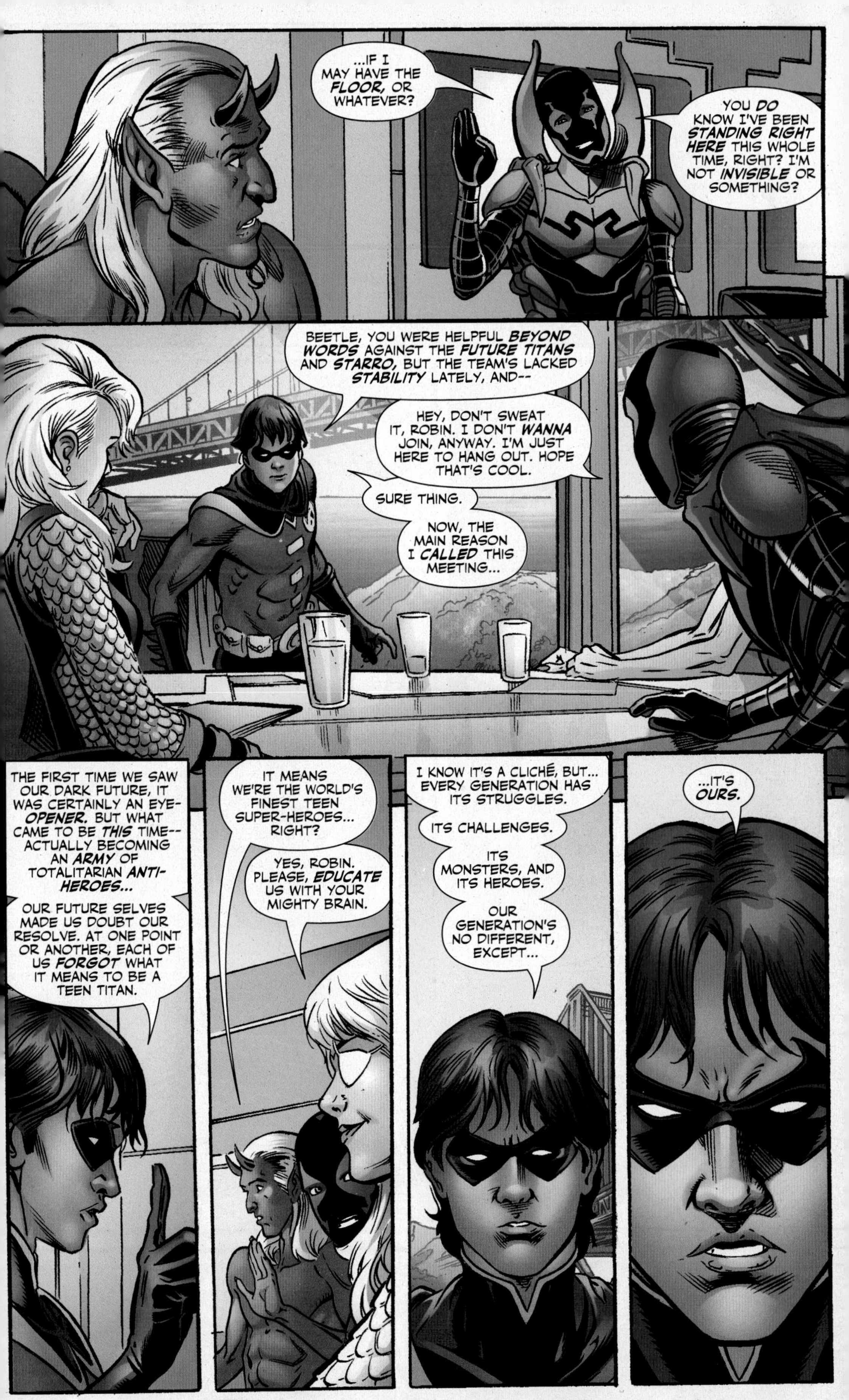
...IF I MAY HAVE THE FLOOR, OR WHATEVER?
YOU DO KNOW I'VE BEEN STANDING RIGHT HERE THIS WHOLE TIME, RIGHT? I'M NOT INVISIBLE OR SOMETHING?
BEETLE, YOU WERE HELPFUL BEYOND WORDS AGAINST THE FUTURE TITANS AND STARRO, BUT THE TEAM'S LACKED STABILITY LATELY, AND--
HEY, DON'T SWEAT IT, ROBIN. I DON'T WANNA JOIN, ANYWAY. I'M JUST HERE TO HANG OUT. HOPE THAT'S COOL.
SURE THING.
NOW, THE MAIN REASON I CALLED THIS MEETING...
THE FIRST TIME WE SAW OUR DARK FUTURE, IT WAS CERTAINLY AN EYE-OPENER. BUT WHAT CAME TO BE THIS TIME--ACTUALLY BECOMING AN ARMY OF TOTALITARIAN ANTI-HEROES...
OUR FUTURE SELVES MADE US DOUBT OUR RESOLVE. AT ONE POINT OR ANOTHER, EACH OF US FORGOT WHAT IT MEANS TO BE A TEEN TITAN.
IT MEANS WE'RE THE WORLD'S FINEST TEEN SUPER-HEROES... RIGHT?
YES, ROBIN. PLEASE, EDUCATE US WITH YOUR MIGHTY BRAIN.
I KNOW IT'S A CLICHÉ, BUT... EVERY GENERATION HAS ITS STRUGGLES.
ITS CHALLENGES.
ITS MONSTERS, AND ITS HEROES.
OUR GENERATION'S NO DIFFERENT, EXCEPT...
...IT'S OURS.

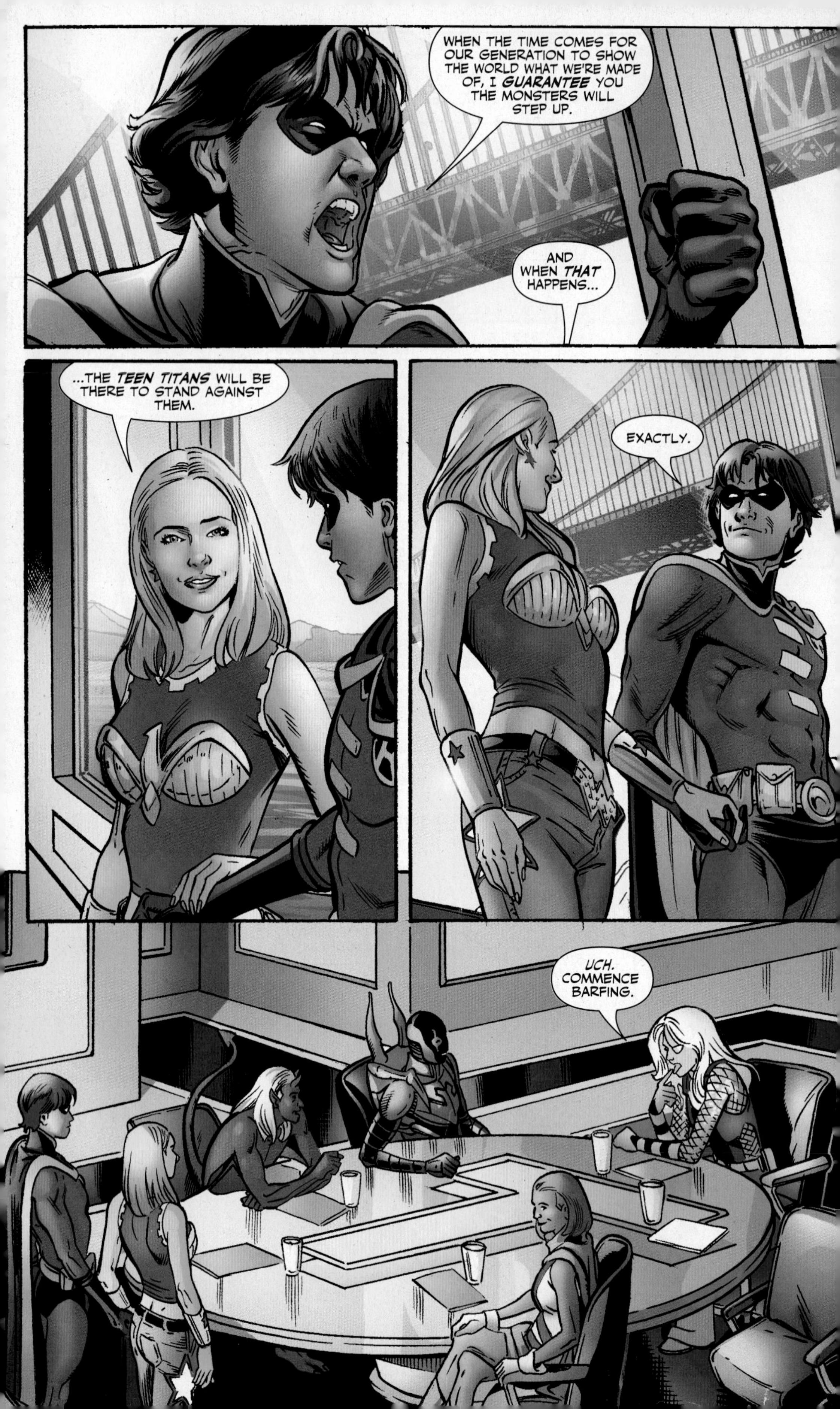
WHEN THE TIME COMES FOR OUR GENERATION TO SHOW THE WORLD WHAT WE'RE MADE OF, I *GUARANTEE* YOU THE MONSTERS WILL STEP UP.
AND WHEN *THAT* HAPPENS...
...THE *TEEN TITANS* WILL BE THERE TO STAND AGAINST THEM.
EXACTLY.
UCH. COMMENCE BARFING.

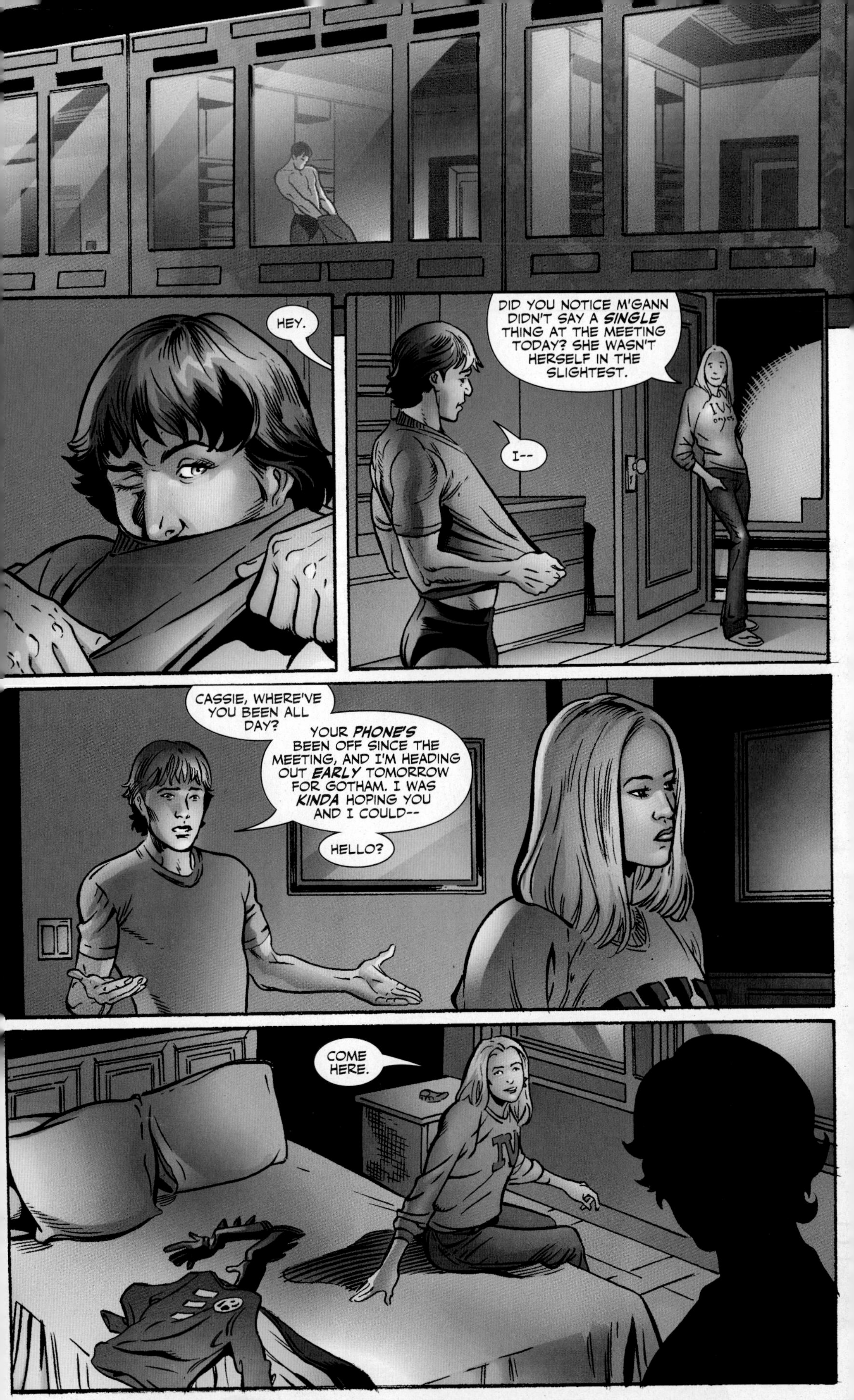
HEY.
DID YOU NOTICE M'GANN DIDN'T SAY A SINGLE THING AT THE MEETING TODAY? SHE WASN'T HERSELF IN THE SLIGHTEST.
I--
CASSIE, WHERE'VE YOU BEEN ALL DAY?
YOUR PHONE'S BEEN OFF SINCE THE MEETING, AND I'M HEADING OUT EARLY TOMORROW FOR GOTHAM. I WAS KINDA HOPING YOU AND I COULD--
HELLO?
COME HERE.

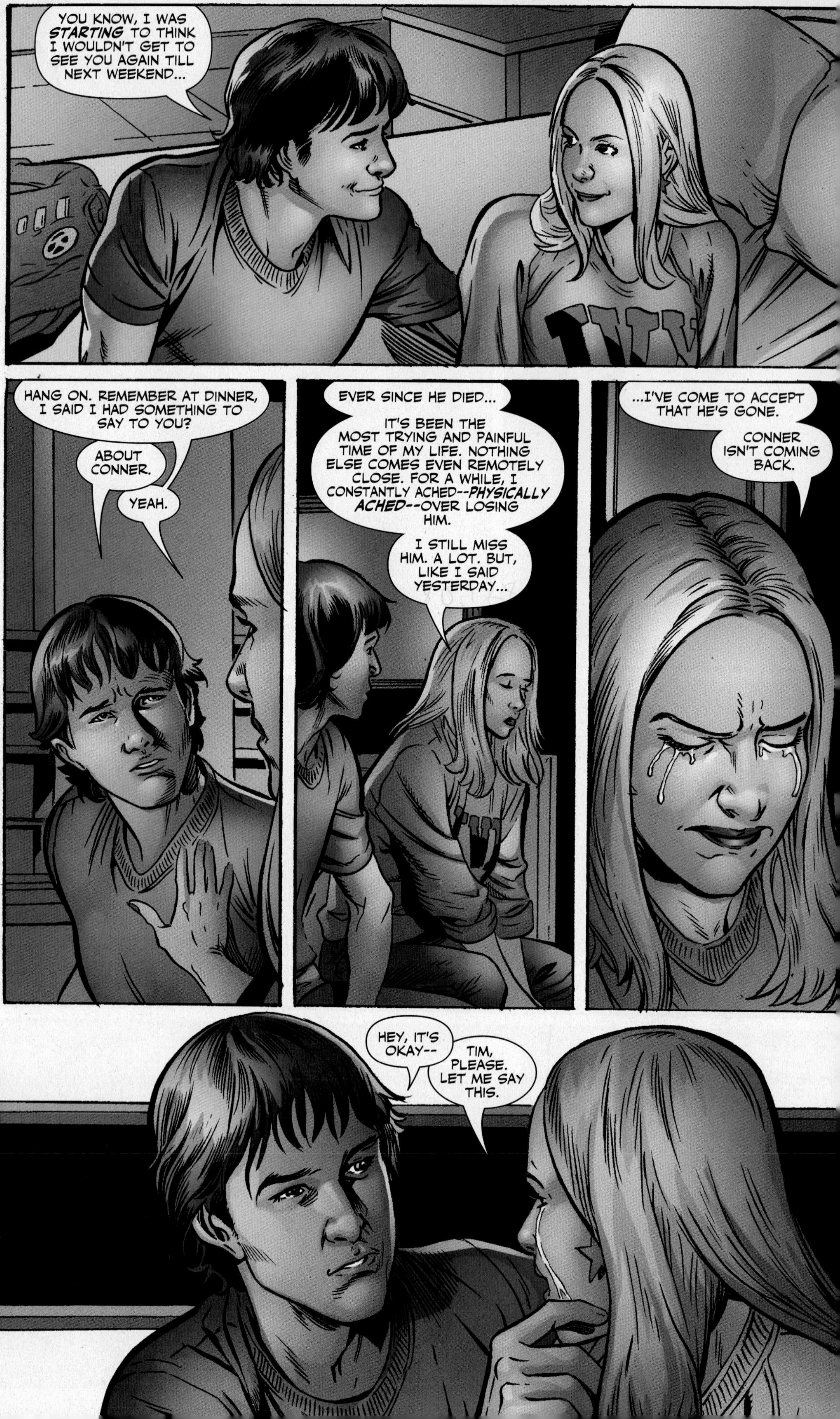

YOU KNOW, I WAS STARTING TO THINK I WOULDN'T GET TO SEE YOU AGAIN TILL NEXT WEEKEND...
HANG ON. REMEMBER AT DINNER, I SAID I HAD SOMETHING TO SAY TO YOU?
ABOUT CONNER.
YEAH.
EVER SINCE HE DIED...
IT'S BEEN THE MOST TRYING AND PAINFUL TIME OF MY LIFE. NOTHING ELSE COMES EVEN REMOTELY CLOSE. FOR A WHILE, I CONSTANTLY ACHED--PHYSICALLY ACHED--OVER LOSING HIM.
I STILL MISS HIM. A LOT. BUT, LIKE I SAID YESTERDAY...
...I'VE COME TO ACCEPT THAT HE'S GONE.
CONNER ISN'T COMING BACK.
HEY, IT'S OKAY--
TIM, PLEASE. LET ME SAY THIS.

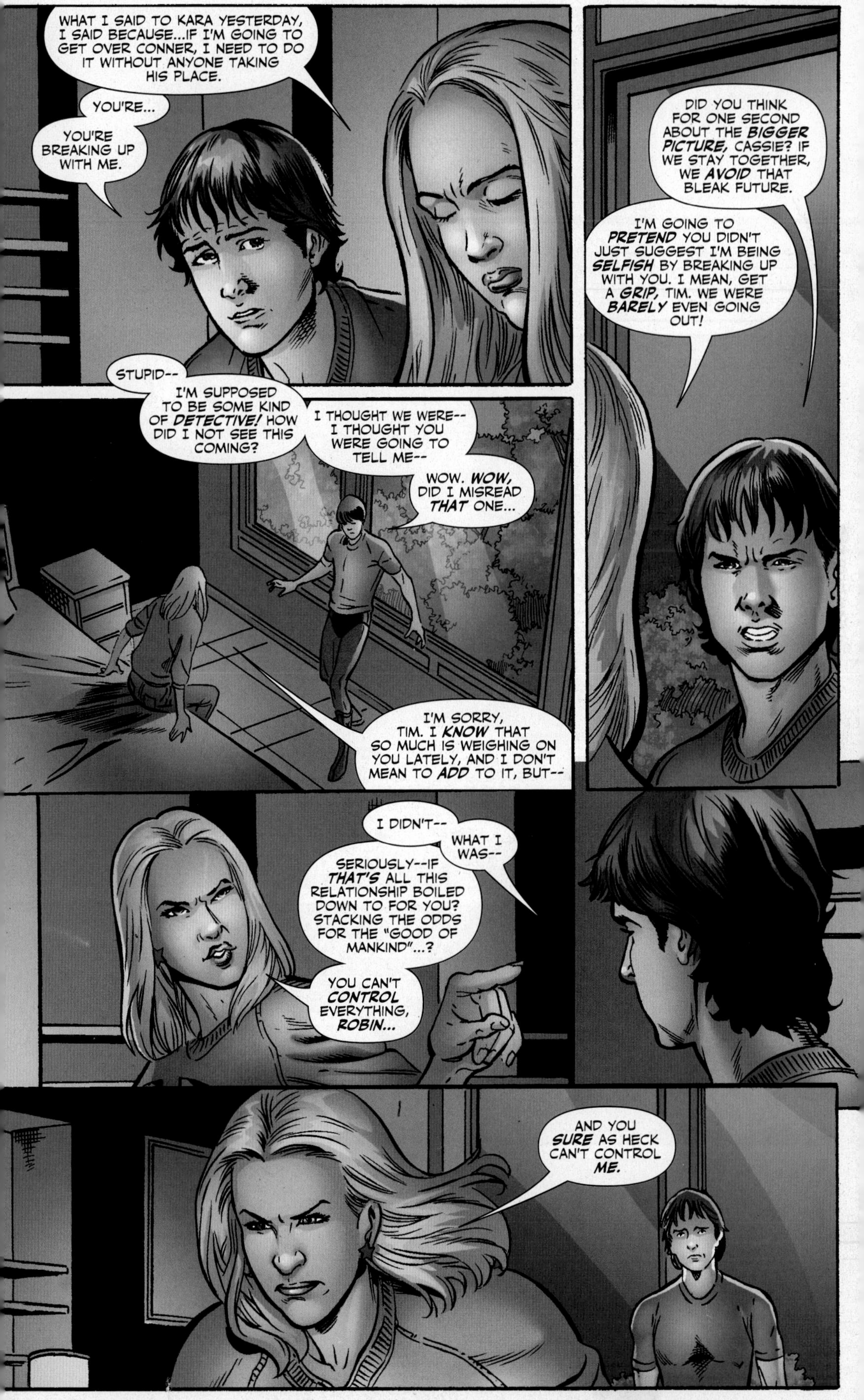
WHAT I SAID TO KARA YESTERDAY, I SAID BECAUSE...IF I'M GOING TO GET OVER CONNER, I NEED TO DO IT WITHOUT ANYONE TAKING HIS PLACE.
YOU'RE...
YOU'RE BREAKING UP WITH ME.
DID YOU THINK FOR ONE SECOND ABOUT THE BIGGER PICTURE, CASSIE? IF WE STAY TOGETHER, WE AVOID THAT BLEAK FUTURE.
I'M GOING TO PRETEND YOU DIDN'T JUST SUGGEST I'M BEING SELFISH BY BREAKING UP WITH YOU. I MEAN, GET A GRIP, TIM. WE WERE BARELY EVEN GOING OUT!
STUPID--
I'M SUPPOSED TO BE SOME KIND OF DETECTIVE! HOW DID I NOT SEE THIS COMING?
I THOUGHT WE WERE-- I THOUGHT YOU WERE GOING TO TELL ME--
WOW. WOW, DID I MISREAD THAT ONE...
I'M SORRY, TIM. I KNOW THAT SO MUCH IS WEIGHING ON YOU LATELY, AND I DON'T MEAN TO ADD TO IT, BUT--
I DIDN'T--
WHAT I WAS--
SERIOUSLY--IF THAT'S ALL THIS RELATIONSHIP BOILED DOWN TO FOR YOU? STACKING THE ODDS FOR THE "GOOD OF MANKIND"...?
YOU CAN'T CONTROL EVERYTHING, ROBIN...
AND YOU SURE AS HECK CAN'T CONTROL ME.

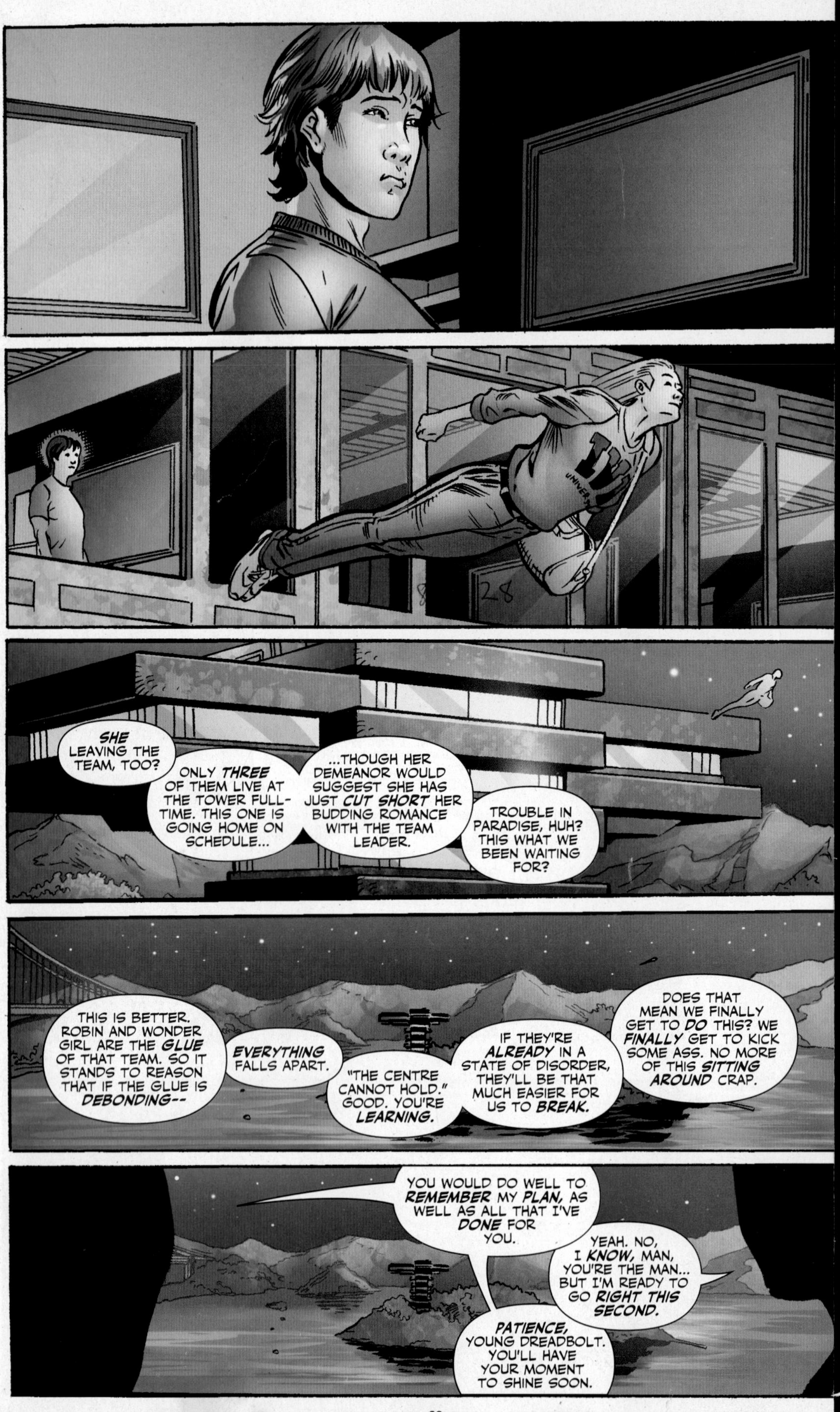
SHE LEAVING THE TEAM, TOO?
ONLY THREE OF THEM LIVE AT THE TOWER FULL-TIME. THIS ONE IS GOING HOME ON SCHEDULE...
...THOUGH HER DEMEANOR WOULD SUGGEST SHE HAS JUST CUT SHORT HER BUDDING ROMANCE WITH THE TEAM LEADER.
TROUBLE IN PARADISE, HUH? THIS WHAT WE BEEN WAITING FOR?
THIS IS BETTER. ROBIN AND WONDER GIRL ARE THE GLUE OF THAT TEAM. SO IT STANDS TO REASON THAT IF THE GLUE IS DEBONDING--
EVERYTHING FALLS APART.
"THE CENTRE CANNOT HOLD." GOOD. YOU'RE LEARNING.
IF THEY'RE ALREADY IN A STATE OF DISORDER, THEY'LL BE THAT MUCH EASIER FOR US TO BREAK.
DOES THAT MEAN WE FINALLY GET TO DO THIS? WE FINALLY GET TO KICK SOME ASS. NO MORE OF THIS SITTING AROUND CRAP.
YOU WOULD DO WELL TO REMEMBER MY PLAN, AS WELL AS ALL THAT I'VE DONE FOR YOU.
YEAH. NO, I KNOW, MAN, YOU'RE THE MAN... BUT I'M READY TO GO RIGHT THIS SECOND.
PATIENCE, YOUNG DREADBOLT. YOU'LL HAVE YOUR MOMENT TO SHINE SOON.

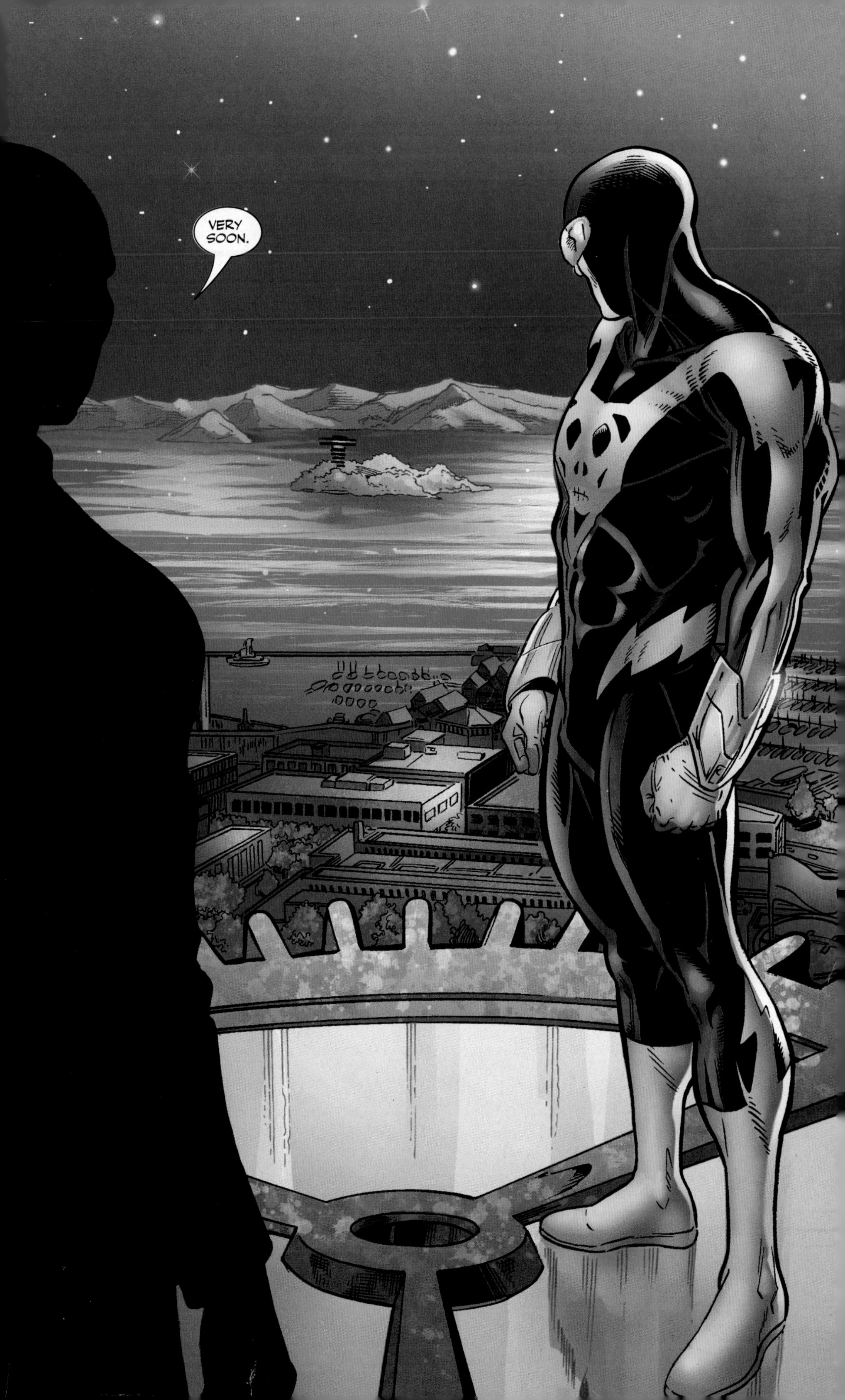
VERY SOON.

TEEN TITANS 56 - Eddy Barrows, Julio Ferreira and Rod Reis

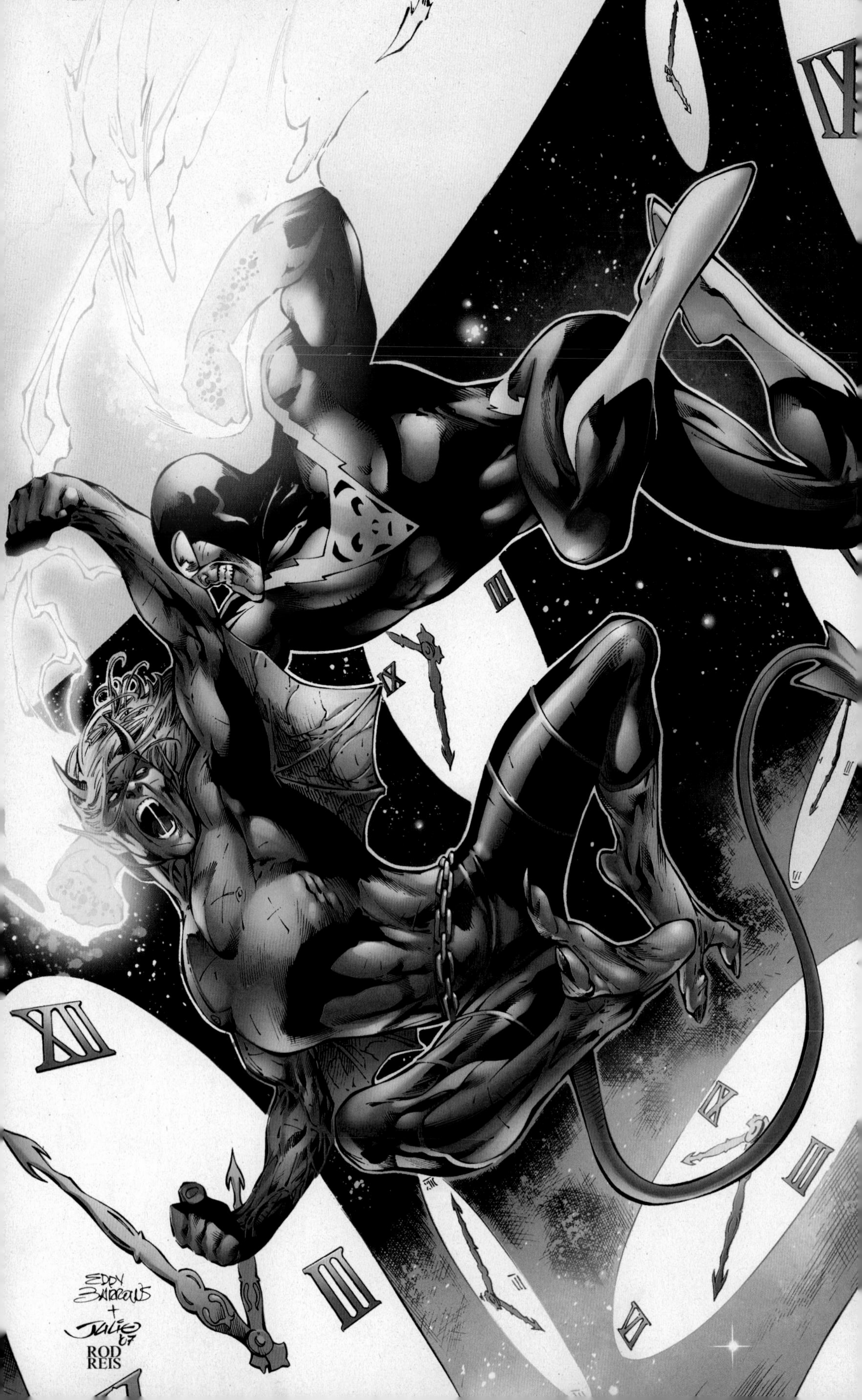
EDDY BARROWS + JULIO 07
ROD REIS

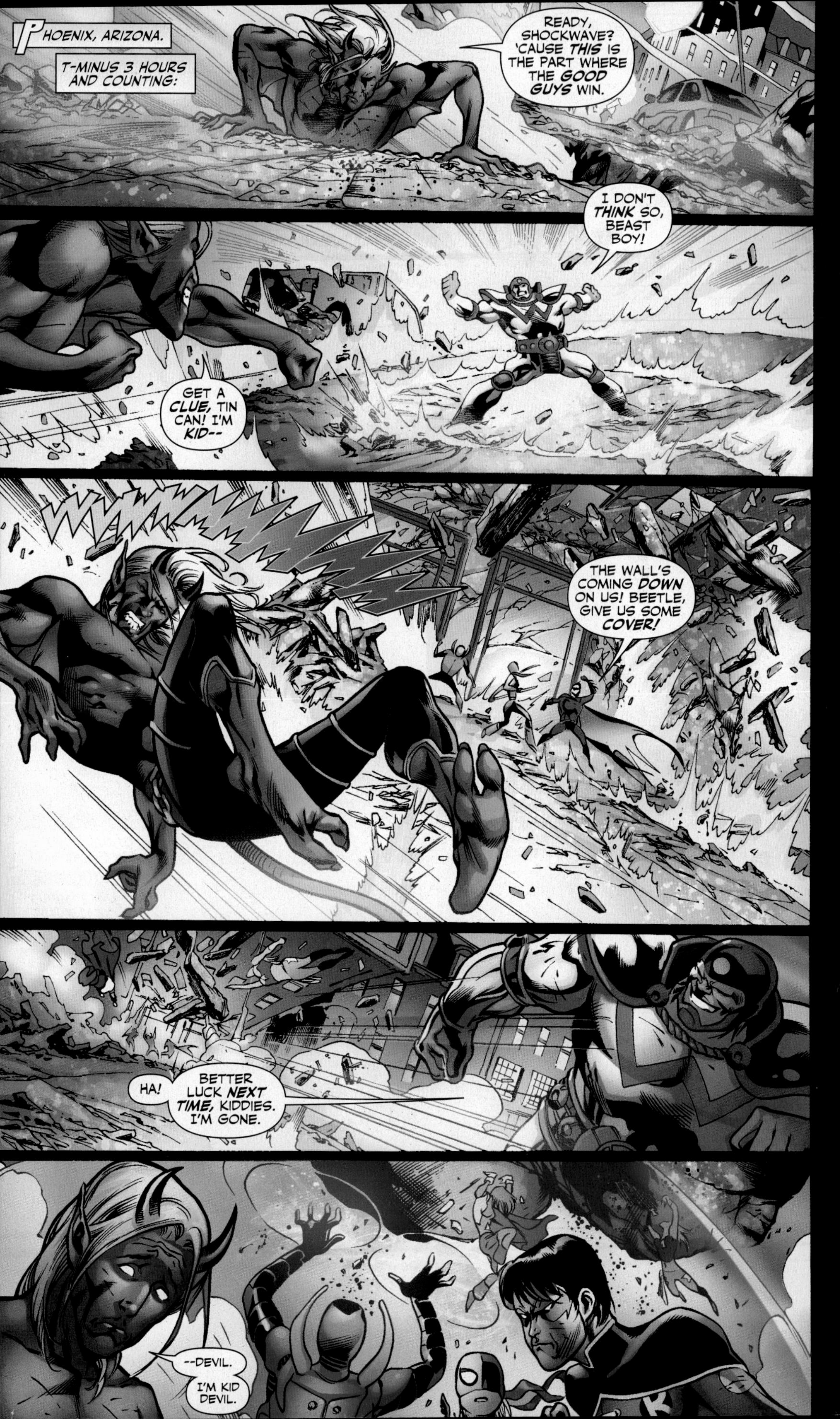
PHOENIX, ARIZONA.
T-MINUS 3 HOURS AND COUNTING:
READY, SHOCKWAVE? 'CAUSE THIS IS THE PART WHERE THE GOOD GUYS WIN.
I DON'T THINK SO, BEAST BOY!
GET A CLUE, TIN CAN! I'M KID--
WVMMMMMM
THE WALL'S COMING DOWN ON US! BEETLE, GIVE US SOME COVER!
HA!
BETTER LUCK NEXT TIME, KIDDIES. I'M GONE.
--DEVIL.
I'M KID DEVIL.

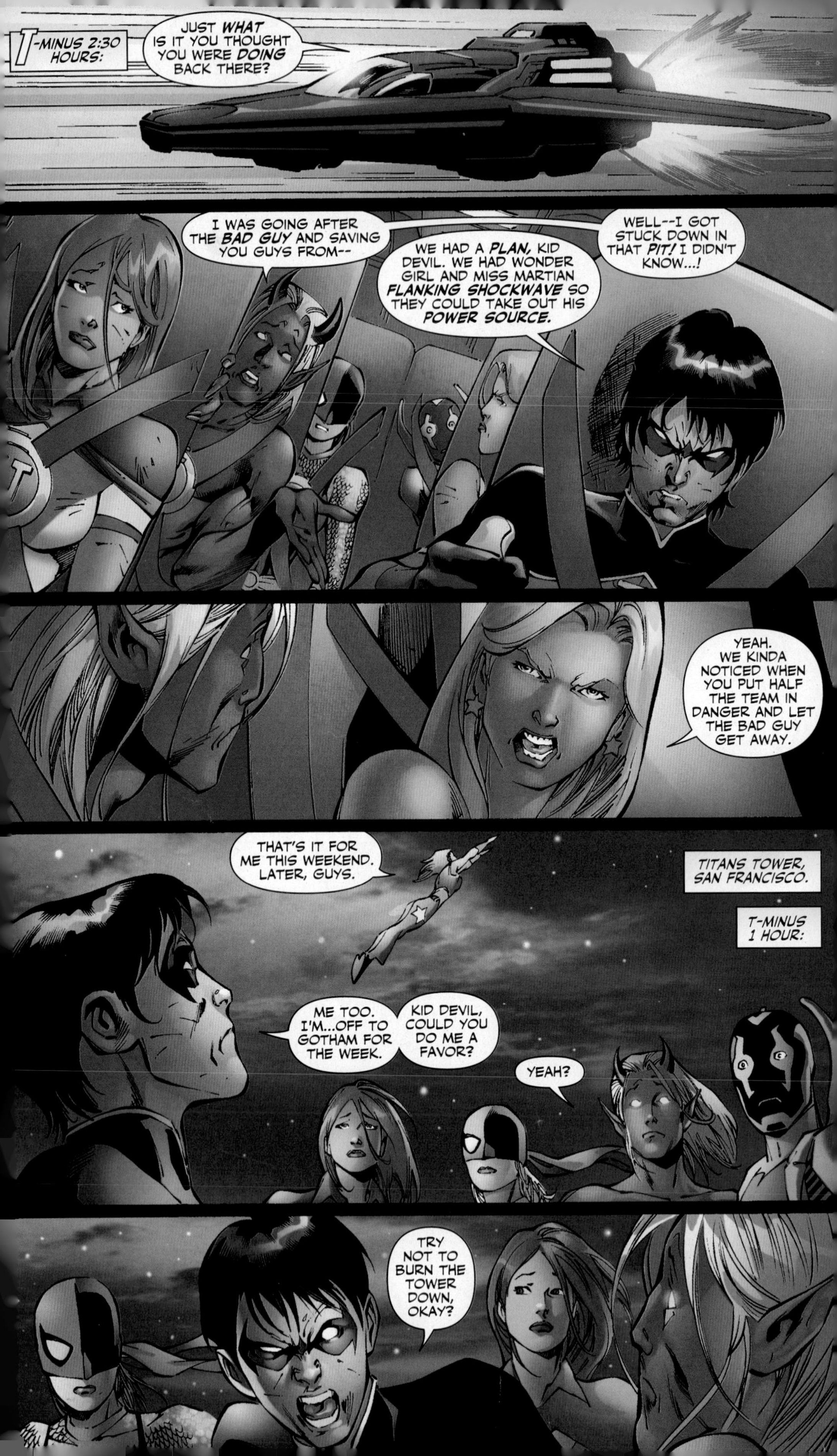
T-MINUS 2:30 HOURS:
JUST WHAT IS IT YOU THOUGHT YOU WERE DOING BACK THERE?
I WAS GOING AFTER THE BAD GUY AND SAVING YOU GUYS FROM--
WE HAD A PLAN, KID DEVIL. WE HAD WONDER GIRL AND MISS MARTIAN FLANKING SHOCKWAVE SO THEY COULD TAKE OUT HIS POWER SOURCE.
WELL--I GOT STUCK DOWN IN THAT PIT! I DIDN'T KNOW...!
YEAH. WE KINDA NOTICED WHEN YOU PUT HALF THE TEAM IN DANGER AND LET THE BAD GUY GET AWAY.
TITANS TOWER, SAN FRANCISCO.
T-MINUS 1 HOUR:
THAT'S IT FOR ME THIS WEEKEND. LATER, GUYS.
ME TOO. I'M...OFF TO GOTHAM FOR THE WEEK.
KID DEVIL, COULD YOU DO ME A FAVOR?
YEAH?
TRY NOT TO BURN THE TOWER DOWN, OKAY?

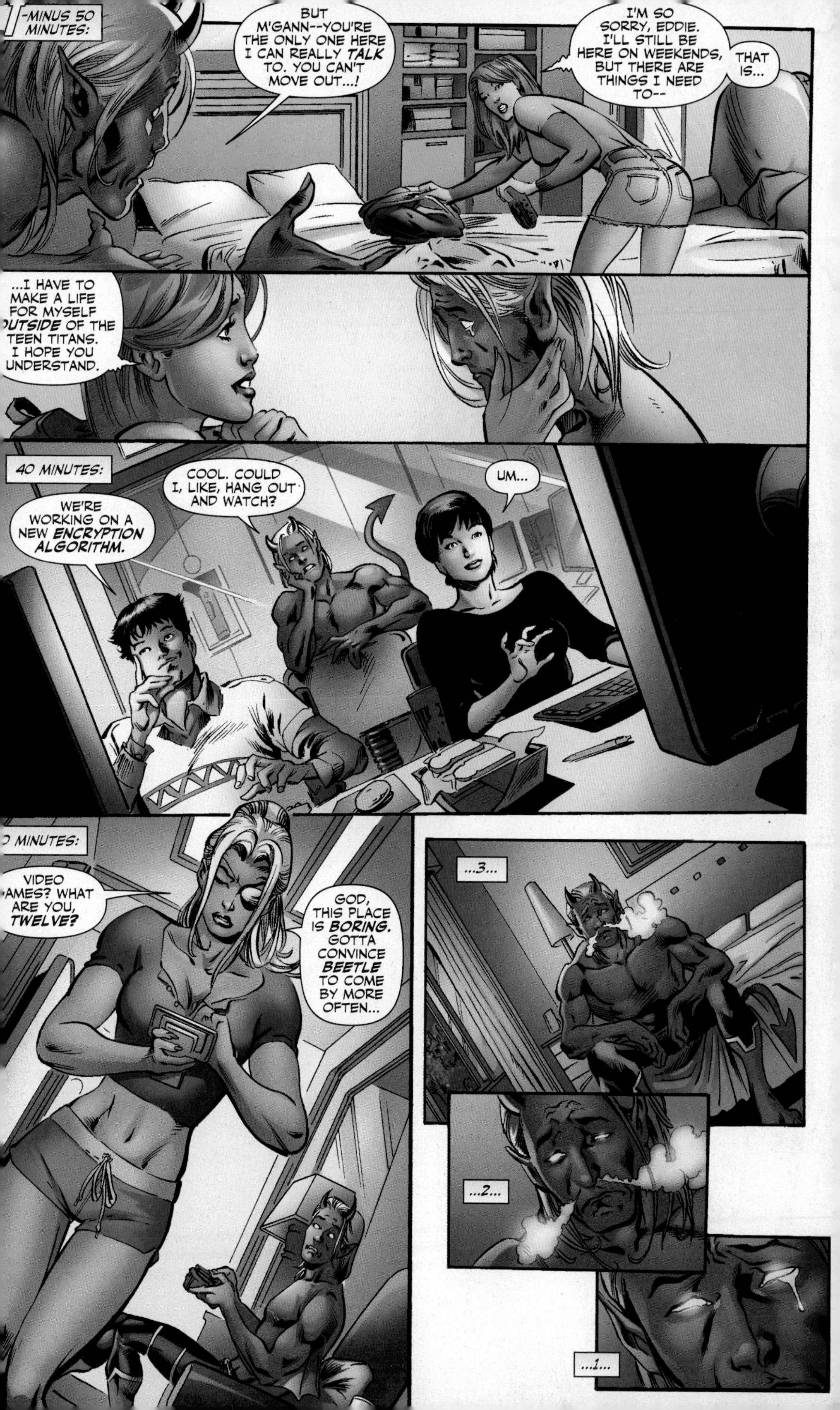

-MINUS 50 MINUTES:
BUT M'GANN--YOU'RE THE ONLY ONE HERE I CAN REALLY *TALK* TO. YOU CAN'T MOVE OUT...!
I'M SO SORRY, EDDIE. I'LL STILL BE HERE ON WEEKENDS, BUT THERE ARE THINGS I NEED TO--
THAT IS...
...I HAVE TO MAKE A LIFE FOR MYSELF *OUTSIDE* OF THE TEEN TITANS. I HOPE YOU UNDERSTAND.
40 MINUTES:
WE'RE WORKING ON A NEW *ENCRYPTION ALGORITHM.*
COOL. COULD I, LIKE, HANG OUT AND WATCH?
UM...
MINUTES:
VIDEO AMES? WHAT ARE YOU, *TWELVE?*
GOD, THIS PLACE IS *BORING.* GOTTA CONVINCE *BEETLE* TO COME BY MORE OFTEN...
...3...
...2...
...1...

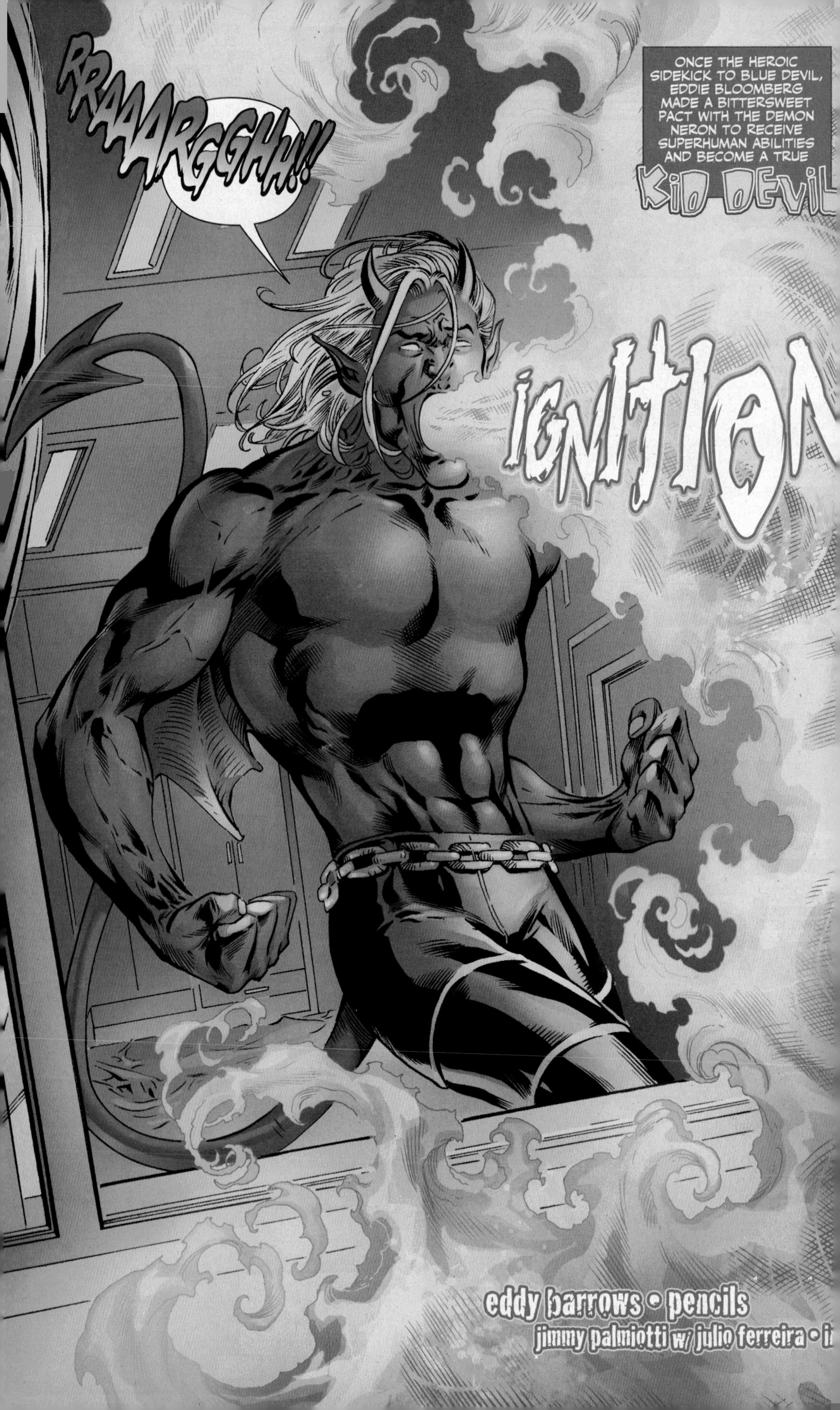
RRAAARGGHH!!
ONCE THE HEROIC SIDEKICK TO BLUE DEVIL, EDDIE BLOOMBERG MADE A BITTERSWEET PACT WITH THE DEMON NERON TO RECEIVE SUPERHUMAN ABILITIES AND BECOME A TRUE
KID DEVIL
IGNITION
eddy barrows • pencils
jimmy palmiotti w/ julio ferreira •

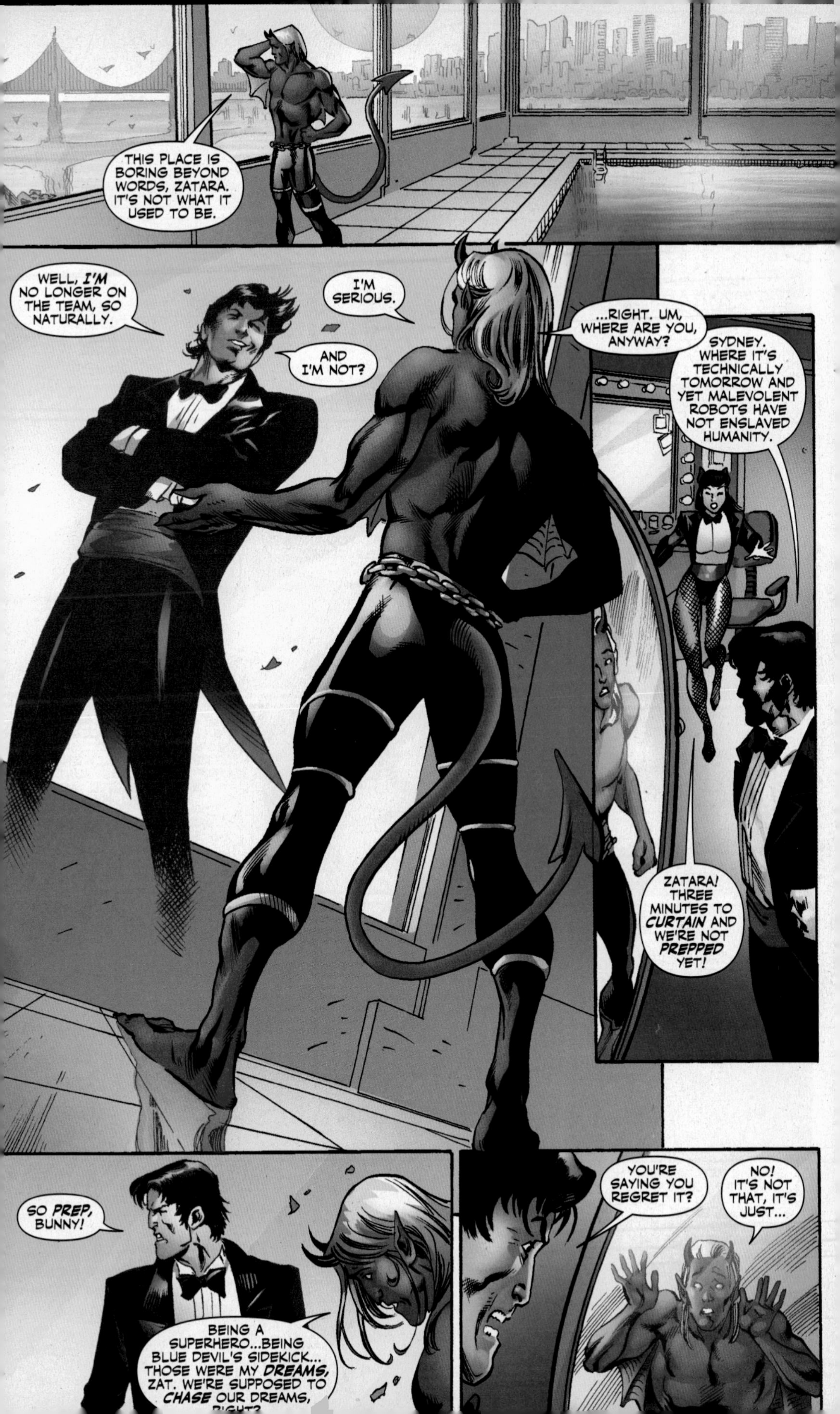
THIS PLACE IS BORING BEYOND WORDS, ZATARA. IT'S NOT WHAT IT USED TO BE.
WELL, I'M NO LONGER ON THE TEAM, SO NATURALLY.
I'M SERIOUS.
AND I'M NOT?
...RIGHT. UM, WHERE ARE YOU, ANYWAY?
SYDNEY. WHERE IT'S TECHNICALLY TOMORROW AND YET MALEVOLENT ROBOTS HAVE NOT ENSLAVED HUMANITY.
ZATARA! THREE MINUTES TO CURTAIN AND WE'RE NOT PREPPED YET!
SO PREP, BUNNY!
BEING A SUPERHERO...BEING BLUE DEVIL'S SIDEKICK... THOSE WERE MY DREAMS, ZAT. WE'RE SUPPOSED TO CHASE OUR DREAMS,
YOU'RE SAYING YOU REGRET IT?
NO! IT'S NOT THAT, IT'S JUST...

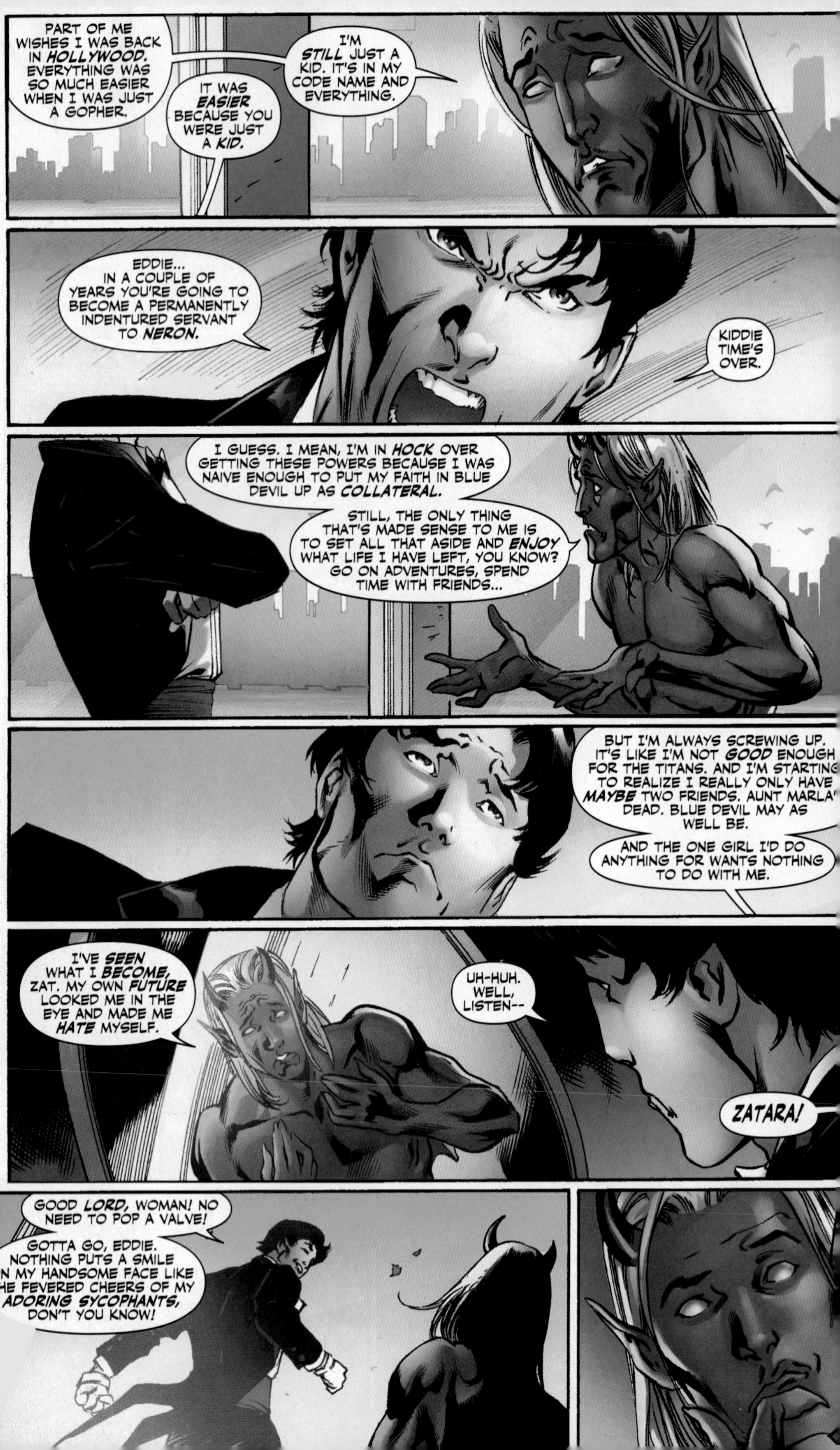
PART OF ME WISHES I WAS BACK IN HOLLYWOOD. EVERYTHING WAS SO MUCH EASIER WHEN I WAS JUST A GOPHER.
IT WAS EASIER BECAUSE YOU WERE JUST A KID.
I'M STILL JUST A KID. IT'S IN MY CODE NAME AND EVERYTHING.
EDDIE... IN A COUPLE OF YEARS YOU'RE GOING TO BECOME A PERMANENTLY INDENTURED SERVANT TO NERON.
KIDDIE TIME'S OVER.
I GUESS. I MEAN, I'M IN HOCK OVER GETTING THESE POWERS BECAUSE I WAS NAIVE ENOUGH TO PUT MY FAITH IN BLUE DEVIL UP AS COLLATERAL.
STILL, THE ONLY THING THAT'S MADE SENSE TO ME IS TO SET ALL THAT ASIDE AND ENJOY WHAT LIFE I HAVE LEFT, YOU KNOW? GO ON ADVENTURES, SPEND TIME WITH FRIENDS...
BUT I'M ALWAYS SCREWING UP. IT'S LIKE I'M NOT GOOD ENOUGH FOR THE TITANS. AND I'M STARTING TO REALIZE I REALLY ONLY HAVE MAYBE TWO FRIENDS. AUNT MARLA' DEAD. BLUE DEVIL MAY AS WELL BE.
AND THE ONE GIRL I'D DO ANYTHING FOR WANTS NOTHING TO DO WITH ME.
I'VE SEEN WHAT I BECOME, ZAT. MY OWN FUTURE LOOKED ME IN THE EYE AND MADE ME HATE MYSELF.
UH-HUH. WELL, LISTEN--
ZATARA!
GOOD LORD, WOMAN! NO NEED TO POP A VALVE!
GOTTA GO, EDDIE. NOTHING PUTS A SMILE ON MY HANDSOME FACE LIKE THE FEVERED CHEERS OF MY ADORING SYCOPHANTS, DON'T YOU KNOW!

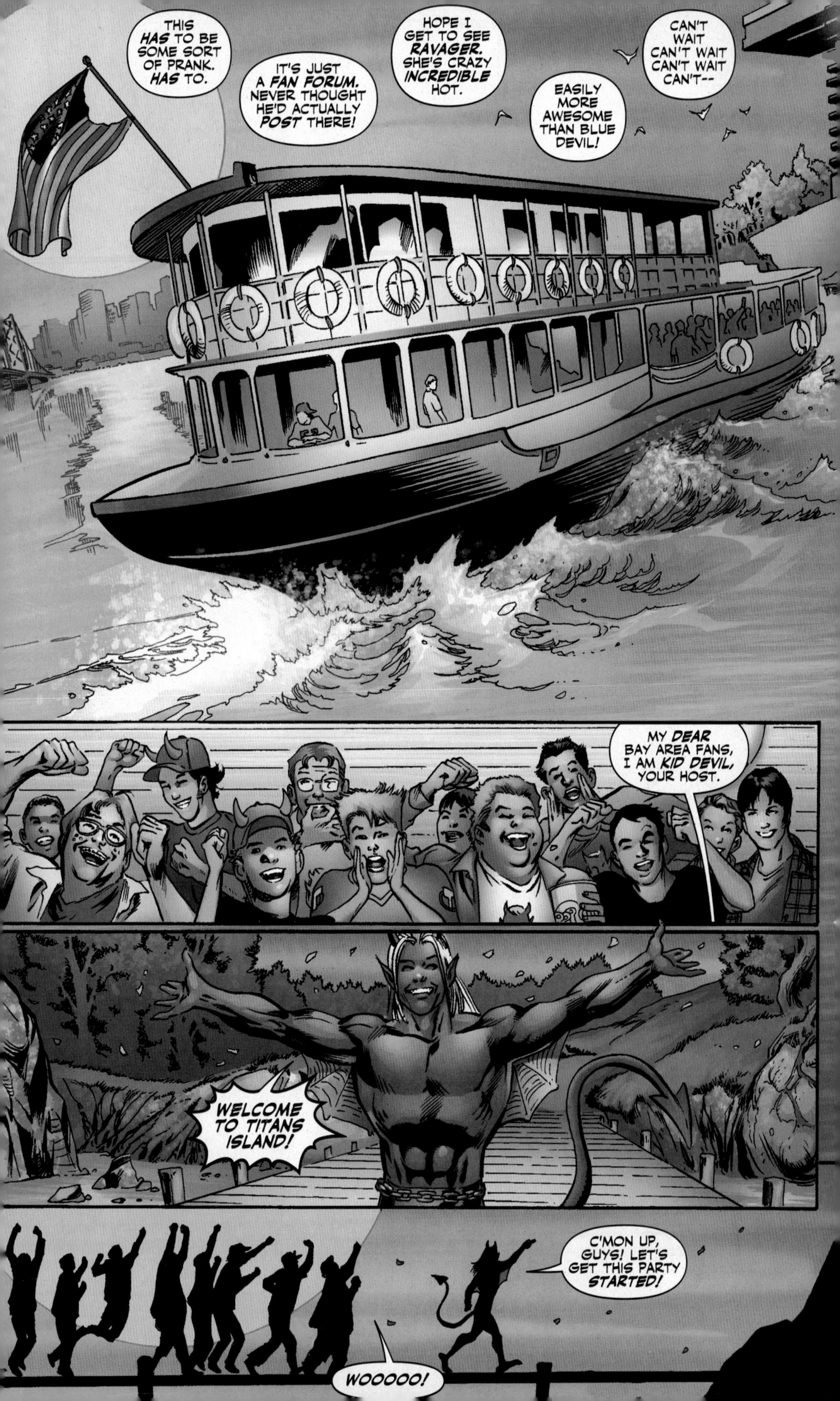

THIS HAS TO BE SOME SORT OF PRANK. HAS TO.
IT'S JUST A FAN FORUM. NEVER THOUGHT HE'D ACTUALLY POST THERE!
HOPE I GET TO SEE RAVAGER. SHE'S CRAZY INCREDIBLE HOT.
EASILY MORE AWESOME THAN BLUE DEVIL!
CAN'T WAIT CAN'T WAIT CAN'T WAIT CAN'T--
MY DEAR BAY AREA FANS, I AM KID DEVIL, YOUR HOST.
WELCOME TO TITANS ISLAND!
C'MON UP, GUYS! LET'S GET THIS PARTY STARTED!
WOOOOO!

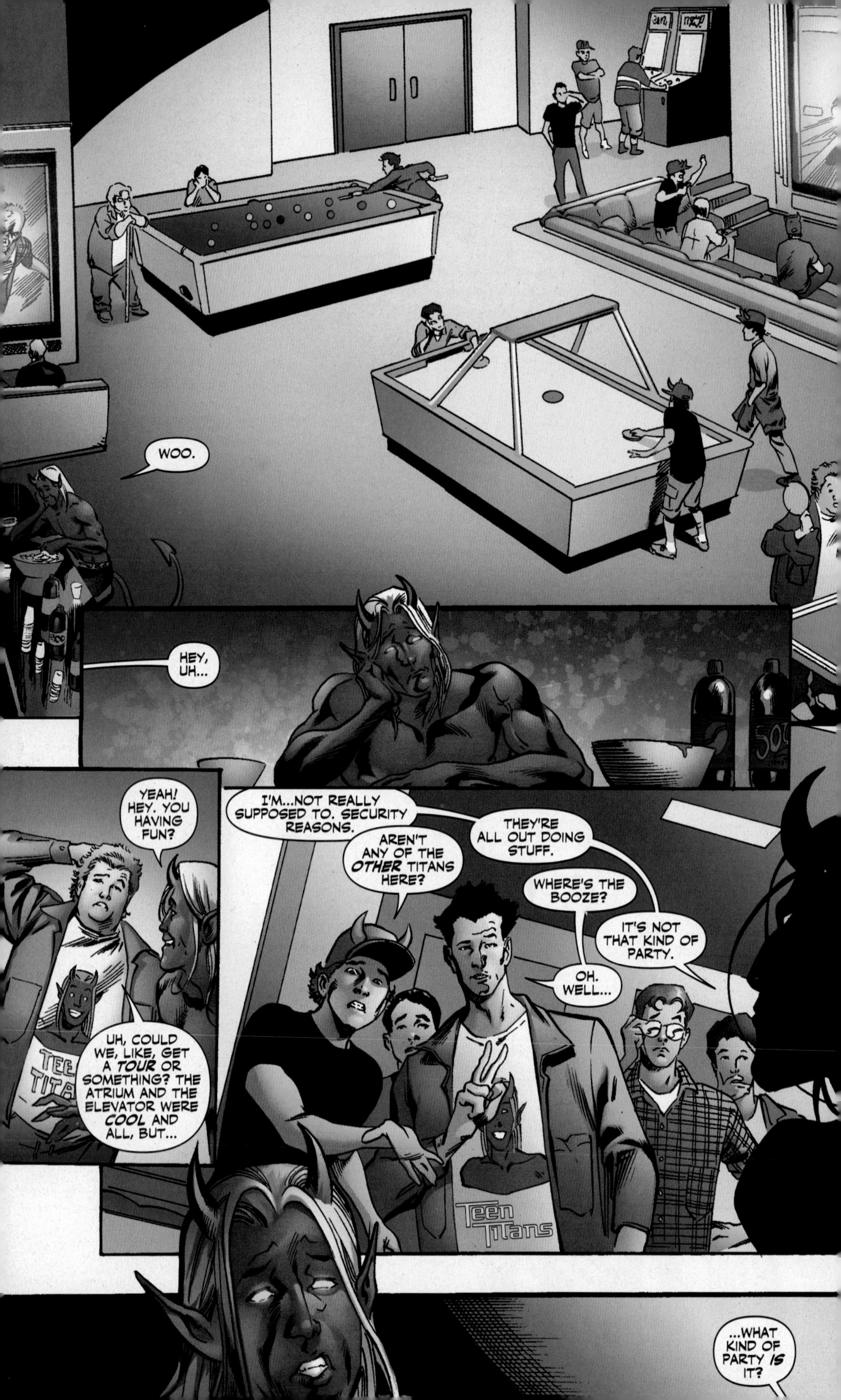
WOO.
HEY, UH...
YEAH! HEY. YOU HAVING FUN?
UH, COULD WE, LIKE, GET A TOUR OR SOMETHING? THE ATRIUM AND THE ELEVATOR WERE COOL AND ALL, BUT...
I'M...NOT REALLY SUPPOSED TO. SECURITY REASONS.
AREN'T ANY OF THE OTHER TITANS HERE?
THEY'RE ALL OUT DOING STUFF.
WHERE'S THE BOOZE?
IT'S NOT THAT KIND OF PARTY.
OH. WELL...
TEEN TITANS
TEEN TITANS
...WHAT KIND OF PARTY IS IT?

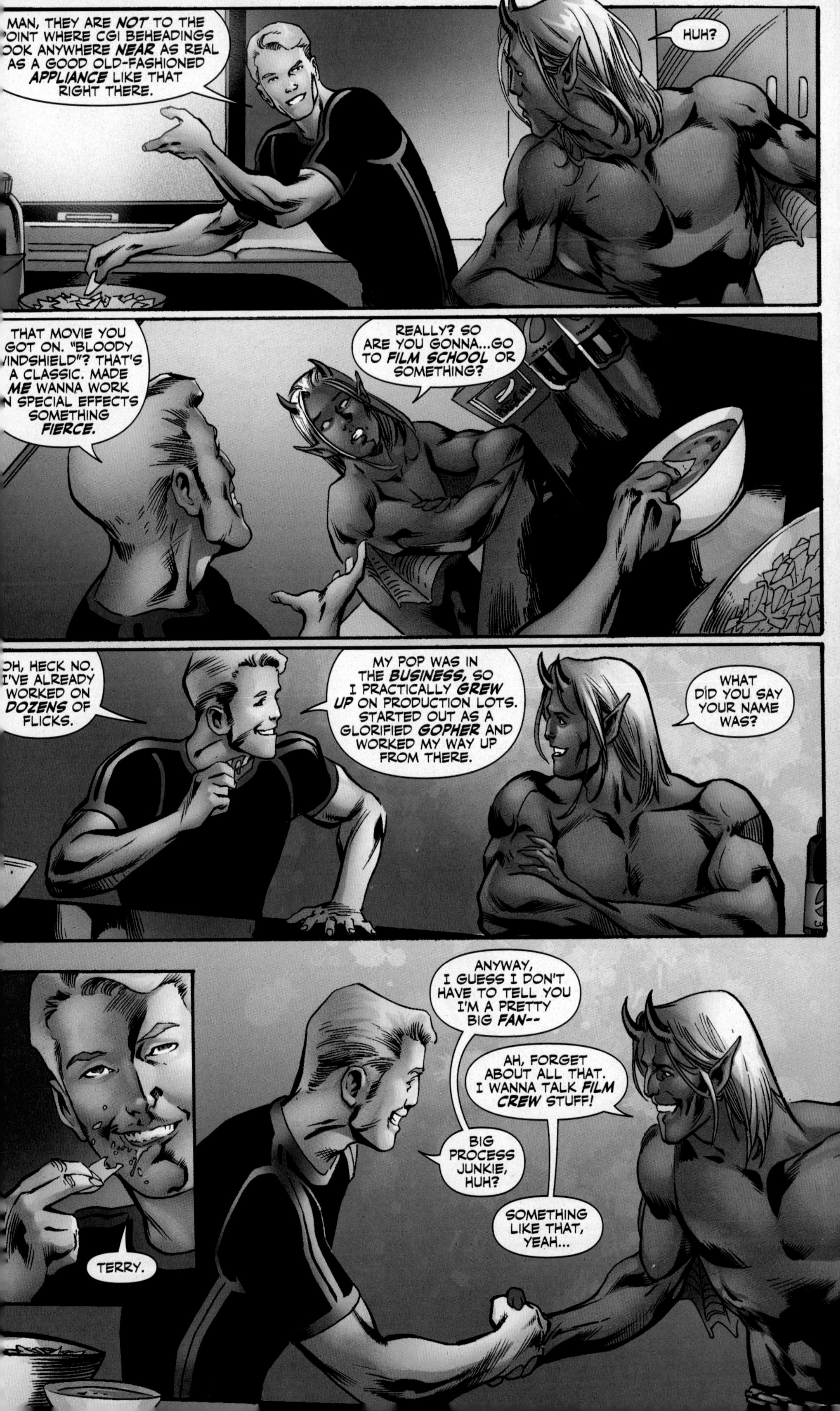
MAN, THEY ARE NOT TO THE POINT WHERE CGI BEHEADINGS LOOK ANYWHERE NEAR AS REAL AS A GOOD OLD-FASHIONED APPLIANCE LIKE THAT RIGHT THERE.
HUH?
THAT MOVIE YOU GOT ON. "BLOODY WINDSHIELD"? THAT'S A CLASSIC. MADE ME WANNA WORK IN SPECIAL EFFECTS SOMETHING FIERCE.
REALLY? SO ARE YOU GONNA...GO TO FILM SCHOOL OR SOMETHING?
OH, HECK NO. I'VE ALREADY WORKED ON DOZENS OF FLICKS.
MY POP WAS IN THE BUSINESS, SO I PRACTICALLY GREW UP ON PRODUCTION LOTS. STARTED OUT AS A GLORIFIED GOPHER AND WORKED MY WAY UP FROM THERE.
WHAT DID YOU SAY YOUR NAME WAS?
TERRY.
ANYWAY, I GUESS I DON'T HAVE TO TELL YOU I'M A PRETTY BIG FAN--
AH, FORGET ABOUT ALL THAT. I WANNA TALK FILM CREW STUFF!
BIG PROCESS JUNKIE, HUH?
SOMETHING LIKE THAT, YEAH...

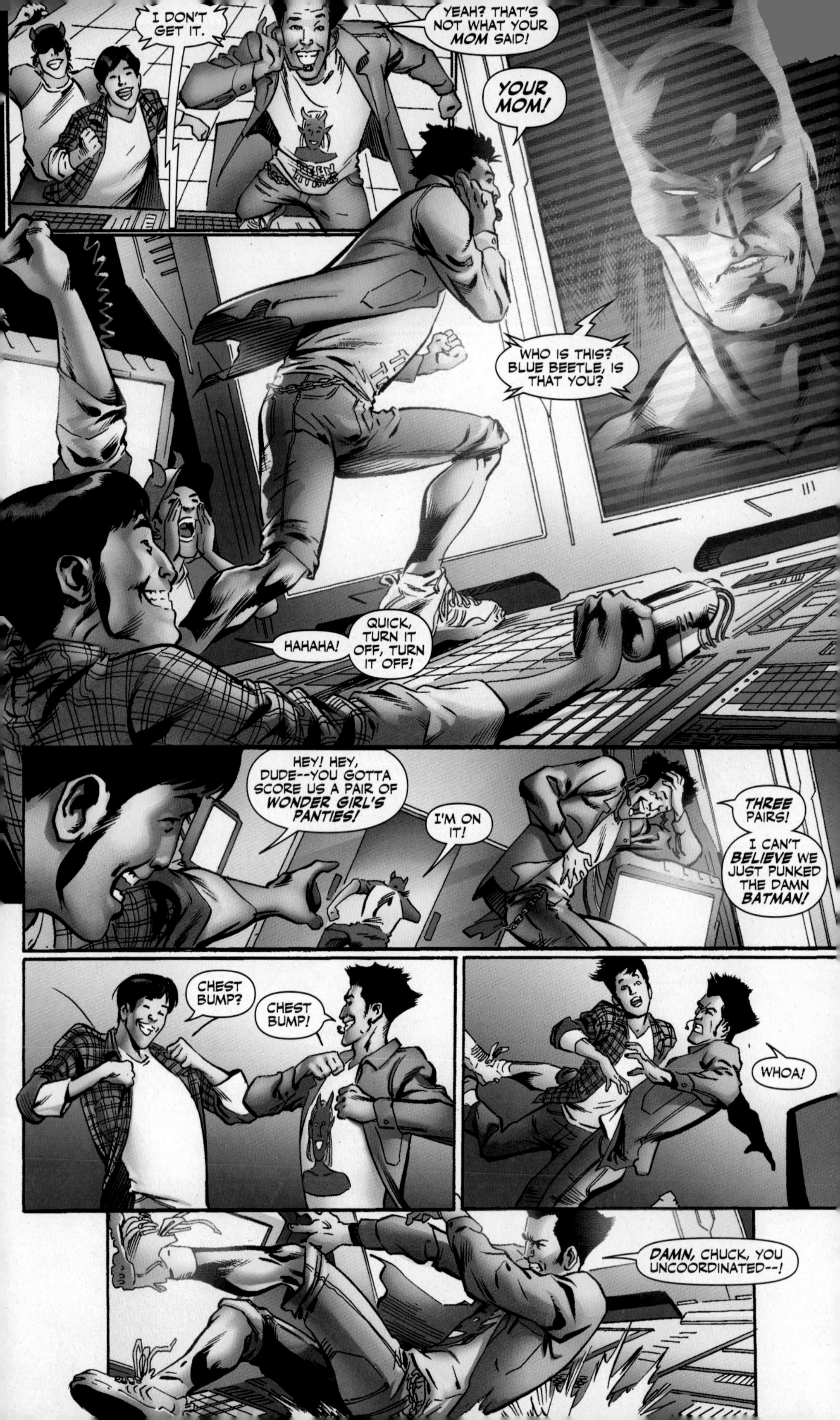

I DON'T GET IT.
YEAH? THAT'S NOT WHAT YOUR MOM SAID!
YOUR MOM!
WHO IS THIS? BLUE BEETLE, IS THAT YOU?
HAHAHA!
QUICK, TURN IT OFF, TURN IT OFF!
HEY! HEY, DUDE--YOU GOTTA SCORE US A PAIR OF WONDER GIRL'S PANTIES!
I'M ON IT!
THREE PAIRS!
I CAN'T BELIEVE WE JUST PUNKED THE DAMN BATMAN!
CHEST BUMP?
CHEST BUMP!
WHOA!
DAMN, CHUCK, YOU UNCOORDINATED--!

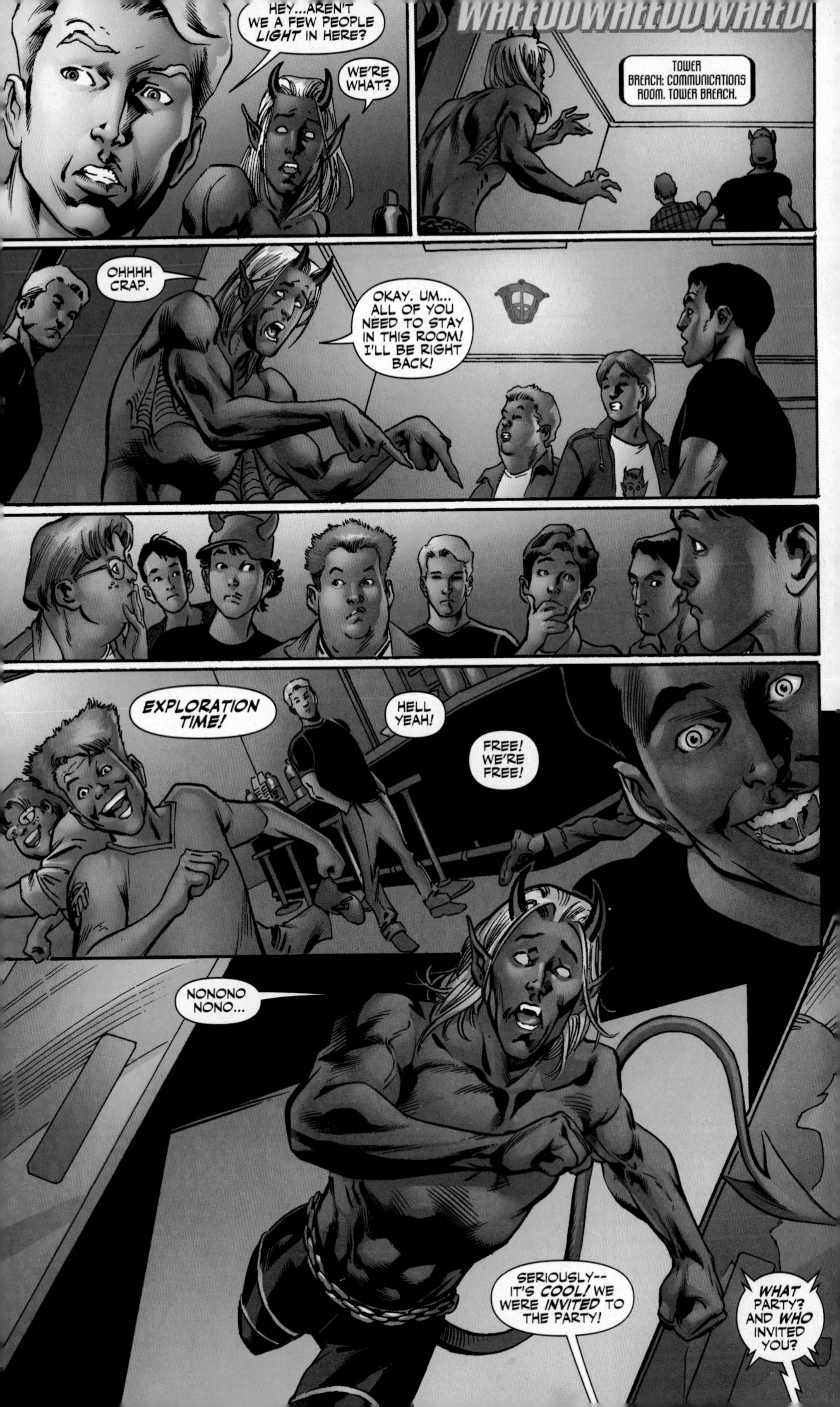
HEY...AREN'T WE A FEW PEOPLE LIGHT IN HERE?
WE'RE WHAT?
TOWER BREACH: COMMUNICATIONS ROOM. TOWER BREACH.
OHHHH CRAP.
OKAY. UM... ALL OF YOU NEED TO STAY IN THIS ROOM! I'LL BE RIGHT BACK!
EXPLORATION TIME!
HELL YEAH!
FREE! WE'RE FREE!
NONONO NONO...
SERIOUSLY-- IT'S COOL! WE WERE INVITED TO THE PARTY!
WHAT PARTY? AND WHO INVITED YOU?

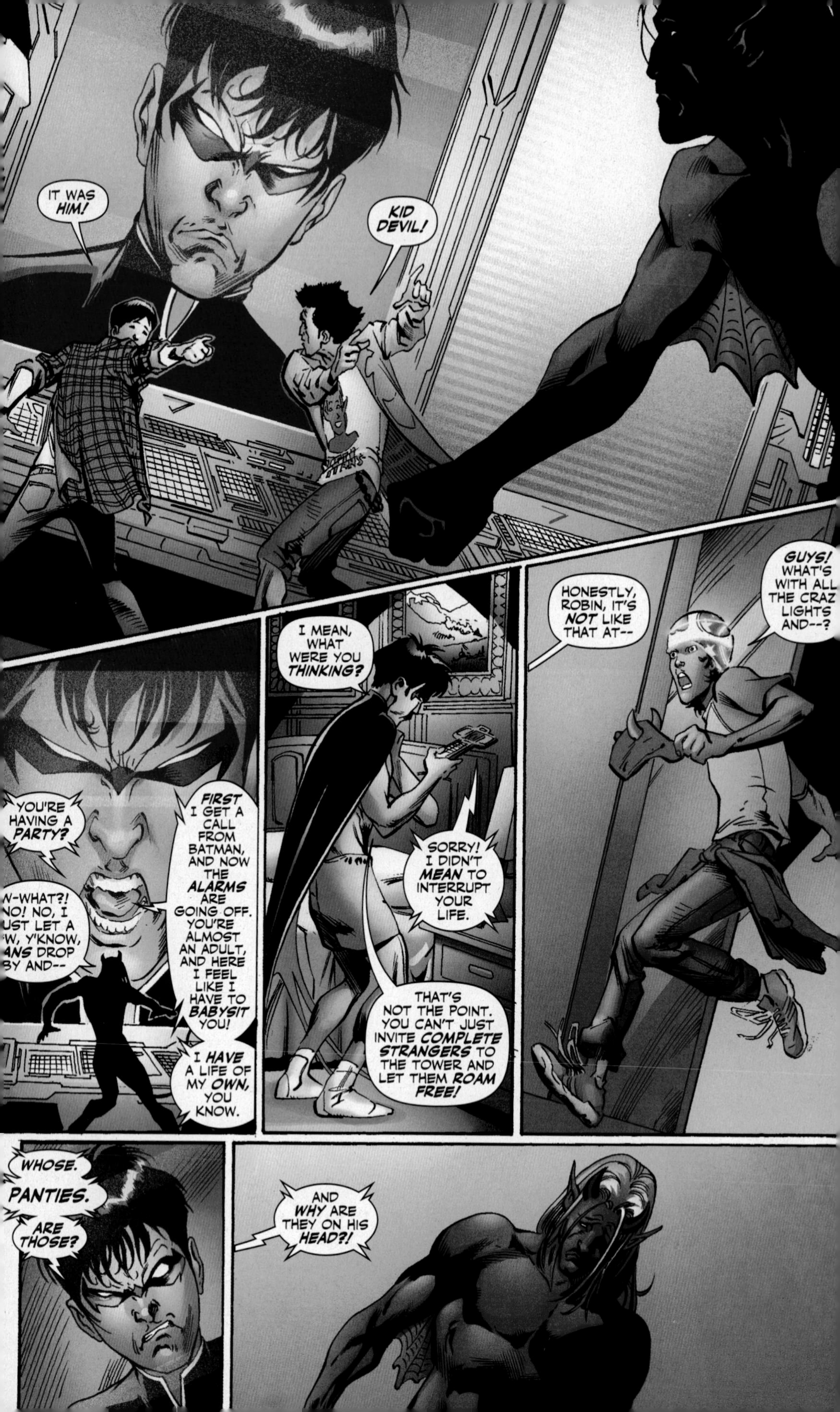
IT WAS HIM!
KID DEVIL!
HONESTLY, ROBIN, IT'S NOT LIKE THAT AT--
GUYS! WHAT'S WITH ALL THE CRAZ LIGHTS AND--?
YOU'RE HAVING A PARTY?
W-WHAT?! NO! NO, I UST LET A W, Y'KNOW, ANS DROP BY AND--
FIRST I GET A CALL FROM BATMAN, AND NOW THE ALARMS ARE GOING OFF. YOU'RE ALMOST AN ADULT, AND HERE I FEEL LIKE I HAVE TO BABYSIT YOU!
I HAVE A LIFE OF MY OWN, YOU KNOW.
I MEAN, WHAT WERE YOU THINKING?
SORRY! I DIDN'T MEAN TO INTERRUPT YOUR LIFE.
THAT'S NOT THE POINT. YOU CAN'T JUST INVITE COMPLETE STRANGERS TO THE TOWER AND LET THEM ROAM FREE!
WHOSE.
PANTIES.
ARE THOSE?
AND WHY ARE THEY ON HIS HEAD?!

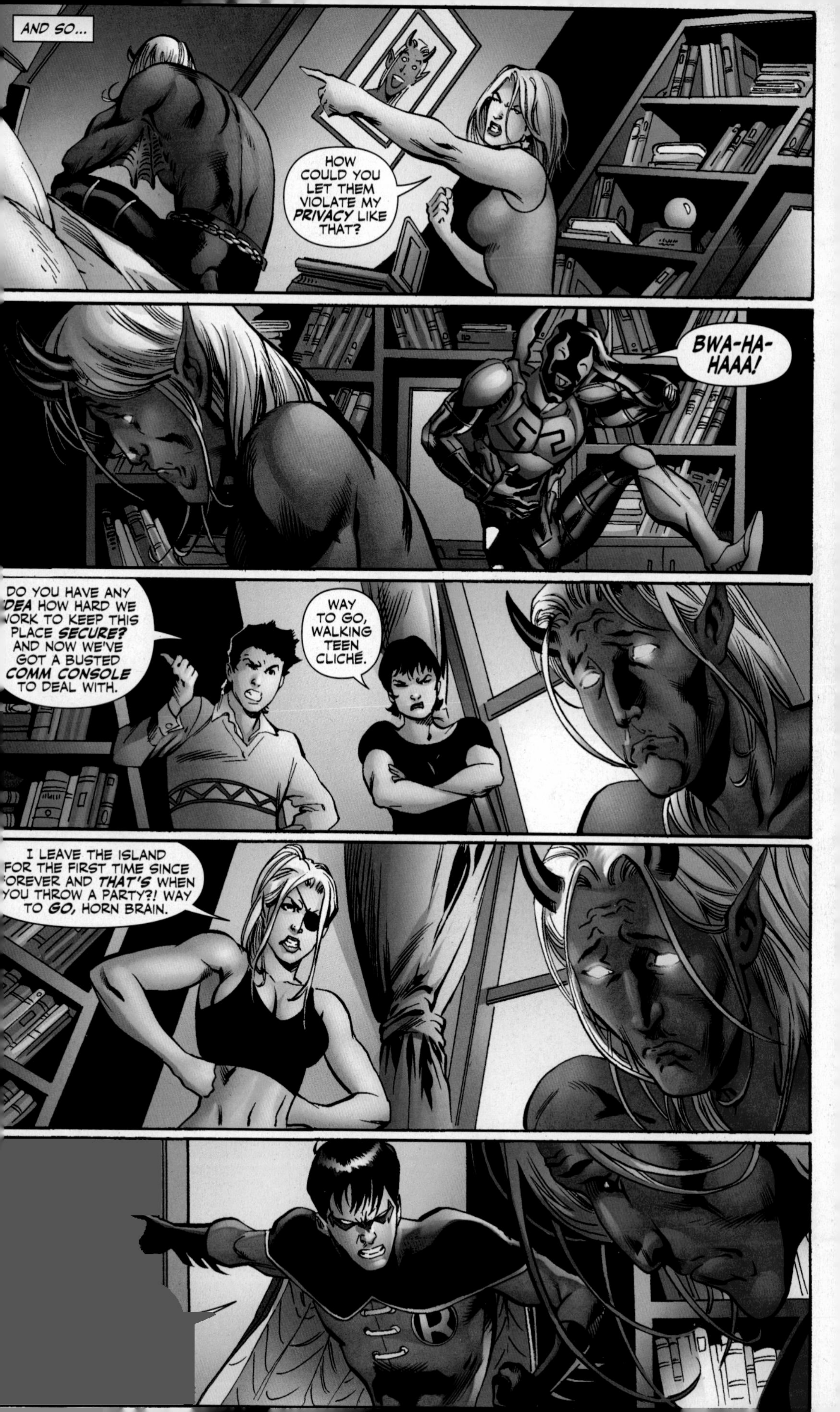
AND SO...
HOW COULD YOU LET THEM VIOLATE MY PRIVACY LIKE THAT?
BWA-HA-HAAA!
DO YOU HAVE ANY IDEA HOW HARD WE WORK TO KEEP THIS PLACE SECURE? AND NOW WE'VE GOT A BUSTED COMM CONSOLE TO DEAL WITH.
WAY TO GO, WALKING TEEN CLICHÉ.
I LEAVE THE ISLAND FOR THE FIRST TIME SINCE FOREVER AND THAT'S WHEN YOU THROW A PARTY?! WAY TO GO, HORN BRAIN.

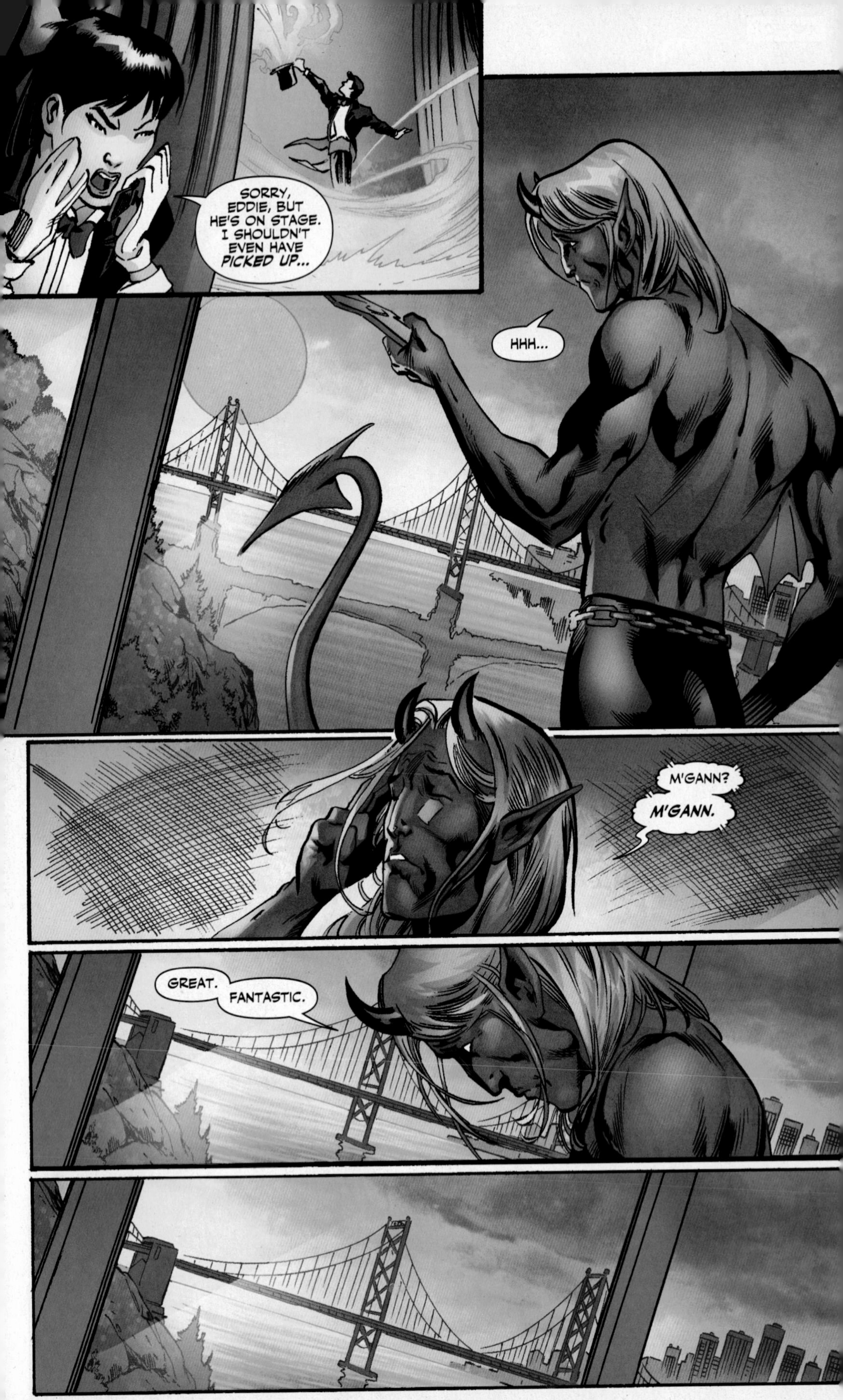
SORRY, EDDIE, BUT HE'S ON STAGE. I SHOULDN'T EVEN HAVE PICKED UP...
HHH...
M'GANN?
M'GANN.
GREAT.
FANTASTIC.

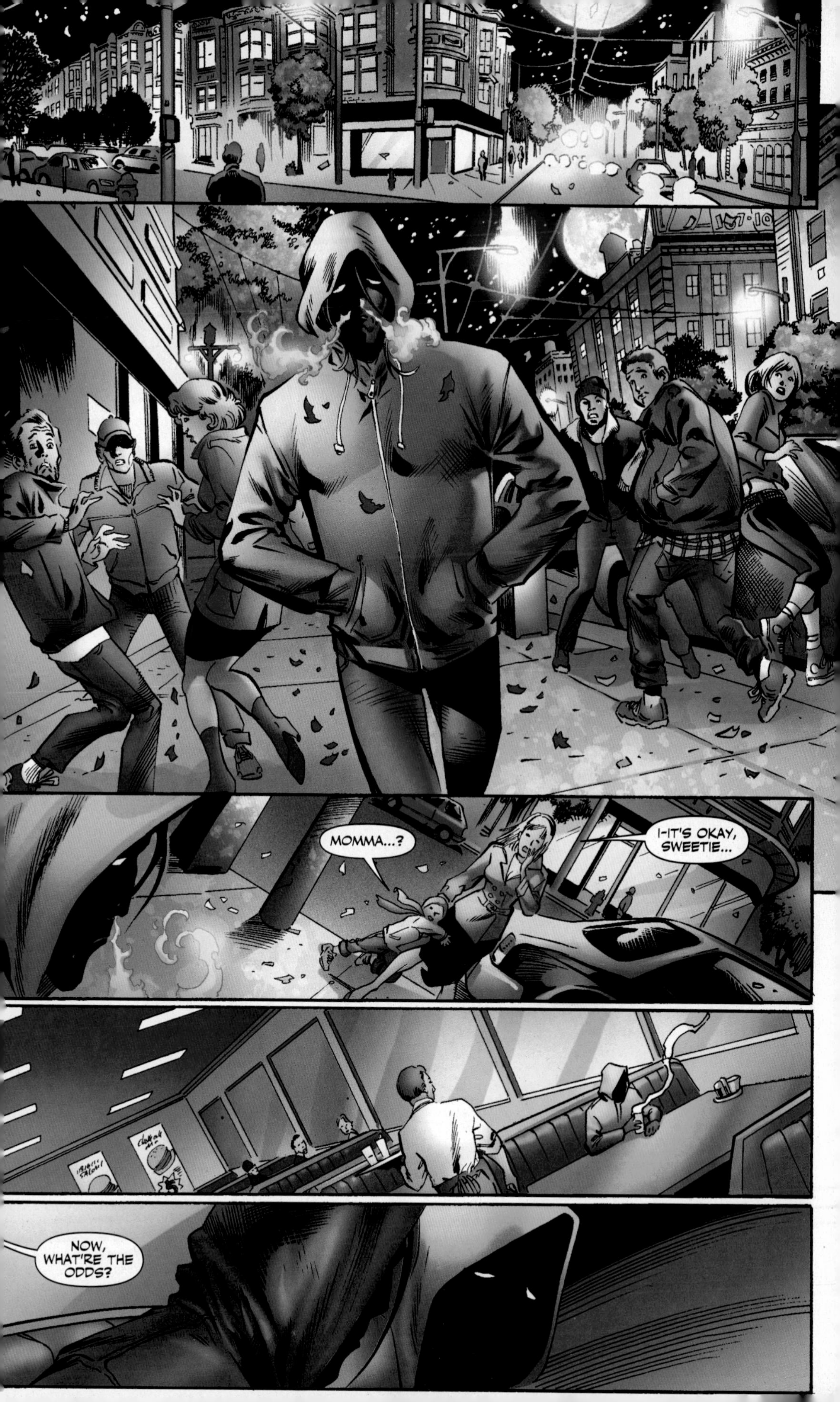
MOMMA...?
I-IT'S OKAY, SWEETIE...
NOW, WHAT'RE THE ODDS?

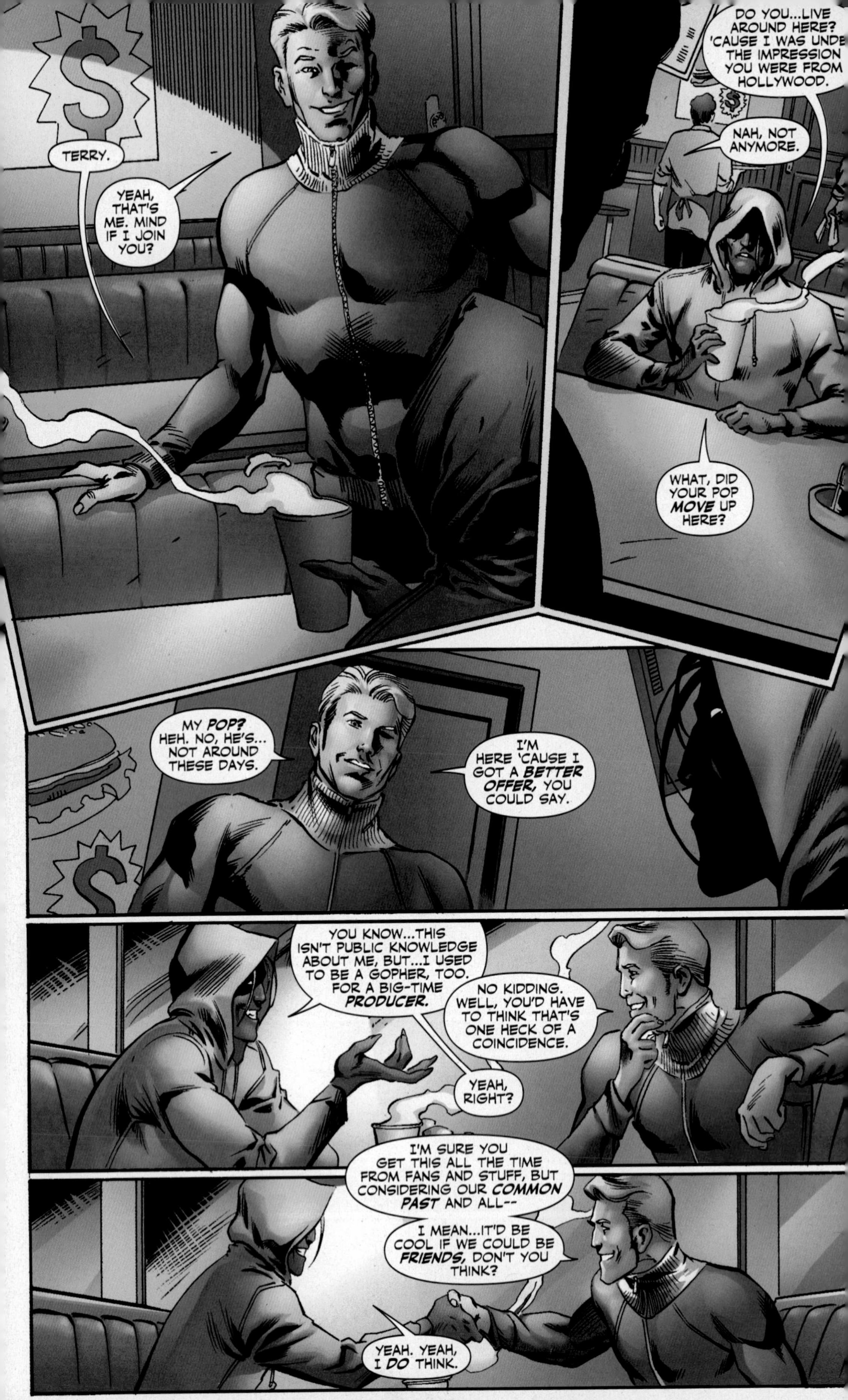
TERRY.
YEAH, THAT'S ME. MIND IF I JOIN YOU?
DO YOU...LIVE AROUND HERE? 'CAUSE I WAS UNDE THE IMPRESSION YOU WERE FROM HOLLYWOOD.
NAH, NOT ANYMORE.
WHAT, DID YOUR POP MOVE UP HERE?
MY POP? HEH. NO, HE'S... NOT AROUND THESE DAYS.
I'M HERE 'CAUSE I GOT A BETTER OFFER, YOU COULD SAY.
YOU KNOW...THIS ISN'T PUBLIC KNOWLEDGE ABOUT ME, BUT...I USED TO BE A GOPHER, TOO. FOR A BIG-TIME PRODUCER.
NO KIDDING. WELL, YOU'D HAVE TO THINK THAT'S ONE HECK OF A COINCIDENCE.
YEAH, RIGHT?
I'M SURE YOU GET THIS ALL THE TIME FROM FANS AND STUFF, BUT CONSIDERING OUR COMMON PAST AND ALL--
I MEAN...IT'D BE COOL IF WE COULD BE FRIENDS, DON'T YOU THINK?
YEAH. YEAH, I DO THINK.

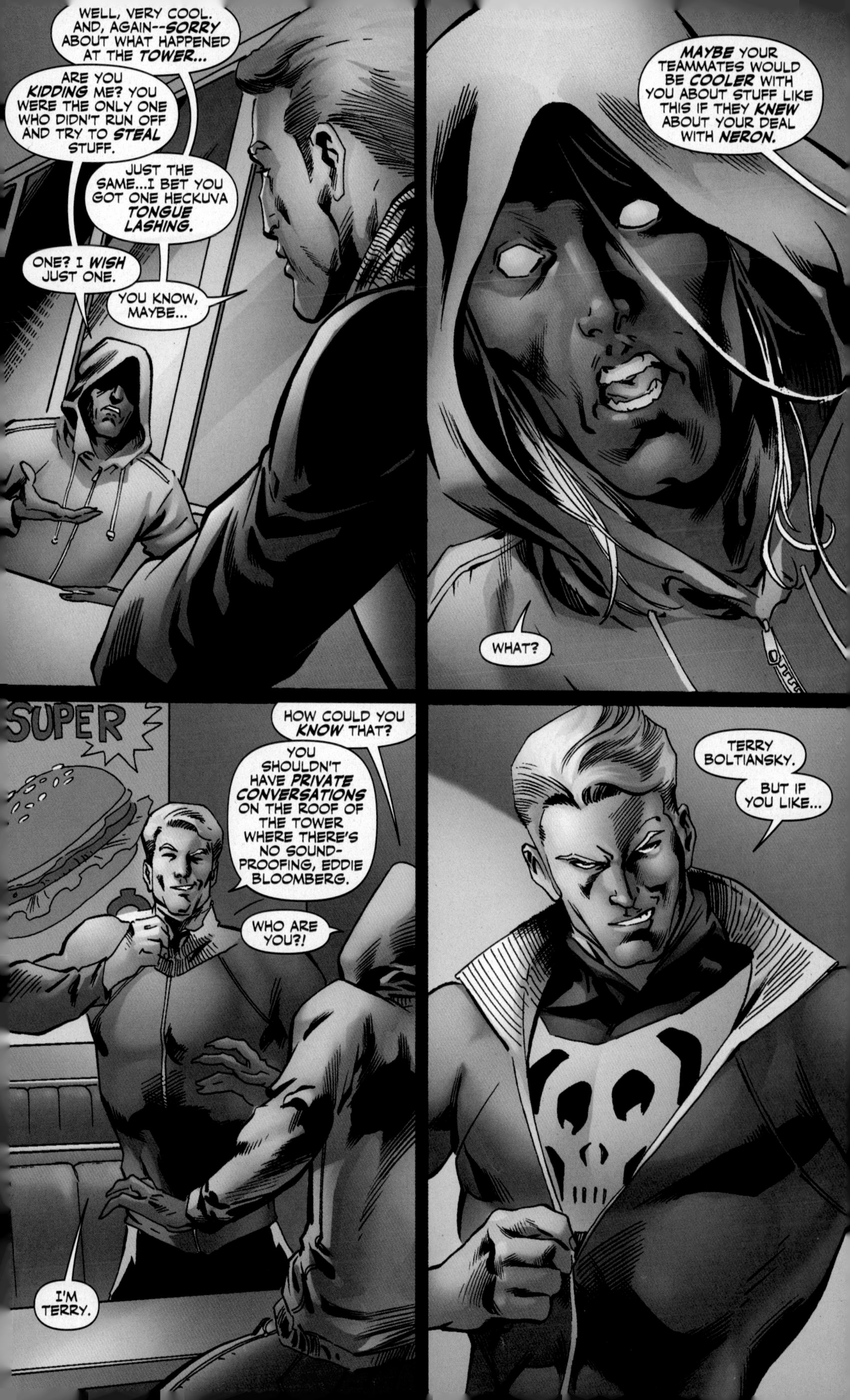
WELL, VERY COOL. AND, AGAIN--SORRY ABOUT WHAT HAPPENED AT THE TOWER...
ARE YOU KIDDING ME? YOU WERE THE ONLY ONE WHO DIDN'T RUN OFF AND TRY TO STEAL STUFF.
JUST THE SAME...I BET YOU GOT ONE HECKUVA TONGUE LASHING.
ONE? I WISH JUST ONE.
YOU KNOW, MAYBE...
MAYBE YOUR TEAMMATES WOULD BE COOLER WITH YOU ABOUT STUFF LIKE THIS IF THEY KNEW ABOUT YOUR DEAL WITH NERON.
WHAT?
SUPER
HOW COULD YOU KNOW THAT?
YOU SHOULDN'T HAVE PRIVATE CONVERSATIONS ON THE ROOF OF THE TOWER WHERE THERE'S NO SOUND-PROOFING, EDDIE BLOOMBERG.
WHO ARE YOU?!
I'M TERRY.
TERRY BOLTIANSKY.
BUT IF YOU LIKE...

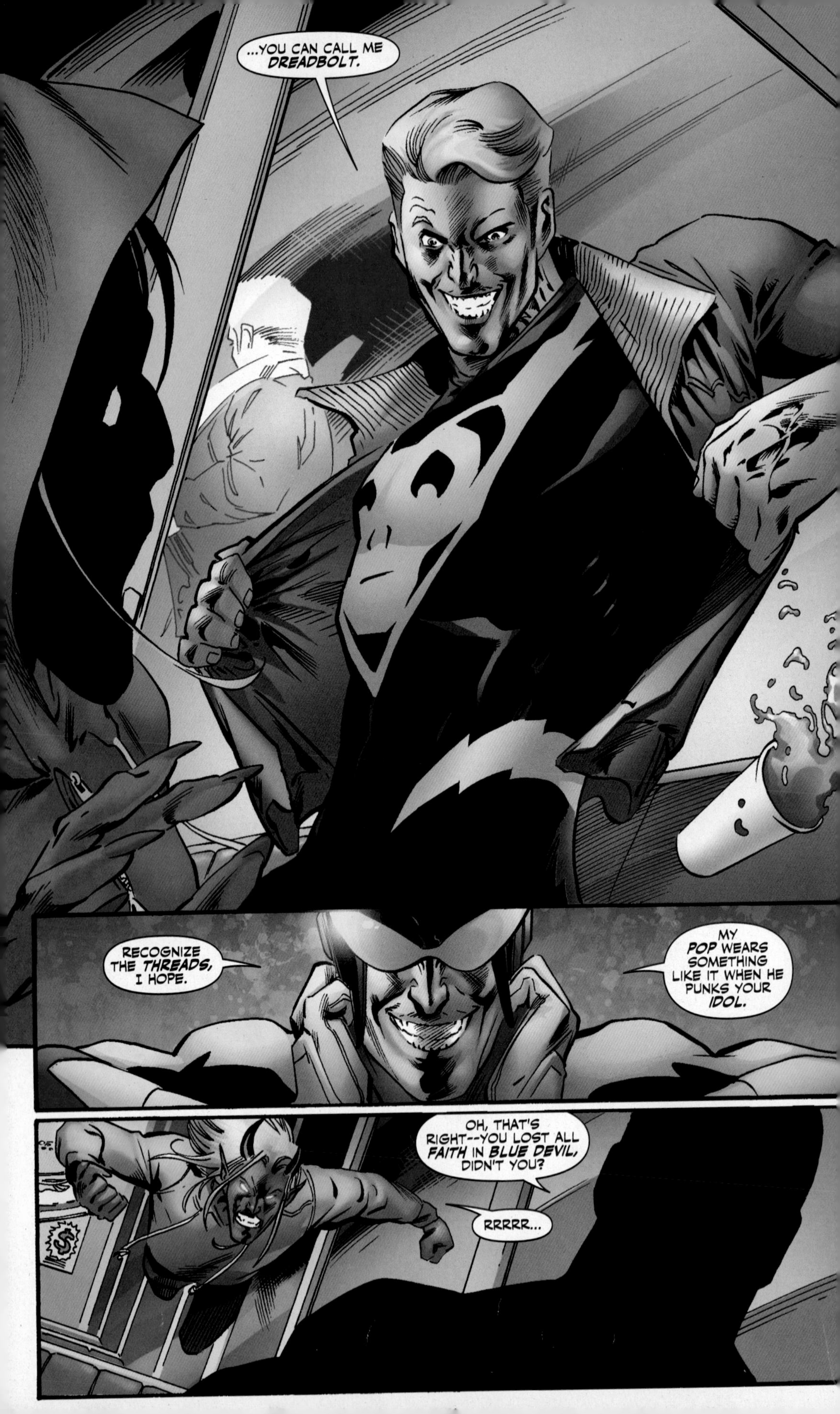
...YOU CAN CALL ME DREADBOLT.
RECOGNIZE THE THREADS, I HOPE.
MY POP WEARS SOMETHING LIKE IT WHEN HE PUNKS YOUR IDOL.
OH, THAT'S RIGHT--YOU LOST ALL FAITH IN BLUE DEVIL, DIDN'T YOU?
RRRRR...

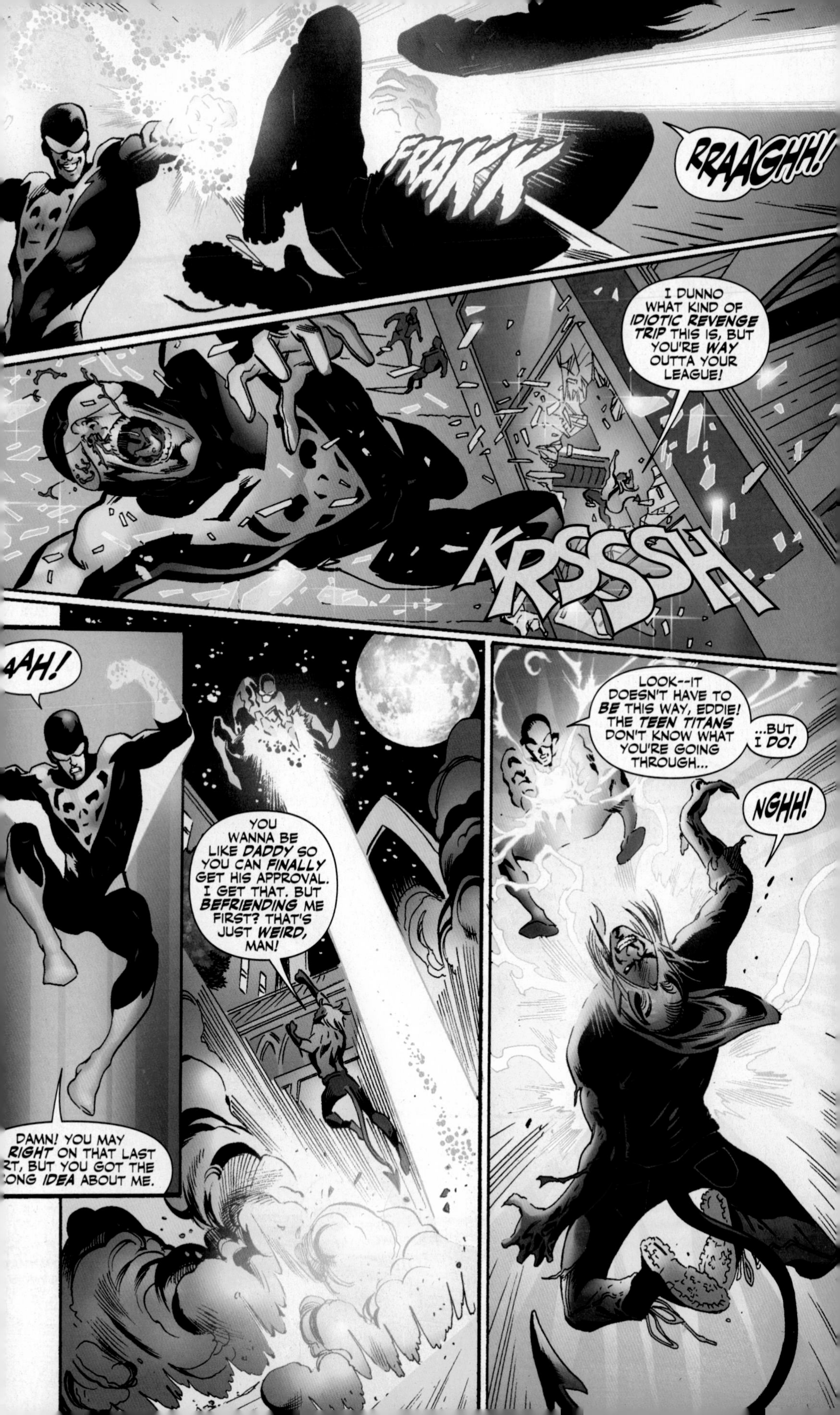
FRAKK
RRAAGHH!
I DUNNO WHAT KIND OF IDIOTIC REVENGE TRIP THIS IS, BUT YOU'RE WAY OUTTA YOUR LEAGUE!
KRSSSH
AAH!
YOU WANNA BE LIKE DADDY SO YOU CAN FINALLY GET HIS APPROVAL. I GET THAT. BUT BEFRIENDING ME FIRST? THAT'S JUST WEIRD, MAN!
DAMN! YOU MAY RIGHT ON THAT LAST RT, BUT YOU GOT THE ONG IDEA ABOUT ME.
LOOK--IT DOESN'T HAVE TO BE THIS WAY, EDDIE! THE TEEN TITANS DON'T KNOW WHAT YOU'RE GOING THROUGH...
...BUT I DO!
NGHH!

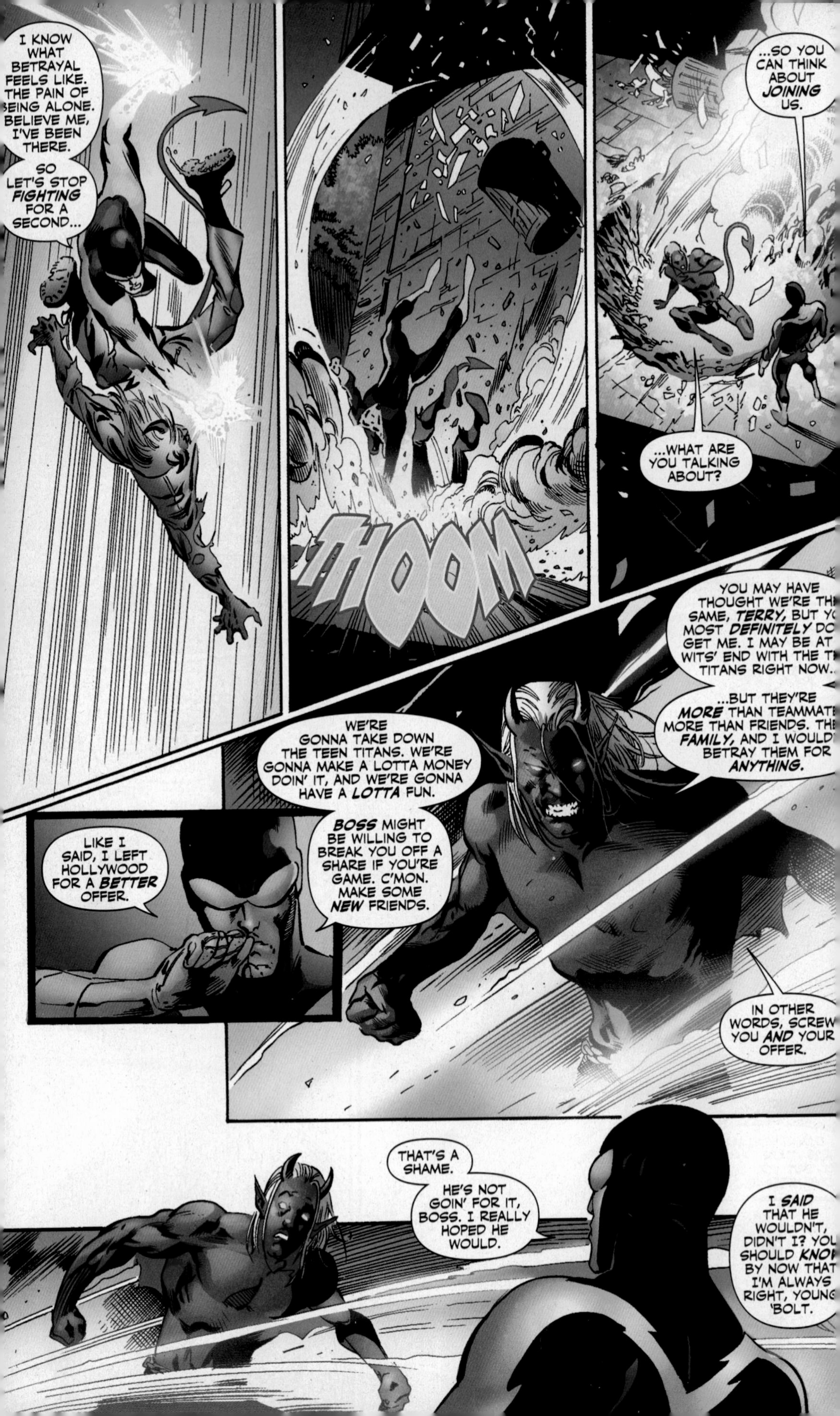

I KNOW WHAT BETRAYAL FEELS LIKE. THE PAIN OF BEING ALONE. BELIEVE ME, I'VE BEEN THERE.
SO LET'S STOP FIGHTING FOR A SECOND...
THOOM
...SO YOU CAN THINK ABOUT JOINING US.
...WHAT ARE YOU TALKING ABOUT?
WE'RE GONNA TAKE DOWN THE TEEN TITANS. WE'RE GONNA MAKE A LOTTA MONEY DOIN' IT, AND WE'RE GONNA HAVE A LOTTA FUN.
BOSS MIGHT BE WILLING TO BREAK YOU OFF A SHARE IF YOU'RE GAME. C'MON. MAKE SOME NEW FRIENDS.
LIKE I SAID, I LEFT HOLLYWOOD FOR A BETTER OFFER.
YOU MAY HAVE THOUGHT WE'RE TH SAME, TERRY, BUT YO MOST DEFINITELY DO GET ME. I MAY BE AT WITS' END WITH THE TI TITANS RIGHT NOW...
...BUT THEY'RE MORE THAN TEAMMATE MORE THAN FRIENDS. THE FAMILY, AND I WOULD BETRAY THEM FOR ANYTHING.
IN OTHER WORDS, SCREW YOU AND YOUR OFFER.
THAT'S A SHAME.
HE'S NOT GOIN' FOR IT, BOSS. I REALLY HOPED HE WOULD.
I SAID THAT HE WOULDN'T, DIDN'T I? YOU SHOULD KNOW BY NOW THAT I'M ALWAYS RIGHT, YOUNG 'BOLT.

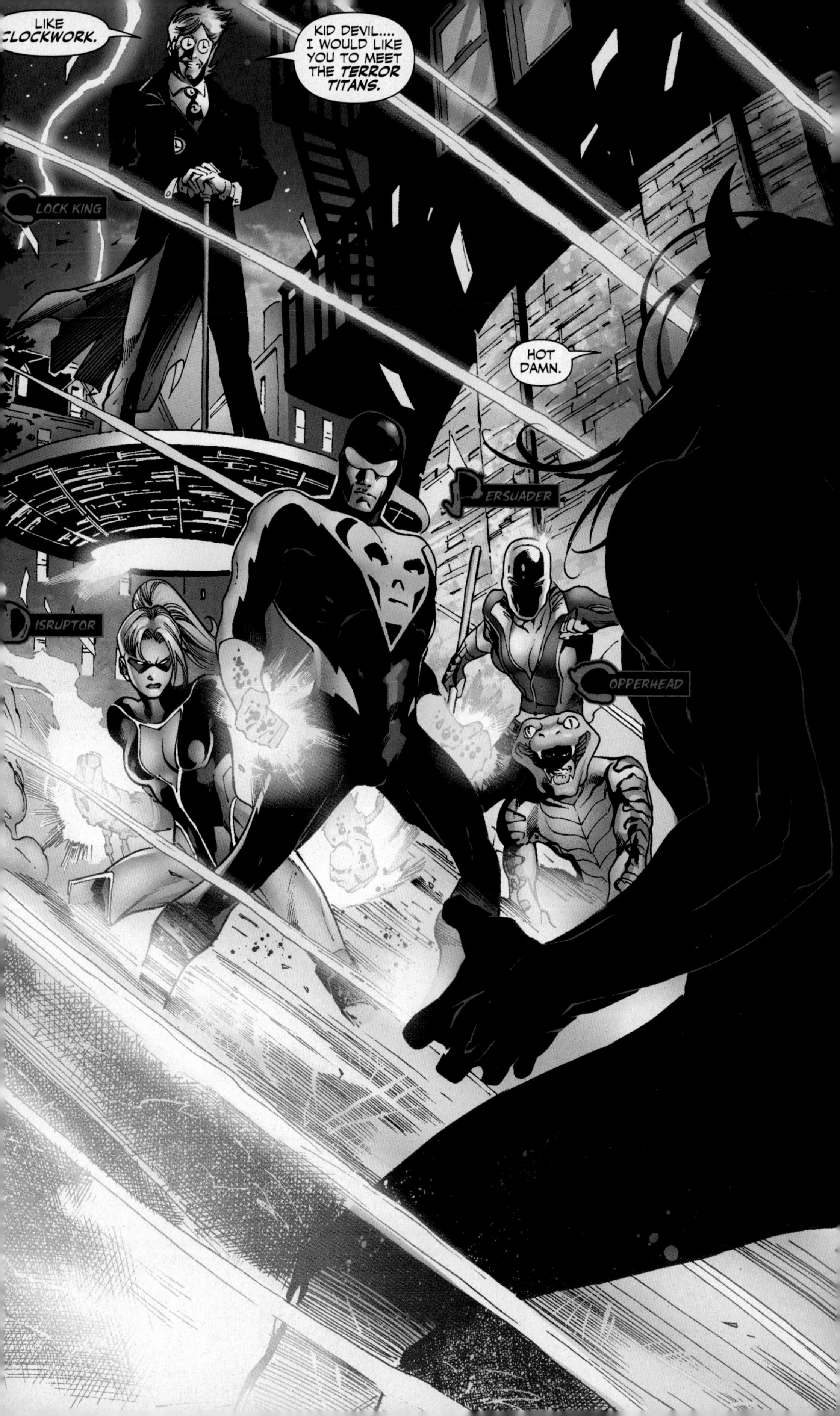
LIKE CLOCKWORK.
KID DEVIL.... I WOULD LIKE YOU TO MEET THE TERROR TITANS.
CLOCK KING
HOT DAMN.
PERSUADER
DISRUPTOR
COPPERHEAD

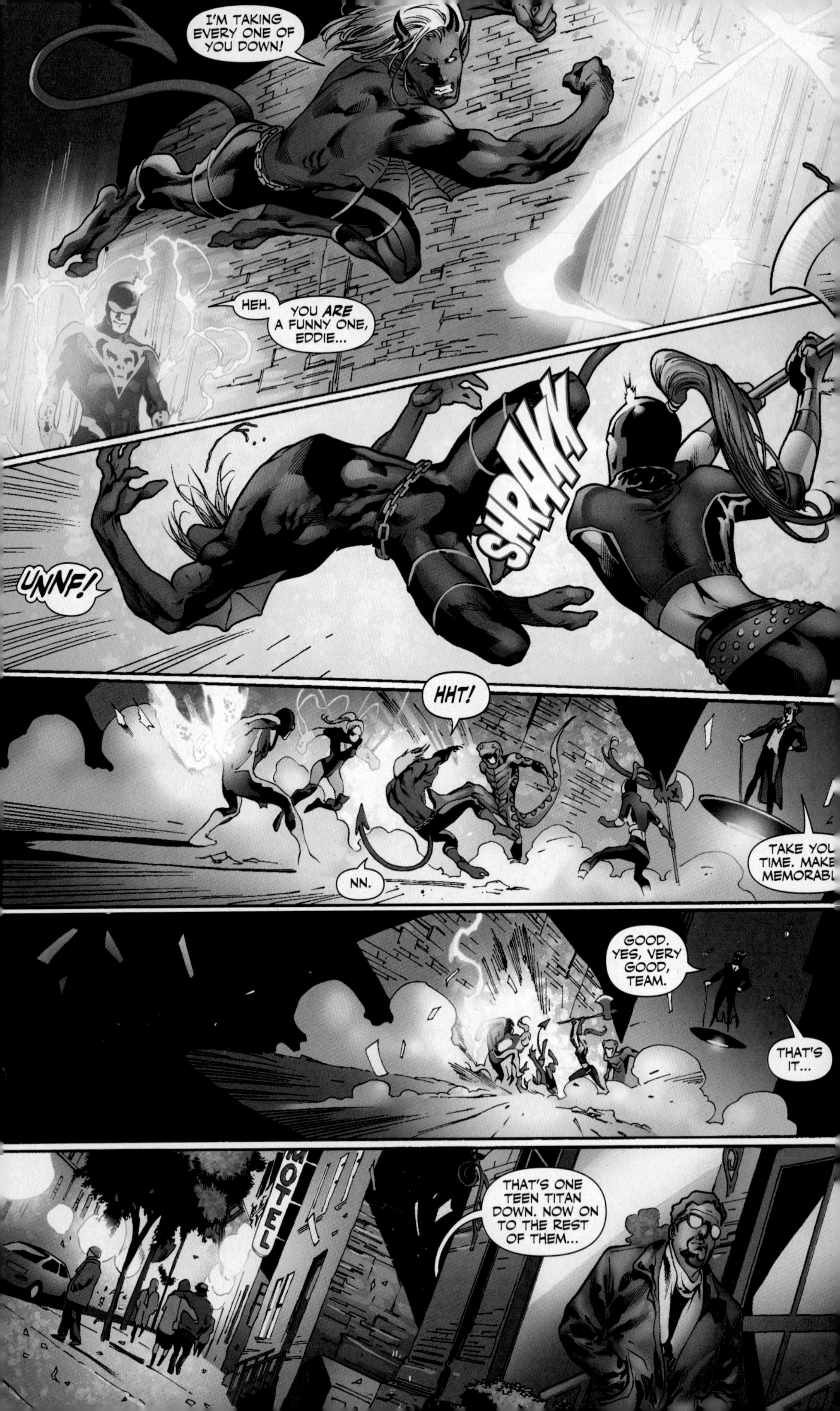

I'M TAKING EVERY ONE OF YOU DOWN!
HEH.
YOU *ARE* A FUNNY ONE, EDDIE...
SHRAKK
UNNF!
HHT!
NN.
TAKE YOU
TIME. MAKE
MEMORABL
GOOD. YES, VERY GOOD, TEAM.
THAT'S IT...
MOTEL
THAT'S ONE TEEN TITAN DOWN. NOW ON TO THE REST OF THEM...

TEEN TITANS 57 - Eddy Barrows, Julio Ferreira and Rod Reis

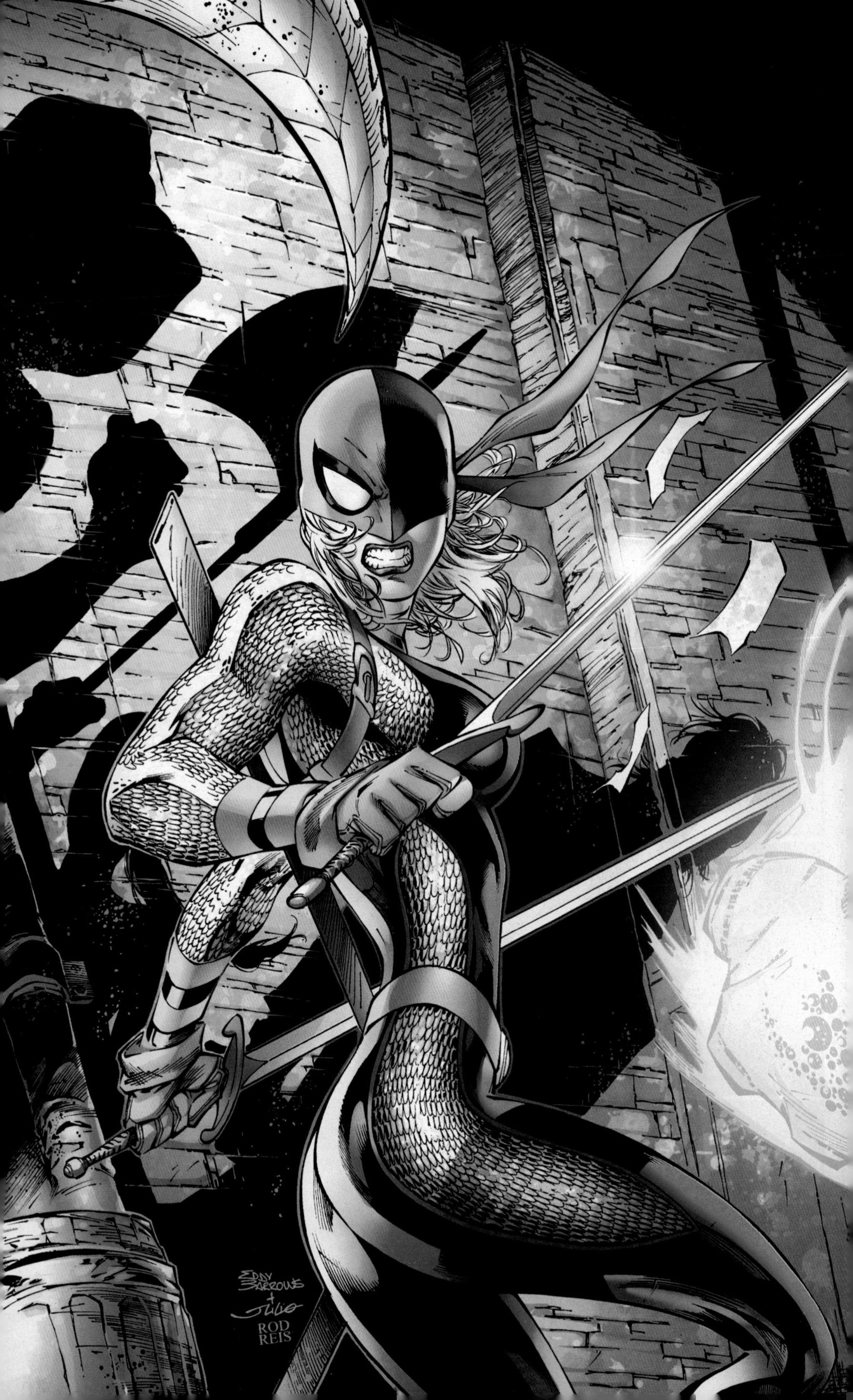
EDDY BARROWS + JULIO
ROD REIS

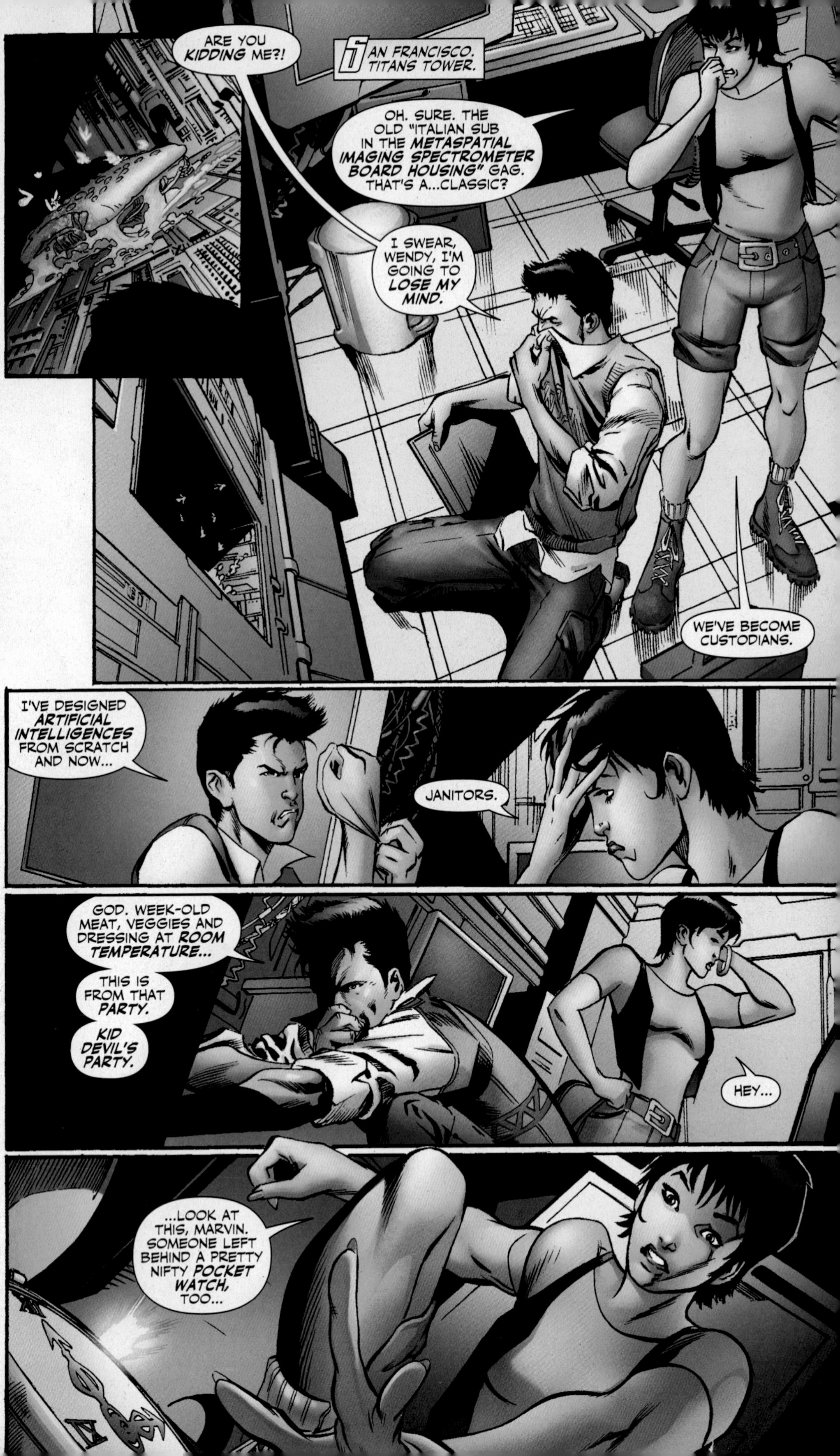
SAN FRANCISCO. TITANS TOWER.
ARE YOU KIDDING ME?!
OH. SURE. THE OLD "ITALIAN SUB IN THE METASPATIAL IMAGING SPECTROMETER BOARD HOUSING" GAG. THAT'S A...CLASSIC?
I SWEAR, WENDY, I'M GOING TO LOSE MY MIND.
WE'VE BECOME CUSTODIANS.
I'VE DESIGNED ARTIFICIAL INTELLIGENCES FROM SCRATCH AND NOW...
JANITORS.
GOD. WEEK-OLD MEAT, VEGGIES AND DRESSING AT ROOM TEMPERATURE...
THIS IS FROM THAT PARTY.
KID DEVIL'S PARTY.
HEY...
...LOOK AT THIS, MARVIN. SOMEONE LEFT BEHIND A PRETTY NIFTY POCKET WATCH, TOO...

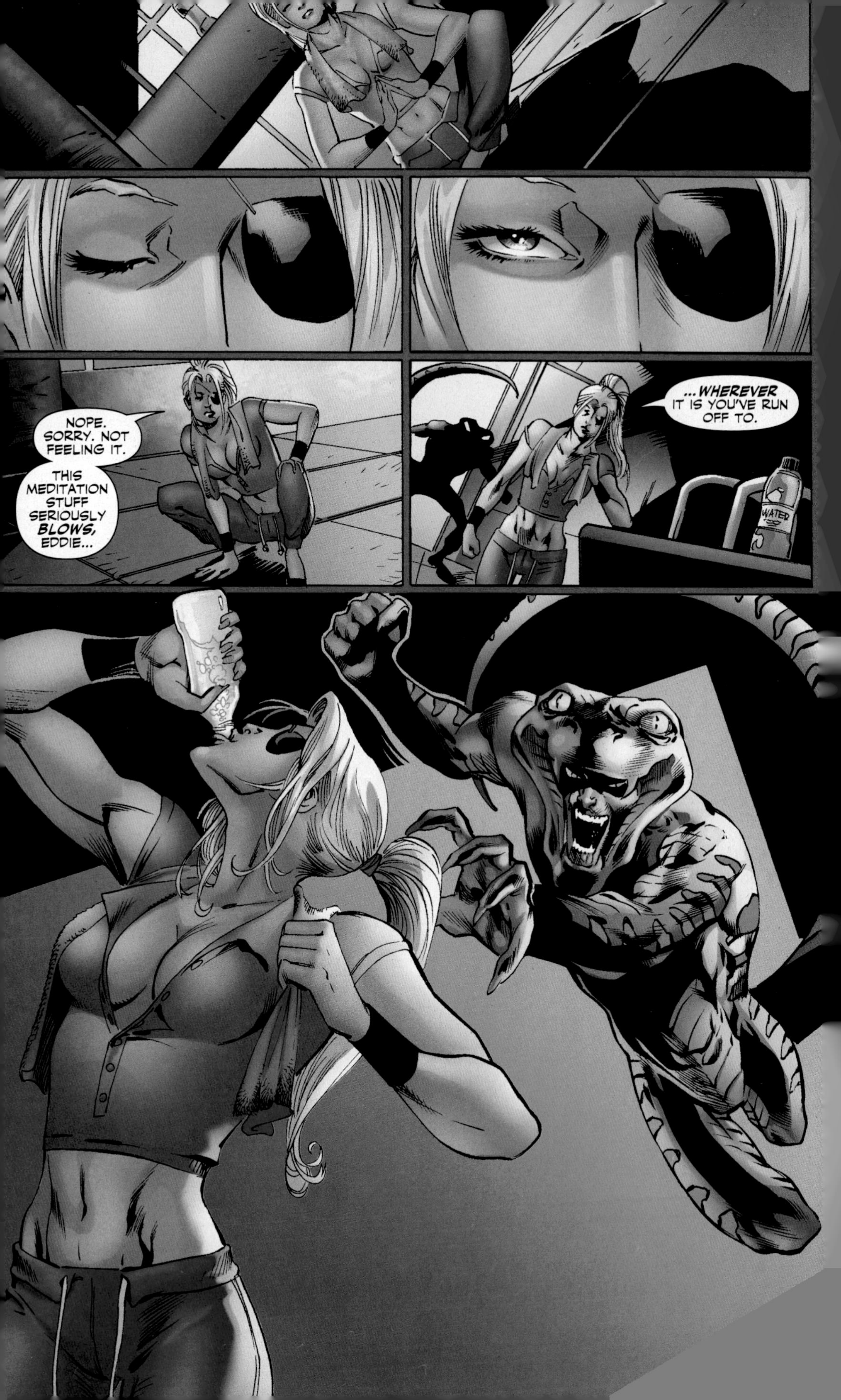

NOPE. SORRY. NOT FEELING IT.
THIS MEDITATION STUFF SERIOUSLY BLOWS, EDDIE...
...WHEREVER IT IS YOU'VE RUN OFF TO.
WATER

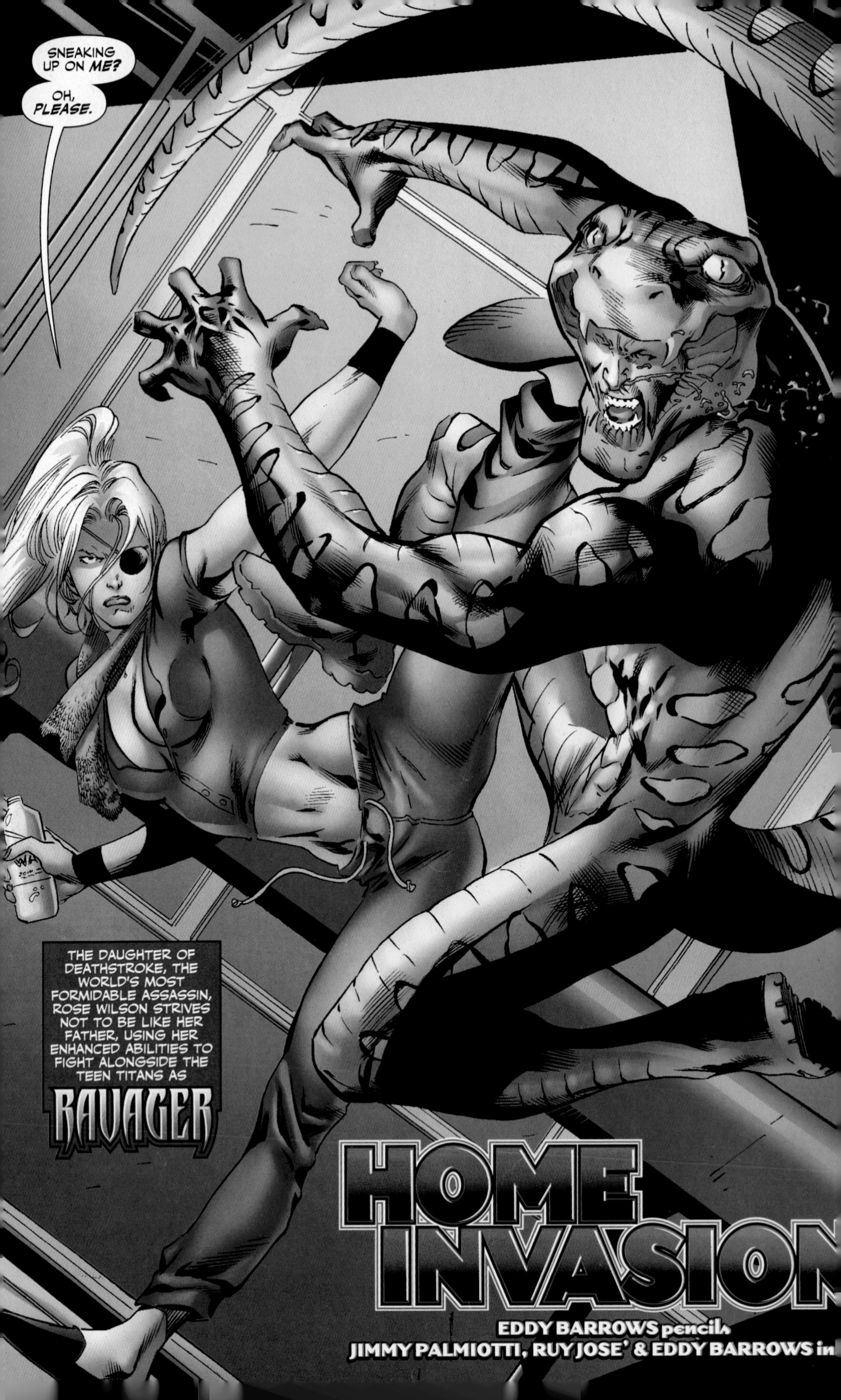
SNEAKING UP ON ME?
OH, PLEASE.
THE DAUGHTER OF DEATHSTROKE, THE WORLD'S MOST FORMIDABLE ASSASSIN, ROSE WILSON STRIVES NOT TO BE LIKE HER FATHER, USING HER ENHANCED ABILITIES TO FIGHT ALONGSIDE THE TEEN TITANS AS
RAVAGER
HOME INVASION
EDDY BARROWS pencils
JIMMY PALMIOTTI, RUY JOSE' & EDDY BARROWS in

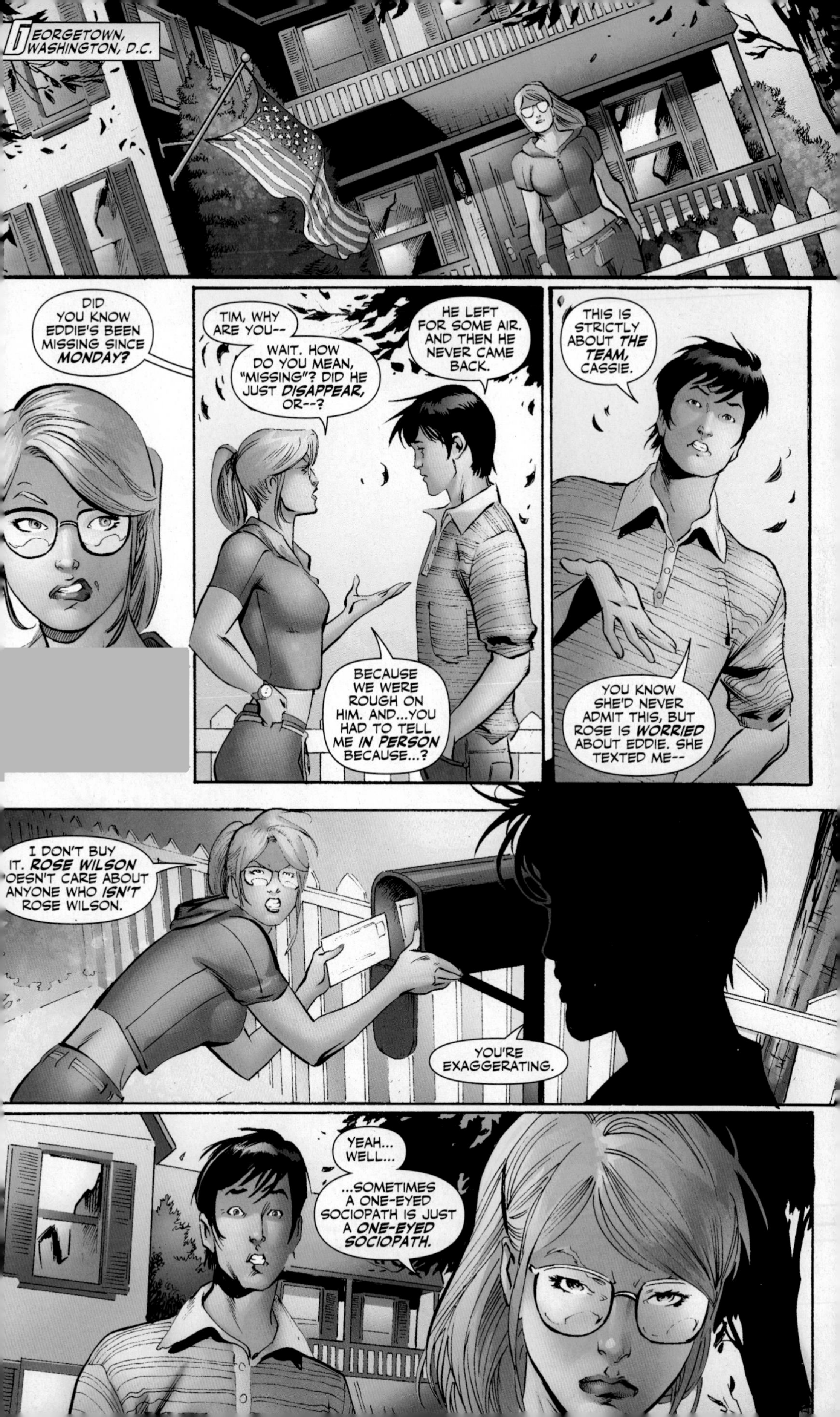
GEORGETOWN, WASHINGTON, D.C.
DID YOU KNOW EDDIE'S BEEN MISSING SINCE MONDAY?
TIM, WHY ARE YOU--
WAIT. HOW DO YOU MEAN, "MISSING"? DID HE JUST DISAPPEAR, OR--?
HE LEFT FOR SOME AIR. AND THEN HE NEVER CAME BACK.
BECAUSE WE WERE ROUGH ON HIM. AND...YOU HAD TO TELL ME IN PERSON BECAUSE...?
THIS IS STRICTLY ABOUT THE TEAM, CASSIE.
YOU KNOW SHE'D NEVER ADMIT THIS, BUT ROSE IS WORRIED ABOUT EDDIE. SHE TEXTED ME--
I DON'T BUY IT. ROSE WILSON OESN'T CARE ABOUT ANYONE WHO ISN'T ROSE WILSON.
YOU'RE EXAGGERATING.
YEAH... WELL...
...SOMETIMES A ONE-EYED SOCIOPATH IS JUST A ONE-EYED SOCIOPATH.

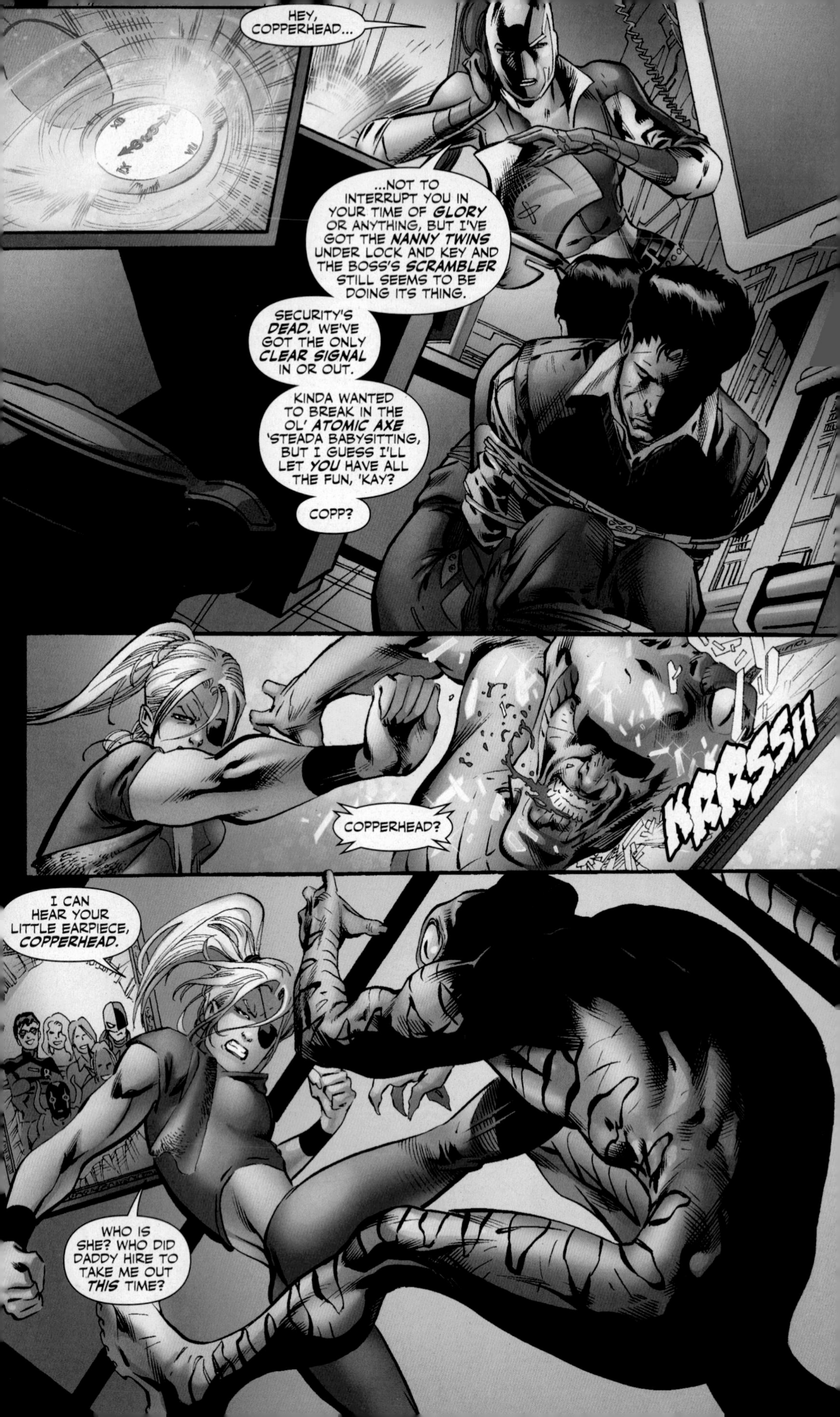
HEY, COPPERHEAD...
...NOT TO INTERRUPT YOU IN YOUR TIME OF GLORY OR ANYTHING, BUT I'VE GOT THE NANNY TWINS UNDER LOCK AND KEY AND THE BOSS'S SCRAMBLER STILL SEEMS TO BE DOING ITS THING.
SECURITY'S DEAD. WE'VE GOT THE ONLY CLEAR SIGNAL IN OR OUT.
KINDA WANTED TO BREAK IN THE OL' ATOMIC AXE 'STEADA BABYSITTING, BUT I GUESS I'LL LET YOU HAVE ALL THE FUN, 'KAY?
COPP?
COPPERHEAD?
KRASSH
I CAN HEAR YOUR LITTLE EARPIECE, COPPERHEAD.
WHO IS SHE? WHO DID DADDY HIRE TO TAKE ME OUT THIS TIME?

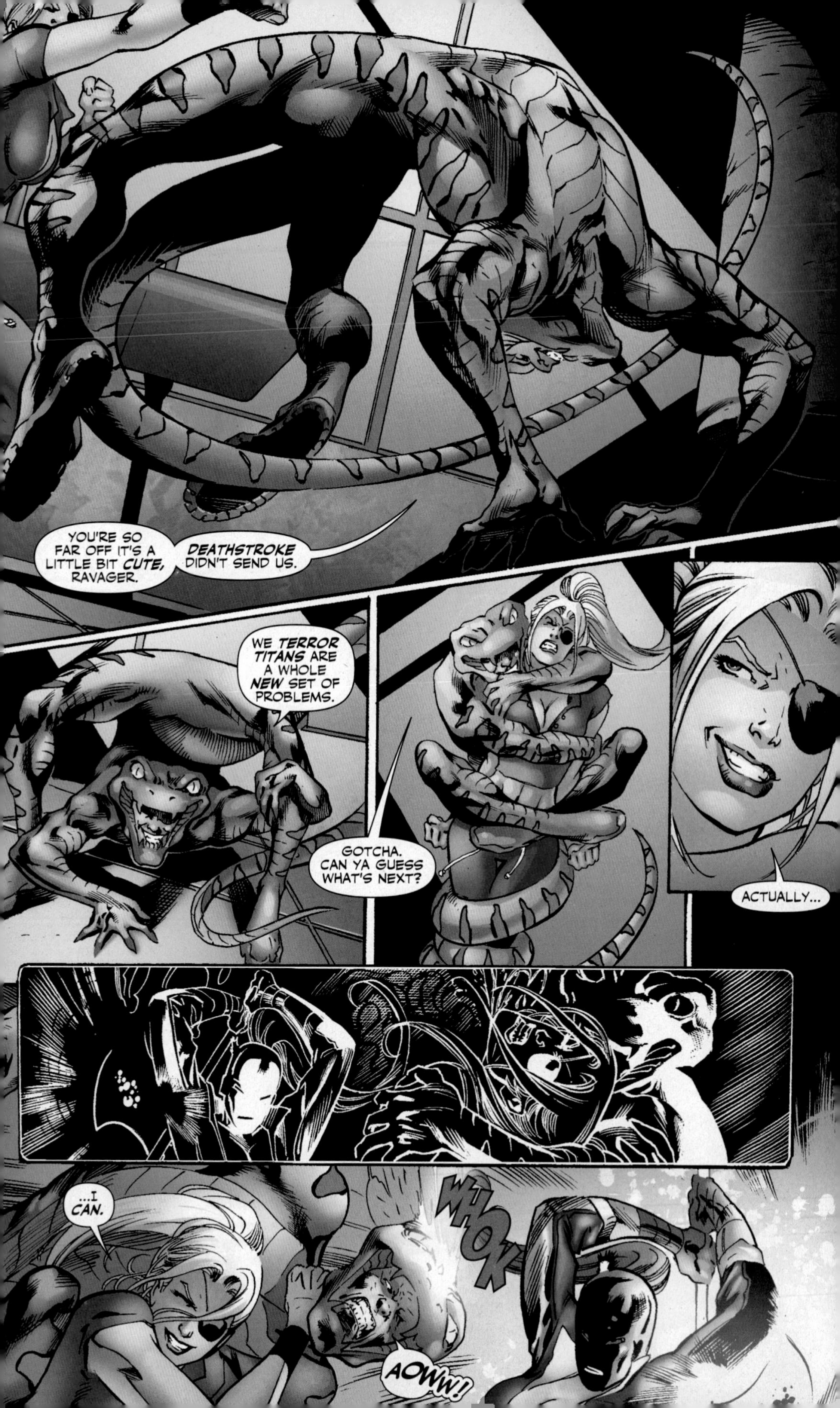
YOU'RE SO FAR OFF IT'S A LITTLE BIT CUTE, RAVAGER.
DEATHSTROKE DIDN'T SEND US.
WE TERROR TITANS ARE A WHOLE NEW SET OF PROBLEMS.
GOTCHA. CAN YA GUESS WHAT'S NEXT?
ACTUALLY...
...I CAN.
WHOK
AOWW!

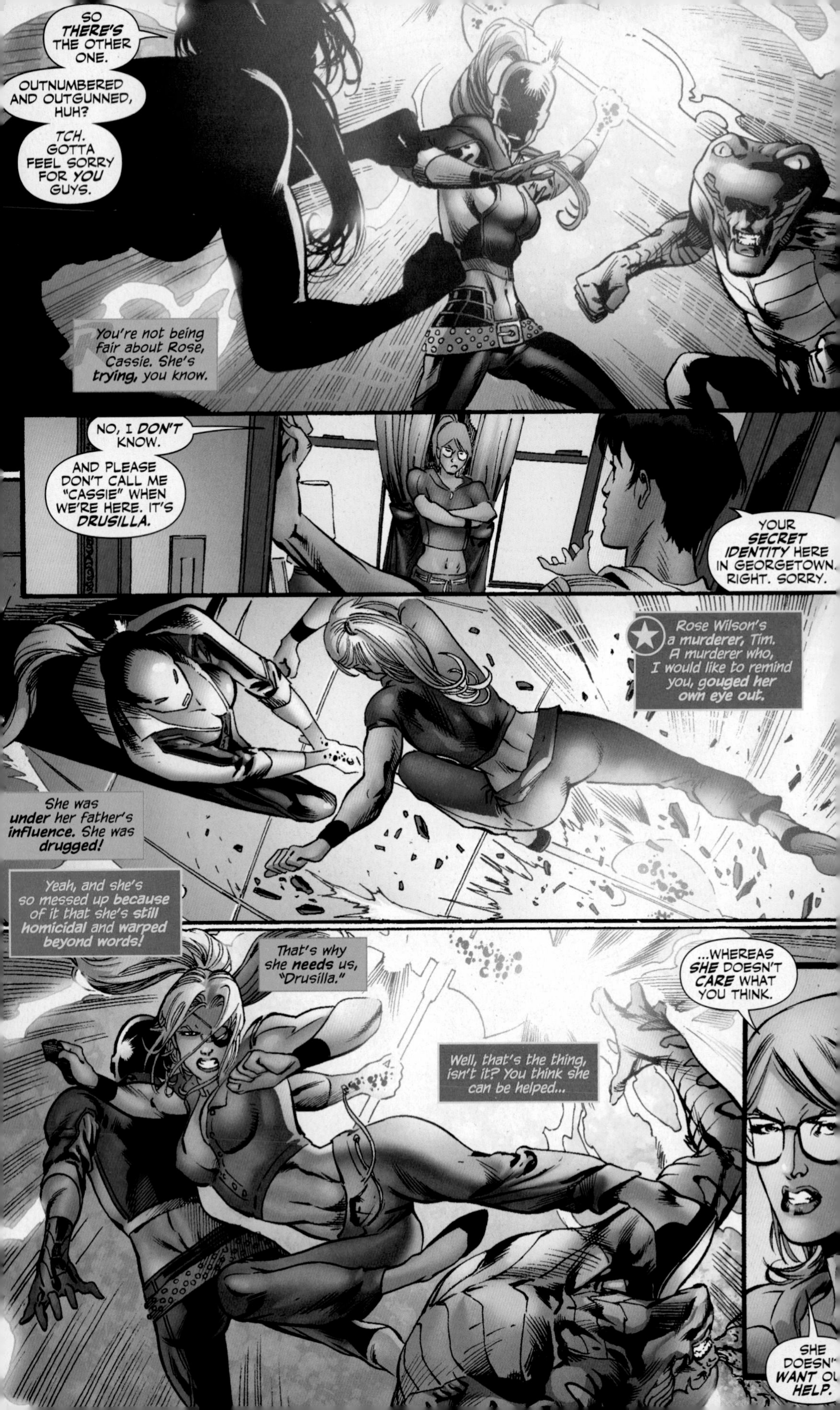
SO THERE'S THE OTHER ONE.
OUTNUMBERED AND OUTGUNNED, HUH?
TCH. GOTTA FEEL SORRY FOR YOU GUYS.
You're not being fair about Rose, Cassie. She's trying, you know.
NO, I DON'T KNOW.
AND PLEASE DON'T CALL ME "CASSIE" WHEN WE'RE HERE. IT'S DRUSILLA.
YOUR SECRET IDENTITY HERE IN GEORGETOWN. RIGHT. SORRY.
Rose Wilson's a murderer, Tim. A murderer who, I would like to remind you, gouged her own eye out.
She was under her father's influence. She was drugged!
Yeah, and she's so messed up because of it that she's still homicidal and warped beyond words!
That's why she needs us, "Drusilla."
Well, that's the thing, isn't it? You think she can be helped...
...WHEREAS SHE DOESN'T CARE WHAT YOU THINK.
SHE DOESN' WANT OU HELP.

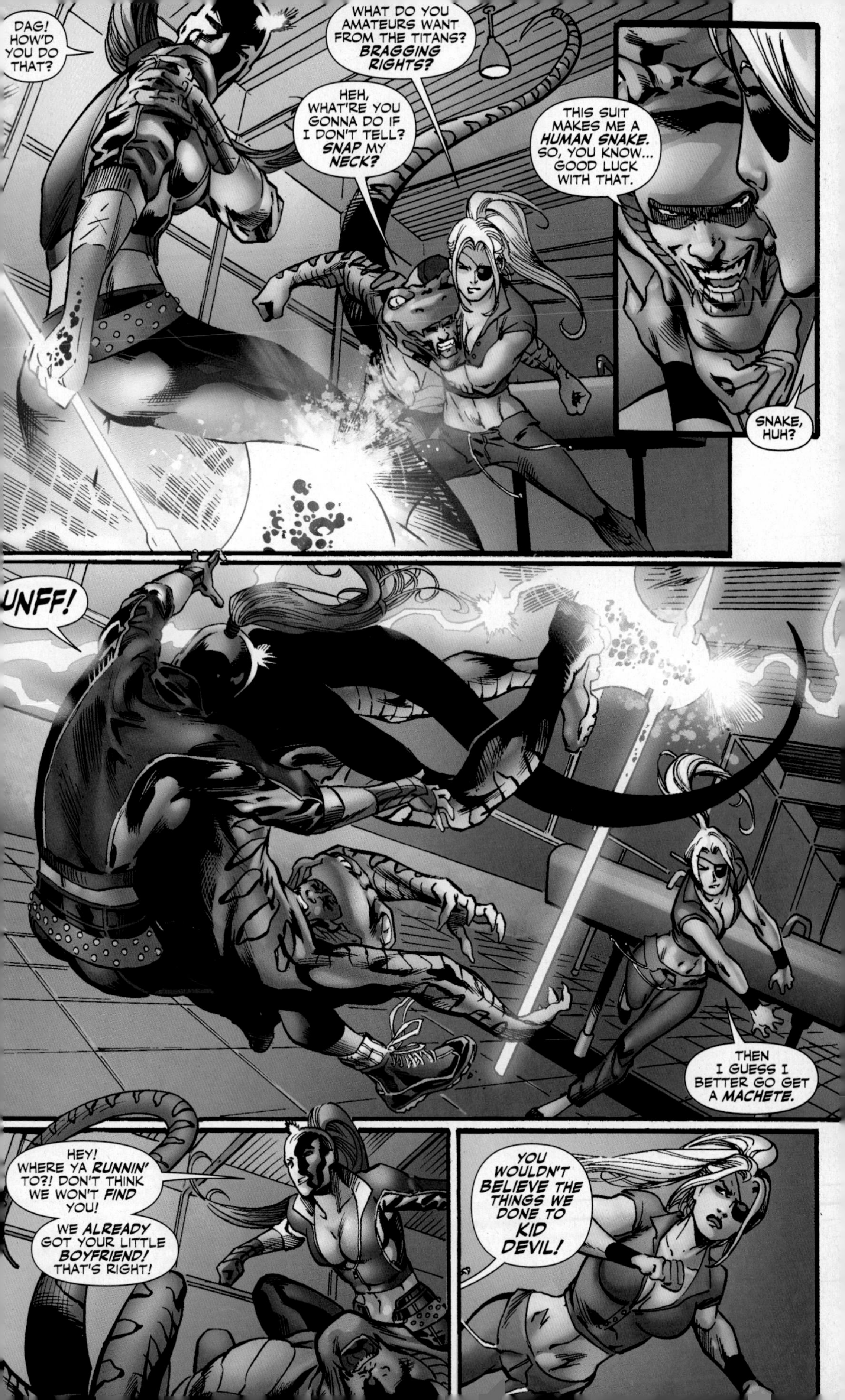
DAG! HOW'D YOU DO THAT?
WHAT DO YOU AMATEURS WANT FROM THE TITANS? BRAGGING RIGHTS?
HEH, WHAT'RE YOU GONNA DO IF I DON'T TELL? SNAP MY NECK?
THIS SUIT MAKES ME A HUMAN SNAKE. SO, YOU KNOW... GOOD LUCK WITH THAT.
SNAKE, HUH?
UNFF!
THEN I GUESS I BETTER GO GET A MACHETE.
HEY! WHERE YA RUNNIN' TO?! DON'T THINK WE WON'T FIND YOU!
WE ALREADY GOT YOUR LITTLE BOYFRIEND! THAT'S RIGHT!
YOU WOULDN'T BELIEVE THE THINGS WE DONE TO KID DEVIL!

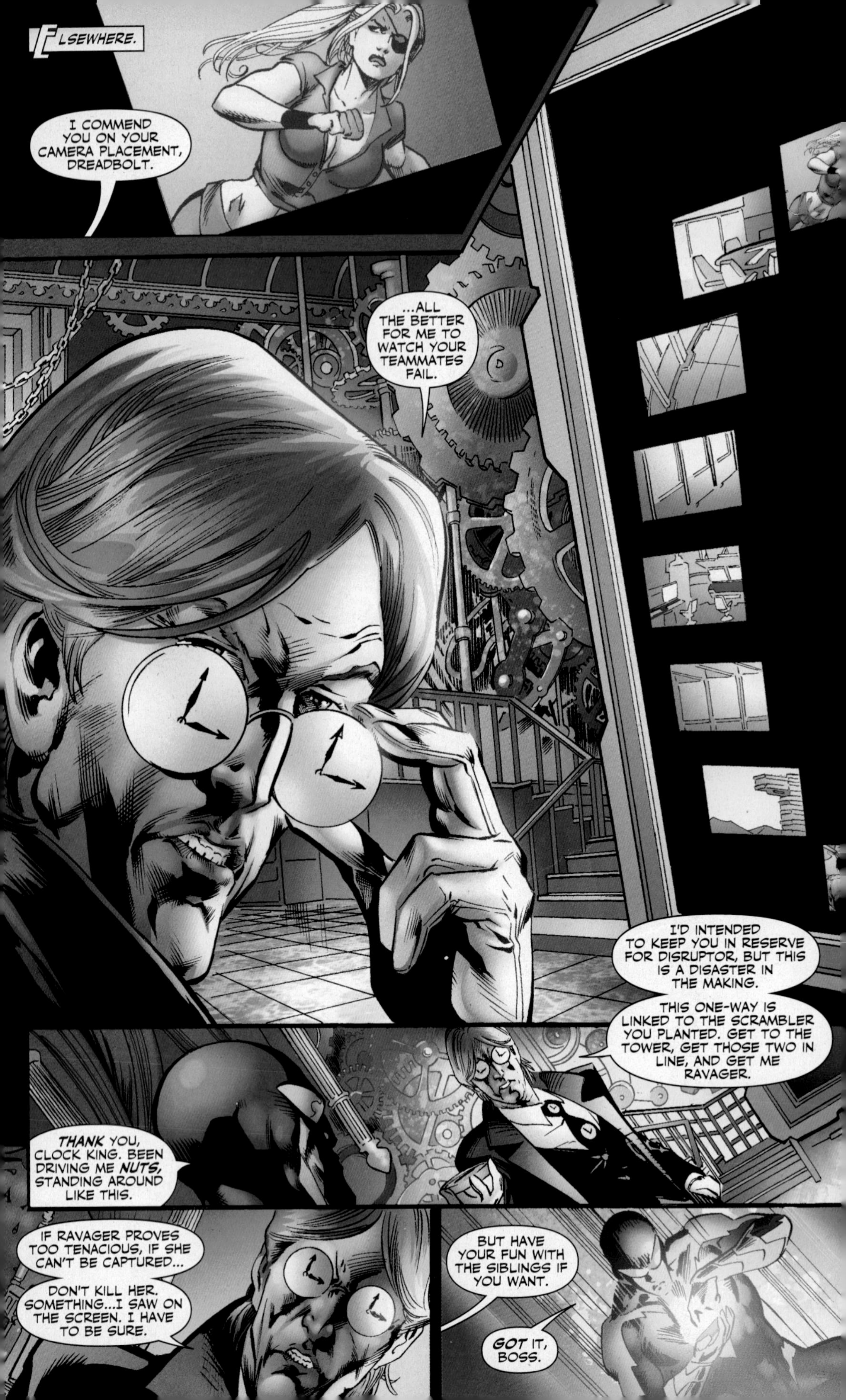
ELSEWHERE.
I COMMEND YOU ON YOUR CAMERA PLACEMENT, DREADBOLT.
...ALL THE BETTER FOR ME TO WATCH YOUR TEAMMATES FAIL.
I'D INTENDED TO KEEP YOU IN RESERVE FOR DISRUPTOR, BUT THIS IS A DISASTER IN THE MAKING.
THIS ONE-WAY IS LINKED TO THE SCRAMBLER YOU PLANTED. GET TO THE TOWER, GET THOSE TWO IN LINE, AND GET ME RAVAGER.
THANK YOU, CLOCK KING. BEEN DRIVING ME NUTS, STANDING AROUND LIKE THIS.
IF RAVAGER PROVES TOO TENACIOUS, IF SHE CAN'T BE CAPTURED...
DON'T KILL HER. SOMETHING...I SAW ON THE SCREEN. I HAVE TO BE SURE.
BUT HAVE YOUR FUN WITH THE SIBLINGS IF YOU WANT.
GOT IT, BOSS.

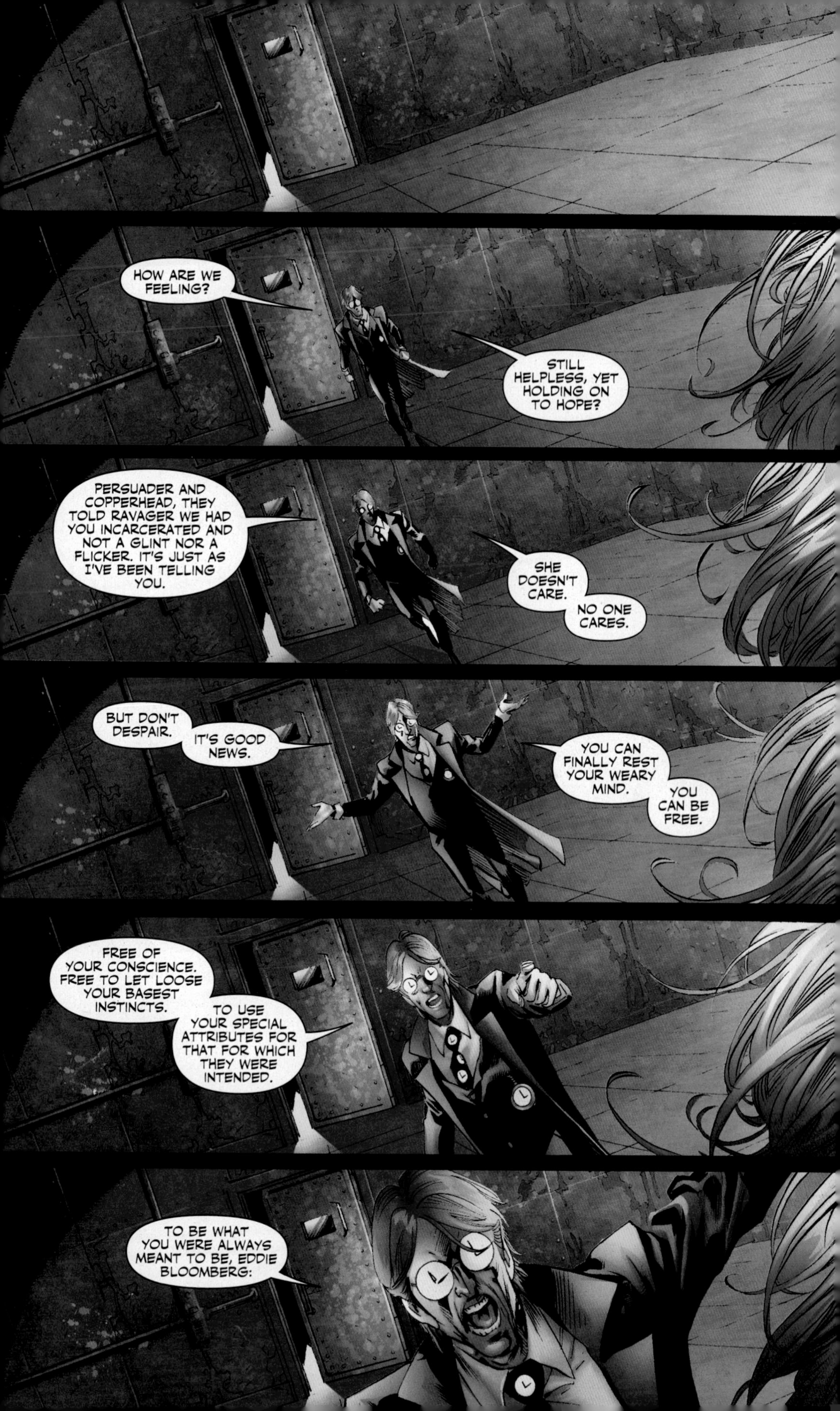
HOW ARE WE FEELING?
STILL HELPLESS, YET HOLDING ON TO HOPE?
PERSUADER AND COPPERHEAD, THEY TOLD RAVAGER WE HAD YOU INCARCERATED AND NOT A GLINT NOR A FLICKER. IT'S JUST AS I'VE BEEN TELLING YOU.
SHE DOESN'T CARE.
NO ONE CARES.
BUT DON'T DESPAIR.
IT'S GOOD NEWS.
YOU CAN FINALLY REST YOUR WEARY MIND.
YOU CAN BE FREE.
FREE OF YOUR CONSCIENCE. FREE TO LET LOOSE YOUR BASEST INSTINCTS.
TO USE YOUR SPECIAL ATTRIBUTES FOR THAT FOR WHICH THEY WERE INTENDED.
TO BE WHAT YOU WERE ALWAYS MEANT TO BE, EDDIE BLOOMBERG:

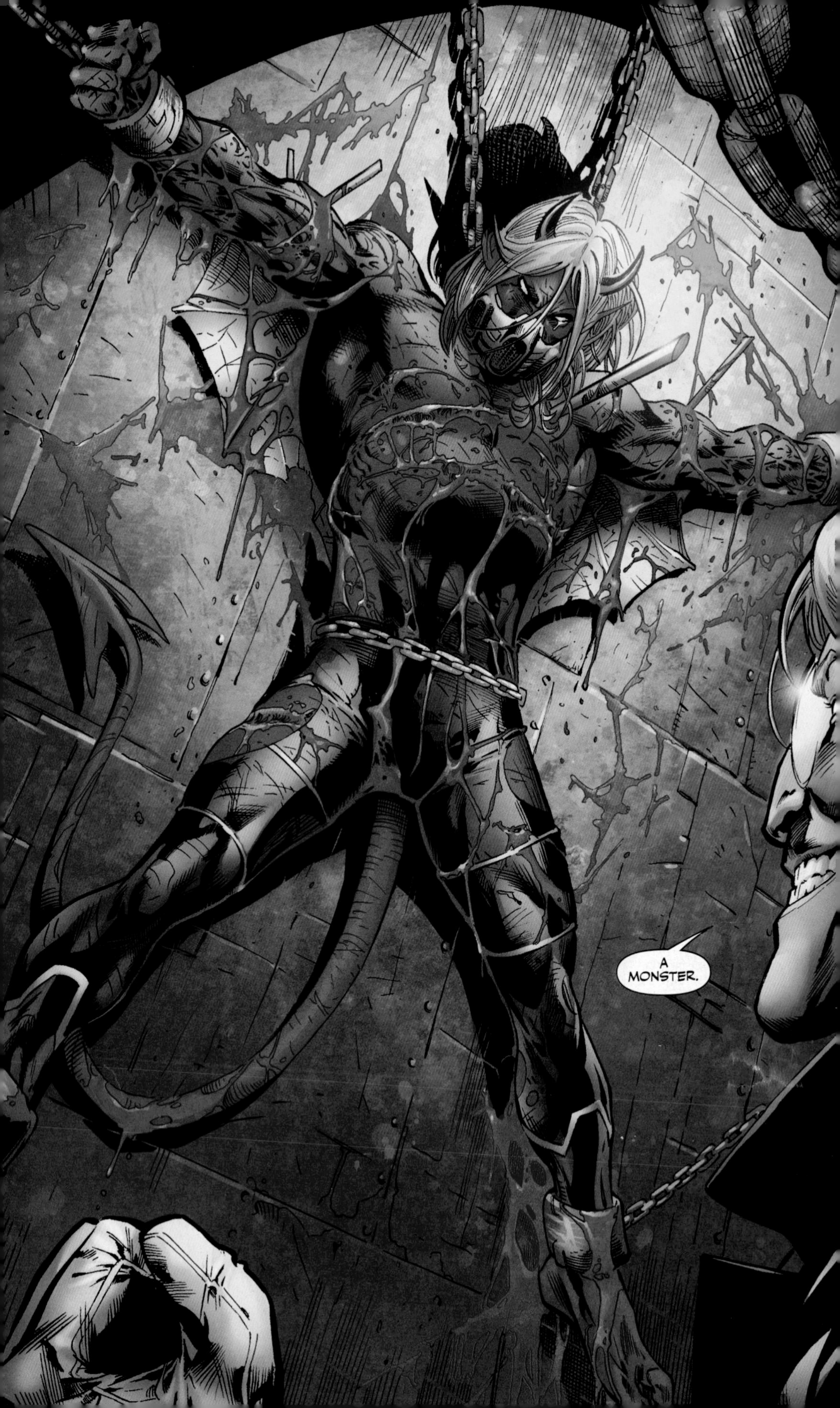
A MONSTER.

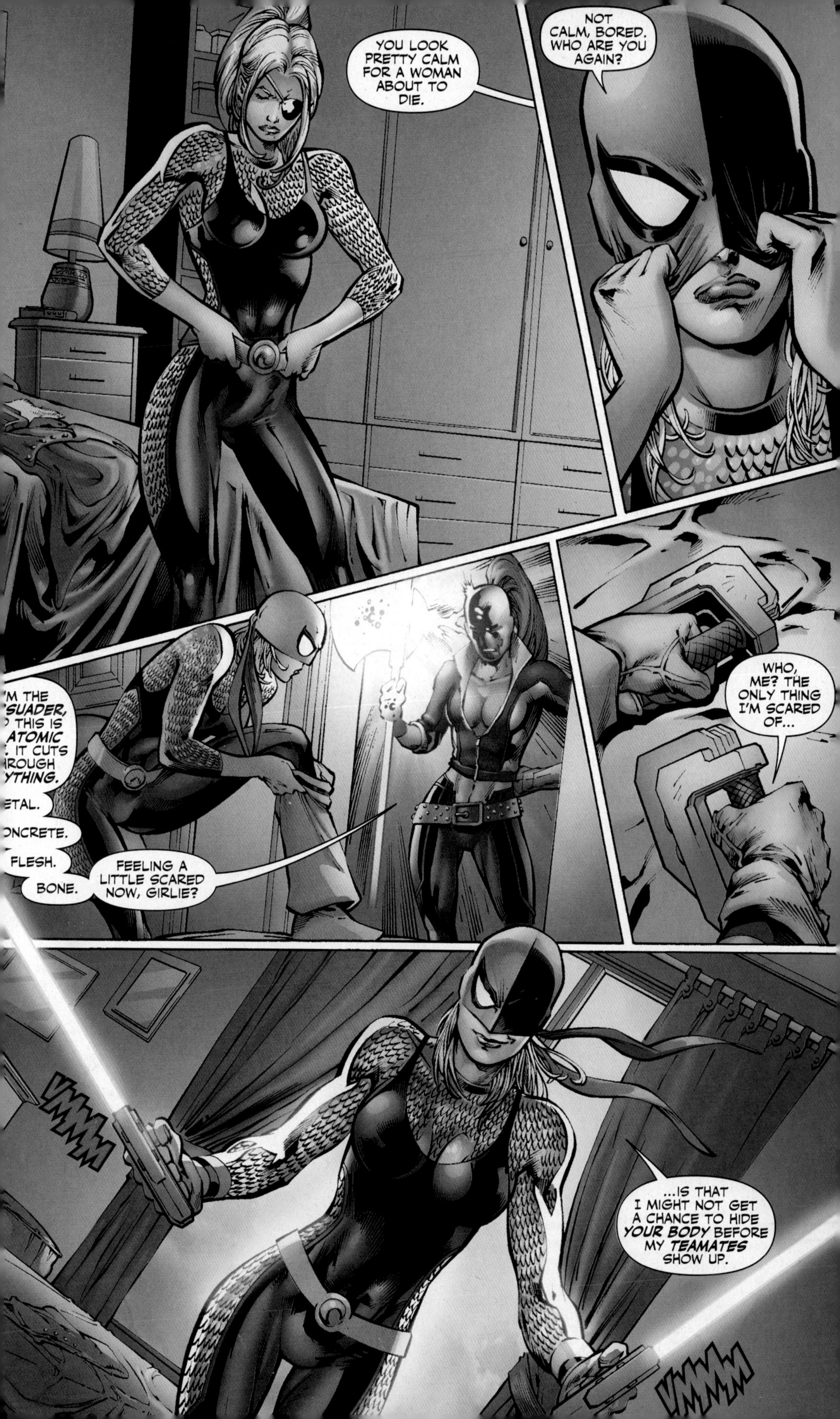
YOU LOOK PRETTY CALM FOR A WOMAN ABOUT TO DIE.
NOT CALM, BORED. WHO ARE YOU AGAIN?
'M THE
SUADER,
THIS IS
ATOMIC
IT CUTS
ROUGH
YTHING.
ETAL.
ONCRETE.
FLESH.
BONE.
FEELING A LITTLE SCARED NOW, GIRLIE?
WHO, ME? THE ONLY THING I'M SCARED OF...
...IS THAT I MIGHT NOT GET A CHANCE TO HIDE *YOUR BODY* BEFORE MY *TEAMATES* SHOW UP.
VMMM
VMMM

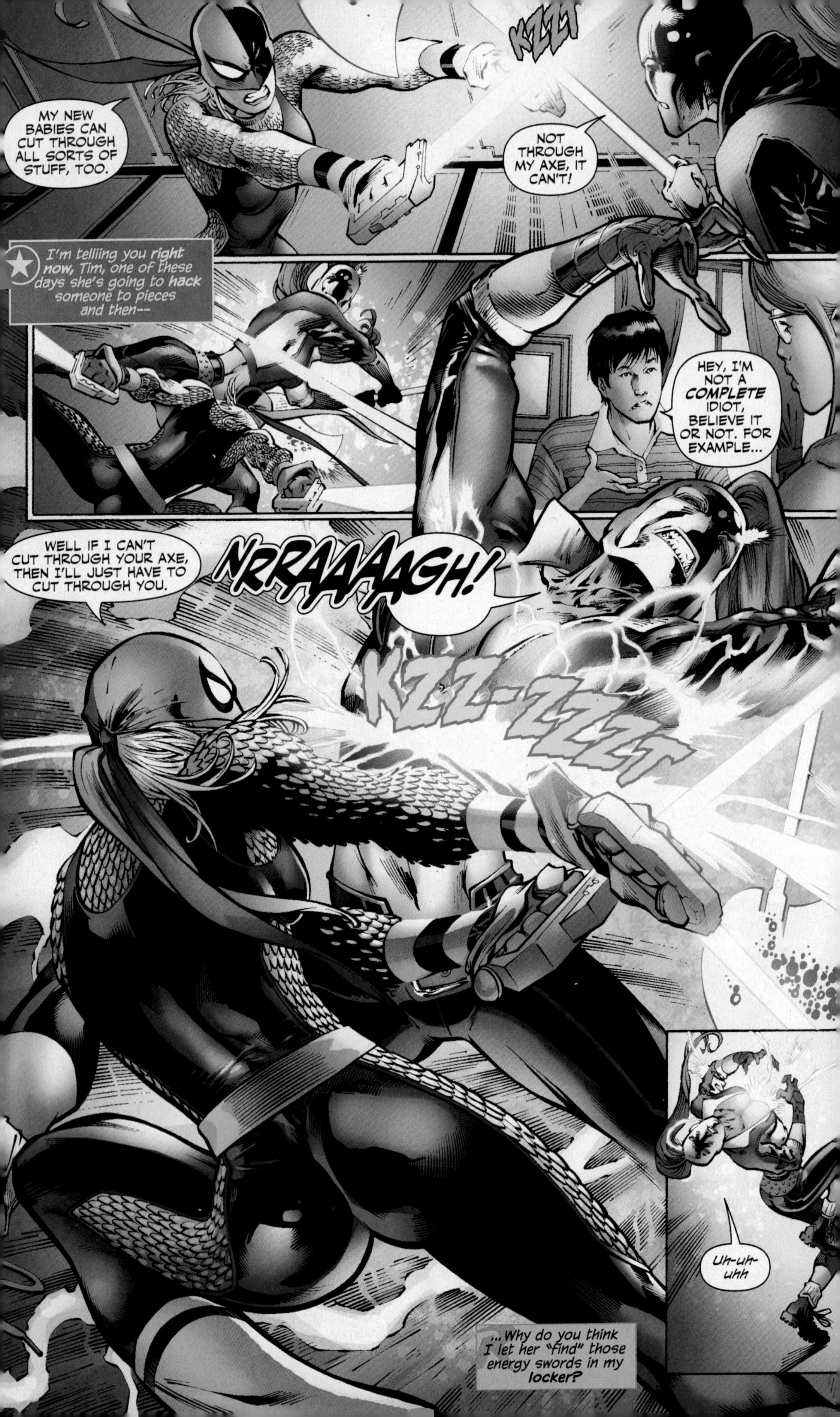
KZZZT
MY NEW BABIES CAN CUT THROUGH ALL SORTS OF STUFF, TOO.
NOT THROUGH MY AXE, IT CAN'T!
I'm telliing you right now, Tim, one of these days she's going to hack someone to pieces and then--
HEY, I'M NOT A COMPLETE IDIOT, BELIEVE IT OR NOT. FOR EXAMPLE...
WELL IF I CAN'T CUT THROUGH YOUR AXE, THEN I'LL JUST HAVE TO CUT THROUGH YOU.
NRRAAAAAGH!
KZZ-ZZZT
Uh-uh-uhh
...Why do you think I let her "find" those energy swords in my locker?

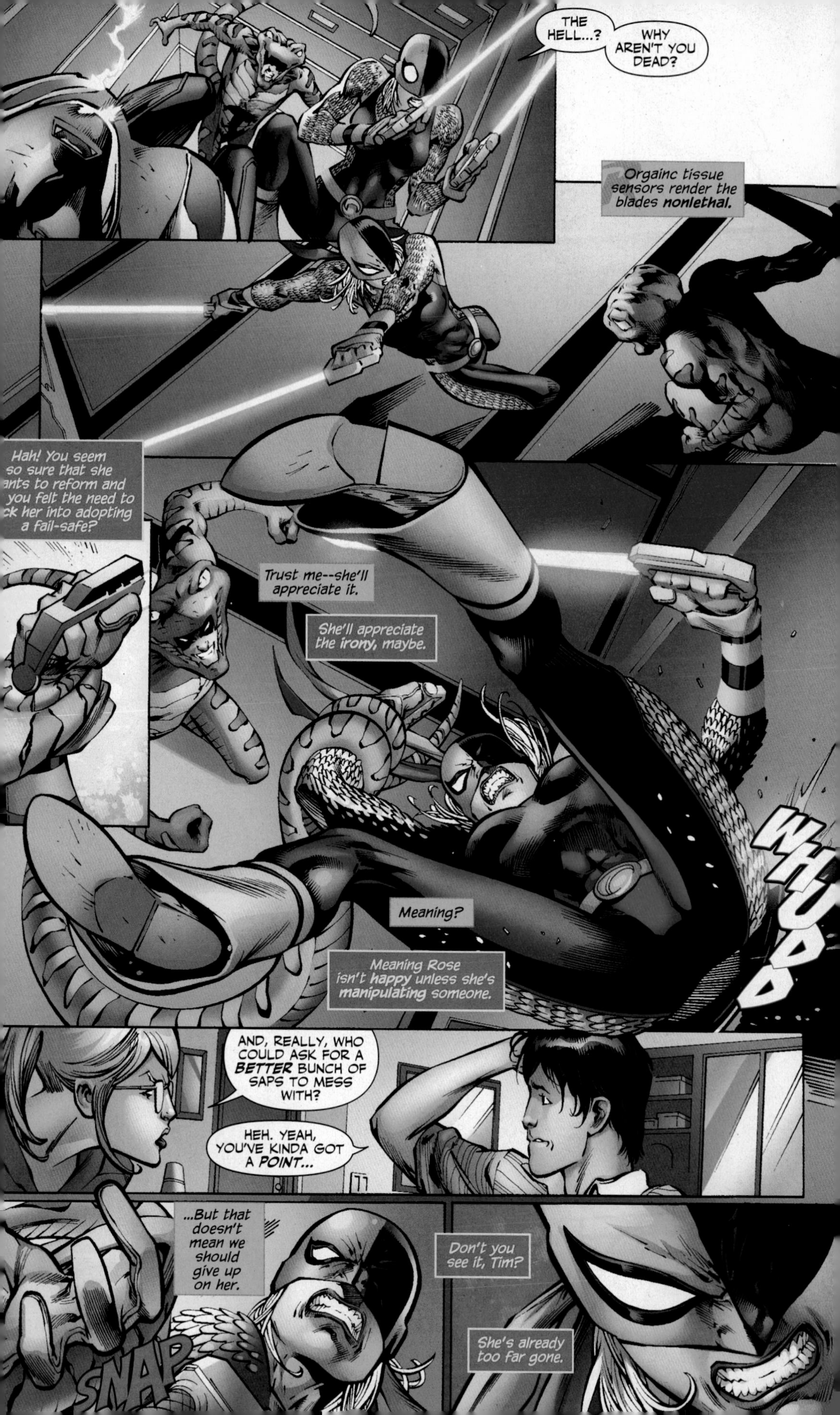
THE HELL...?
WHY AREN'T YOU DEAD?
Orgainc tissue sensors render the blades nonlethal.
Hah! You seem so sure that she ants to reform and you felt the need to ck her into adopting a fail-safe?
Trust me--she'll appreciate it.
She'll appreciate the irony, maybe.
WHUDD
Meaning?
Meaning Rose isn't happy unless she's manipulating someone.
AND, REALLY, WHO COULD ASK FOR A BETTER BUNCH OF SAPS TO MESS WITH?
HEH. YEAH, YOU'VE KINDA GOT A POINT...
...But that doesn't mean we should give up on her.
SNAP
Don't you see it, Tim?
She's already too far gone.

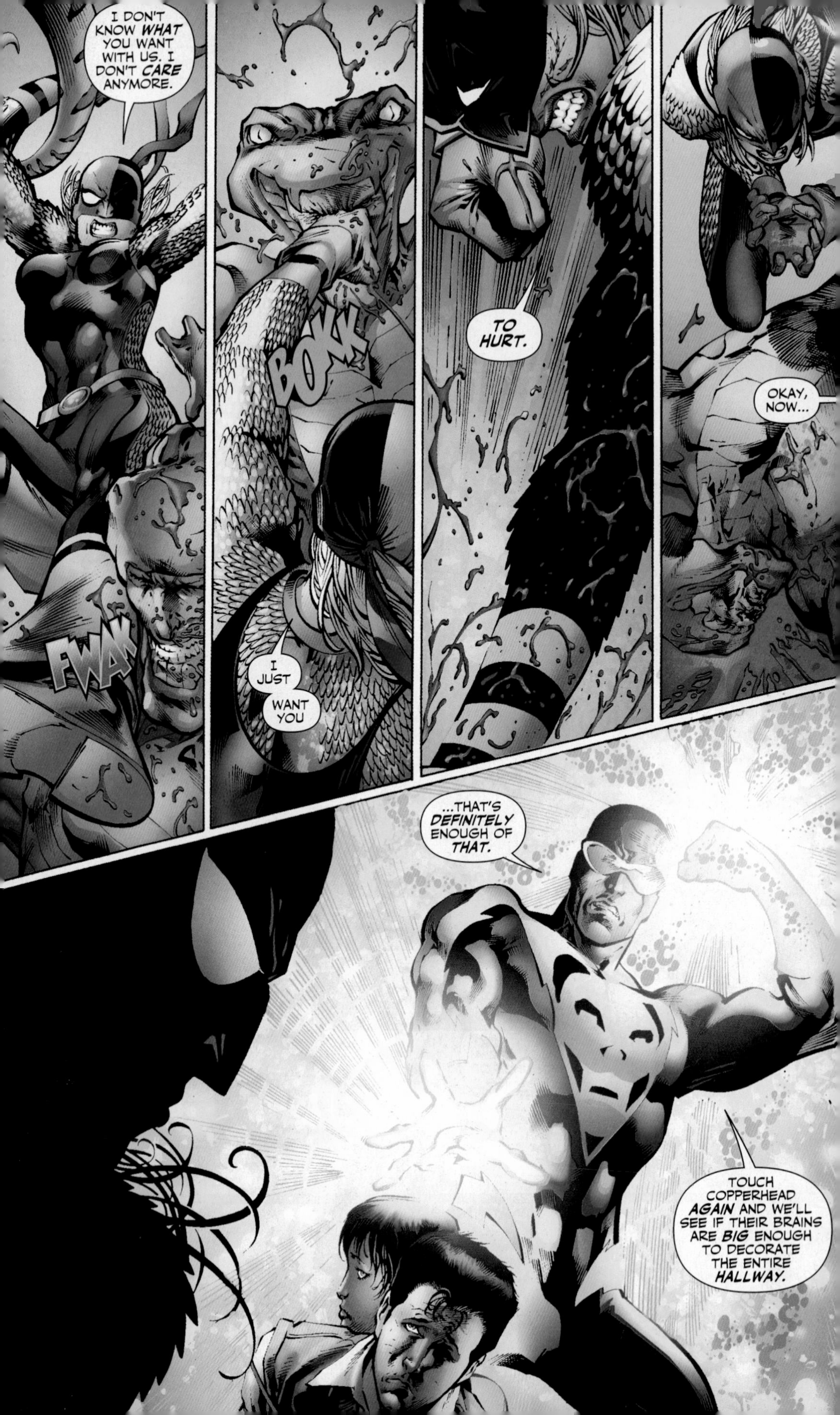
I DON'T KNOW *WHAT* YOU WANT WITH US. I DON'T *CARE* ANYMORE.
FWAK
BOKK
I JUST
WANT YOU
TO HURT.
OKAY, NOW...
...THAT'S *DEFINITELY* ENOUGH OF *THAT.*
TOUCH COPPERHEAD *AGAIN* AND WE'LL SEE IF THEIR BRAINS ARE *BIG* ENOUGH TO DECORATE THE ENTIRE *HALLWAY.*

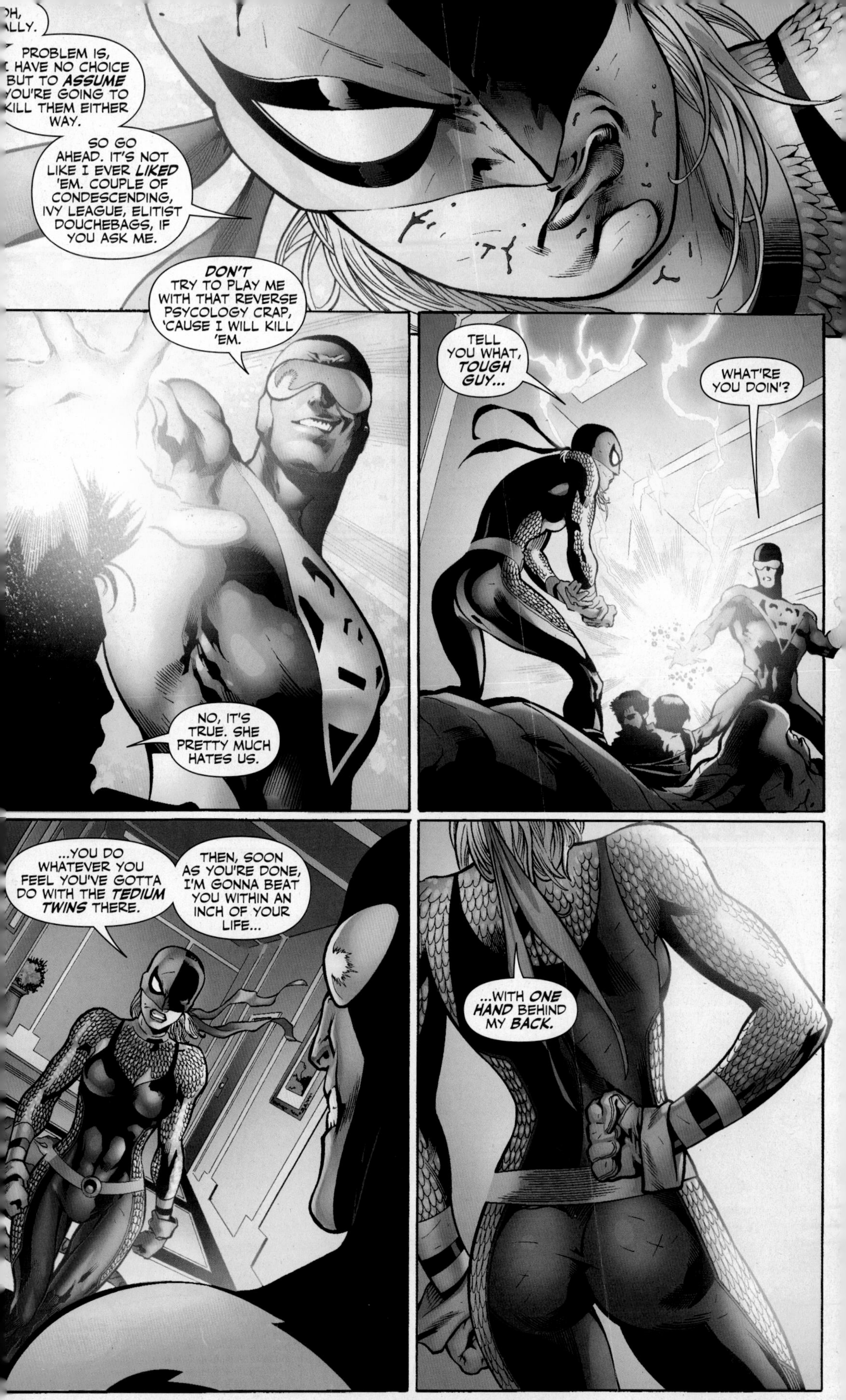
PROBLEM IS, I HAVE NO CHOICE BUT TO ASSUME YOU'RE GOING TO KILL THEM EITHER WAY.
SO GO AHEAD. IT'S NOT LIKE I EVER LIKED 'EM. COUPLE OF CONDESCENDING, IVY LEAGUE, ELITIST DOUCHEBAGS, IF YOU ASK ME.
DON'T TRY TO PLAY ME WITH THAT REVERSE PSYCOLOGY CRAP, 'CAUSE I WILL KILL 'EM.
NO, IT'S TRUE. SHE PRETTY MUCH HATES US.
TELL YOU WHAT, TOUGH GUY...
WHAT'RE YOU DOIN'?
...YOU DO WHATEVER YOU FEEL YOU'VE GOTTA DO WITH THE TEDIUM TWINS THERE.
THEN, SOON AS YOU'RE DONE, I'M GONNA BEAT YOU WITHIN AN INCH OF YOUR LIFE...
...WITH ONE HAND BEHIND MY BACK.

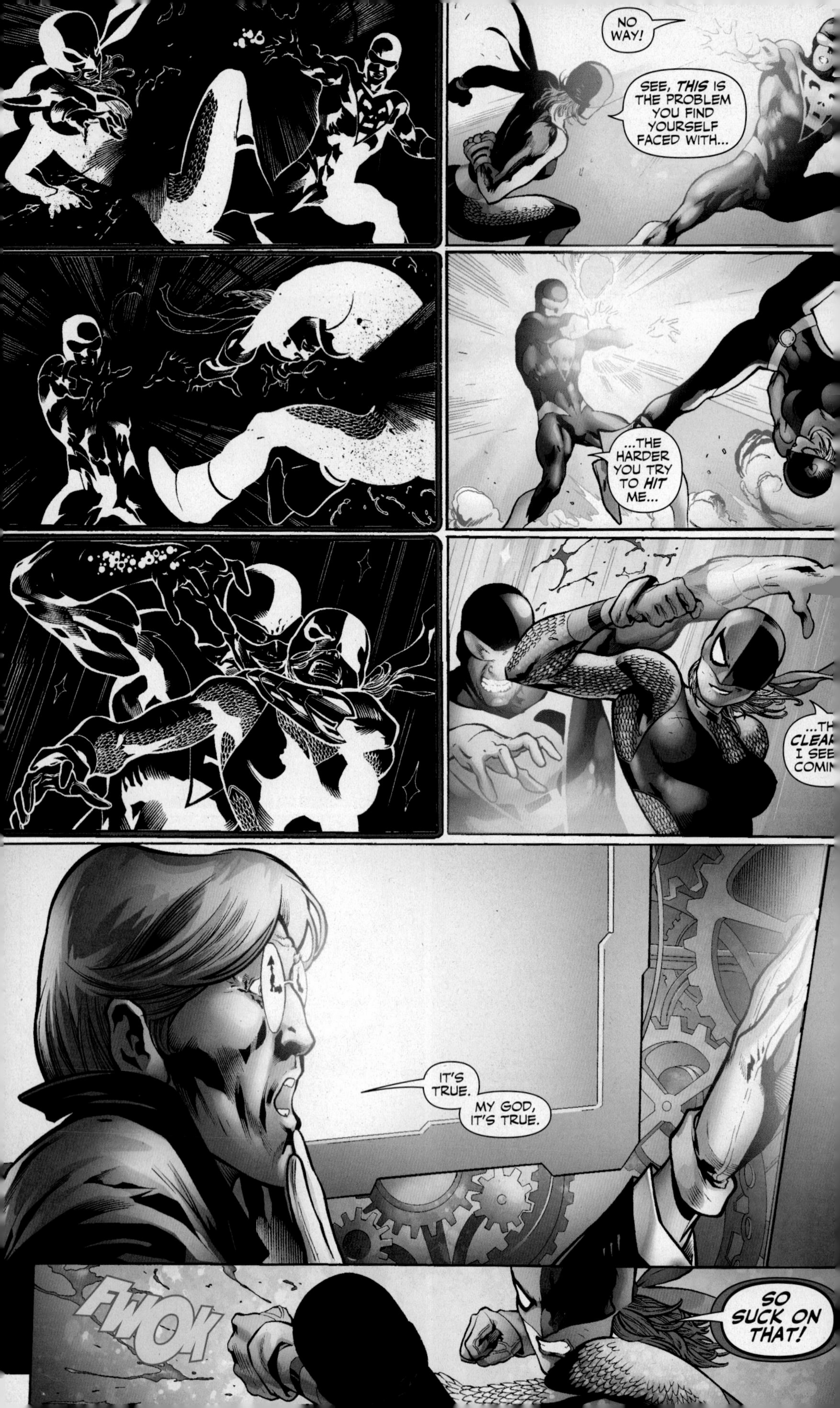
NO WAY!
SEE, THIS IS THE PROBLEM YOU FIND YOURSELF FACED WITH...
...THE HARDER YOU TRY TO HIT ME...
IT'S TRUE.
MY GOD, IT'S TRUE.
FWOK
SO SUCK ON THAT!

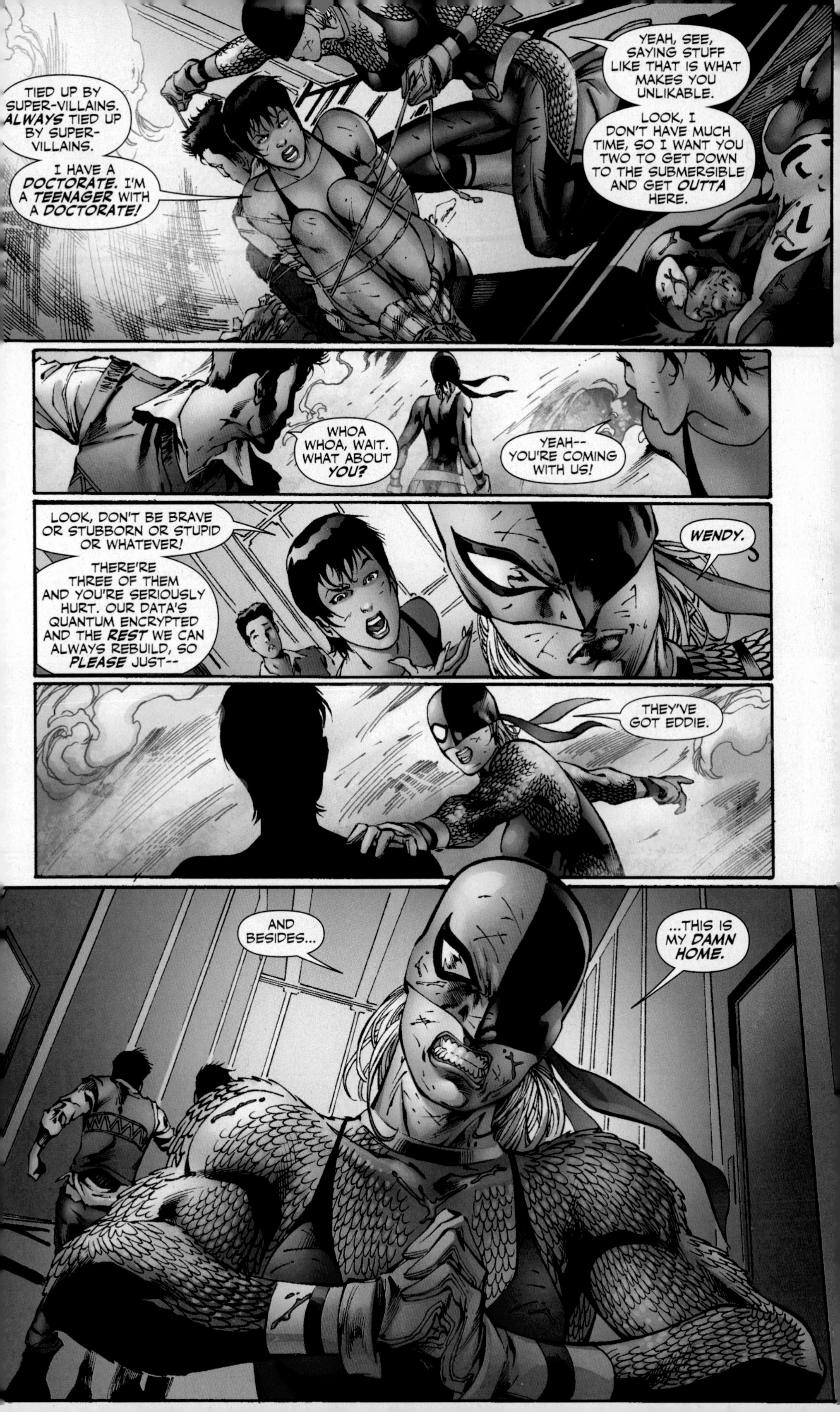
TIED UP BY SUPER-VILLAINS. ALWAYS TIED UP BY SUPER-VILLAINS.
I HAVE A DOCTORATE. I'M A TEENAGER WITH A DOCTORATE!
YEAH, SEE, SAYING STUFF LIKE THAT IS WHAT MAKES YOU UNLIKABLE.
LOOK, I DON'T HAVE MUCH TIME, SO I WANT YOU TWO TO GET DOWN TO THE SUBMERSIBLE AND GET OUTTA HERE.
WHOA WHOA, WAIT. WHAT ABOUT YOU?
YEAH-- YOU'RE COMING WITH US!
LOOK, DON'T BE BRAVE OR STUBBORN OR STUPID OR WHATEVER!
THERE'RE THREE OF THEM AND YOU'RE SERIOUSLY HURT. OUR DATA'S QUANTUM ENCRYPTED AND THE REST WE CAN ALWAYS REBUILD, SO PLEASE JUST--
WENDY.
THEY'VE GOT EDDIE.
AND BESIDES...
...THIS IS MY DAMN HOME.

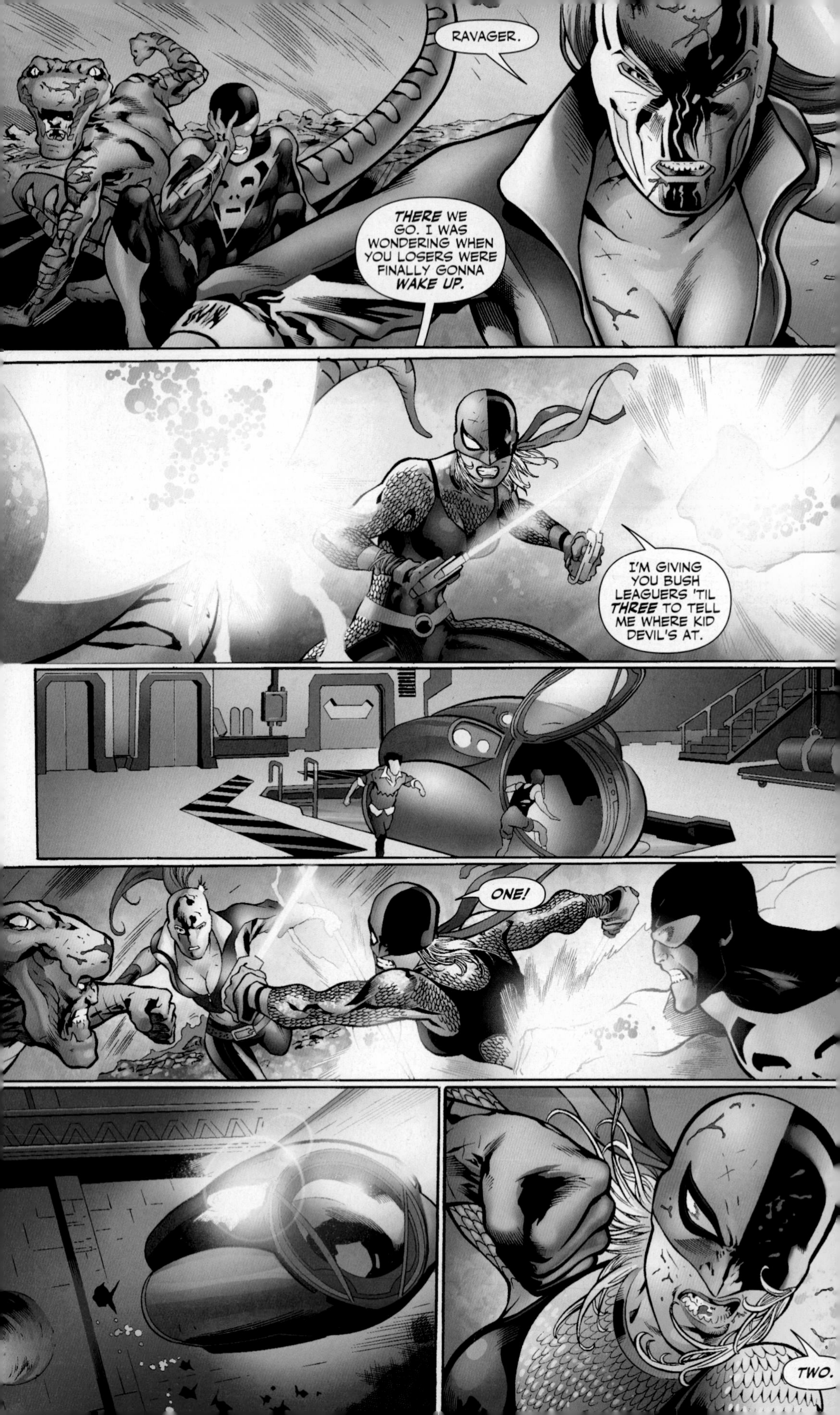
RAVAGER.
THERE WE GO. I WAS WONDERING WHEN YOU LOSERS WERE FINALLY GONNA WAKE UP.
I'M GIVING YOU BUSH LEAGUERS 'TIL THREE TO TELL ME WHERE KID DEVIL'S AT.
ONE!
TWO.

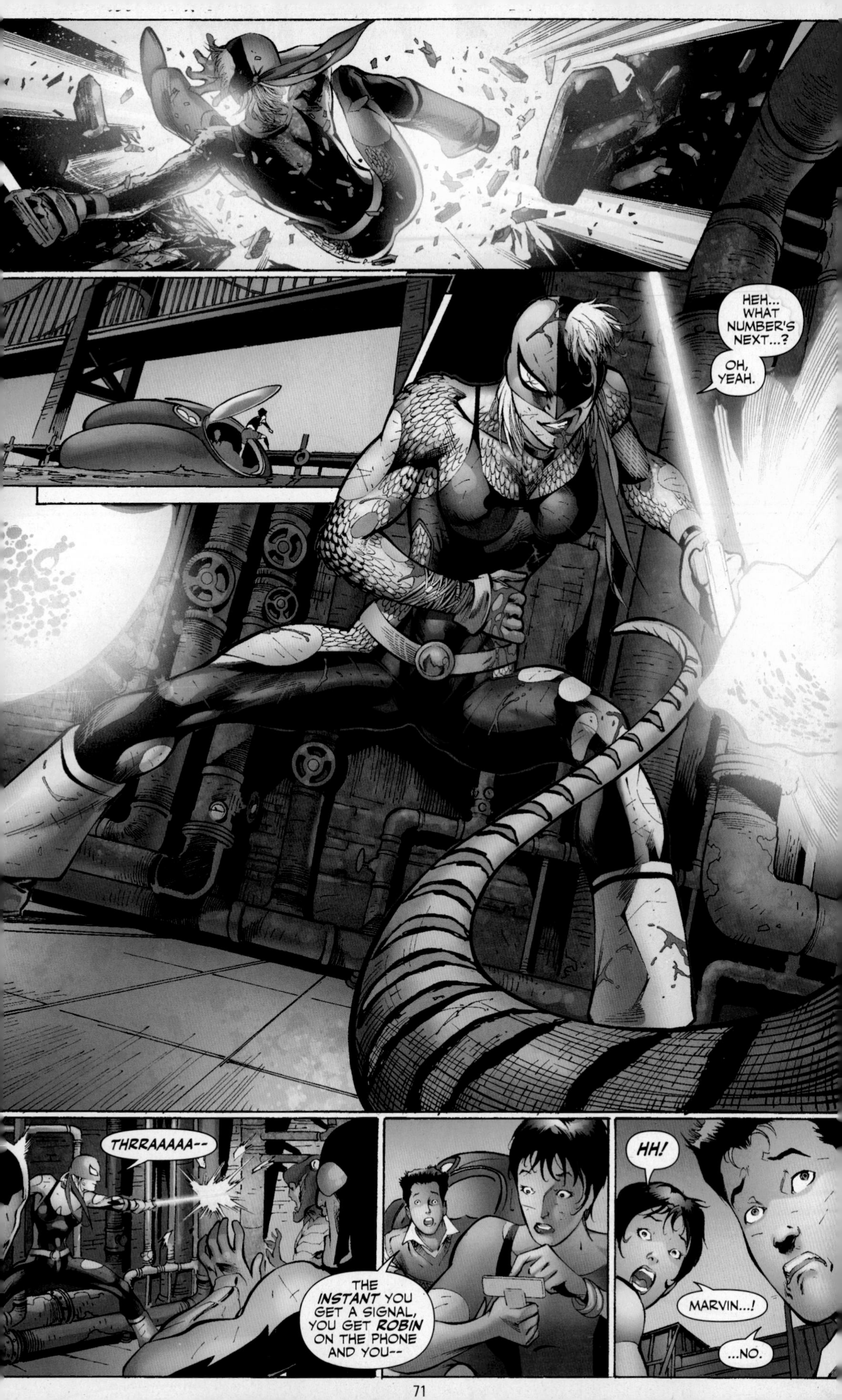
HEH... WHAT NUMBER'S NEXT...?
OH, YEAH.
THRRAAAAA--
THE INSTANT YOU GET A SIGNAL, YOU GET ROBIN ON THE PHONE AND YOU--
HH!
MARVIN...!
...NO.

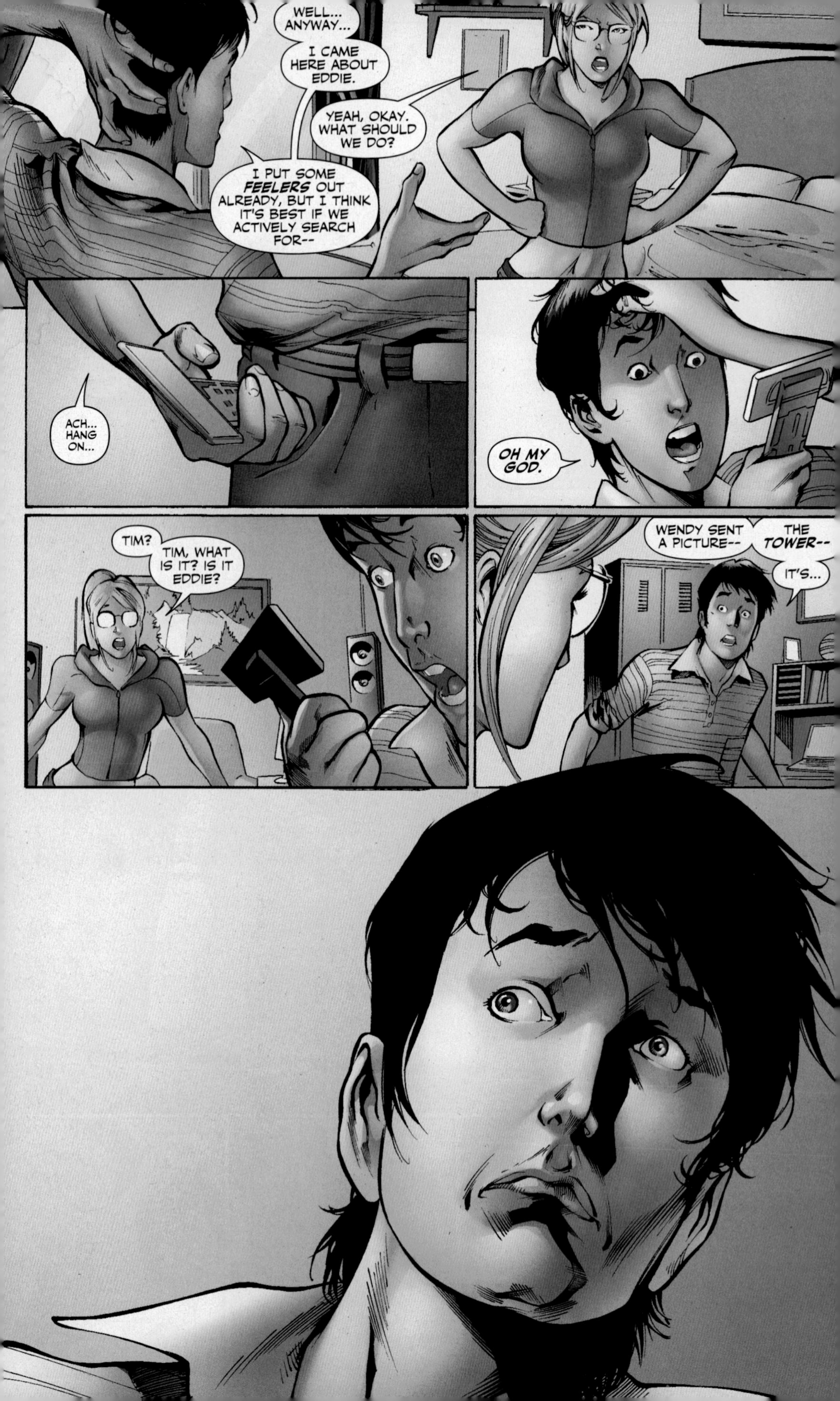
WELL... ANYWAY...
I CAME HERE ABOUT EDDIE.
YEAH, OKAY. WHAT SHOULD WE DO?
I PUT SOME FEELERS OUT ALREADY, BUT I THINK IT'S BEST IF WE ACTIVELY SEARCH FOR--
ACH... HANG ON...
OH MY GOD.
TIM?
TIM, WHAT IS IT? IS IT EDDIE?
WENDY SENT A PICTURE--
THE TOWER--
IT'S...

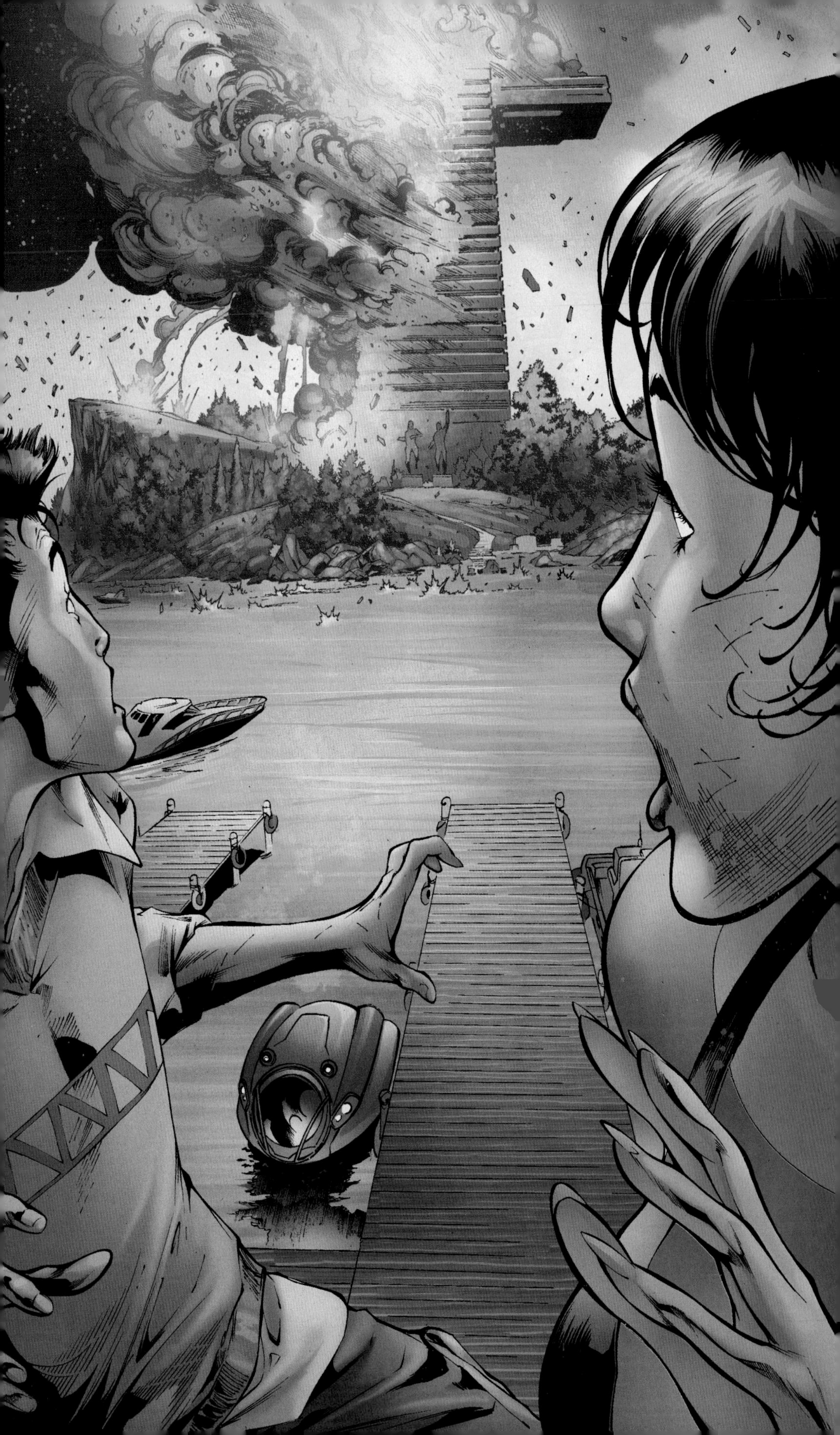

TEEN TITANS 58 - Eddy Barrows, Julio Ferreira and Rod Reis

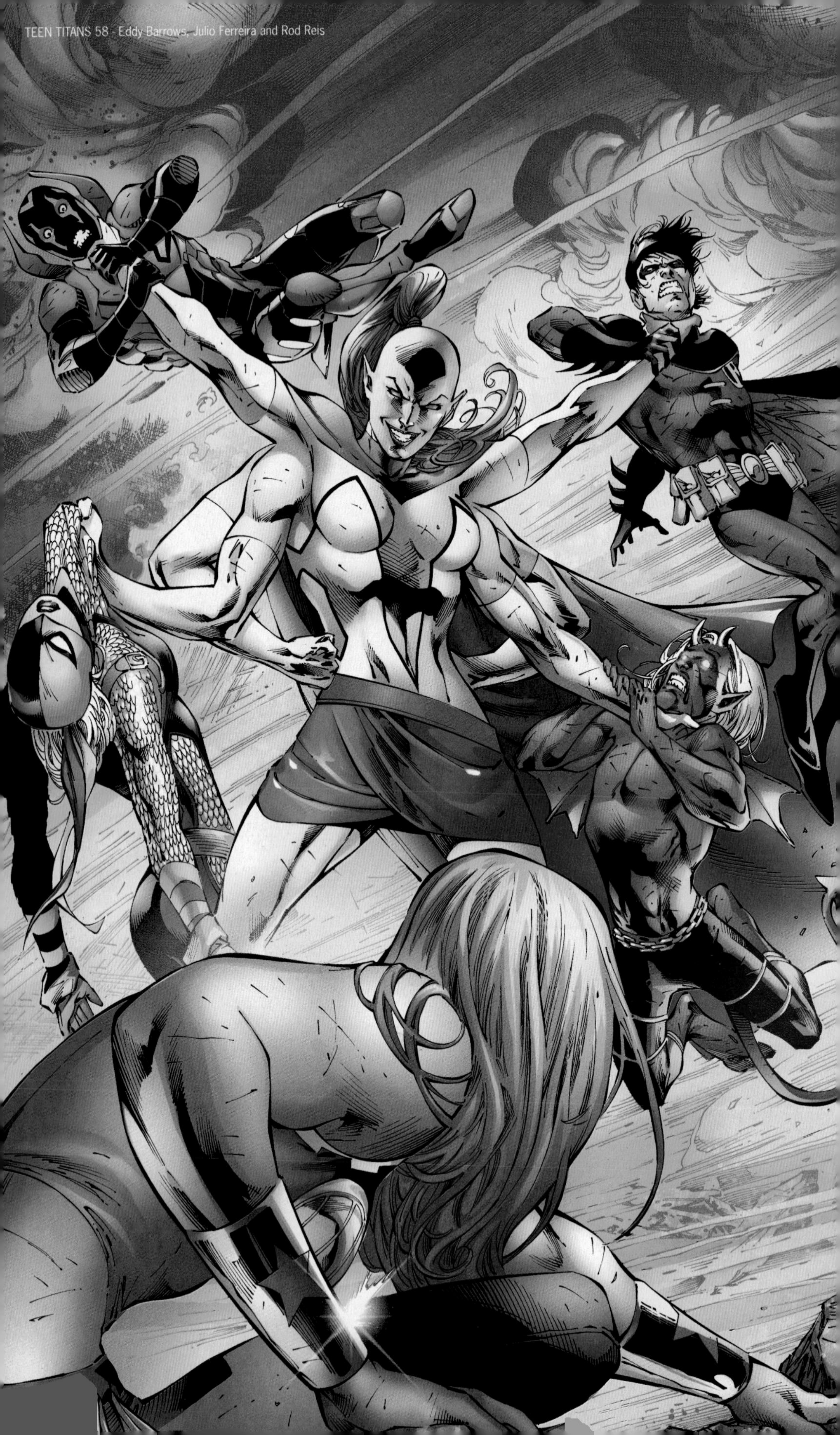

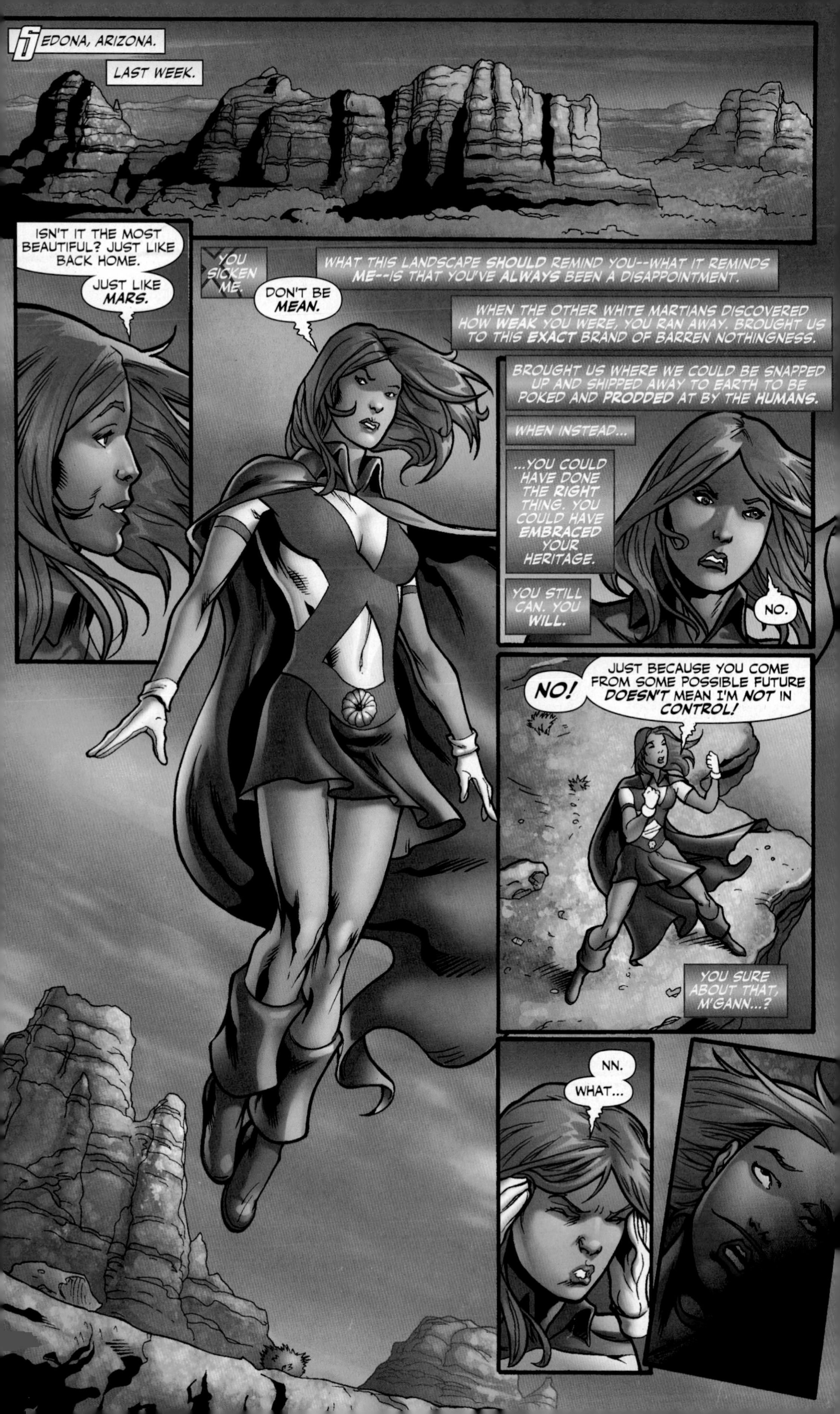
SEDONA, ARIZONA.
LAST WEEK.
ISN'T IT THE MOST BEAUTIFUL? JUST LIKE BACK HOME.
JUST LIKE MARS.
YOU SICKEN ME.
DON'T BE MEAN.
WHAT THIS LANDSCAPE SHOULD REMIND YOU--WHAT IT REMINDS ME--IS THAT YOU'VE ALWAYS BEEN A DISAPPOINTMENT.
WHEN THE OTHER WHITE MARTIANS DISCOVERED HOW WEAK YOU WERE, YOU RAN AWAY. BROUGHT US TO THIS EXACT BRAND OF BARREN NOTHINGNESS.
BROUGHT US WHERE WE COULD BE SNAPPED UP AND SHIPPED AWAY TO EARTH TO BE POKED AND PRODDED AT BY THE HUMANS.
WHEN INSTEAD...
...YOU COULD HAVE DONE THE RIGHT THING. YOU COULD HAVE EMBRACED YOUR HERITAGE.
YOU STILL CAN. YOU WILL.
NO.
NO!
JUST BECAUSE YOU COME FROM SOME POSSIBLE FUTURE DOESN'T MEAN I'M NOT IN CONTROL!
YOU SURE ABOUT THAT, M'GANN...?
NN.
WHAT...

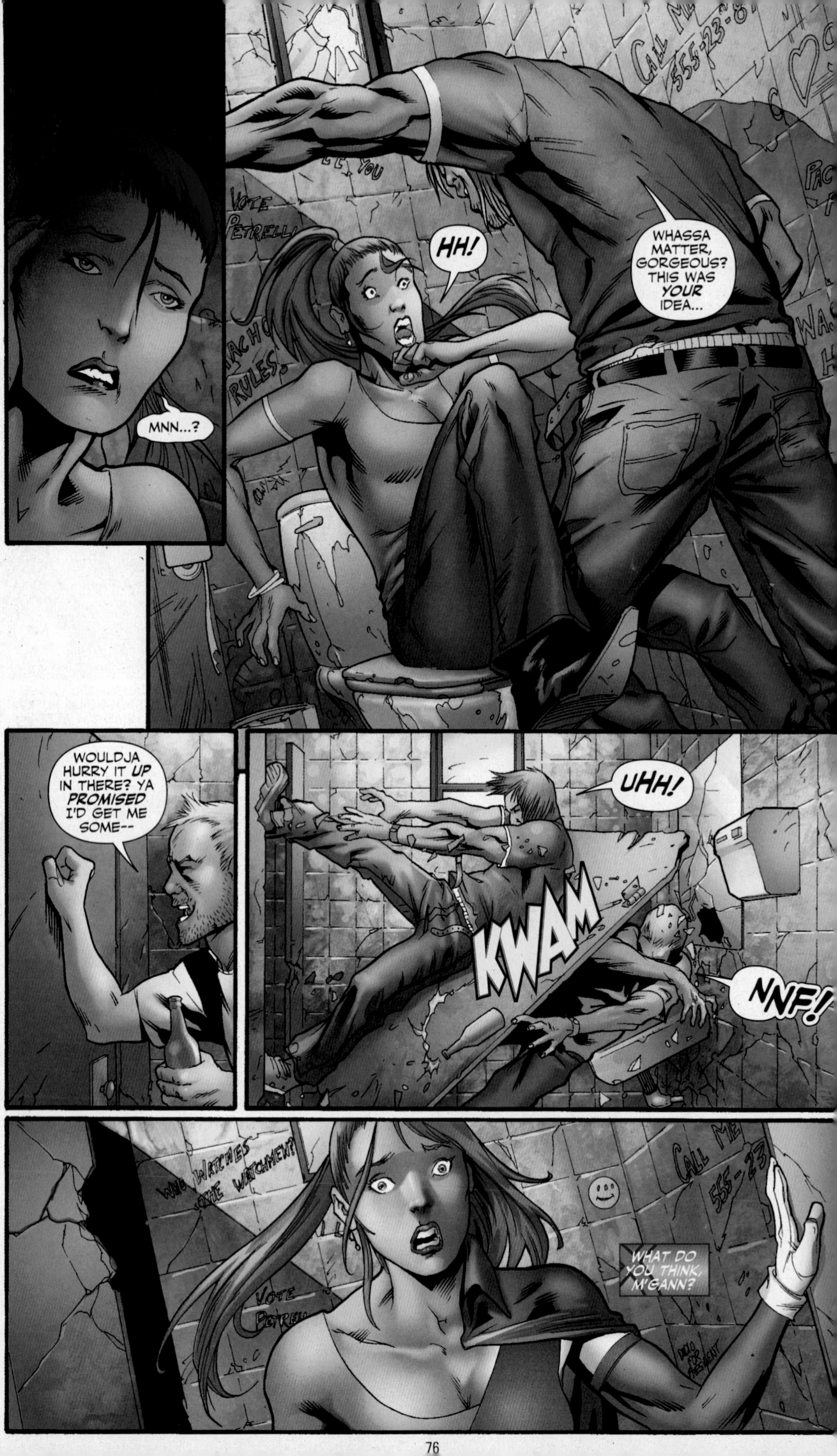
MNN...?
HH!
WHASSA MATTER, GORGEOUS? THIS WAS *YOUR* IDEA...
WOULDJA HURRY IT *UP* IN THERE? YA *PROMISED* I'D GET ME SOME--
UHH!
KWAM
NNF!
WHAT DO YOU THINK, M'GANN?

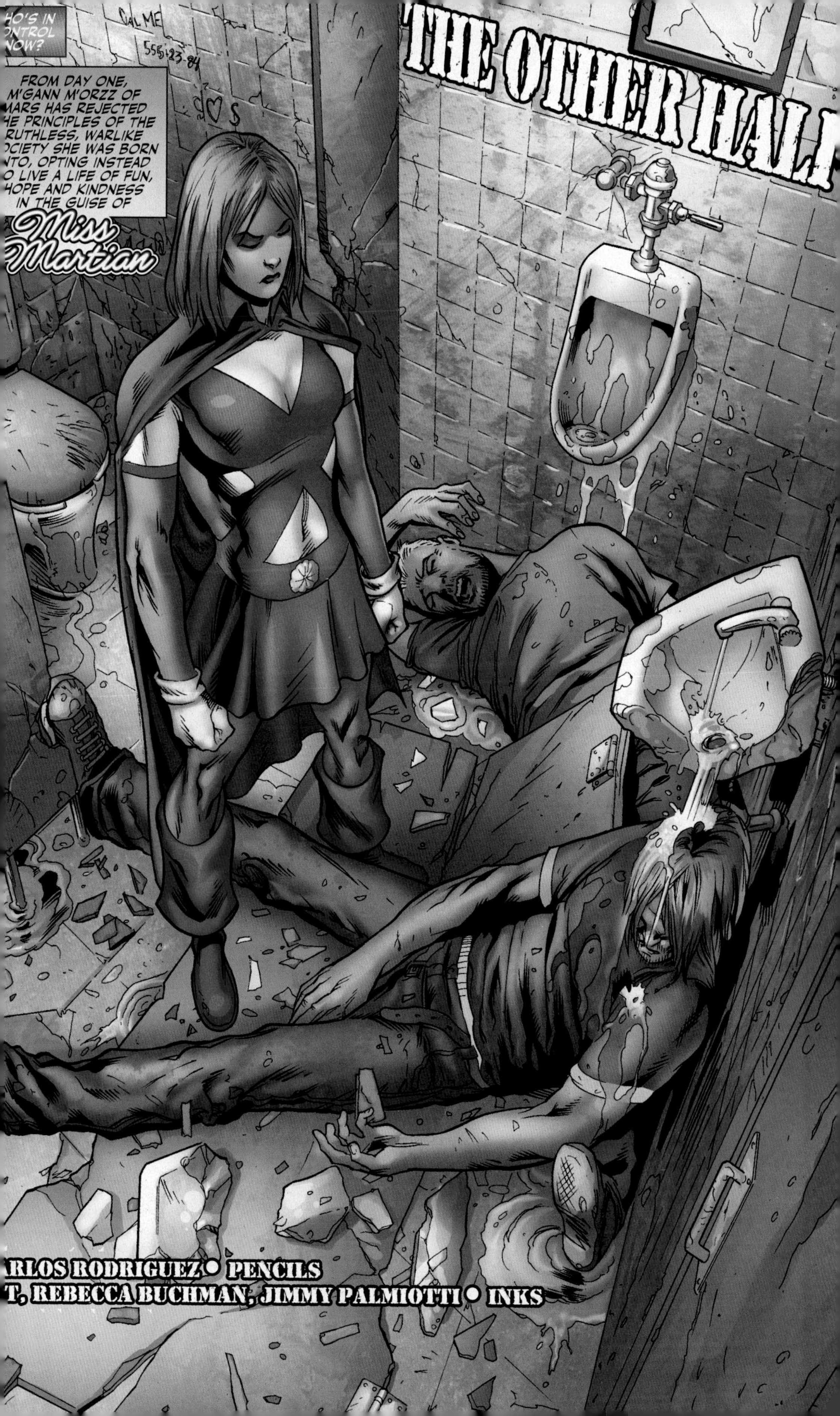
HO'S IN
ONTROL
NOW?
CAL ME
555-123-84
FROM DAY ONE, M'GANN M'ORZZ OF MARS HAS REJECTED HE PRINCIPLES OF THE RUTHLESS, WARLIKE OCIETY SHE WAS BORN NTO, OPTING INSTEAD O LIVE A LIFE OF FUN, HOPE AND KINDNESS IN THE GUISE OF
Miss Martian
THE OTHER HALI
RLOS RODRIGUEZ • PENCILS
T, REBECCA BUCHMAN, JIMMY PALMIOTTI • INKS

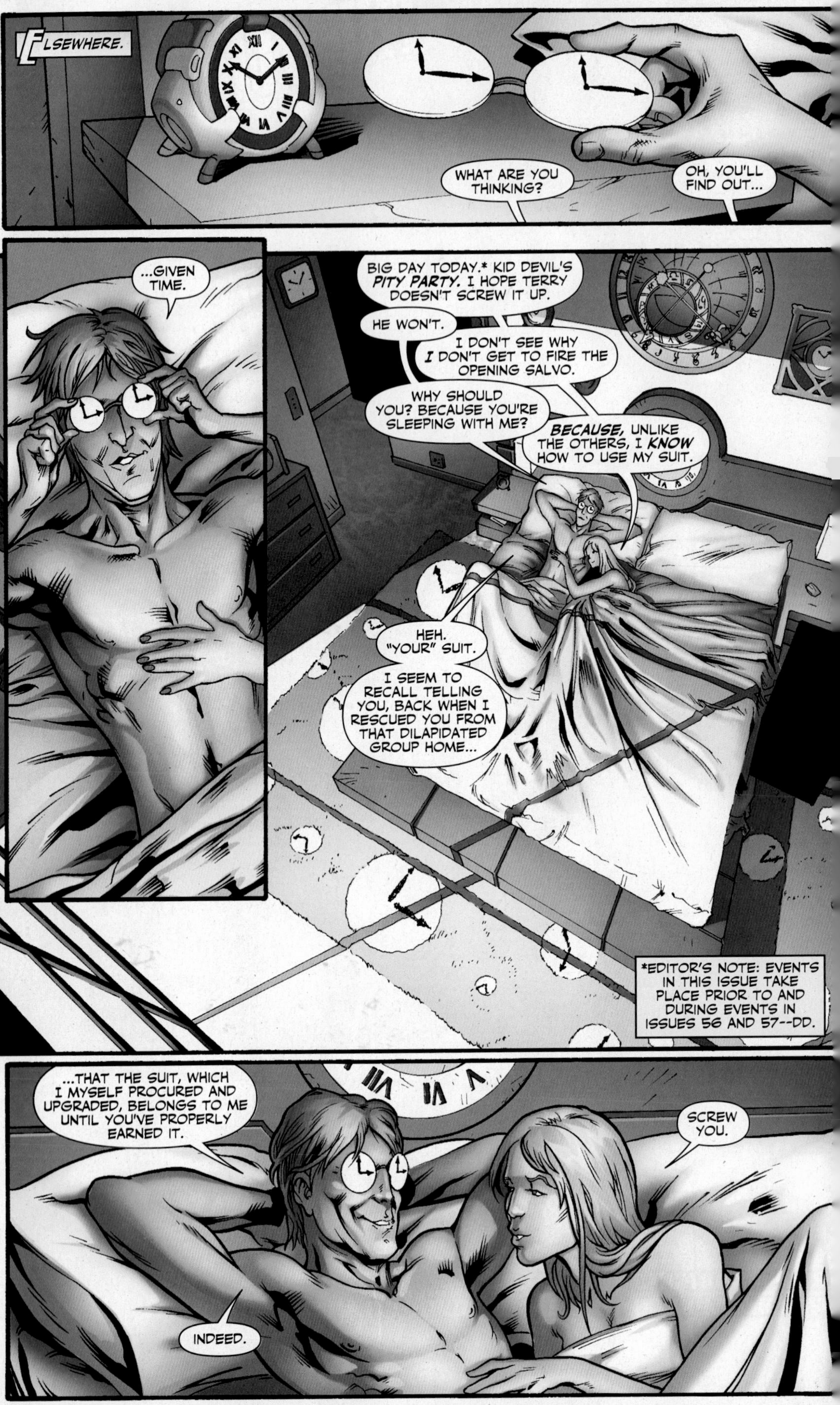
ELSEWHERE.
WHAT ARE YOU THINKING?
OH, YOU'LL FIND OUT...
...GIVEN TIME.
BIG DAY TODAY.* KID DEVIL'S PITY PARTY. I HOPE TERRY DOESN'T SCREW IT UP.
HE WON'T.
I DON'T SEE WHY I DON'T GET TO FIRE THE OPENING SALVO.
WHY SHOULD YOU? BECAUSE YOU'RE SLEEPING WITH ME?
BECAUSE, UNLIKE THE OTHERS, I KNOW HOW TO USE MY SUIT.
HEH. "YOUR" SUIT.
I SEEM TO RECALL TELLING YOU, BACK WHEN I RESCUED YOU FROM THAT DILAPIDATED GROUP HOME...
*EDITOR'S NOTE: EVENTS IN THIS ISSUE TAKE PLACE PRIOR TO AND DURING EVENTS IN ISSUES 56 AND 57--DD.
...THAT THE SUIT, WHICH I MYSELF PROCURED AND UPGRADED, BELONGS TO ME UNTIL YOU'VE PROPERLY EARNED IT.
SCREW YOU.
INDEED.

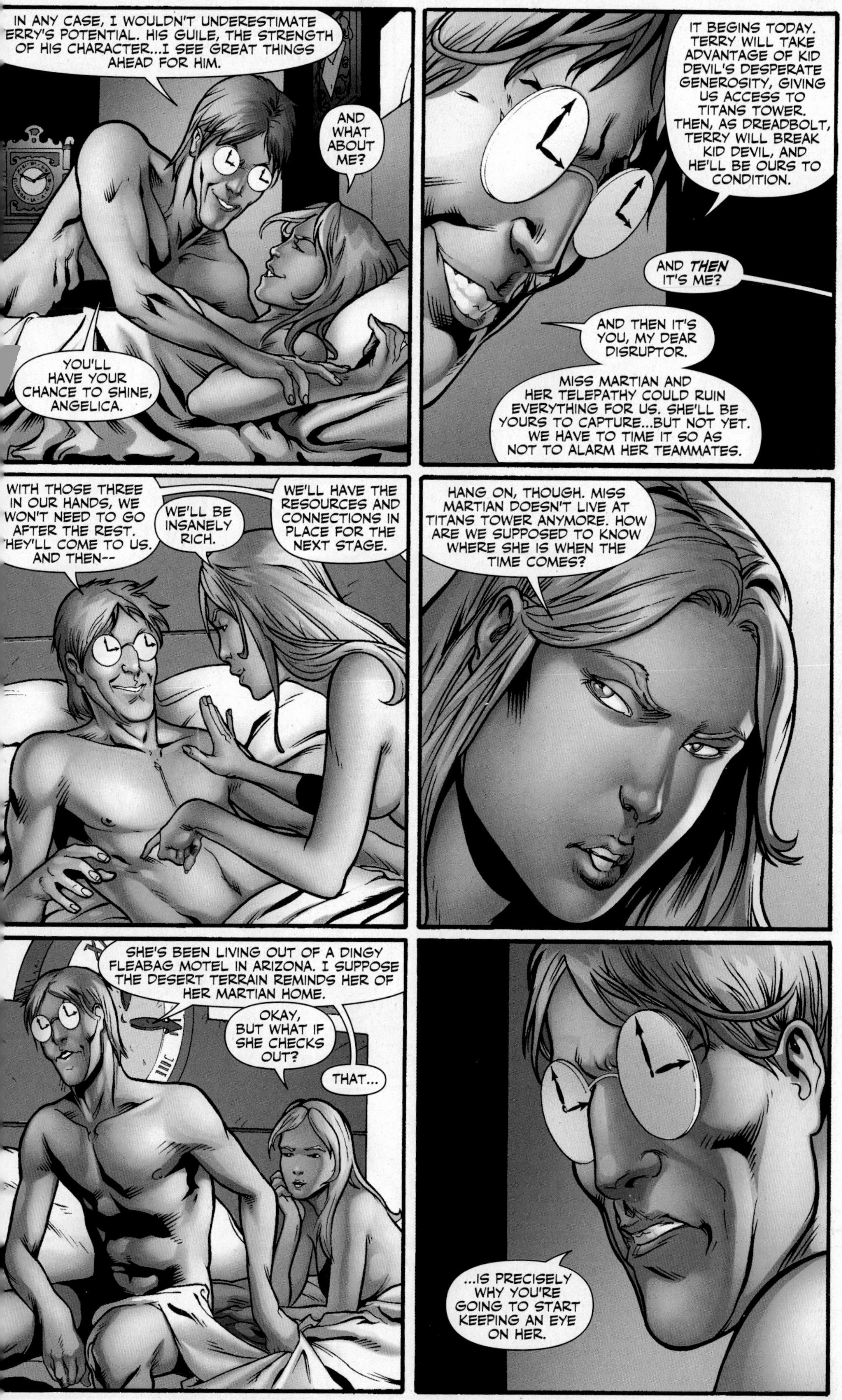
IN ANY CASE, I WOULDN'T UNDERESTIMATE ERRY'S POTENTIAL. HIS GUILE, THE STRENGTH OF HIS CHARACTER...I SEE GREAT THINGS AHEAD FOR HIM.
AND WHAT ABOUT ME?
YOU'LL HAVE YOUR CHANCE TO SHINE, ANGELICA.
IT BEGINS TODAY. TERRY WILL TAKE ADVANTAGE OF KID DEVIL'S DESPERATE GENEROSITY, GIVING US ACCESS TO TITANS TOWER. THEN, AS DREADBOLT, TERRY WILL BREAK KID DEVIL, AND HE'LL BE OURS TO CONDITION.
AND *THEN* IT'S ME?
AND THEN IT'S YOU, MY DEAR DISRUPTOR.
MISS MARTIAN AND HER TELEPATHY COULD RUIN EVERYTHING FOR US. SHE'LL BE YOURS TO CAPTURE...BUT NOT YET. WE HAVE TO TIME IT SO AS NOT TO ALARM HER TEAMMATES.
WITH THOSE THREE IN OUR HANDS, WE WON'T NEED TO GO AFTER THE REST. HEY'LL COME TO US. AND THEN--
WE'LL BE INSANELY RICH.
WE'LL HAVE THE RESOURCES AND CONNECTIONS IN PLACE FOR THE NEXT STAGE.
HANG ON, THOUGH. MISS MARTIAN DOESN'T LIVE AT TITANS TOWER ANYMORE. HOW ARE WE SUPPOSED TO KNOW WHERE SHE IS WHEN THE TIME COMES?
SHE'S BEEN LIVING OUT OF A DINGY FLEABAG MOTEL IN ARIZONA. I SUPPOSE THE DESERT TERRAIN REMINDS HER OF HER MARTIAN HOME.
OKAY, BUT WHAT IF SHE CHECKS OUT?
THAT...
...IS PRECISELY WHY YOU'RE GOING TO START KEEPING AN EYE ON HER.

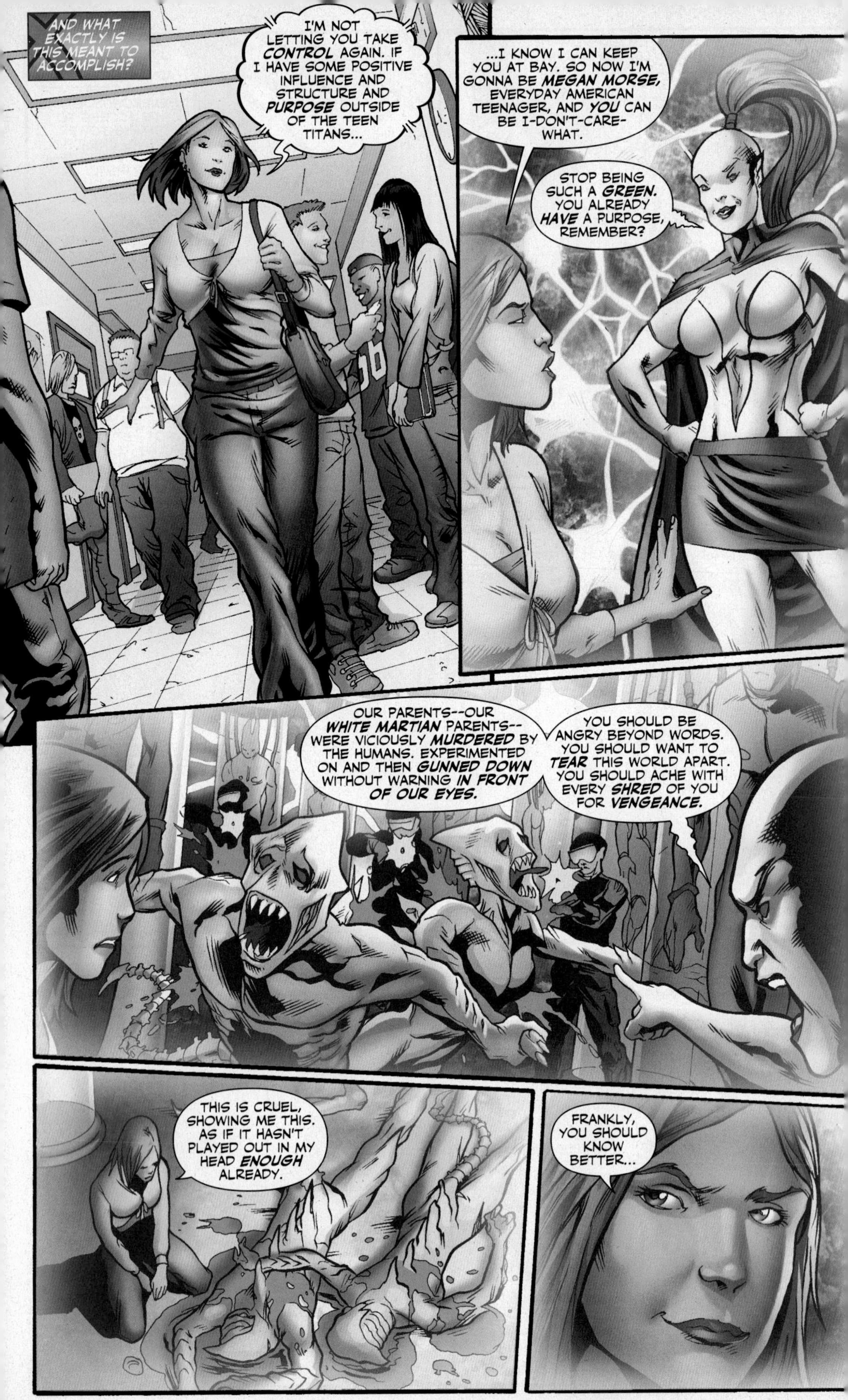
AND WHAT EXACTLY IS THIS MEANT TO ACCOMPLISH?
I'M NOT LETTING YOU TAKE CONTROL AGAIN. IF I HAVE SOME POSITIVE INFLUENCE AND STRUCTURE AND PURPOSE OUTSIDE OF THE TEEN TITANS...
...I KNOW I CAN KEEP YOU AT BAY. SO NOW I'M GONNA BE MEGAN MORSE, EVERYDAY AMERICAN TEENAGER, AND YOU CAN BE I-DON'T-CARE-WHAT.
STOP BEING SUCH A GREEN. YOU ALREADY HAVE A PURPOSE, REMEMBER?
OUR PARENTS--OUR WHITE MARTIAN PARENTS--WERE VICIOUSLY MURDERED BY THE HUMANS. EXPERIMENTED ON AND THEN GUNNED DOWN WITHOUT WARNING IN FRONT OF OUR EYES.
YOU SHOULD BE ANGRY BEYOND WORDS. YOU SHOULD WANT TO TEAR THIS WORLD APART. YOU SHOULD ACHE WITH EVERY SHRED OF YOU FOR VENGEANCE.
THIS IS CRUEL, SHOWING ME THIS. AS IF IT HASN'T PLAYED OUT IN MY HEAD ENOUGH ALREADY.
FRANKLY, YOU SHOULD KNOW BETTER...

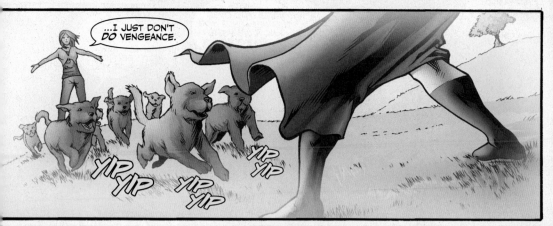

...I JUST DON'T *DO* VENGEANCE.

YIP YIP

YIP YIP

YIP YIP

YIP YIP

YIP YIP YIP

YIP

YIP YIP

AUCHH! THIS IS SO...SO *WRONG!*

AREN'T PUPPY DOGS THE GREATEST?

UH...

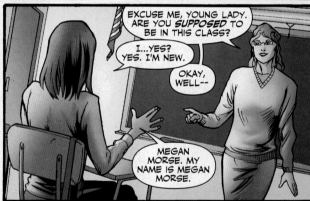

EXCUSE ME, YOUNG LADY. ARE YOU *SUPPOSED* TO BE IN THIS CLASS?

I...YES? YES. I'M NEW.

OKAY, WELL--

MEGAN MORSE. MY NAME IS MEGAN MORSE.

OKAY--*MISS MORSE*--THE OFFICE DIDN'T TELL ME I *HAD* A NEW STUDENT TODAY, BUT THAT'S HARDLY ANYTHING NEW. DO YOU HAVE YOUR SCHEDULE HANDY?

MY SCHEDULE. YEAH, SEE...

OR YOU COULD JUST SHOW ME YOUR *STUDENT I.D.* AND WE CAN GET THIS ALL SORTED OUT.

MY I.D.... RIGHT.

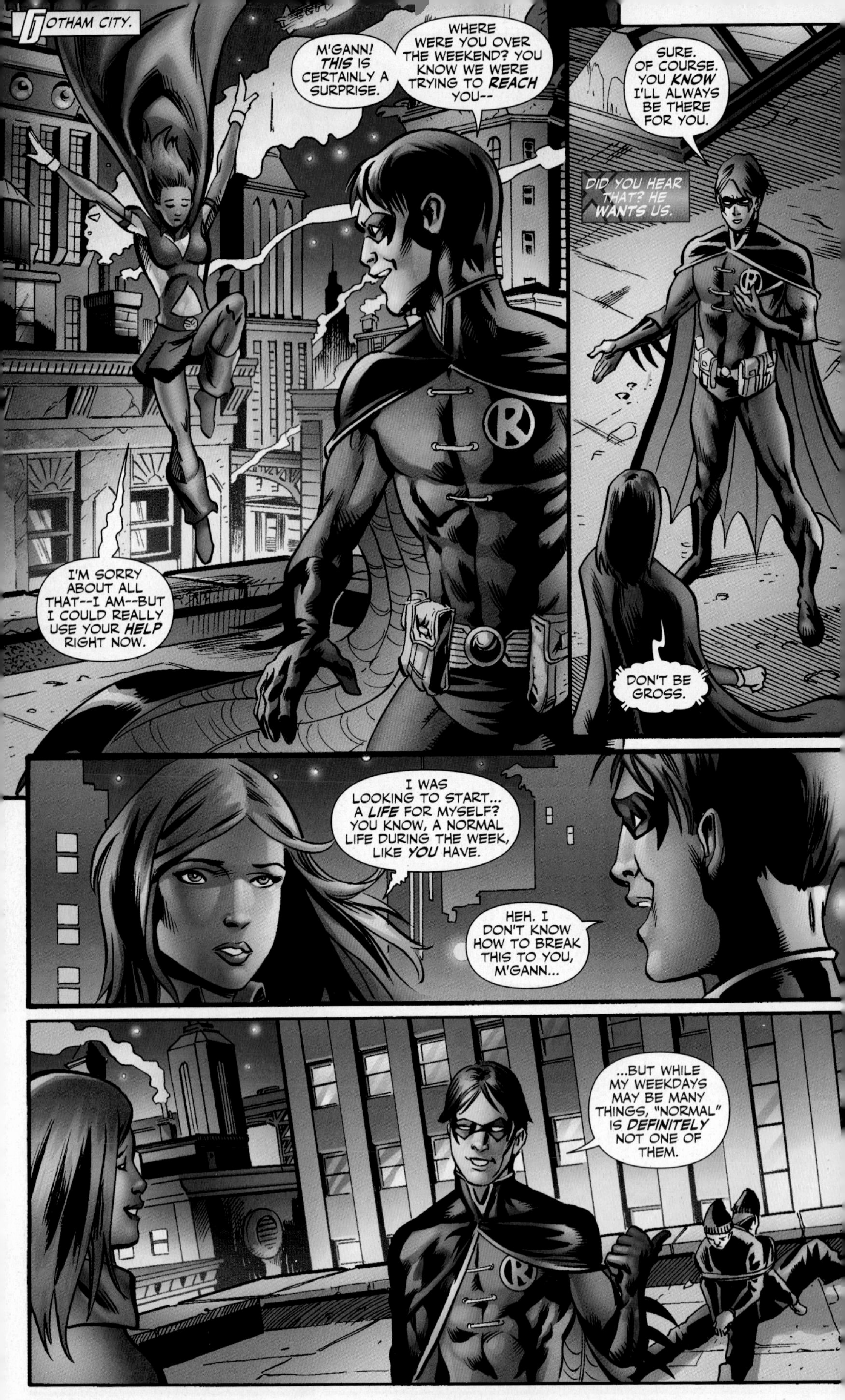
GOTHAM CITY.
M'GANN! THIS IS CERTAINLY A SURPRISE.
WHERE WERE YOU OVER THE WEEKEND? YOU KNOW WE WERE TRYING TO REACH YOU--
I'M SORRY ABOUT ALL THAT--I AM--BUT I COULD REALLY USE YOUR HELP RIGHT NOW.
SURE. OF COURSE. YOU KNOW I'LL ALWAYS BE THERE FOR YOU.
DID YOU HEAR THAT? HE WANTS US.
DON'T BE GROSS.
I WAS LOOKING TO START... A LIFE FOR MYSELF? YOU KNOW, A NORMAL LIFE DURING THE WEEK, LIKE YOU HAVE.
HEH. I DON'T KNOW HOW TO BREAK THIS TO YOU, M'GANN...
...BUT WHILE MY WEEKDAYS MAY BE MANY THINGS, "NORMAL" IS DEFINITELY NOT ONE OF THEM.

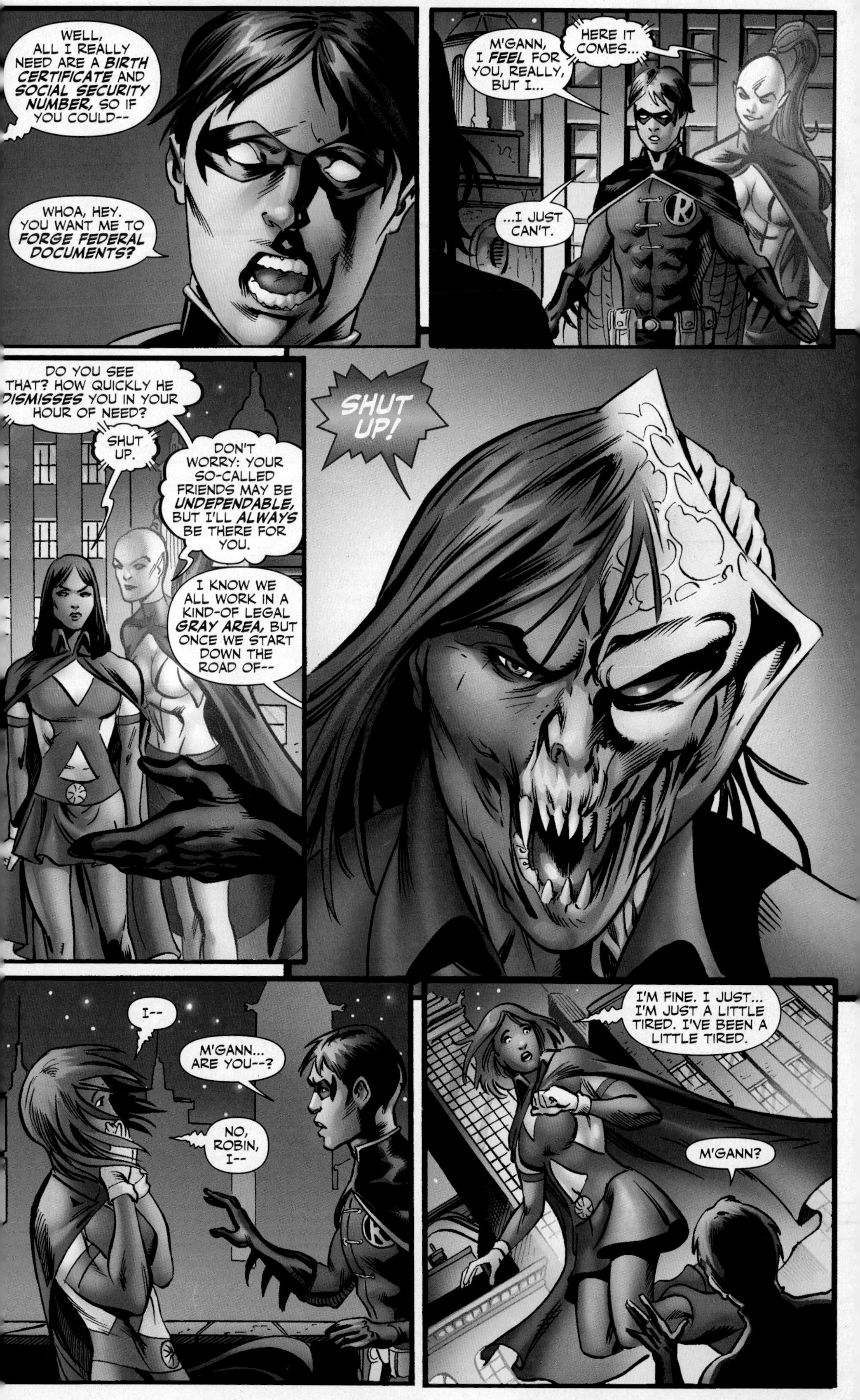
WELL, ALL I REALLY NEED ARE A BIRTH CERTIFICATE AND SOCIAL SECURITY NUMBER, SO IF YOU COULD--
WHOA, HEY. YOU WANT ME TO FORGE FEDERAL DOCUMENTS?
M'GANN, I FEEL FOR YOU, REALLY, BUT I...
HERE IT COMES...
...I JUST CAN'T.
DO YOU SEE THAT? HOW QUICKLY HE DISMISSES YOU IN YOUR HOUR OF NEED?
SHUT UP.
DON'T WORRY: YOUR SO-CALLED FRIENDS MAY BE UNDEPENDABLE, BUT I'LL ALWAYS BE THERE FOR YOU.
I KNOW WE ALL WORK IN A KIND-OF LEGAL GRAY AREA, BUT ONCE WE START DOWN THE ROAD OF--
SHUT UP!
I--
M'GANN... ARE YOU--?
NO, ROBIN, I--
I'M FINE. I JUST... I'M JUST A LITTLE TIRED. I'VE BEEN A LITTLE TIRED.
M'GANN?

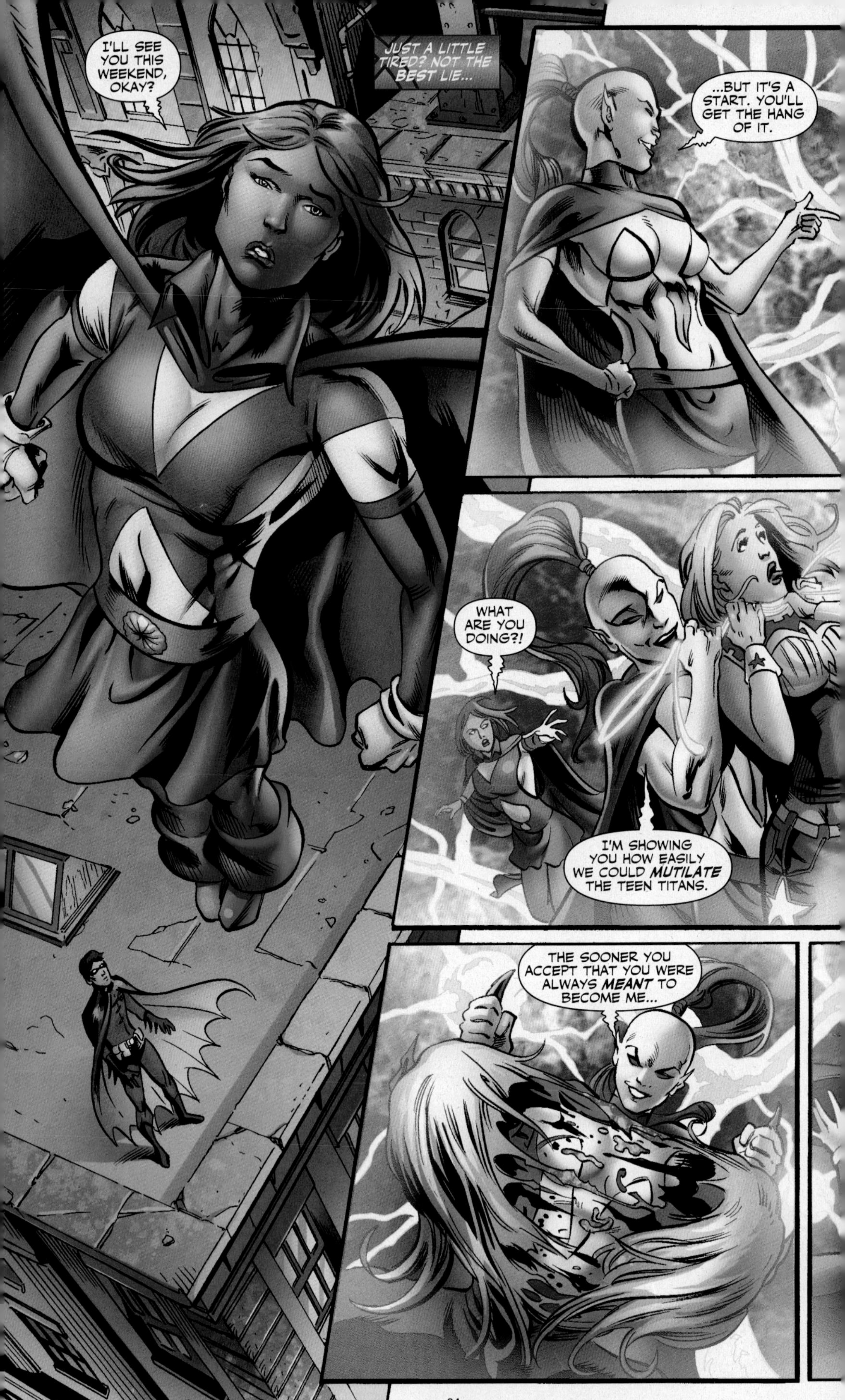

I'LL SEE YOU THIS WEEKEND, OKAY?
JUST A LITTLE TIRED? NOT THE BEST LIE...
...BUT IT'S A START. YOU'LL GET THE HANG OF IT.
WHAT ARE YOU DOING?!
I'M SHOWING YOU HOW EASILY WE COULD MUTILATE THE TEEN TITANS.
THE SOONER YOU ACCEPT THAT YOU WERE ALWAYS MEANT TO BECOME ME...

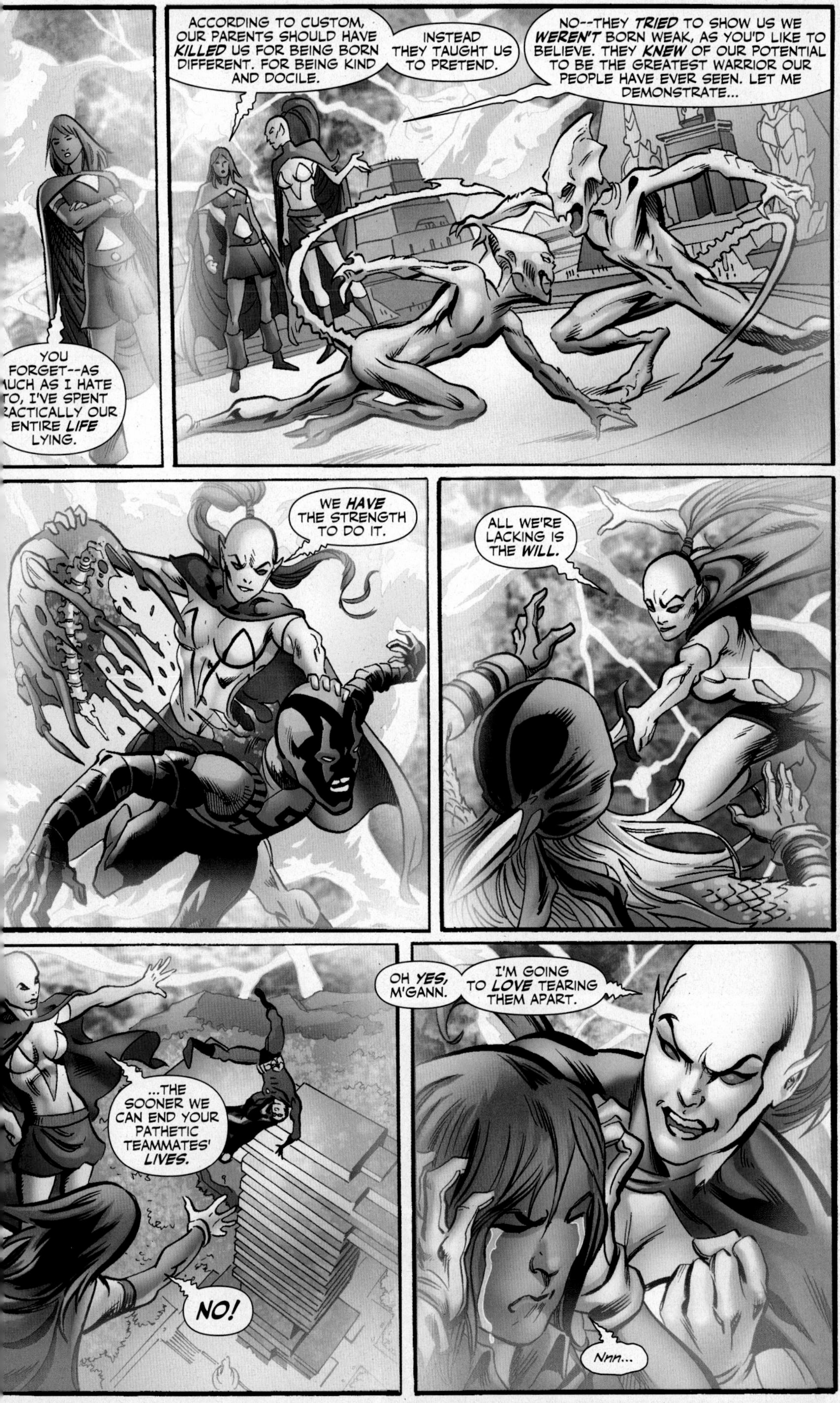

YOU FORGET--AS MUCH AS I HATE TO, I'VE SPENT PRACTICALLY OUR ENTIRE LIFE LYING.
ACCORDING TO CUSTOM, OUR PARENTS SHOULD HAVE KILLED US FOR BEING BORN DIFFERENT. FOR BEING KIND AND DOCILE.
INSTEAD THEY TAUGHT US TO PRETEND.
NO--THEY TRIED TO SHOW US WE WEREN'T BORN WEAK, AS YOU'D LIKE TO BELIEVE. THEY KNEW OF OUR POTENTIAL TO BE THE GREATEST WARRIOR OUR PEOPLE HAVE EVER SEEN. LET ME DEMONSTRATE...
WE HAVE THE STRENGTH TO DO IT.
ALL WE'RE LACKING IS THE WILL.
...THE SOONER WE CAN END YOUR PATHETIC TEAMMATES' LIVES.
NO!
OH YES, M'GANN.
I'M GOING TO LOVE TEARING THEM APART.
Nnn...

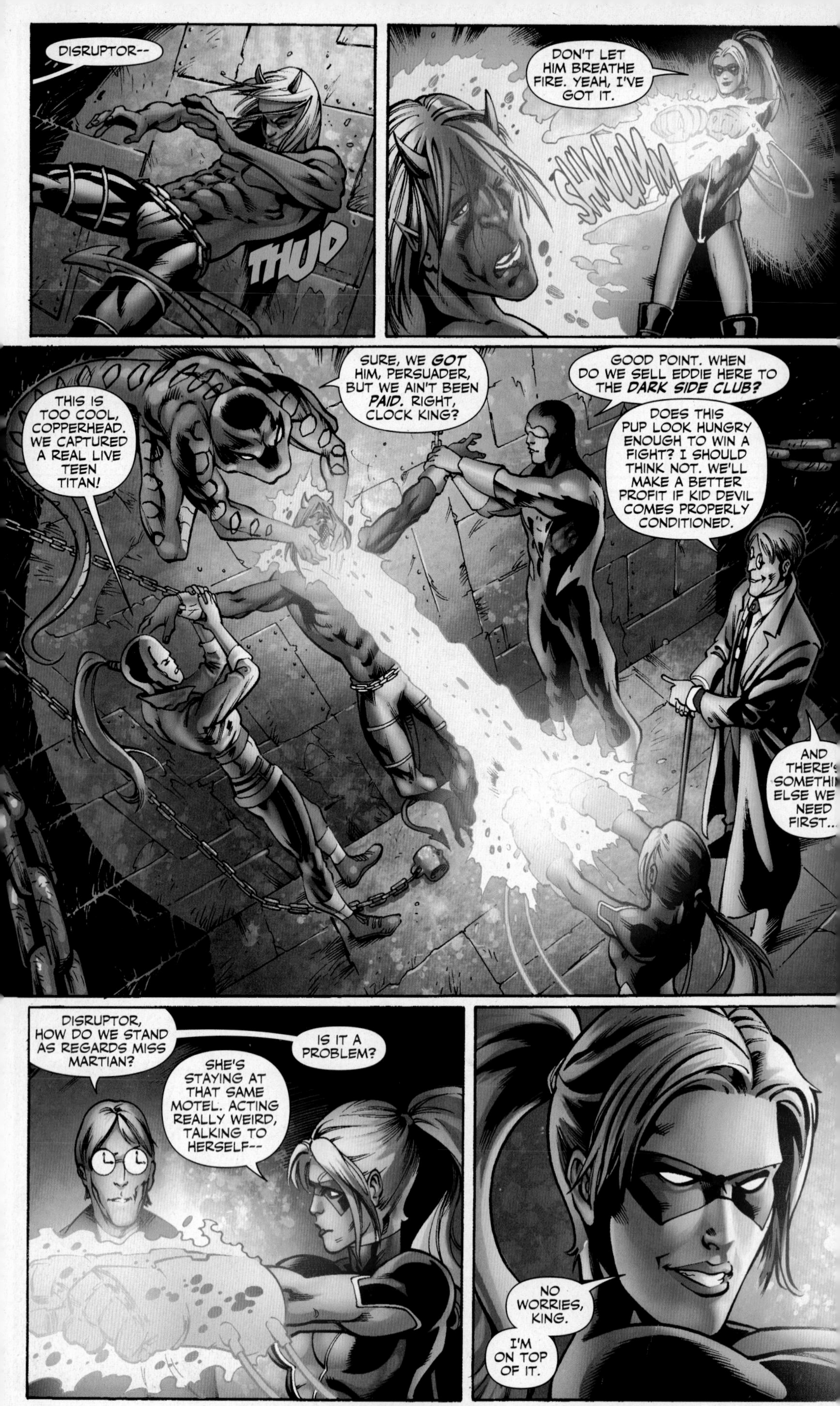
DISRUPTOR--
THUD
DON'T LET HIM BREATHE FIRE. YEAH, I'VE GOT IT.
THIS IS TOO COOL, COPPERHEAD. WE CAPTURED A REAL LIVE TEEN TITAN!
SURE, WE GOT HIM, PERSUADER, BUT WE AIN'T BEEN PAID. RIGHT, CLOCK KING?
GOOD POINT. WHEN DO WE SELL EDDIE HERE TO THE DARK SIDE CLUB?
DOES THIS PUP LOOK HUNGRY ENOUGH TO WIN A FIGHT? I SHOULD THINK NOT. WE'LL MAKE A BETTER PROFIT IF KID DEVIL COMES PROPERLY CONDITIONED.
AND THERE'S SOMETHI ELSE WE NEED FIRST...
DISRUPTOR, HOW DO WE STAND AS REGARDS MISS MARTIAN?
IS IT A PROBLEM?
SHE'S STAYING AT THAT SAME MOTEL. ACTING REALLY WEIRD, TALKING TO HERSELF--
NO WORRIES, KING.
I'M ON TOP OF IT.

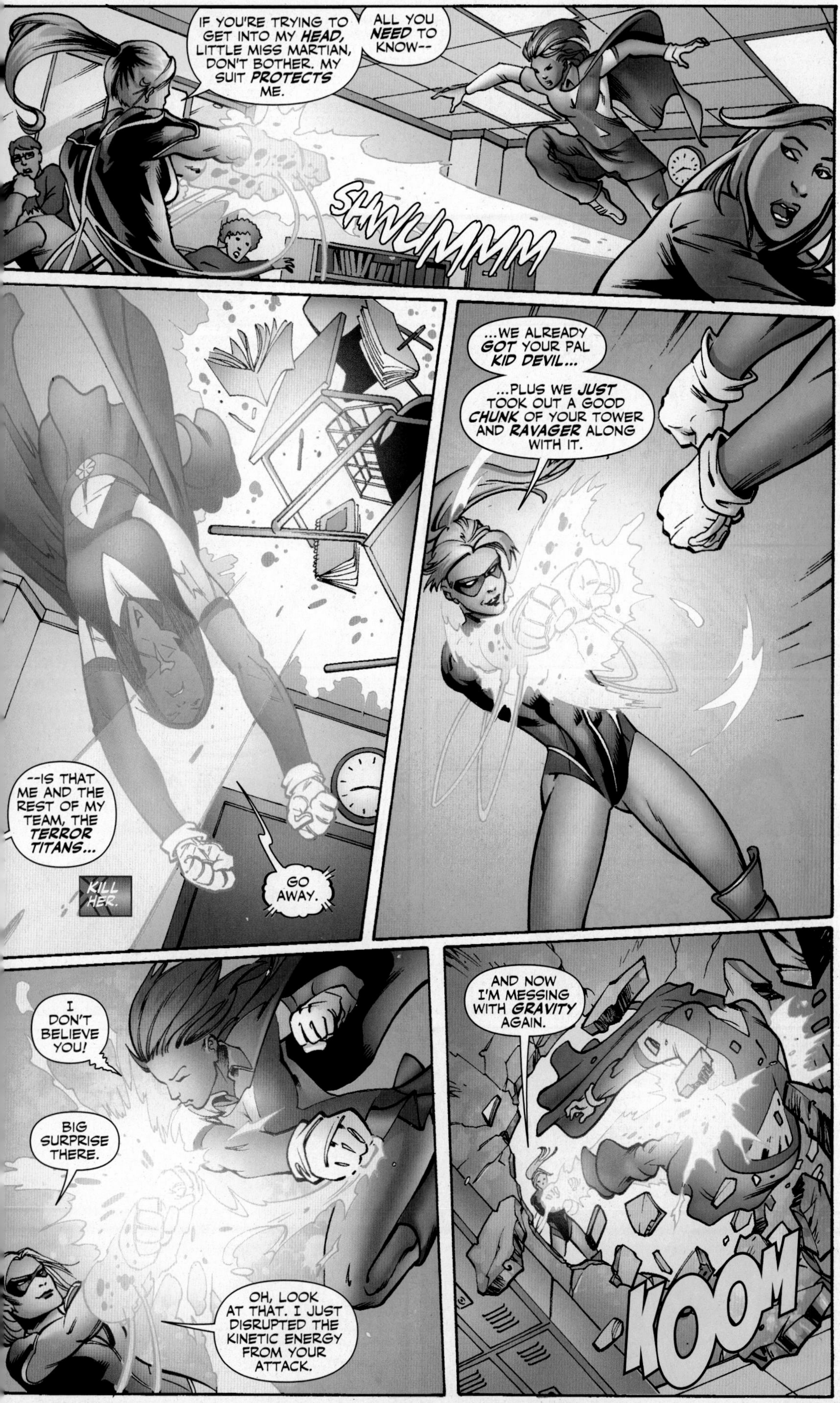
IF YOU'RE TRYING TO GET INTO MY *HEAD*, LITTLE MISS MARTIAN, DON'T BOTHER. MY SUIT *PROTECTS* ME.
ALL YOU *NEED* TO KNOW--
SHVUMMMM
--IS THAT ME AND THE REST OF MY TEAM, THE *TERROR TITANS*...
KILL HER.
GO AWAY.
...WE ALREADY *GOT* YOUR PAL *KID DEVIL*...
...PLUS WE *JUST* TOOK OUT A GOOD *CHUNK* OF YOUR TOWER AND *RAVAGER* ALONG WITH IT.
I DON'T BELIEVE YOU!
BIG SURPRISE THERE.
OH, LOOK AT THAT. I JUST DISRUPTED THE KINETIC ENERGY FROM YOUR ATTACK.
AND NOW I'M MESSING WITH *GRAVITY* AGAIN.
KOOM

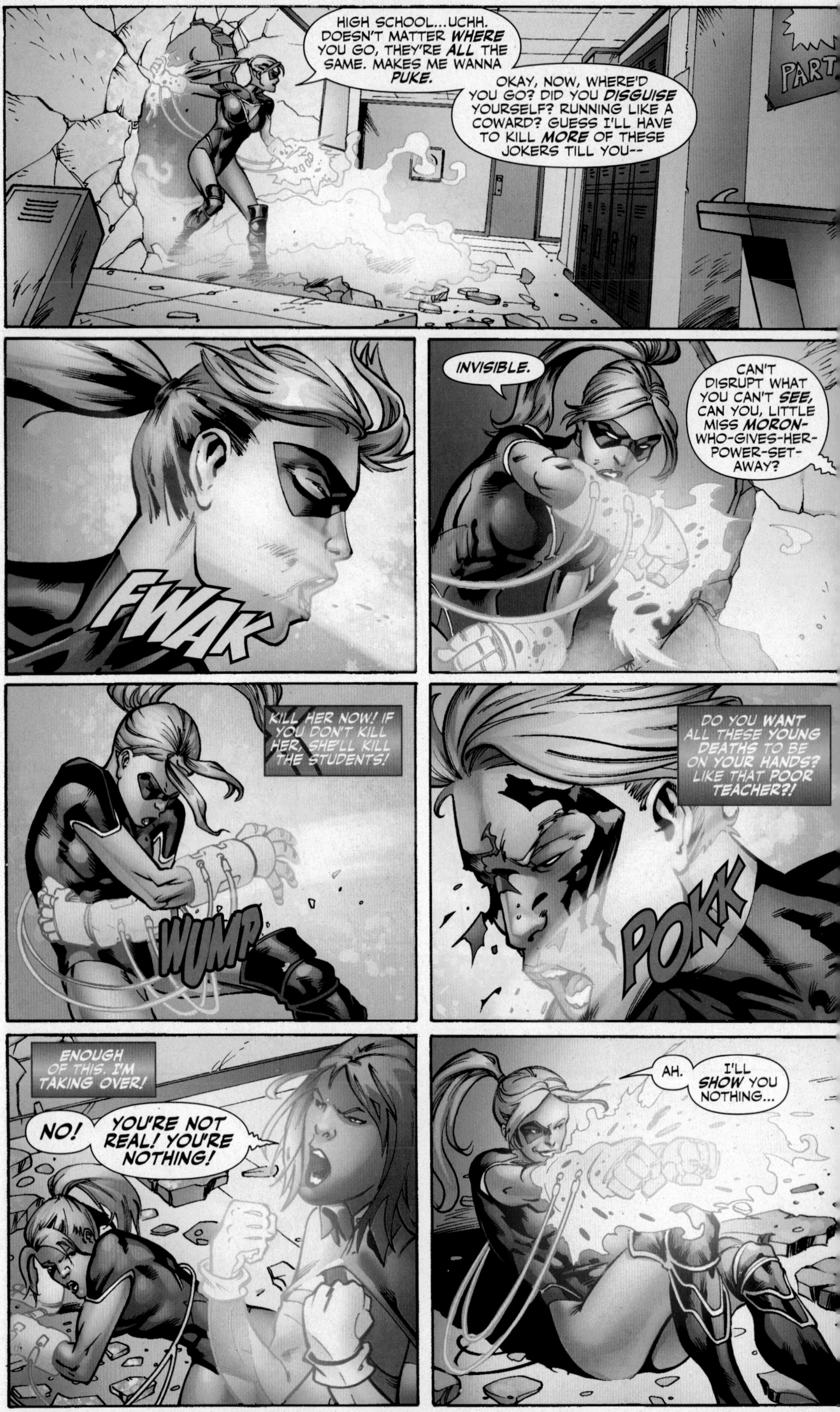

HIGH SCHOOL...UCHH. DOESN'T MATTER WHERE YOU GO, THEY'RE ALL THE SAME. MAKES ME WANNA PUKE.
OKAY, NOW, WHERE'D YOU GO? DID YOU DISGUISE YOURSELF? RUNNING LIKE A COWARD? GUESS I'LL HAVE TO KILL MORE OF THESE JOKERS TILL YOU--
PART
FWAK
INVISIBLE.
CAN'T DISRUPT WHAT YOU CAN'T SEE, CAN YOU, LITTLE MISS MORON-WHO-GIVES-HER-POWER-SET-AWAY?
KILL HER NOW! IF YOU DON'T KILL HER, SHE'LL KILL THE STUDENTS!
WUMP
DO YOU WANT ALL THESE YOUNG DEATHS TO BE ON YOUR HANDS? LIKE THAT POOR TEACHER?!
POKK
ENOUGH OF THIS. I'M TAKING OVER!
NO!
YOU'RE NOT REAL! YOU'RE NOTHING!
AH.
I'LL SHOW YOU NOTHING...

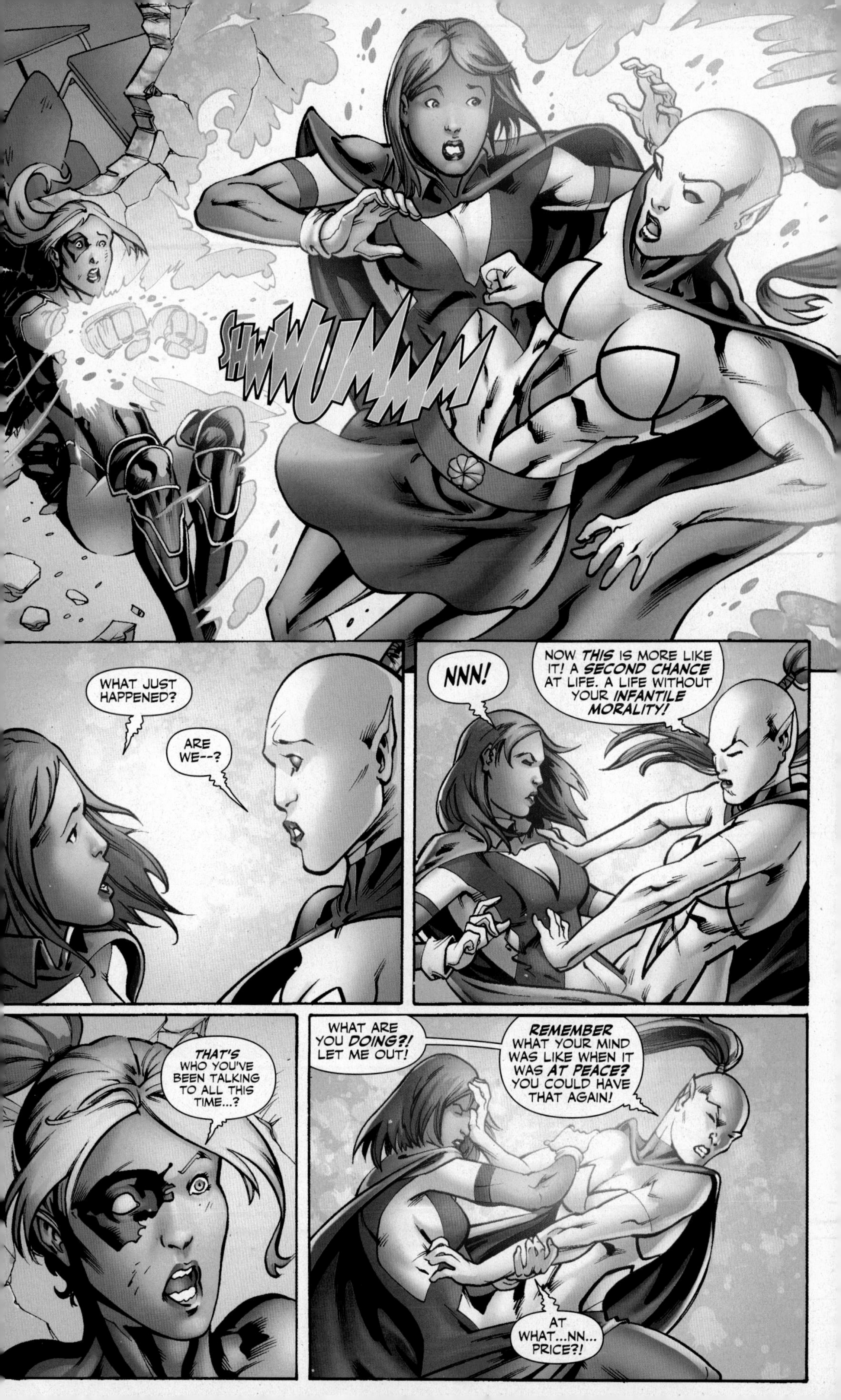
SHWWUMMMM
WHAT JUST HAPPENED?
ARE WE--?
NNN!
NOW THIS IS MORE LIKE IT! A SECOND CHANCE AT LIFE. A LIFE WITHOUT YOUR INFANTILE MORALITY!
THAT'S WHO YOU'VE BEEN TALKING TO ALL THIS TIME...?
WHAT ARE YOU DOING?! LET ME OUT!
REMEMBER WHAT YOUR MIND WAS LIKE WHEN IT WAS AT PEACE? YOU COULD HAVE THAT AGAIN!
AT WHAT...NN... PRICE?!

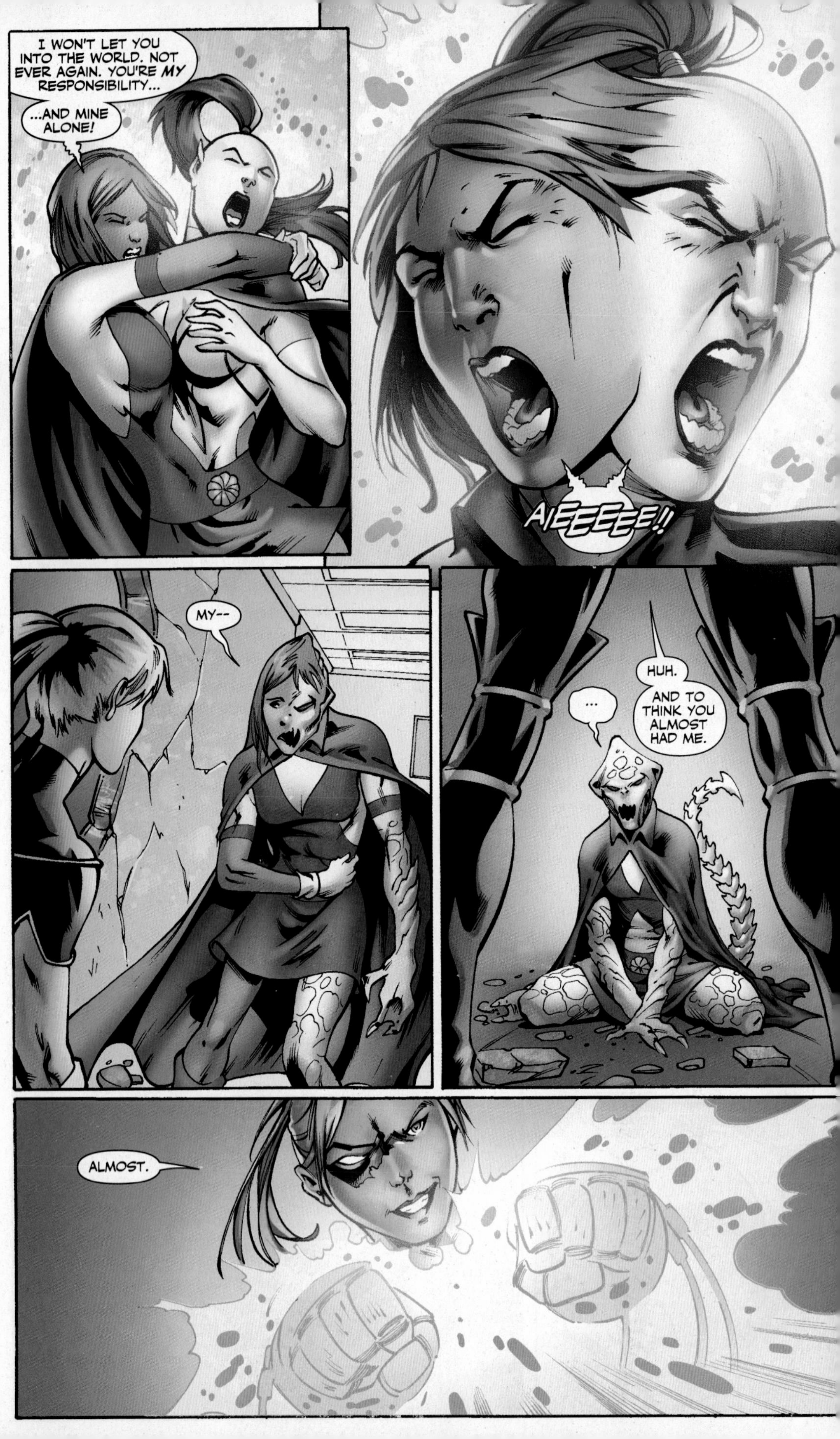
I WON'T LET YOU INTO THE WORLD. NOT EVER AGAIN. YOU'RE *MY* RESPONSIBILITY...
...AND MINE ALONE!
AIEEEEEE!!
MY--
...
HUH.
AND TO THINK YOU ALMOST HAD ME.
ALMOST.

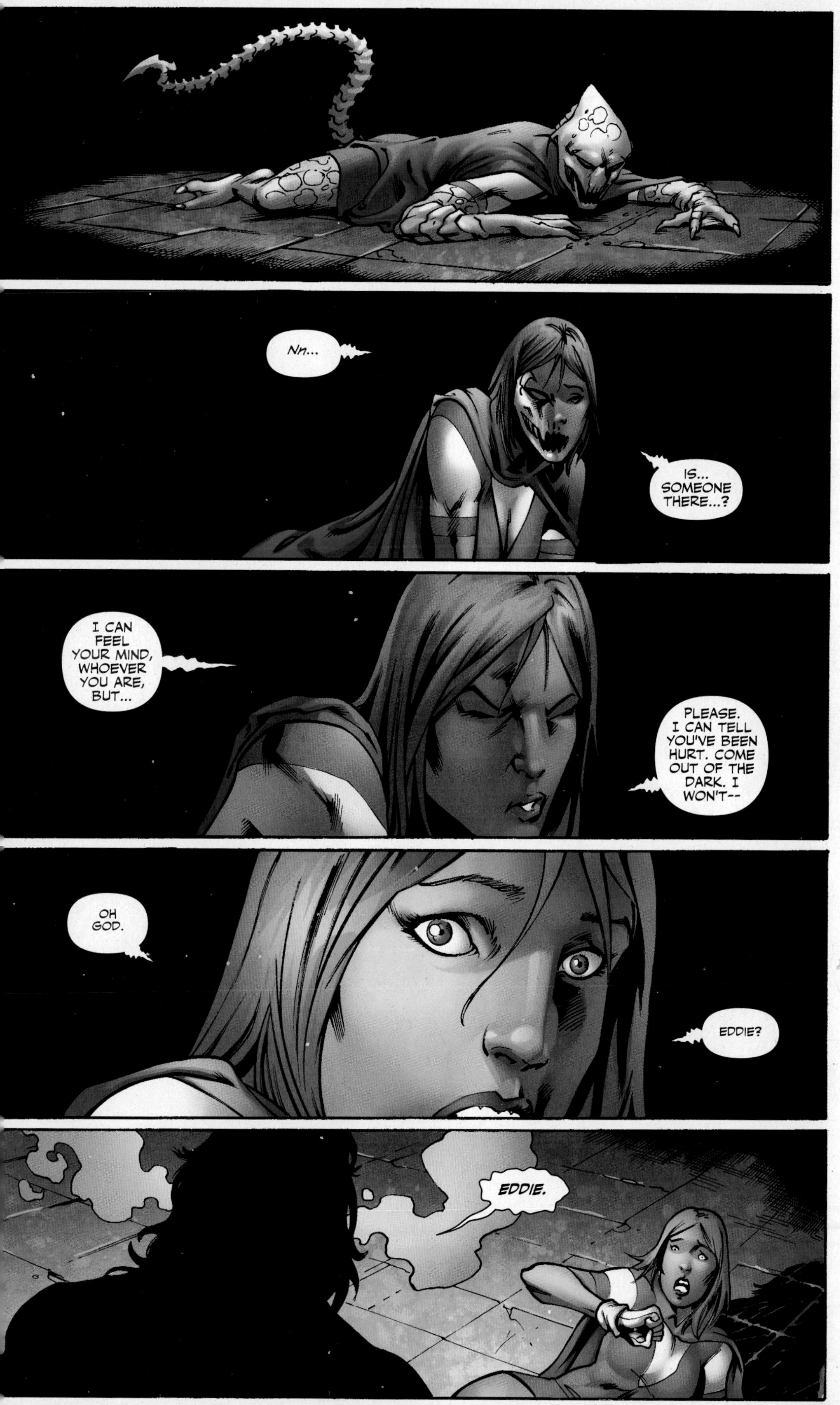

Nn...
IS... SOMEONE THERE...?
I CAN FEEL YOUR MIND, WHOEVER YOU ARE, BUT...
PLEASE. I CAN TELL YOU'VE BEEN HURT. COME OUT OF THE DARK. I WON'T--
OH GOD.
EDDIE?
EDDIE.

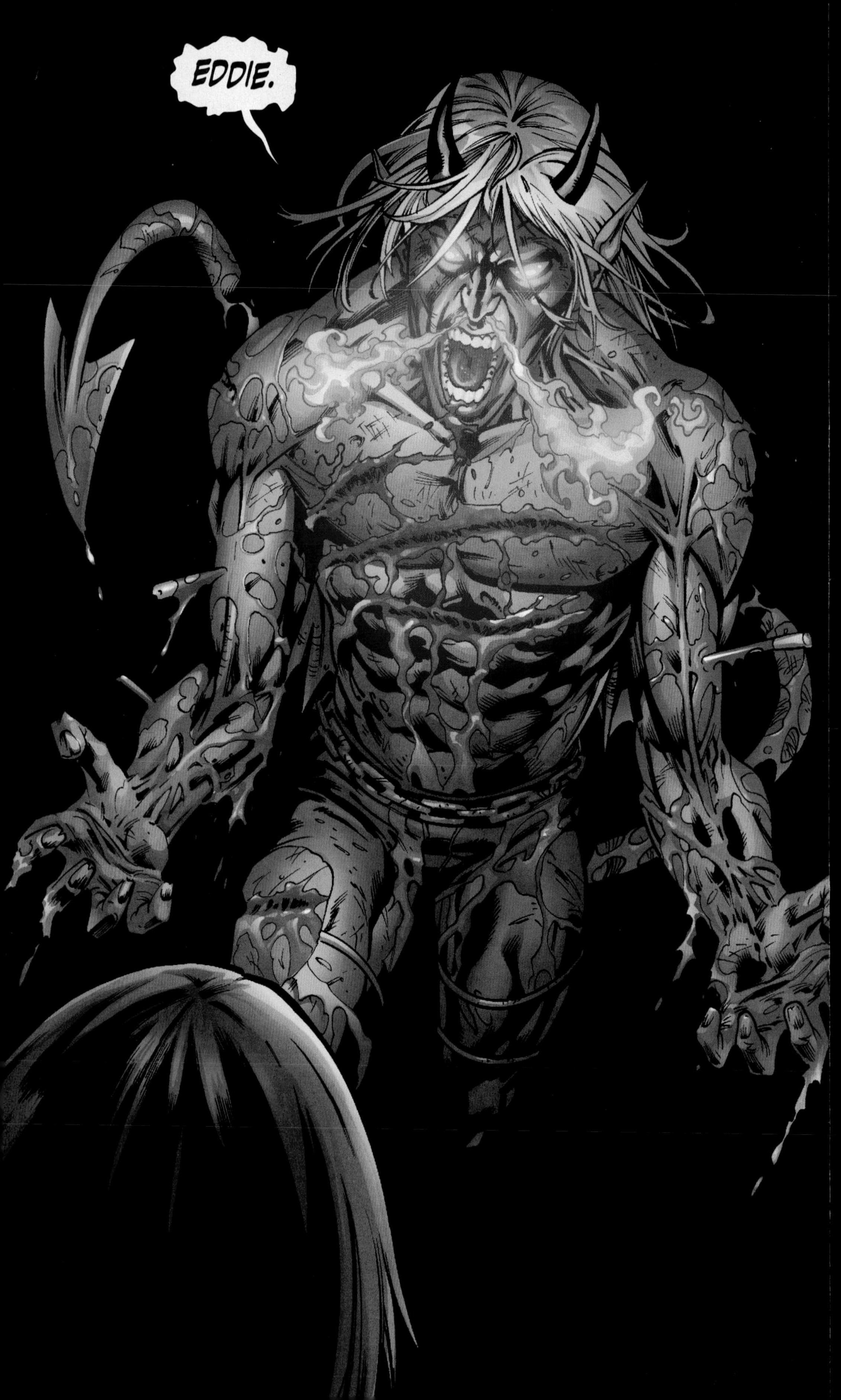
EDDIE.

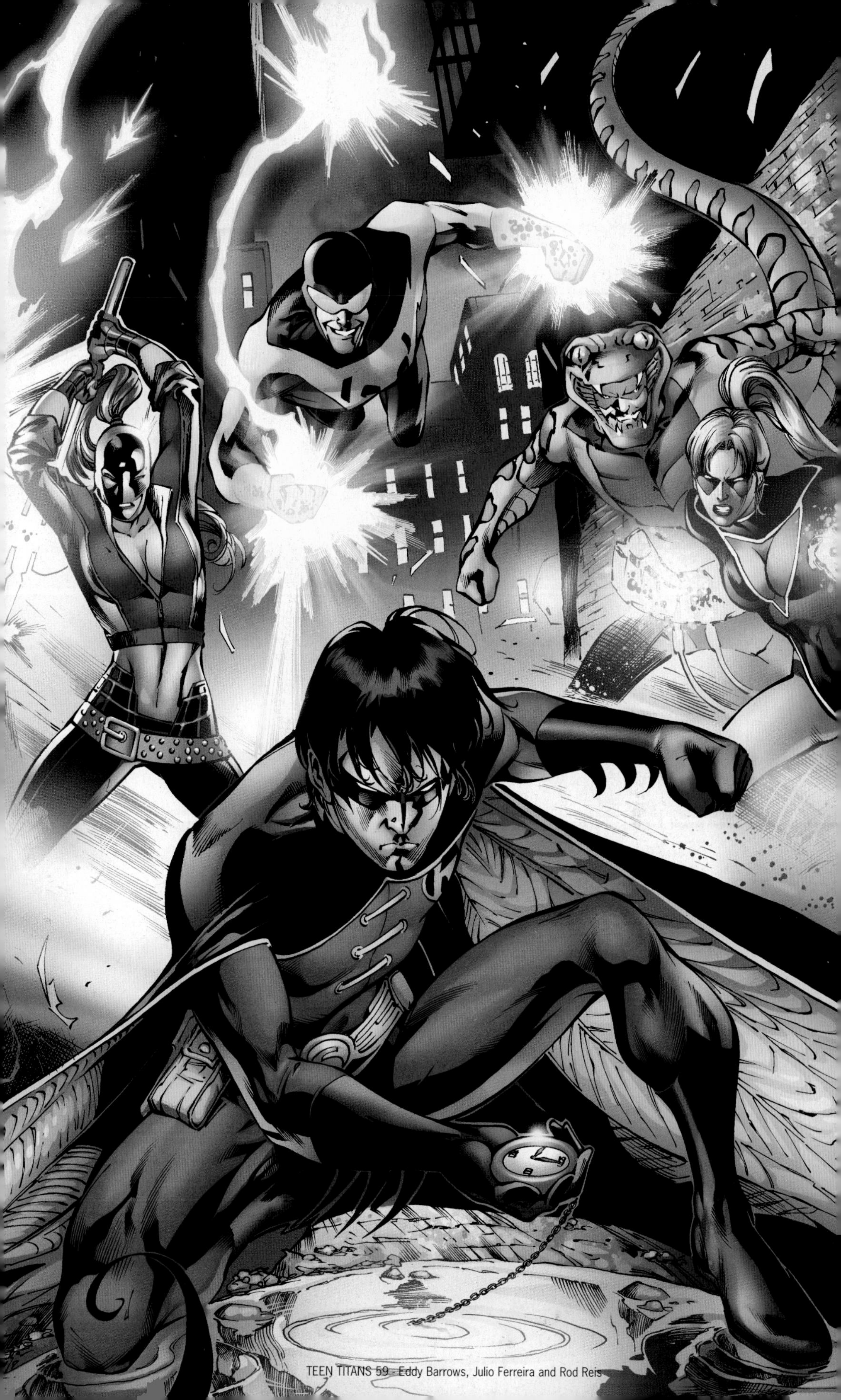

TEEN TITANS 59 - Eddy Barrows, Julio Ferreira and Rod Reis

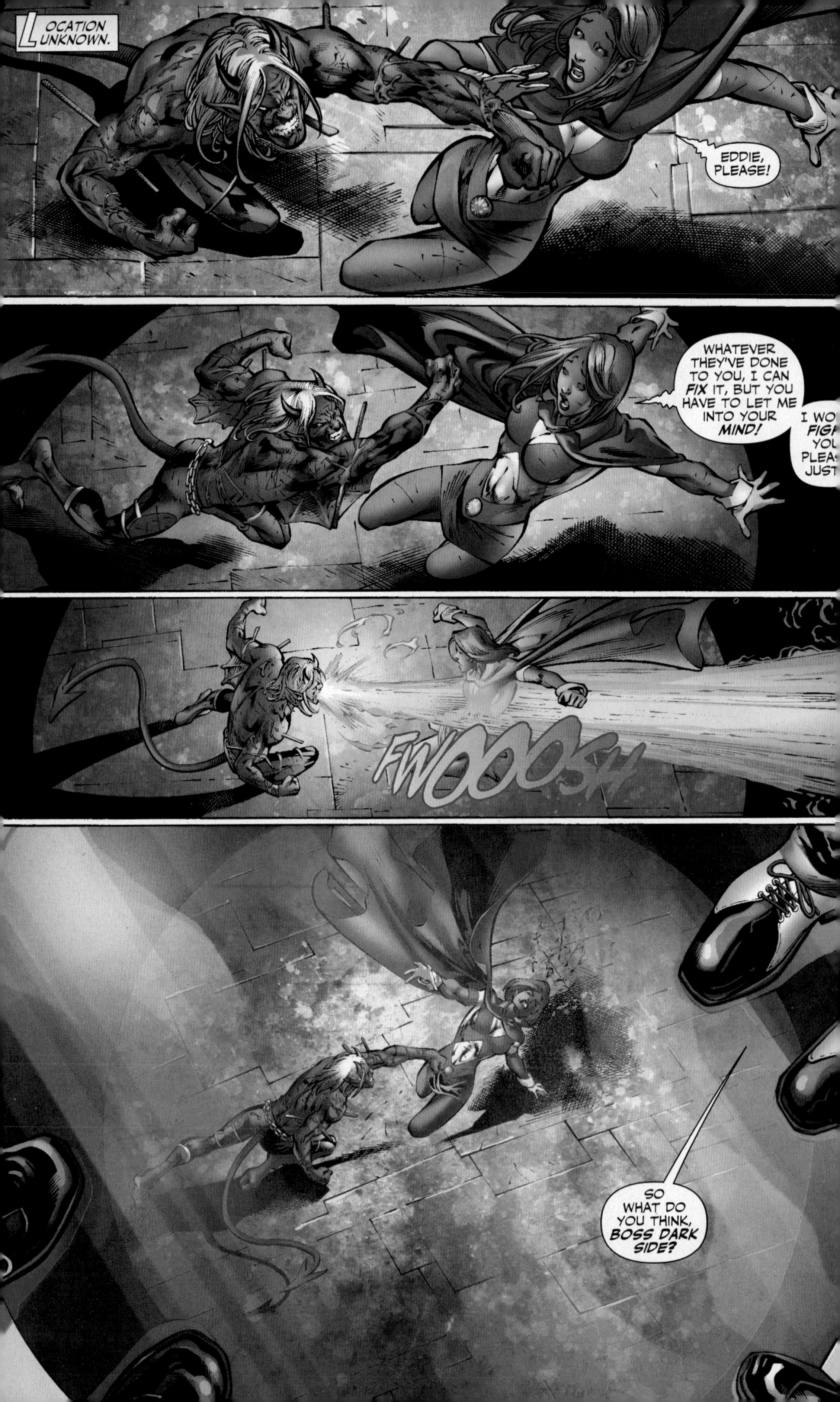
LOCATION UNKNOWN.
EDDIE, PLEASE!
WHATEVER THEY'VE DONE TO YOU, I CAN FIX IT, BUT YOU HAVE TO LET ME INTO YOUR MIND!
FWOOOSH
SO WHAT DO YOU THINK, BOSS DARK SIDE?

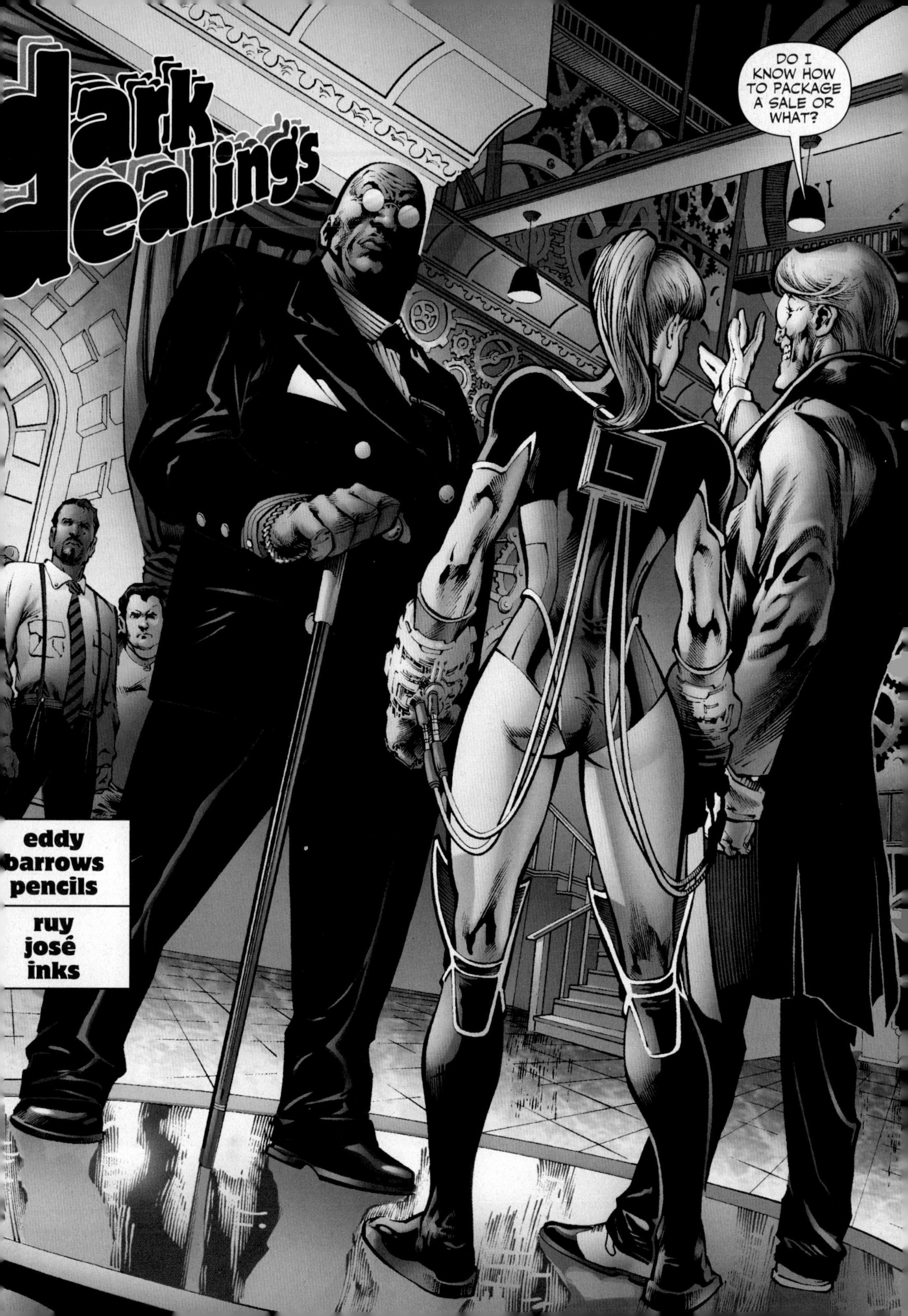
dark dealings
DO I KNOW HOW TO PACKAGE A SALE OR WHAT?
eddy barrows pencils
ruy josé inks

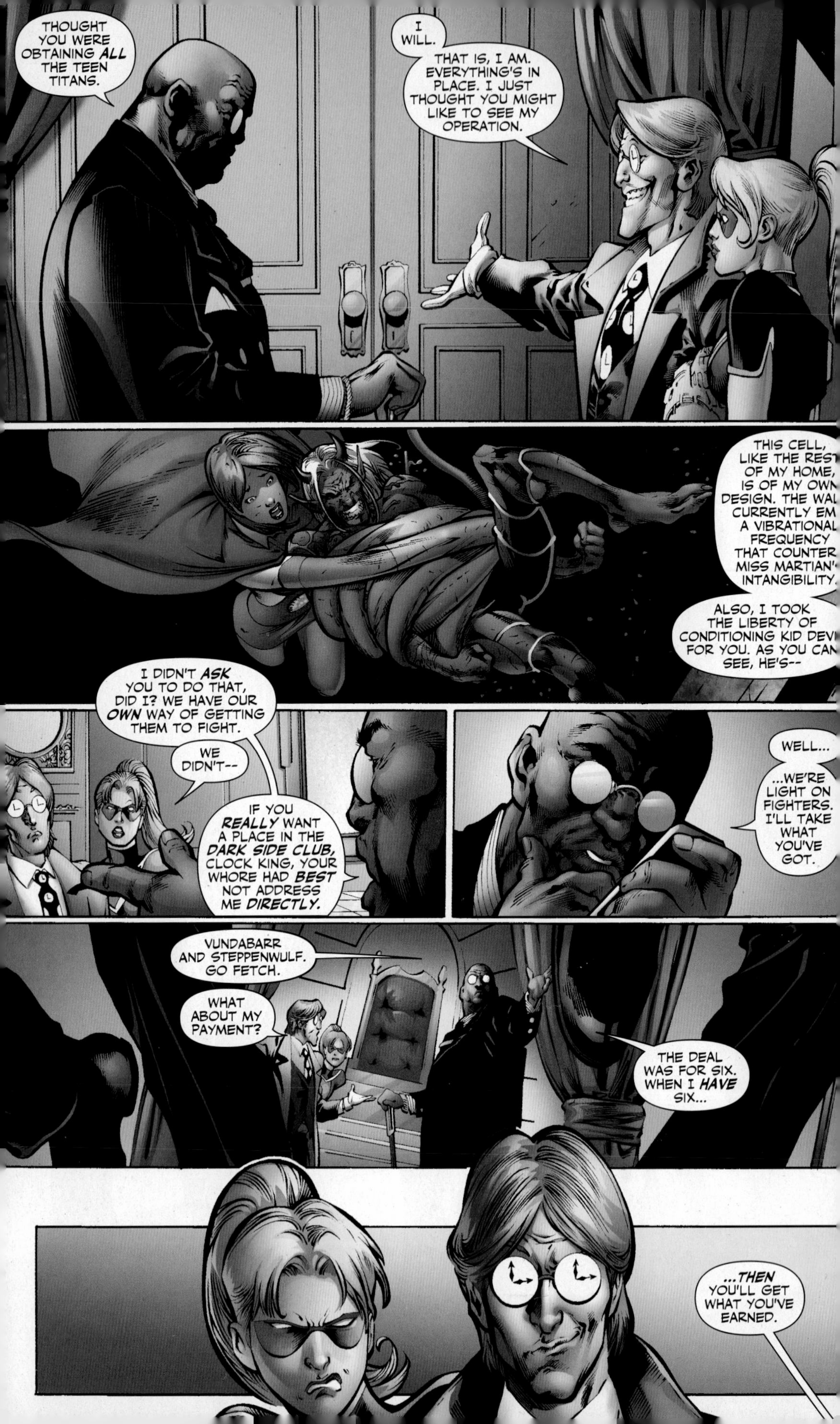
THOUGHT YOU WERE OBTAINING ALL THE TEEN TITANS.
I WILL.
THAT IS, I AM. EVERYTHING'S IN PLACE. I JUST THOUGHT YOU MIGHT LIKE TO SEE MY OPERATION.
THIS CELL, LIKE THE REST OF MY HOME, IS OF MY OWN DESIGN. THE WAL CURRENTLY EM A VIBRATIONAL FREQUENCY THAT COUNTER MISS MARTIAN' INTANGIBILITY.
ALSO, I TOOK THE LIBERTY OF CONDITIONING KID DEV FOR YOU. AS YOU CAN SEE, HE'S--
I DIDN'T ASK YOU TO DO THAT, DID I? WE HAVE OUR OWN WAY OF GETTING THEM TO FIGHT.
WE DIDN'T--
IF YOU REALLY WANT A PLACE IN THE DARK SIDE CLUB, CLOCK KING, YOUR WHORE HAD BEST NOT ADDRESS ME DIRECTLY.
WELL...
...WE'RE LIGHT ON FIGHTERS. I'LL TAKE WHAT YOU'VE GOT.
VUNDABARR AND STEPPENWULF. GO FETCH.
WHAT ABOUT MY PAYMENT?
THE DEAL WAS FOR SIX. WHEN I HAVE SIX...
...THEN YOU'LL GET WHAT YOU'VE EARNED.

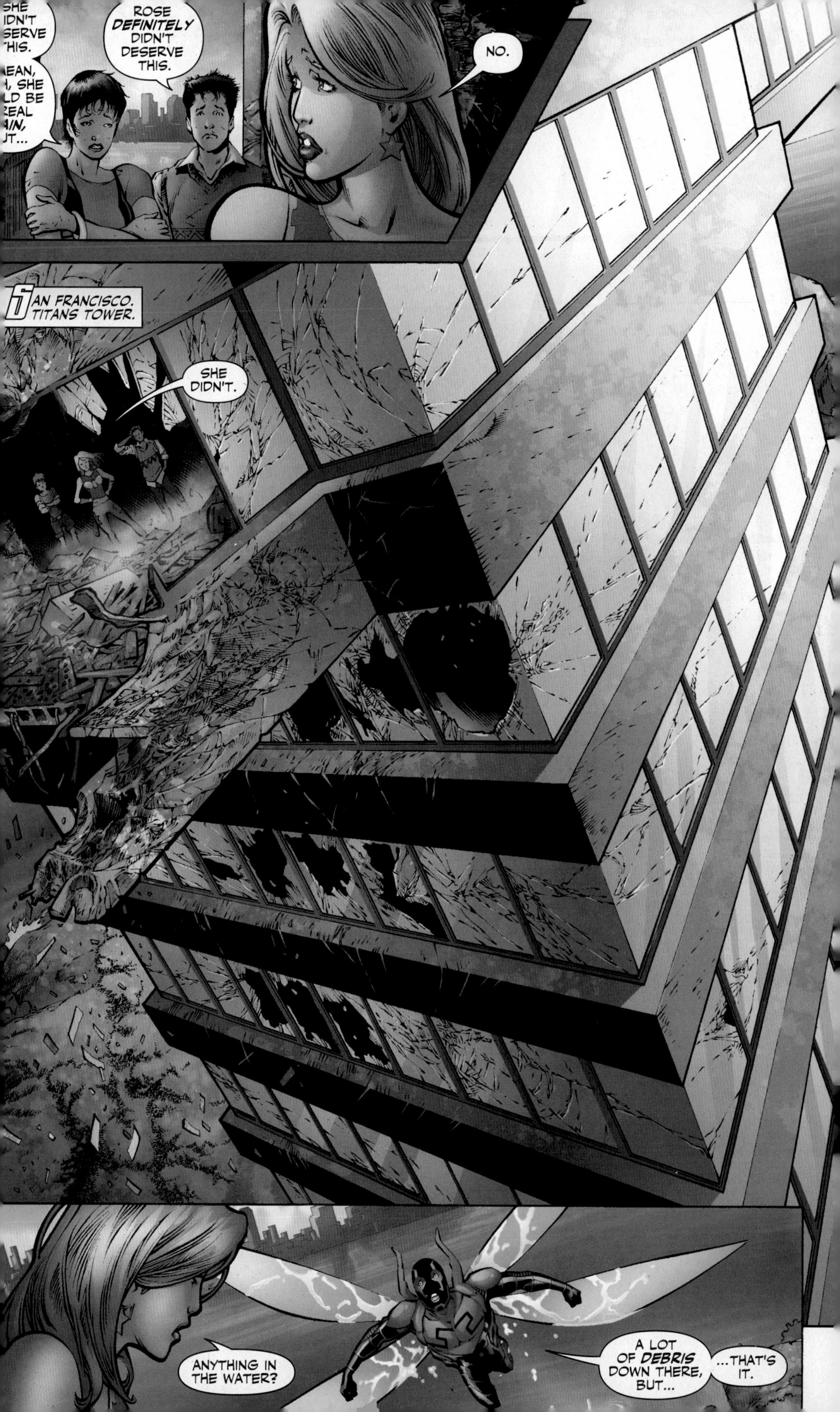
ROSE DEFINITELY DIDN'T DESERVE THIS.
NO.
SAN FRANCISCO. TITANS TOWER.
SHE DIDN'T.
ANYTHING IN THE WATER?
A LOT OF DEBRIS DOWN THERE, BUT...
...THAT'S IT.

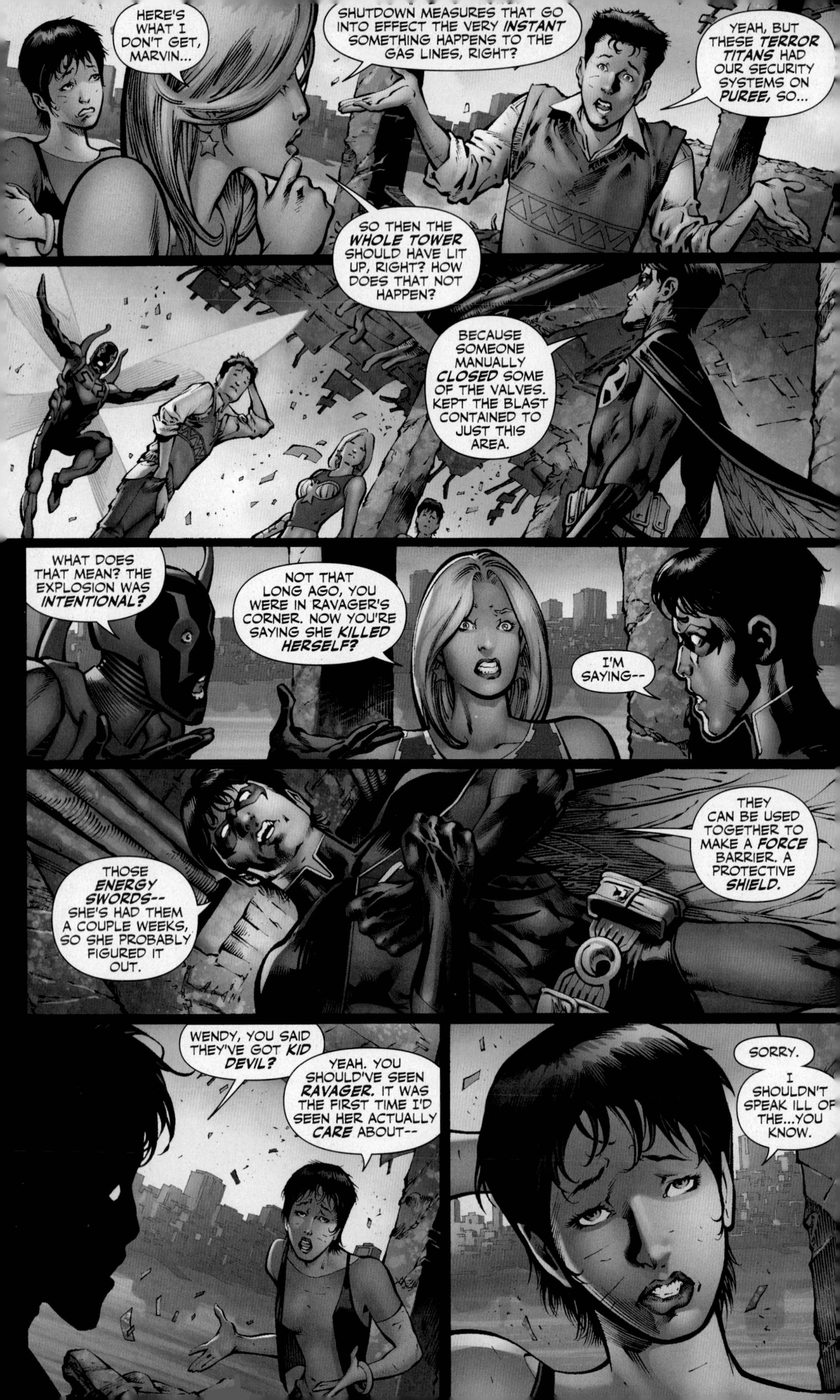
HERE'S WHAT I DON'T GET, MARVIN...
SHUTDOWN MEASURES THAT GO INTO EFFECT THE VERY INSTANT SOMETHING HAPPENS TO THE GAS LINES, RIGHT?
YEAH, BUT THESE TERROR TITANS HAD OUR SECURITY SYSTEMS ON PUREE, SO...
SO THEN THE WHOLE TOWER SHOULD HAVE LIT UP, RIGHT? HOW DOES THAT NOT HAPPEN?
BECAUSE SOMEONE MANUALLY CLOSED SOME OF THE VALVES. KEPT THE BLAST CONTAINED TO JUST THIS AREA.
WHAT DOES THAT MEAN? THE EXPLOSION WAS INTENTIONAL?
NOT THAT LONG AGO, YOU WERE IN RAVAGER'S CORNER. NOW YOU'RE SAYING SHE KILLED HERSELF?
I'M SAYING--
THOSE ENERGY SWORDS-- SHE'S HAD THEM A COUPLE WEEKS, SO SHE PROBABLY FIGURED IT OUT.
THEY CAN BE USED TOGETHER TO MAKE A FORCE BARRIER. A PROTECTIVE SHIELD.
WENDY, YOU SAID THEY'VE GOT KID DEVIL?
YEAH. YOU SHOULD'VE SEEN RAVAGER. IT WAS THE FIRST TIME I'D SEEN HER ACTUALLY CARE ABOUT--
SORRY.
I SHOULDN'T SPEAK ILL OF THE...YOU KNOW.

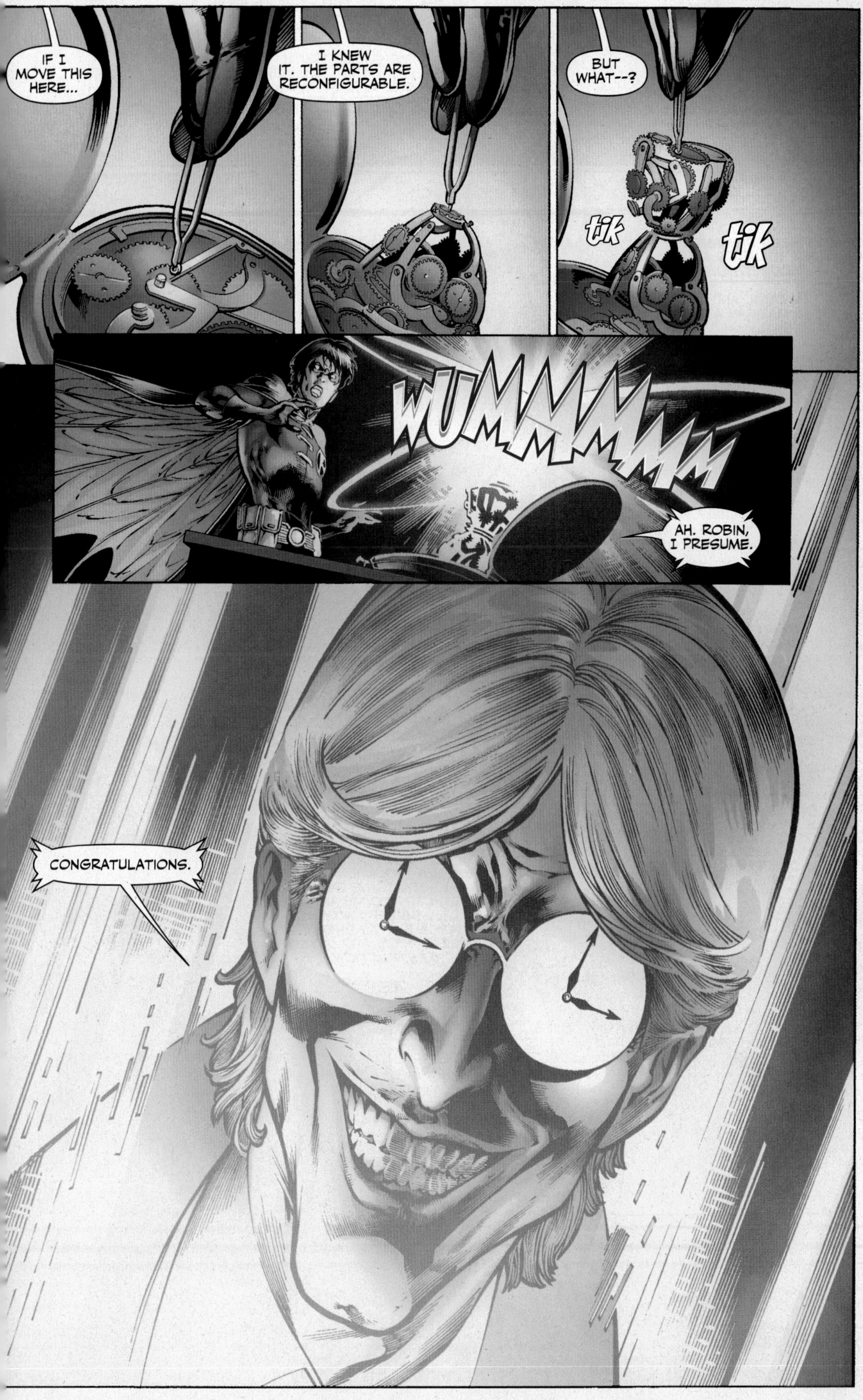

IF I MOVE THIS HERE...
I KNEW IT. THE PARTS ARE RECONFIGURABLE.
BUT WHAT--?
tik
tik
WUMMMMMMMMMM
AH. ROBIN, I PRESUME.
CONGRATULATIONS.

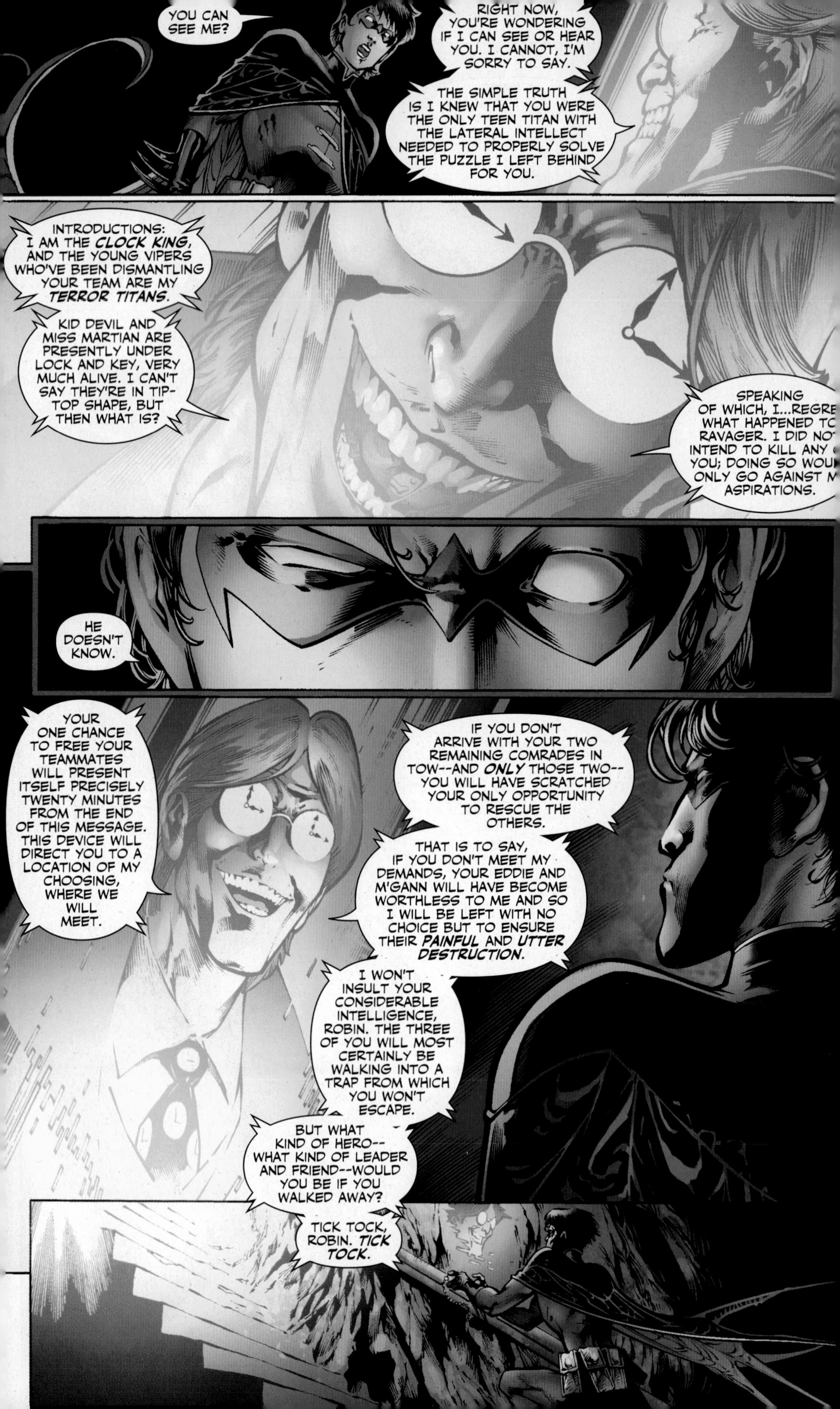
YOU CAN SEE ME?
RIGHT NOW, YOU'RE WONDERING IF I CAN SEE OR HEAR YOU. I CANNOT, I'M SORRY TO SAY.
THE SIMPLE TRUTH IS I KNEW THAT YOU WERE THE ONLY TEEN TITAN WITH THE LATERAL INTELLECT NEEDED TO PROPERLY SOLVE THE PUZZLE I LEFT BEHIND FOR YOU.
INTRODUCTIONS: I AM THE *CLOCK KING*, AND THE YOUNG VIPERS WHO'VE BEEN DISMANTLING YOUR TEAM ARE MY *TERROR TITANS*.
KID DEVIL AND MISS MARTIAN ARE PRESENTLY UNDER LOCK AND KEY, VERY MUCH ALIVE. I CAN'T SAY THEY'RE IN TIP-TOP SHAPE, BUT THEN WHAT IS?
HE DOESN'T KNOW.
YOUR ONE CHANCE TO FREE YOUR TEAMMATES WILL PRESENT ITSELF PRECISELY TWENTY MINUTES FROM THE END OF THIS MESSAGE. THIS DEVICE WILL DIRECT YOU TO A LOCATION OF MY CHOOSING, WHERE WE WILL MEET.
IF YOU DON'T ARRIVE WITH YOUR TWO REMAINING COMRADES IN TOW--AND *ONLY* THOSE TWO--YOU WILL HAVE SCRATCHED YOUR ONLY OPPORTUNITY TO RESCUE THE OTHERS.
THAT IS TO SAY, IF YOU DON'T MEET MY DEMANDS, YOUR EDDIE AND M'GANN WILL HAVE BECOME WORTHLESS TO ME AND SO I WILL BE LEFT WITH NO CHOICE BUT TO ENSURE THEIR *PAINFUL* AND *UTTER DESTRUCTION*.
I WON'T INSULT YOUR CONSIDERABLE INTELLIGENCE, ROBIN. THE THREE OF YOU WILL MOST CERTAINLY BE WALKING INTO A TRAP FROM WHICH YOU WON'T ESCAPE.
BUT WHAT KIND OF HERO--WHAT KIND OF LEADER AND FRIEND--WOULD YOU BE IF YOU WALKED AWAY?
TICK TOCK, ROBIN. *TICK TOCK*.

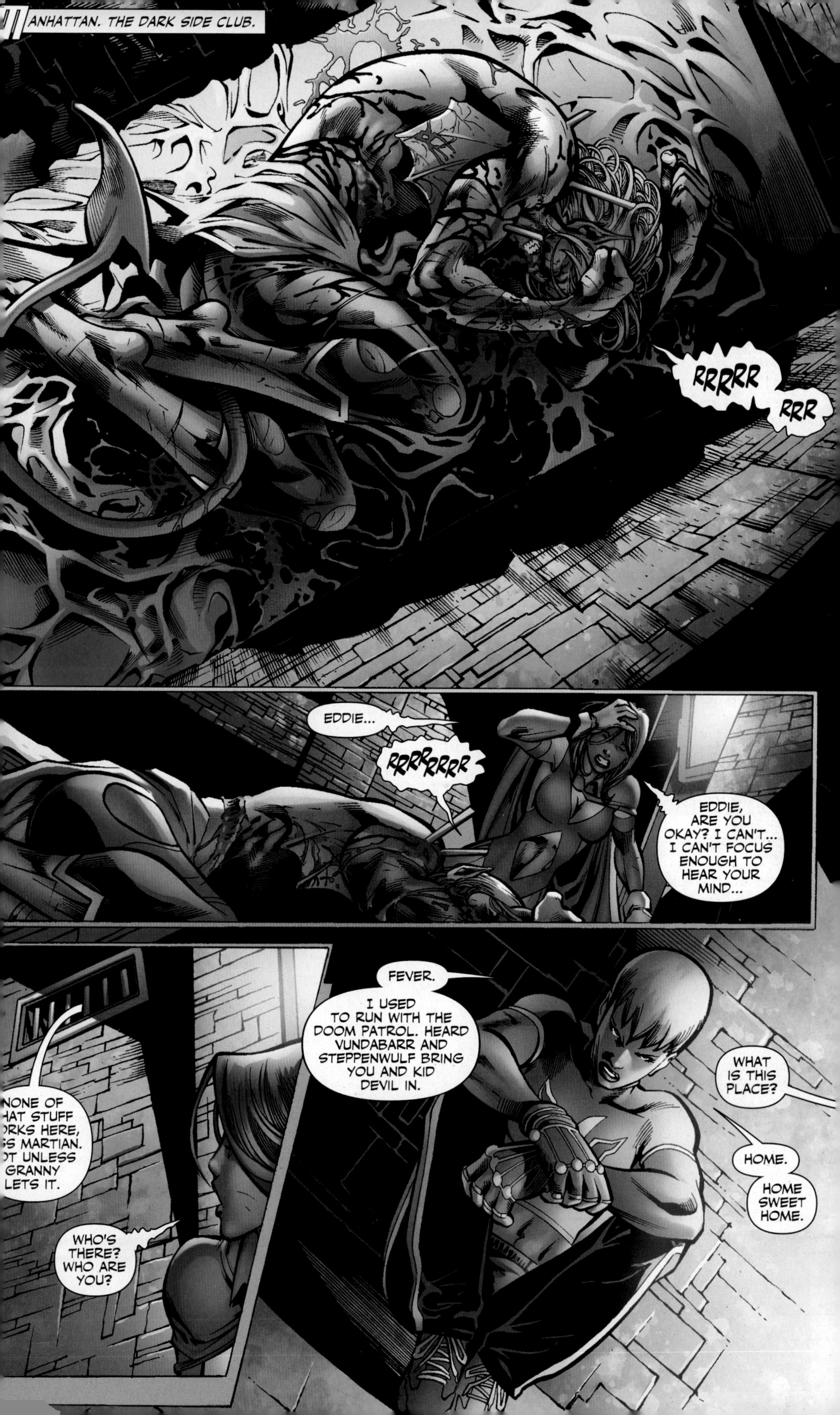

ANHATTAN. THE DARK SIDE CLUB.
RRRRR
RRR
EDDIE...
RRRRRRRR
EDDIE, ARE YOU OKAY? I CAN'T... I CAN'T FOCUS ENOUGH TO HEAR YOUR MIND...
WHAT IS THIS PLACE?
HOME.
HOME SWEET HOME.
WHO'S THERE? WHO ARE YOU?
FEVER.
I USED TO RUN WITH THE DOOM PATROL. HEARD VUNDABARR AND STEPPENWULF BRING YOU AND KID DEVIL IN.
NONE OF HAT STUFF ORKS HERE, SS MARTIAN. OT UNLESS GRANNY LETS IT.

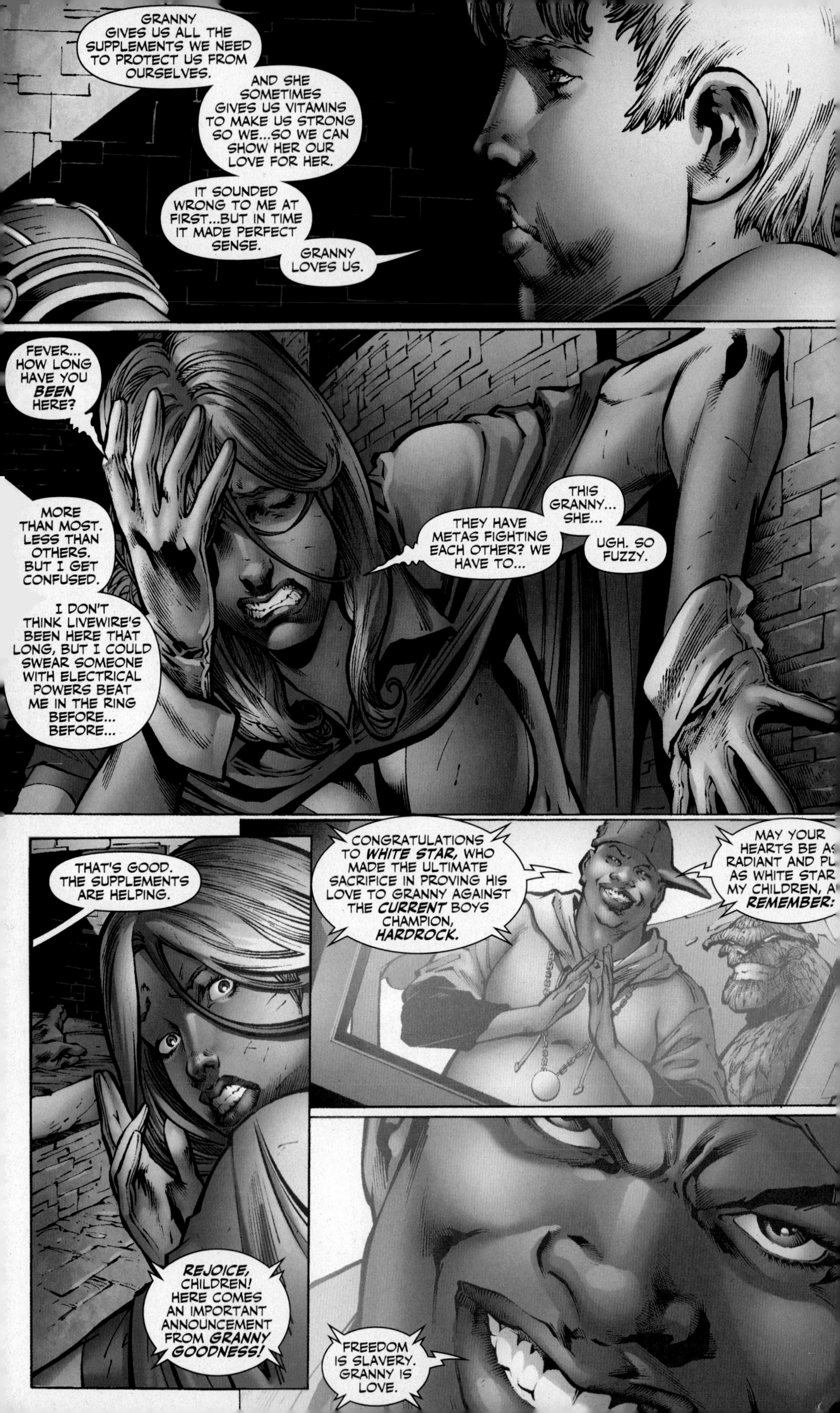
GRANNY GIVES US ALL THE SUPPLEMENTS WE NEED TO PROTECT US FROM OURSELVES.
AND SHE SOMETIMES GIVES US VITAMINS TO MAKE US STRONG SO WE...SO WE CAN SHOW HER OUR LOVE FOR HER.
IT SOUNDED WRONG TO ME AT FIRST...BUT IN TIME IT MADE PERFECT SENSE.
GRANNY LOVES US.
FEVER... HOW LONG HAVE YOU BEEN HERE?
MORE THAN MOST. LESS THAN OTHERS. BUT I GET CONFUSED.
I DON'T THINK LIVEWIRE'S BEEN HERE THAT LONG, BUT I COULD SWEAR SOMEONE WITH ELECTRICAL POWERS BEAT ME IN THE RING BEFORE... BEFORE...
THEY HAVE METAS FIGHTING EACH OTHER? WE HAVE TO...
THIS GRANNY... SHE...
UGH. SO FUZZY.
THAT'S GOOD. THE SUPPLEMENTS ARE HELPING.
CONGRATULATIONS TO WHITE STAR, WHO MADE THE ULTIMATE SACRIFICE IN PROVING HIS LOVE TO GRANNY AGAINST THE CURRENT BOYS CHAMPION, HARDROCK.
REJOICE, CHILDREN! HERE COMES AN IMPORTANT ANNOUNCEMENT FROM GRANNY GOODNESS!
FREEDOM IS SLAVERY. GRANNY IS LOVE.

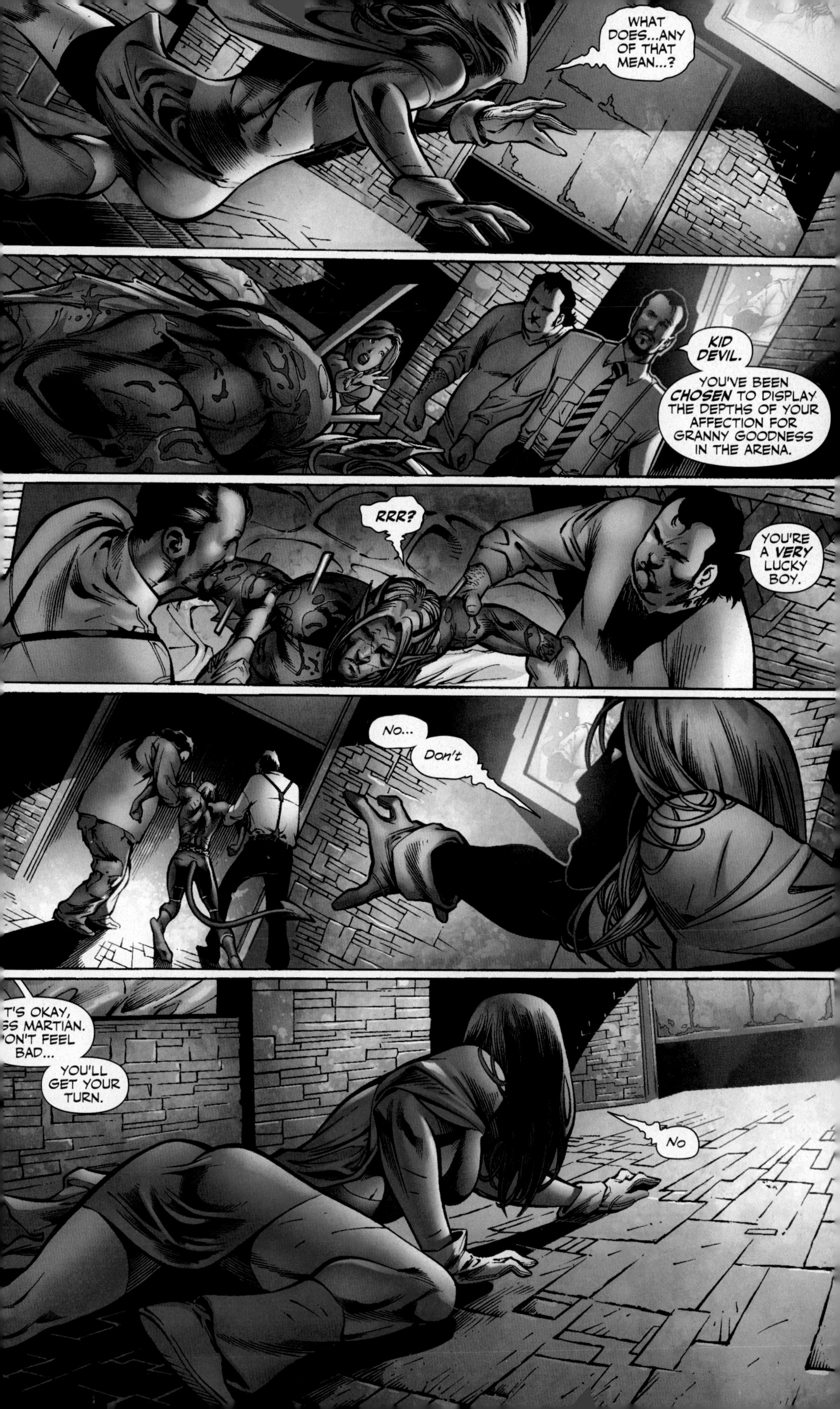

WHAT DOES...ANY OF THAT MEAN...?
KID DEVIL.
YOU'VE BEEN CHOSEN TO DISPLAY THE DEPTHS OF YOUR AFFECTION FOR GRANNY GOODNESS IN THE ARENA.
RRR?
YOU'RE A VERY LUCKY BOY.
No...
Don't
T'S OKAY, SS MARTIAN. ON'T FEEL BAD...
YOU'LL GET YOUR TURN.
No

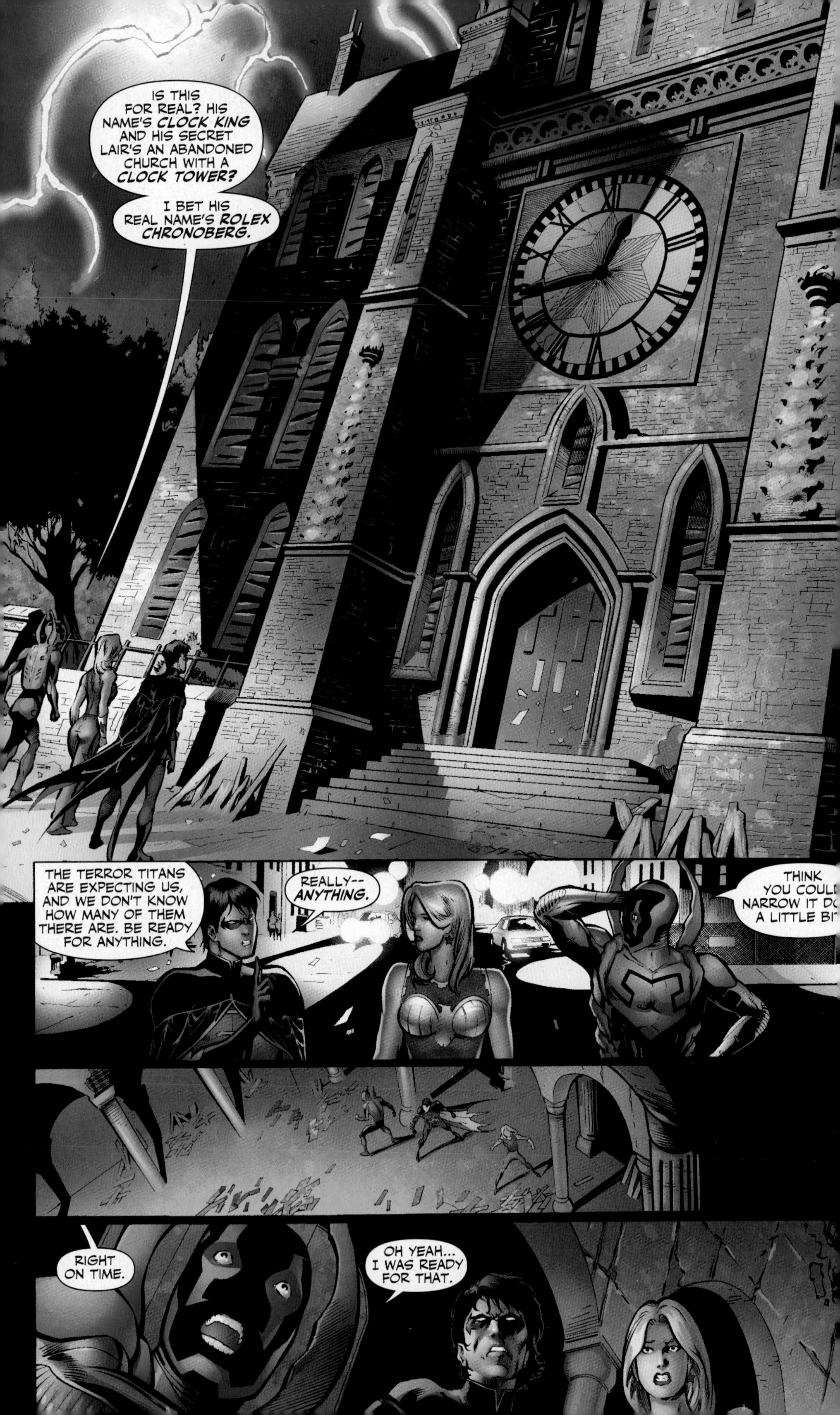
IS THIS FOR REAL? HIS NAME'S CLOCK KING AND HIS SECRET LAIR'S AN ABANDONED CHURCH WITH A CLOCK TOWER?
I BET HIS REAL NAME'S ROLEX CHRONOBERG.
THE TERROR TITANS ARE EXPECTING US, AND WE DON'T KNOW HOW MANY OF THEM THERE ARE. BE READY FOR ANYTHING.
REALLY-- ANYTHING.
THINK YOU COUL NARROW IT DO A LITTLE BI
RIGHT ON TIME.
OH YEAH... I WAS READY FOR THAT.

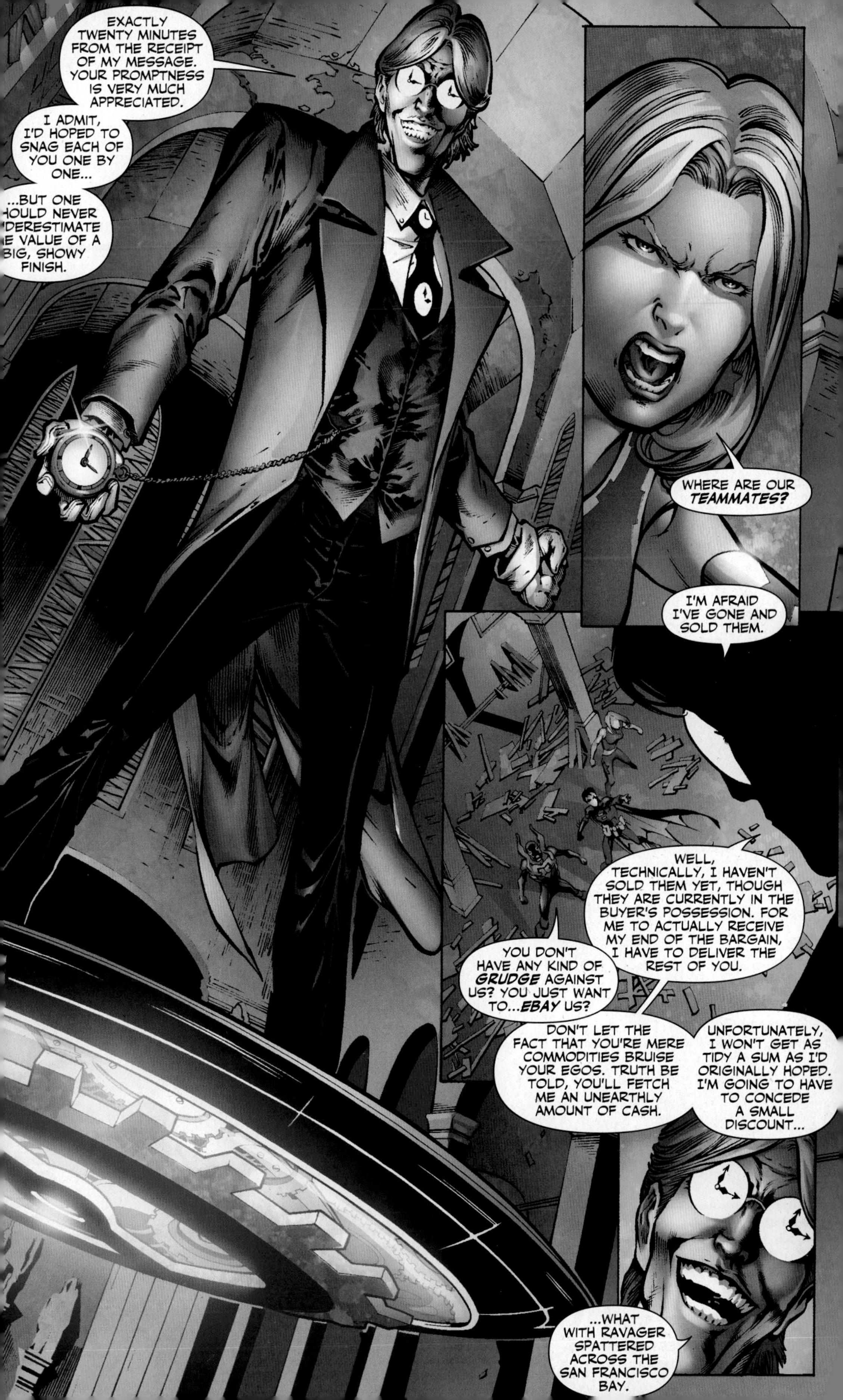
EXACTLY TWENTY MINUTES FROM THE RECEIPT OF MY MESSAGE. YOUR PROMPTNESS IS VERY MUCH APPRECIATED.
I ADMIT, I'D HOPED TO SNAG EACH OF YOU ONE BY ONE...
...BUT ONE HOULD NEVER DERESTIMATE E VALUE OF A BIG, SHOWY FINISH.
WHERE ARE OUR TEAMMATES?
I'M AFRAID I'VE GONE AND SOLD THEM.
WELL, TECHNICALLY, I HAVEN'T SOLD THEM YET, THOUGH THEY ARE CURRENTLY IN THE BUYER'S POSSESSION. FOR ME TO ACTUALLY RECEIVE MY END OF THE BARGAIN, I HAVE TO DELIVER THE REST OF YOU.
YOU DON'T HAVE ANY KIND OF GRUDGE AGAINST US? YOU JUST WANT TO...EBAY US?
DON'T LET THE FACT THAT YOU'RE MERE COMMODITIES BRUISE YOUR EGOS. TRUTH BE TOLD, YOU'LL FETCH ME AN UNEARTHLY AMOUNT OF CASH.
UNFORTUNATELY, I WON'T GET AS TIDY A SUM AS I'D ORIGINALLY HOPED. I'M GOING TO HAVE TO CONCEDE A SMALL DISCOUNT...
...WHAT WITH RAVAGER SPATTERED ACROSS THE SAN FRANCISCO BAY.

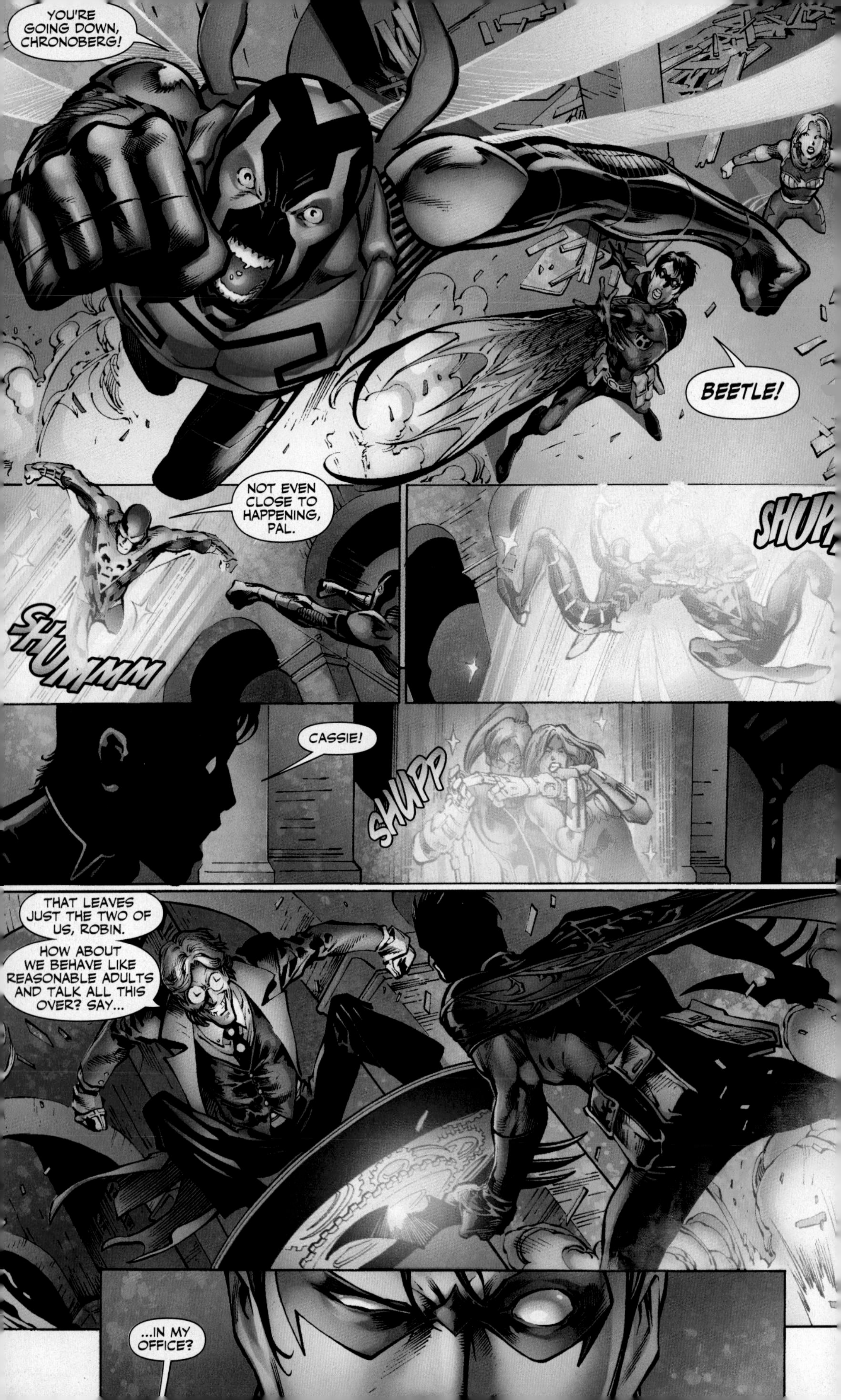

YOU'RE GOING DOWN, CHRONOBERG!
BEETLE!
NOT EVEN CLOSE TO HAPPENING, PAL.
SHUMMM
SHUPP
CASSIE!
SHUPP
THAT LEAVES JUST THE TWO OF US, ROBIN.
HOW ABOUT WE BEHAVE LIKE REASONABLE ADULTS AND TALK ALL THIS OVER? SAY...
...IN MY OFFICE?

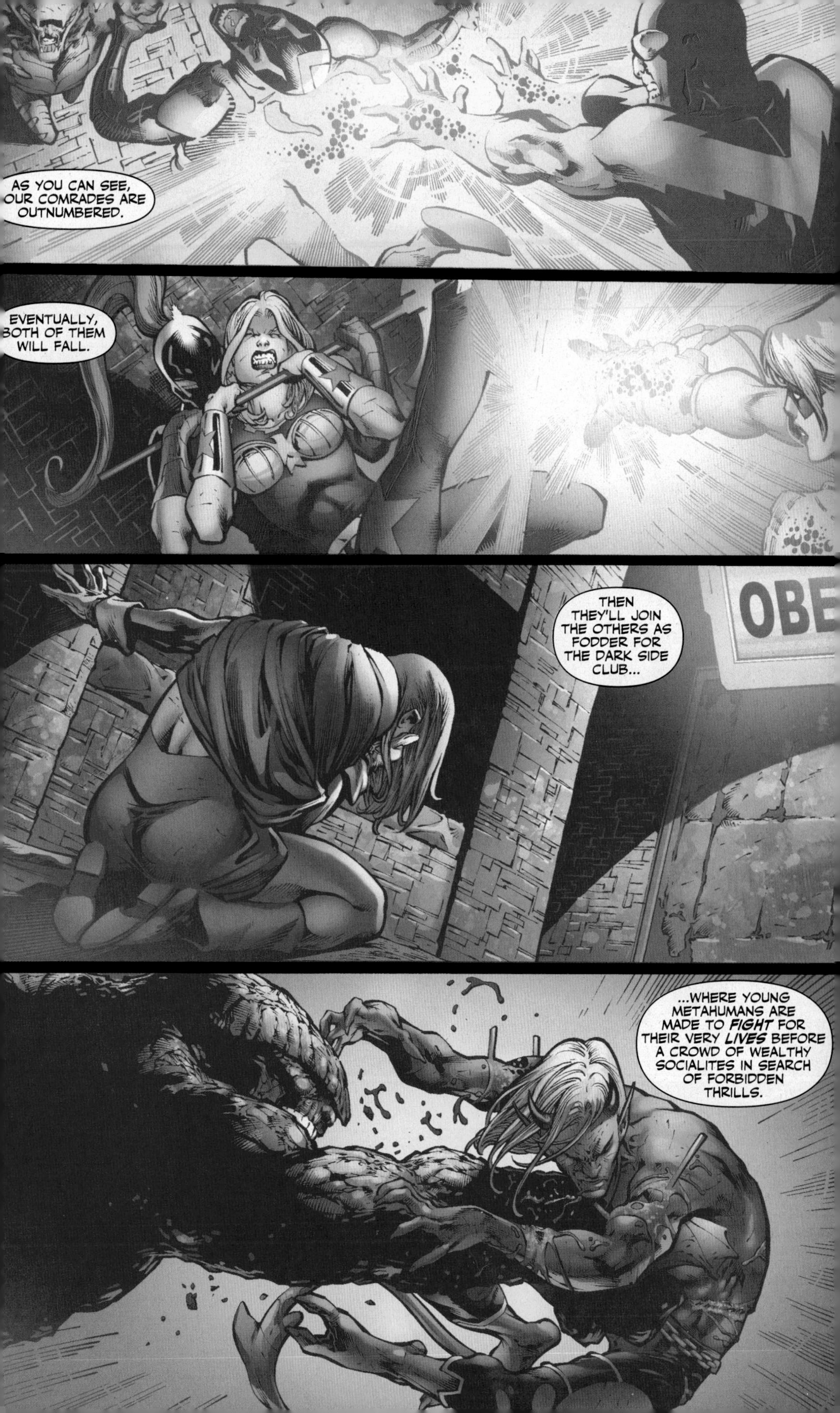
AS YOU CAN SEE, OUR COMRADES ARE OUTNUMBERED.
EVENTUALLY, BOTH OF THEM WILL FALL.
THEN THEY'LL JOIN THE OTHERS AS FODDER FOR THE DARK SIDE CLUB...
OBE
...WHERE YOUNG METAHUMANS ARE MADE TO *FIGHT* FOR THEIR VERY *LIVES* BEFORE A CROWD OF WEALTHY SOCIALITES IN SEARCH OF FORBIDDEN THRILLS.

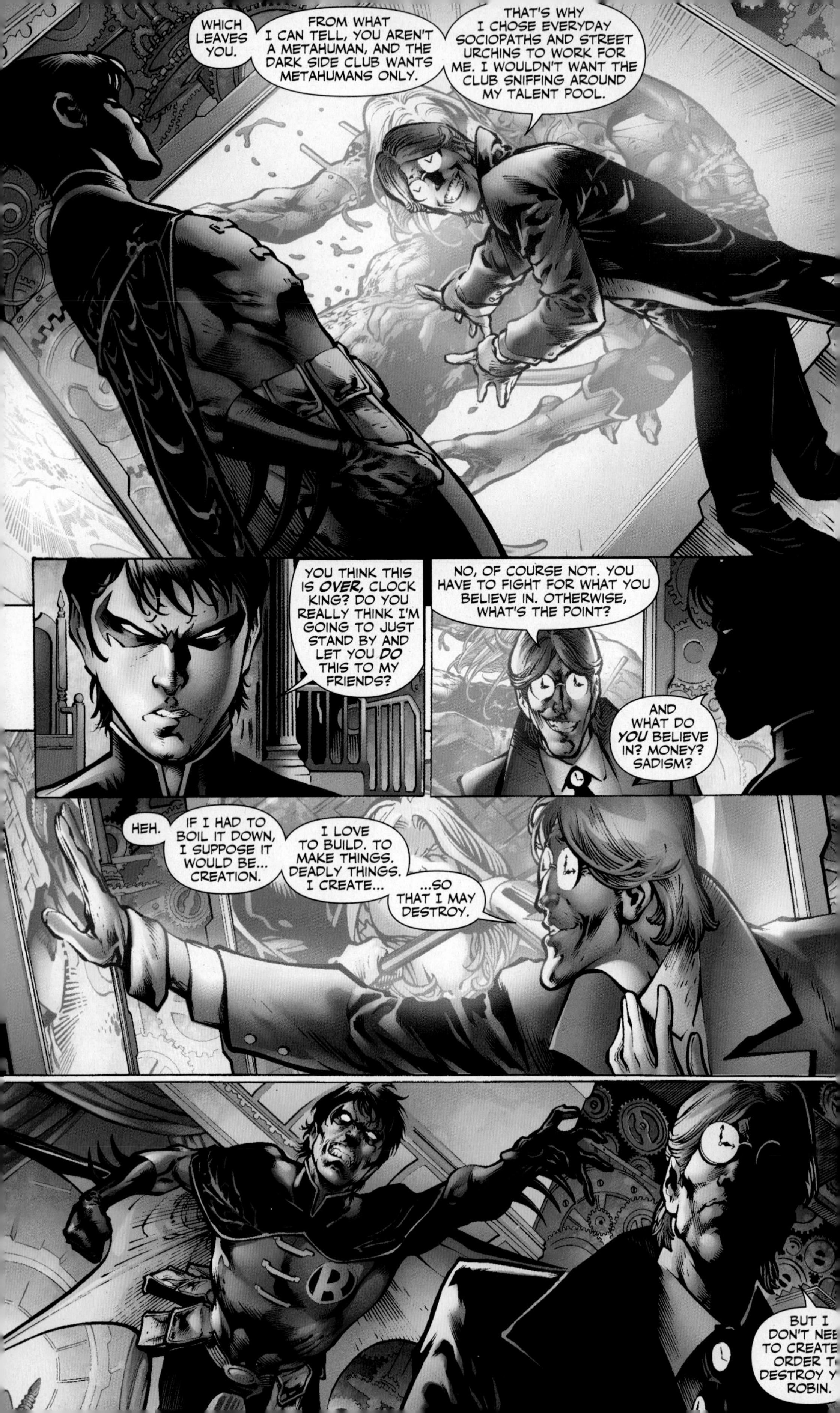
WHICH LEAVES YOU.
FROM WHAT I CAN TELL, YOU AREN'T A METAHUMAN, AND THE DARK SIDE CLUB WANTS METAHUMANS ONLY.
THAT'S WHY I CHOSE EVERYDAY SOCIOPATHS AND STREET URCHINS TO WORK FOR ME. I WOULDN'T WANT THE CLUB SNIFFING AROUND MY TALENT POOL.
YOU THINK THIS IS *OVER,* CLOCK KING? DO YOU REALLY THINK I'M GOING TO JUST STAND BY AND LET YOU *DO* THIS TO MY FRIENDS?
NO, OF COURSE NOT. YOU HAVE TO FIGHT FOR WHAT YOU BELIEVE IN. OTHERWISE, WHAT'S THE POINT?
AND WHAT DO *YOU* BELIEVE IN? MONEY? SADISM?
HEH.
IF I HAD TO BOIL IT DOWN, I SUPPOSE IT WOULD BE... CREATION.
I LOVE TO BUILD. TO MAKE THINGS. DEADLY THINGS. I CREATE...
...SO THAT I MAY DESTROY.
BUT I DON'T NEE TO CREATE ORDER T DESTROY Y ROBIN.

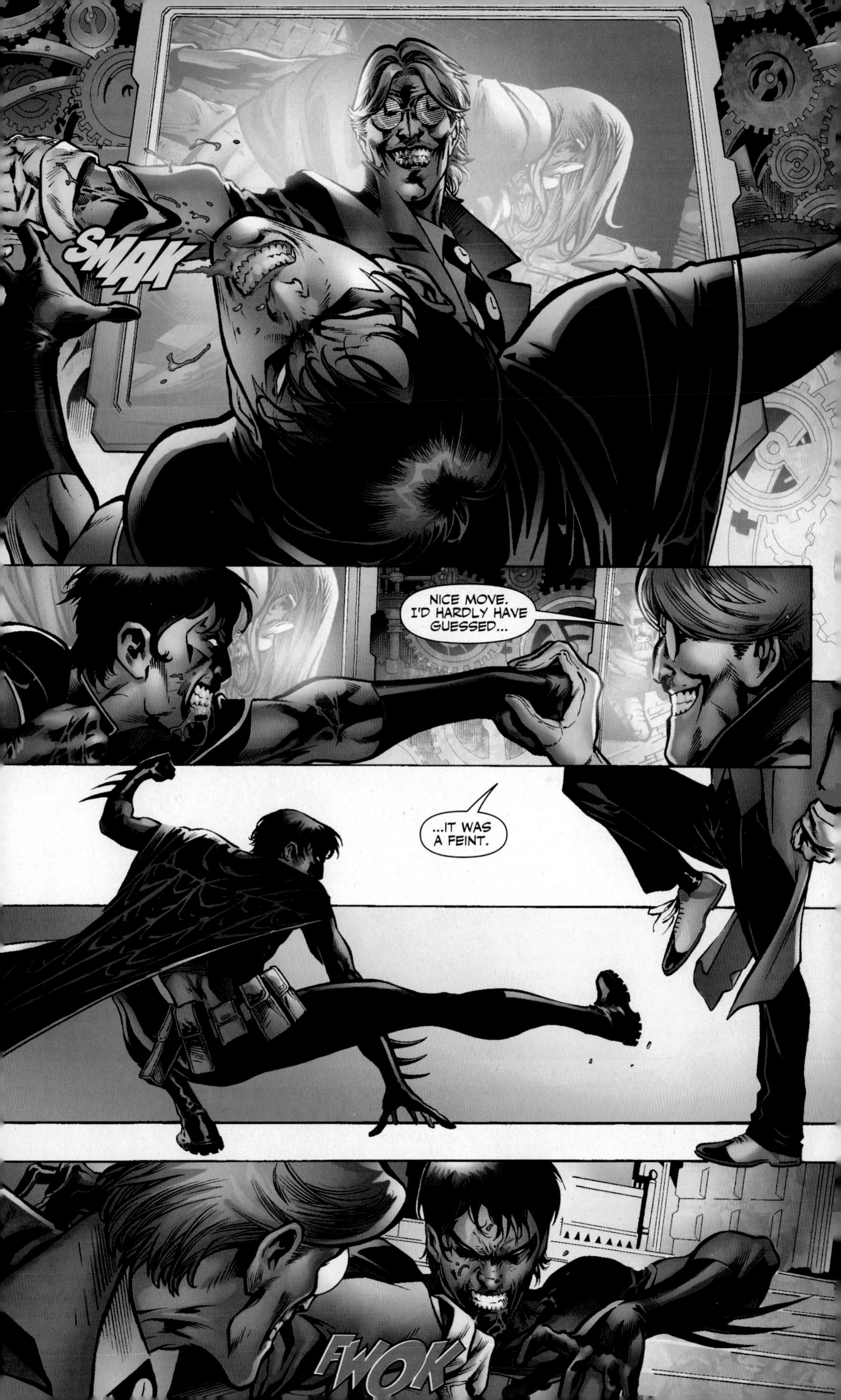
SMAK
NICE MOVE. I'D HARDLY HAVE GUESSED...
...IT WAS A FEINT.
FWOK

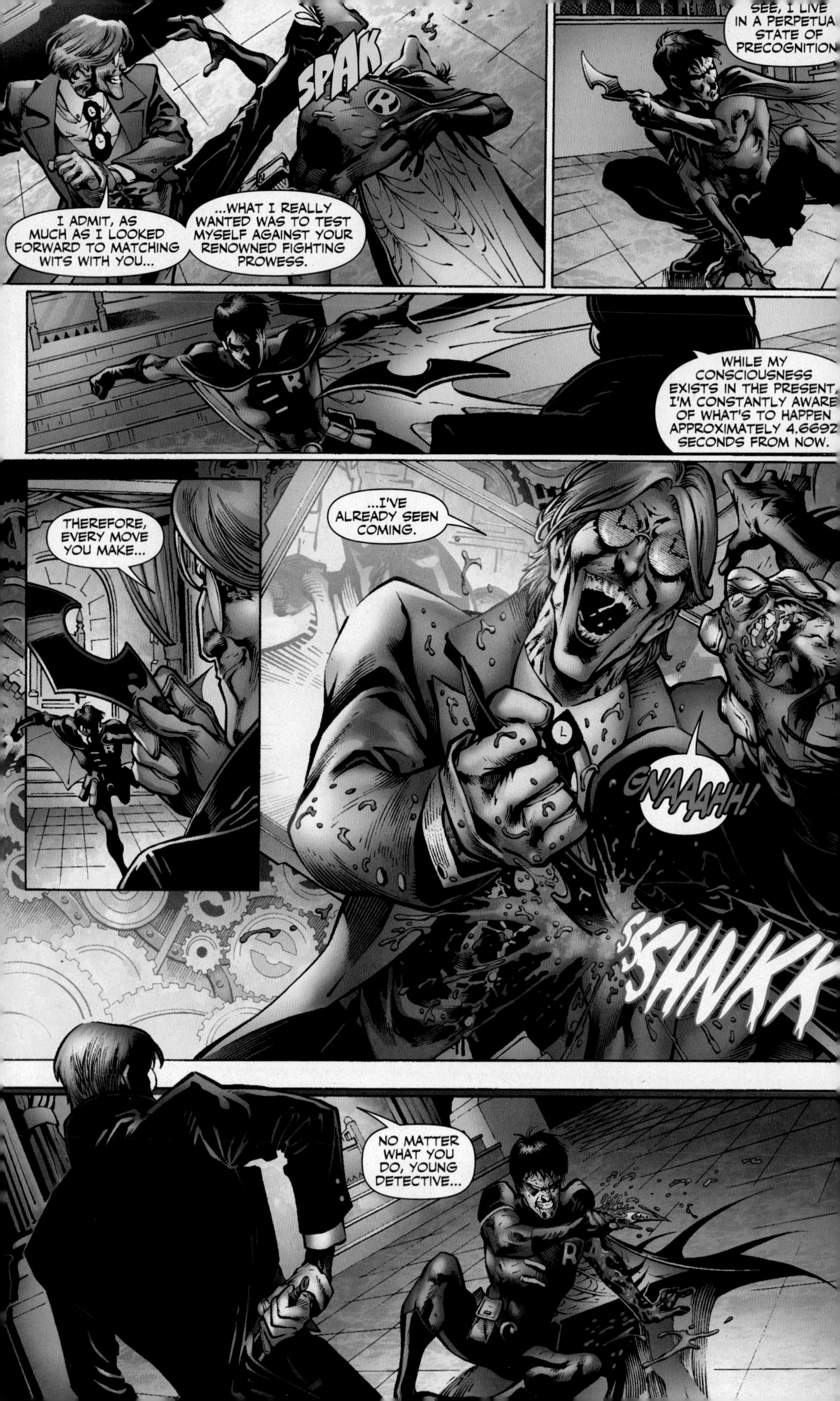
SPAK
I ADMIT, AS MUCH AS I LOOKED FORWARD TO MATCHING WITS WITH YOU...
...WHAT I REALLY WANTED WAS TO TEST MYSELF AGAINST YOUR RENOWNED FIGHTING PROWESS.
SEE, I LIVE IN A PERPETUA STATE OF PRECOGNITION
WHILE MY CONSCIOUSNESS EXISTS IN THE PRESENT, I'M CONSTANTLY AWARE OF WHAT'S TO HAPPEN APPROXIMATELY 4.6692 SECONDS FROM NOW.
THEREFORE, EVERY MOVE YOU MAKE...
...I'VE ALREADY SEEN COMING.
GNAAAHH!
SSHNKK
NO MATTER WHAT YOU DO, YOUNG DETECTIVE...

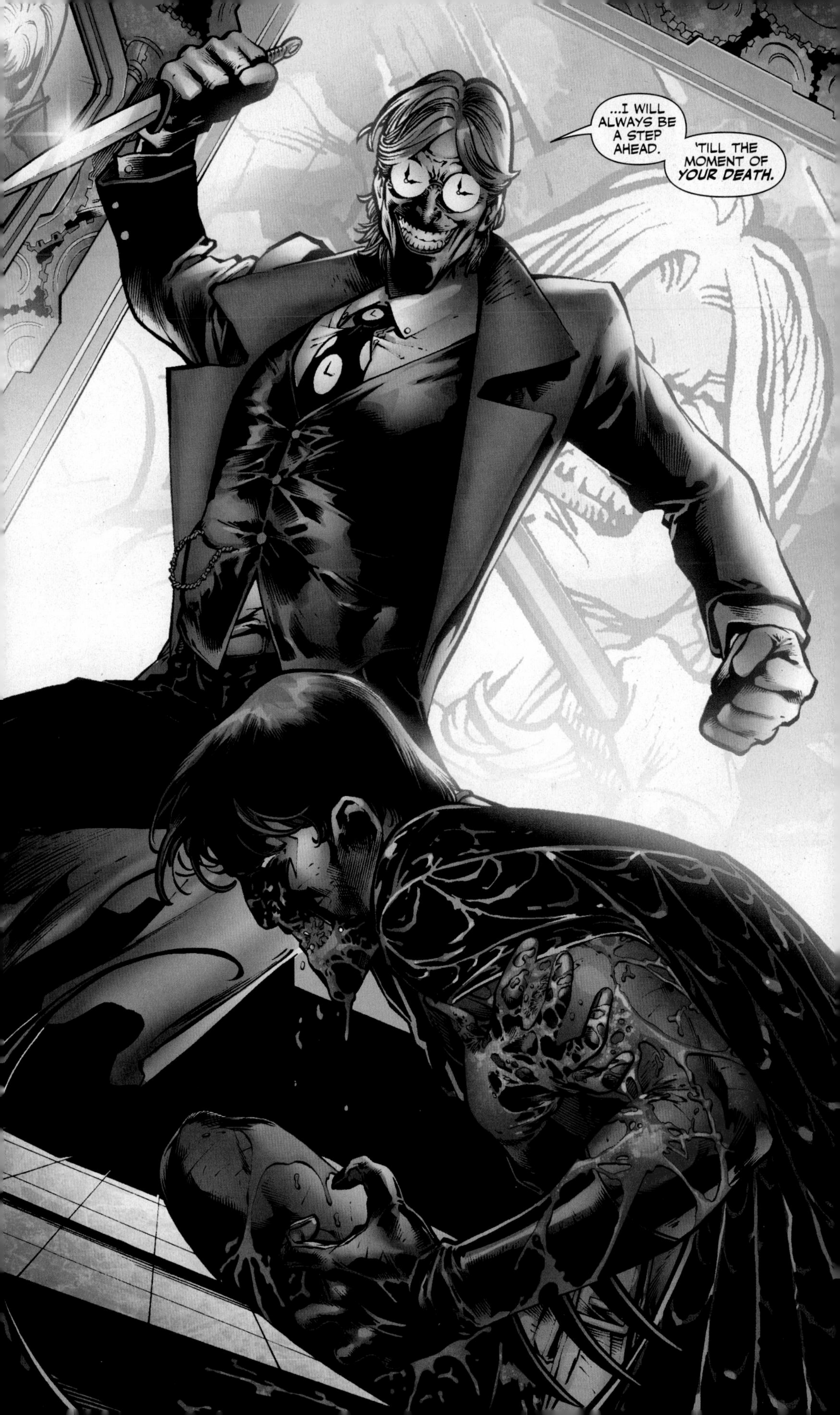
...I WILL ALWAYS BE A STEP AHEAD.
'TILL THE MOMENT OF YOUR DEATH.

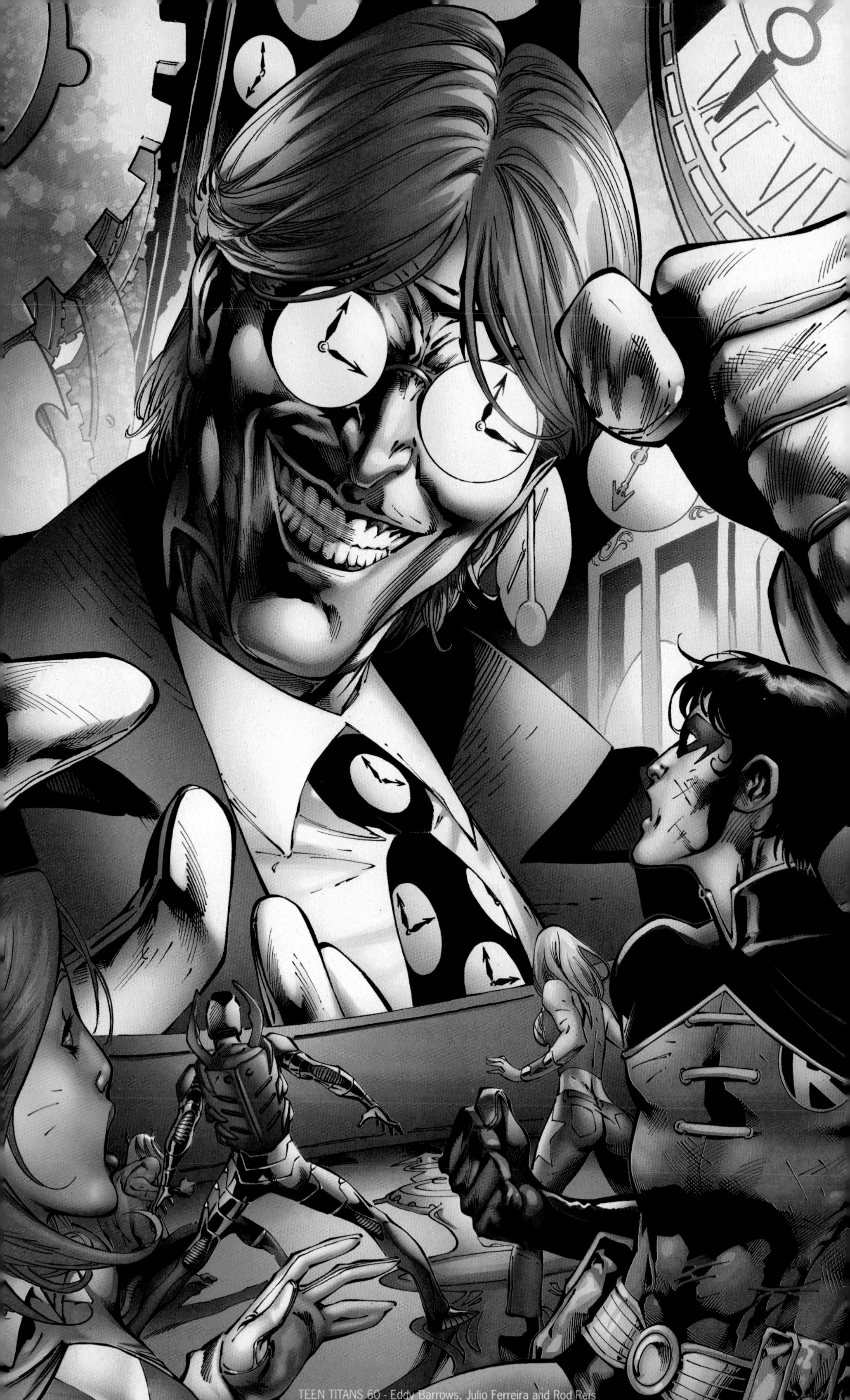

TEEN TITANS 60 - Eddy Barrows, Julio Ferreira and Rod Reis

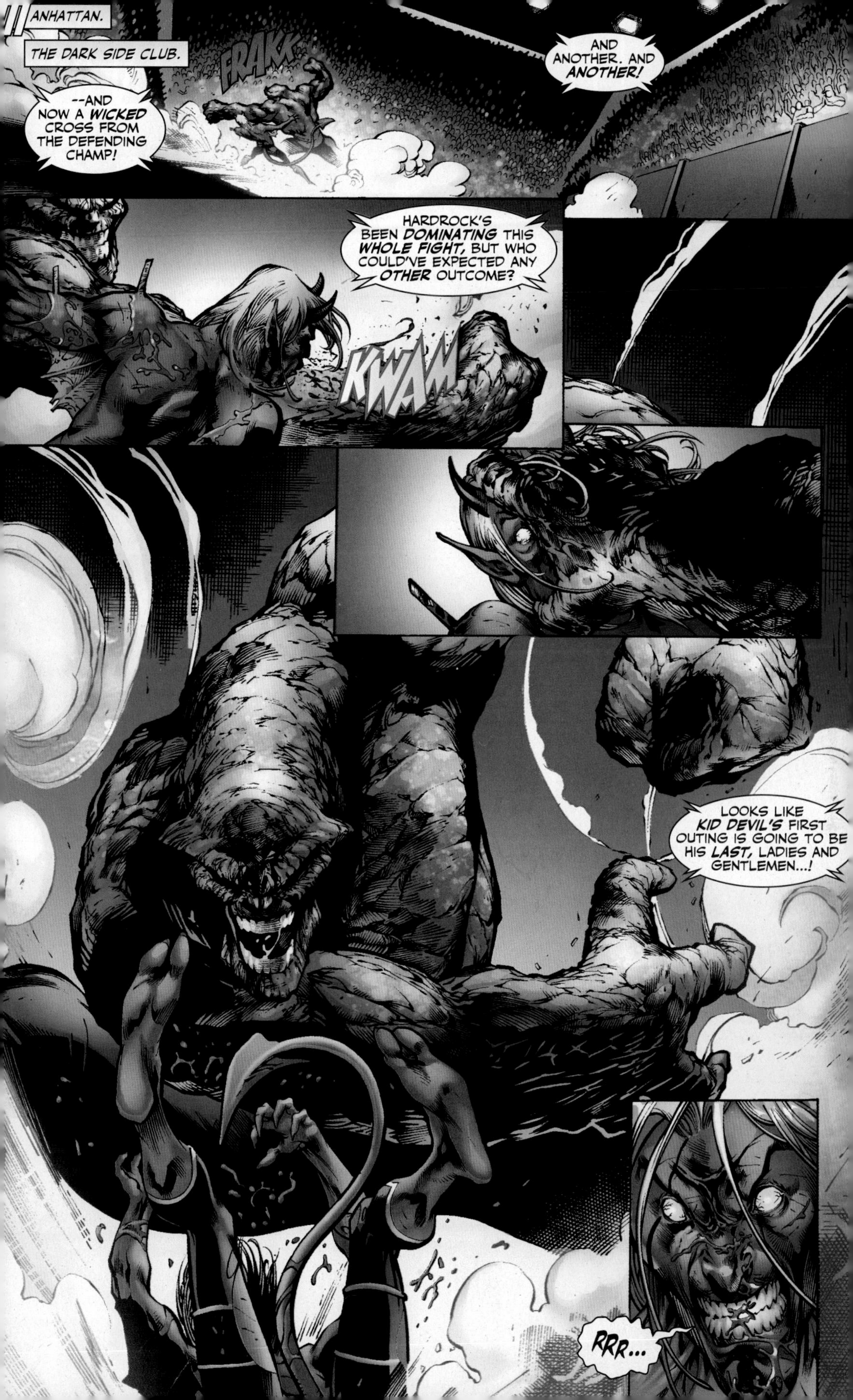
MANHATTAN.
THE DARK SIDE CLUB.
--AND NOW A WICKED CROSS FROM THE DEFENDING CHAMP!
FRAKK
AND ANOTHER. AND ANOTHER!
HARDROCK'S BEEN DOMINATING THIS WHOLE FIGHT, BUT WHO COULD'VE EXPECTED ANY OTHER OUTCOME?
KWAM
LOOKS LIKE KID DEVIL'S FIRST OUTING IS GOING TO BE HIS LAST, LADIES AND GENTLEMEN...!
RRR...

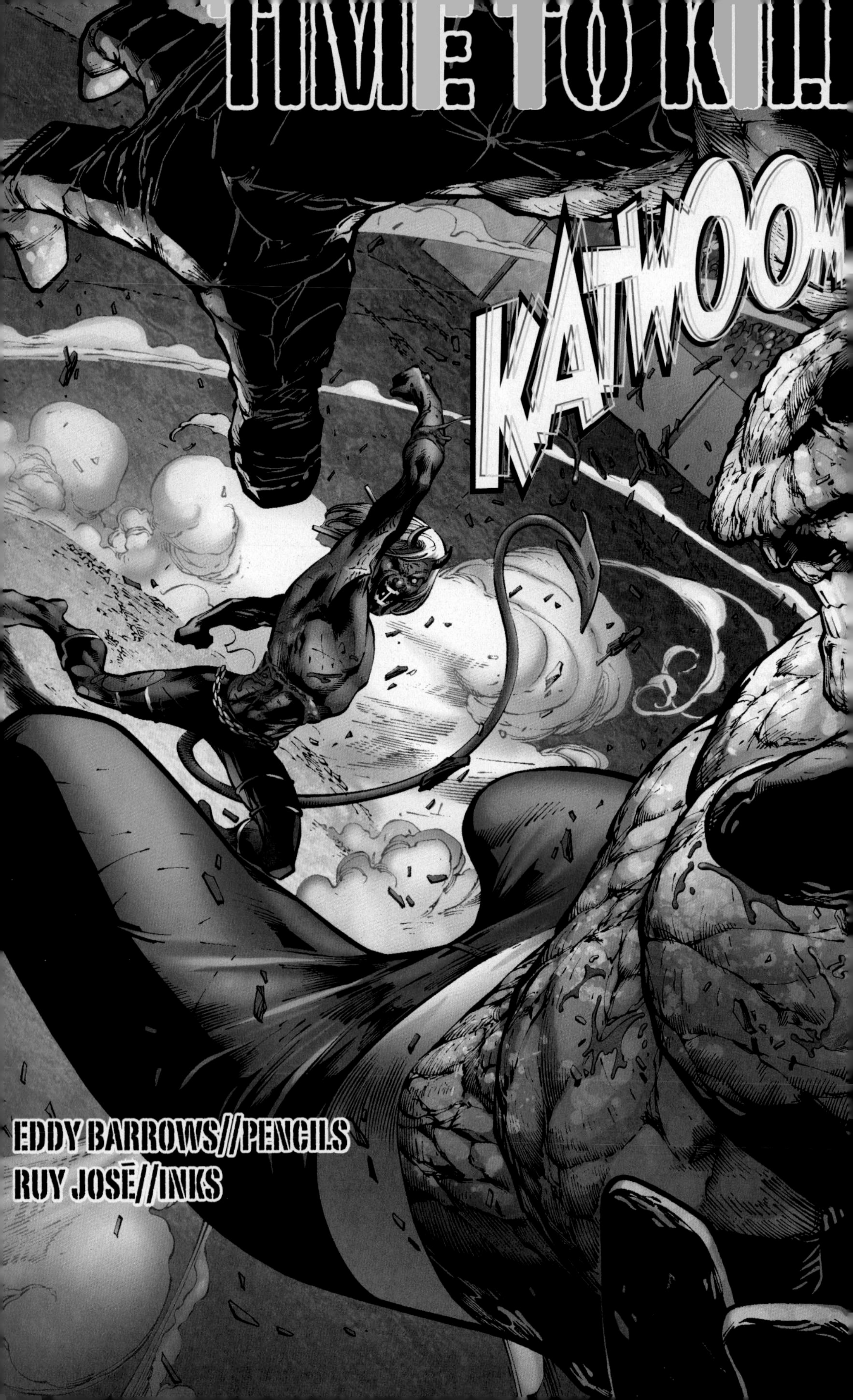
TIME TO KILL
KATWOOM
EDDY BARROWS//PENCILS
RUY JOSÉ//INKS

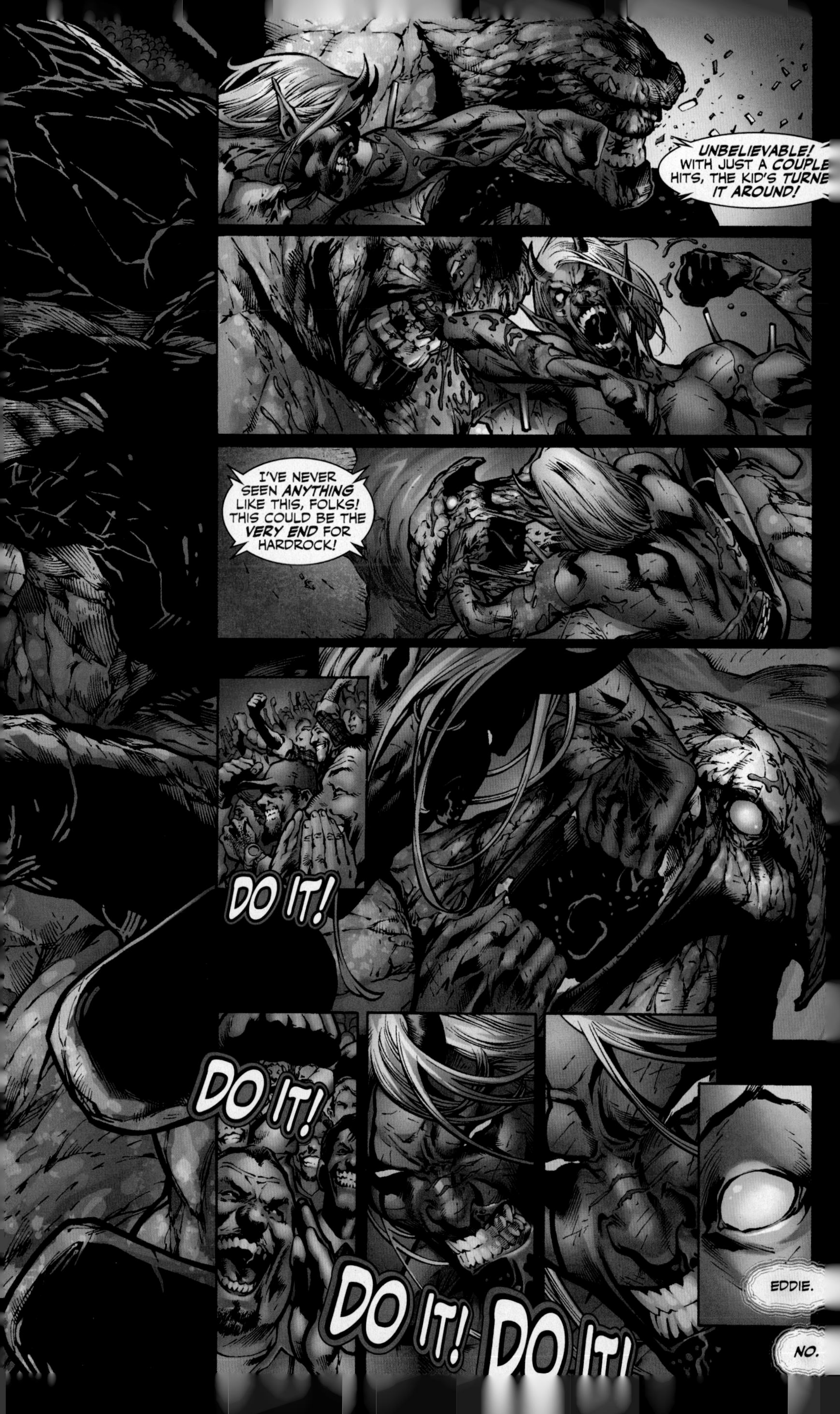
UNBELIEVABLE! WITH JUST A COUPLE HITS, THE KID'S TURNE IT AROUND!
I'VE NEVER SEEN ANYTHING LIKE THIS, FOLKS! THIS COULD BE THE VERY END FOR HARDROCK!
DO IT!
DO IT!
DO IT! DO IT!
EDDIE.
NO.

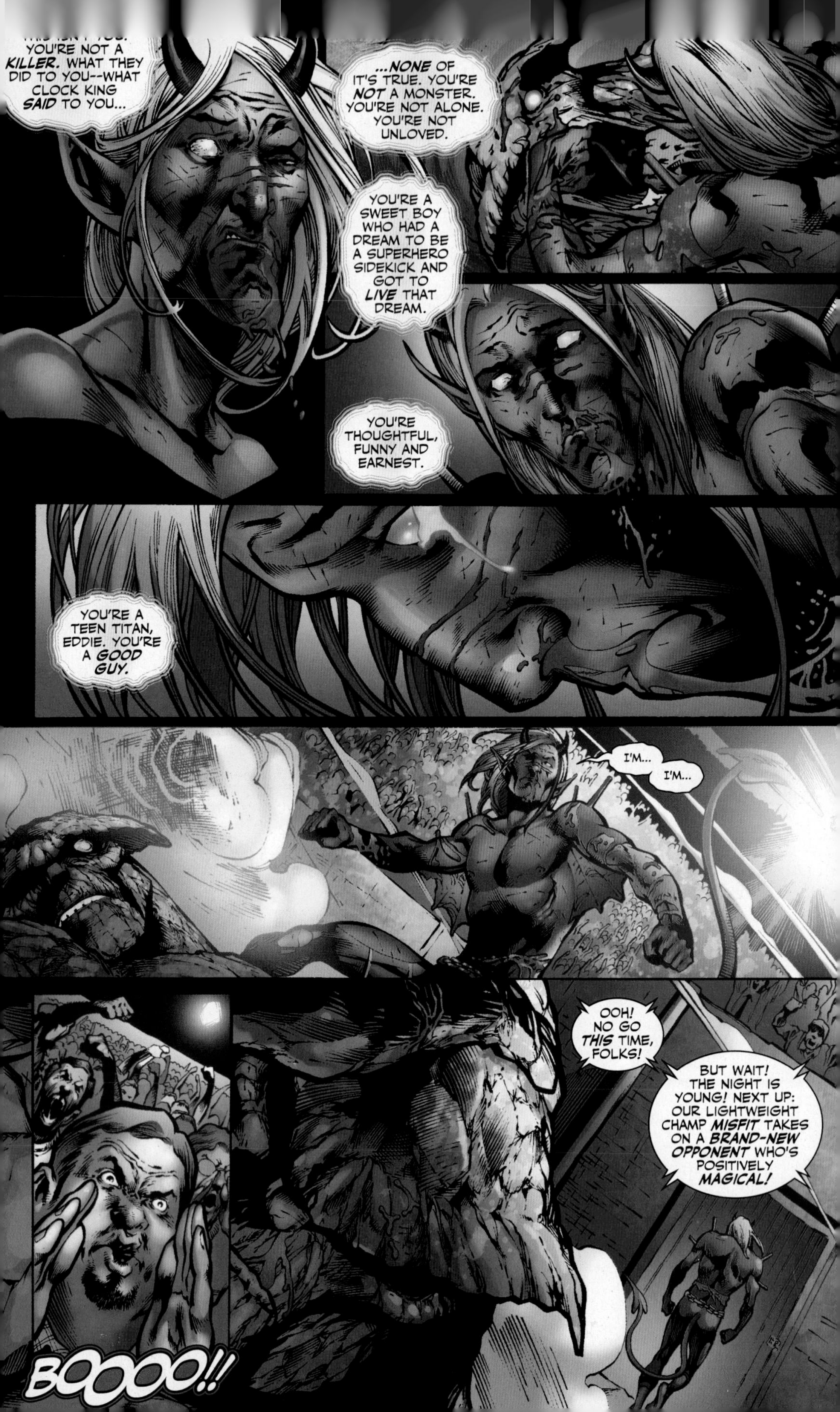
YOU'RE NOT A KILLER. WHAT THEY DID TO YOU--WHAT CLOCK KING SAID TO YOU...
...NONE OF IT'S TRUE. YOU'RE NOT A MONSTER. YOU'RE NOT ALONE. YOU'RE NOT UNLOVED.
YOU'RE A SWEET BOY WHO HAD A DREAM TO BE A SUPERHERO SIDEKICK AND GOT TO LIVE THAT DREAM.
YOU'RE THOUGHTFUL, FUNNY AND EARNEST.
YOU'RE A TEEN TITAN, EDDIE. YOU'RE A GOOD GUY.
I'M...
I'M...
OOH! NO GO THIS TIME, FOLKS!
BUT WAIT! THE NIGHT IS YOUNG! NEXT UP: OUR LIGHTWEIGHT CHAMP MISFIT TAKES ON A BRAND-NEW OPPONENT WHO'S POSITIVELY MAGICAL!
BOOOO!!

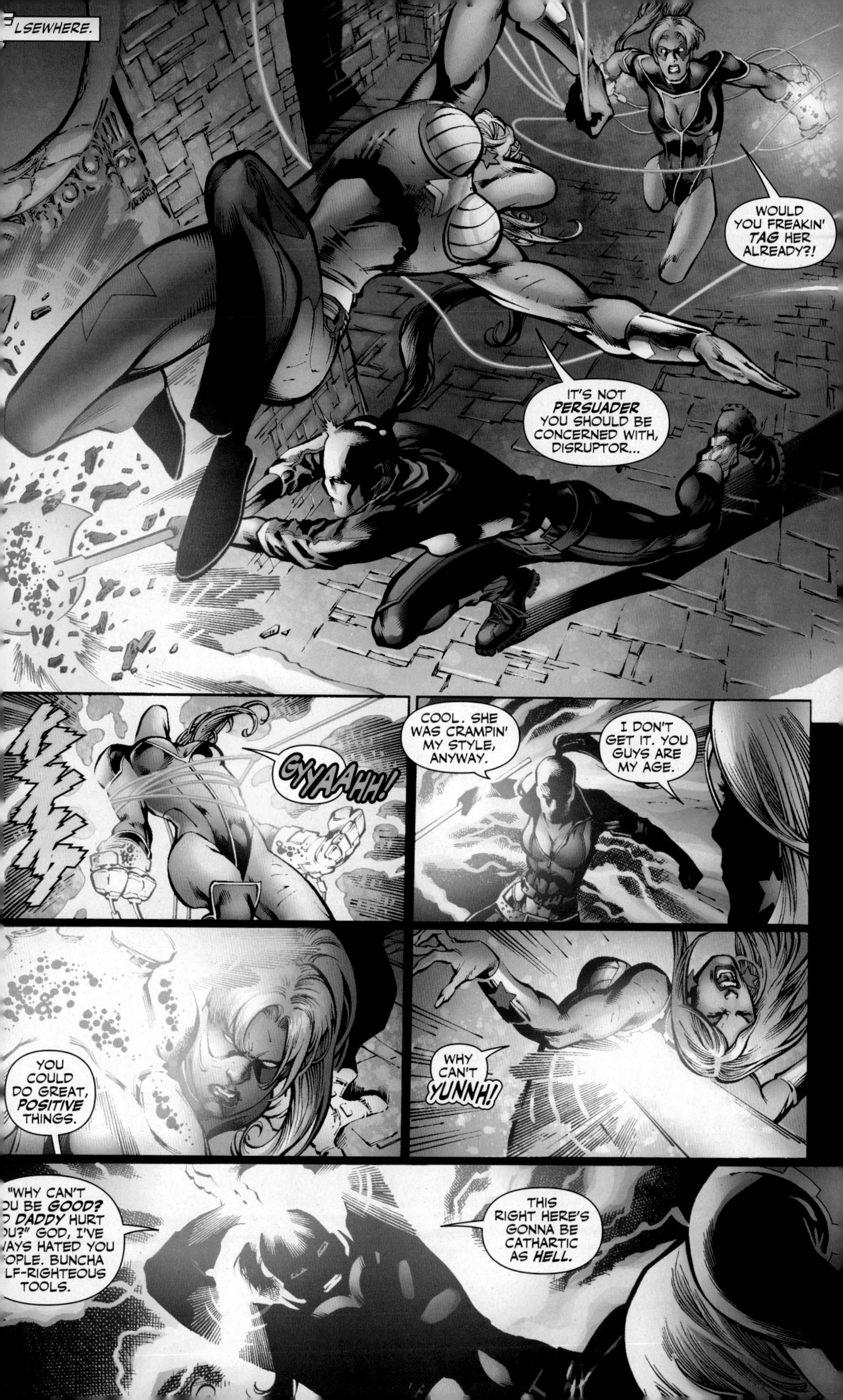
ELSEWHERE.
WOULD YOU FREAKIN' TAG HER ALREADY?!
IT'S NOT PERSUADER YOU SHOULD BE CONCERNED WITH, DISRUPTOR...
GYYAAHH!
COOL. SHE WAS CRAMPIN' MY STYLE, ANYWAY.
I DON'T GET IT. YOU GUYS ARE MY AGE.
YOU COULD DO GREAT, POSITIVE THINGS.
WHY CAN'T YUNNH!
"WHY CAN'T
OU BE GOOD?
D DADDY HURT
OU?" GOD, I'VE
AYS HATED YOU
OPLE. BUNCHA
LF-RIGHTEOUS
TOOLS.
THIS RIGHT HERE'S GONNA BE CATHARTIC AS HELL.

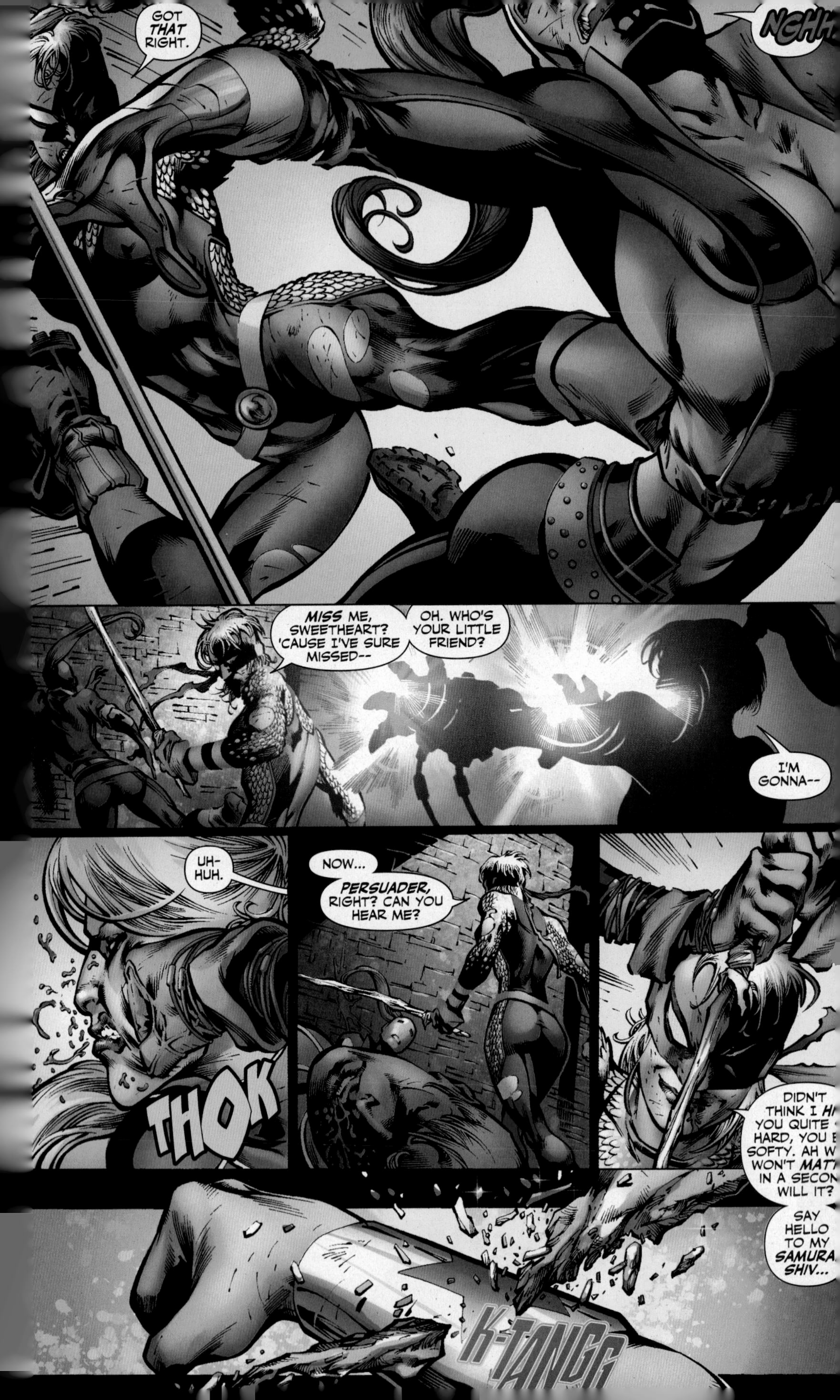
GOT THAT RIGHT.
NGHH
MISS ME, SWEETHEART? 'CAUSE I'VE SURE MISSED--
OH. WHO'S YOUR LITTLE FRIEND?
I'M GONNA--
UH-HUH.
THOK
NOW... PERSUADER, RIGHT? CAN YOU HEAR ME?
K-TANGG

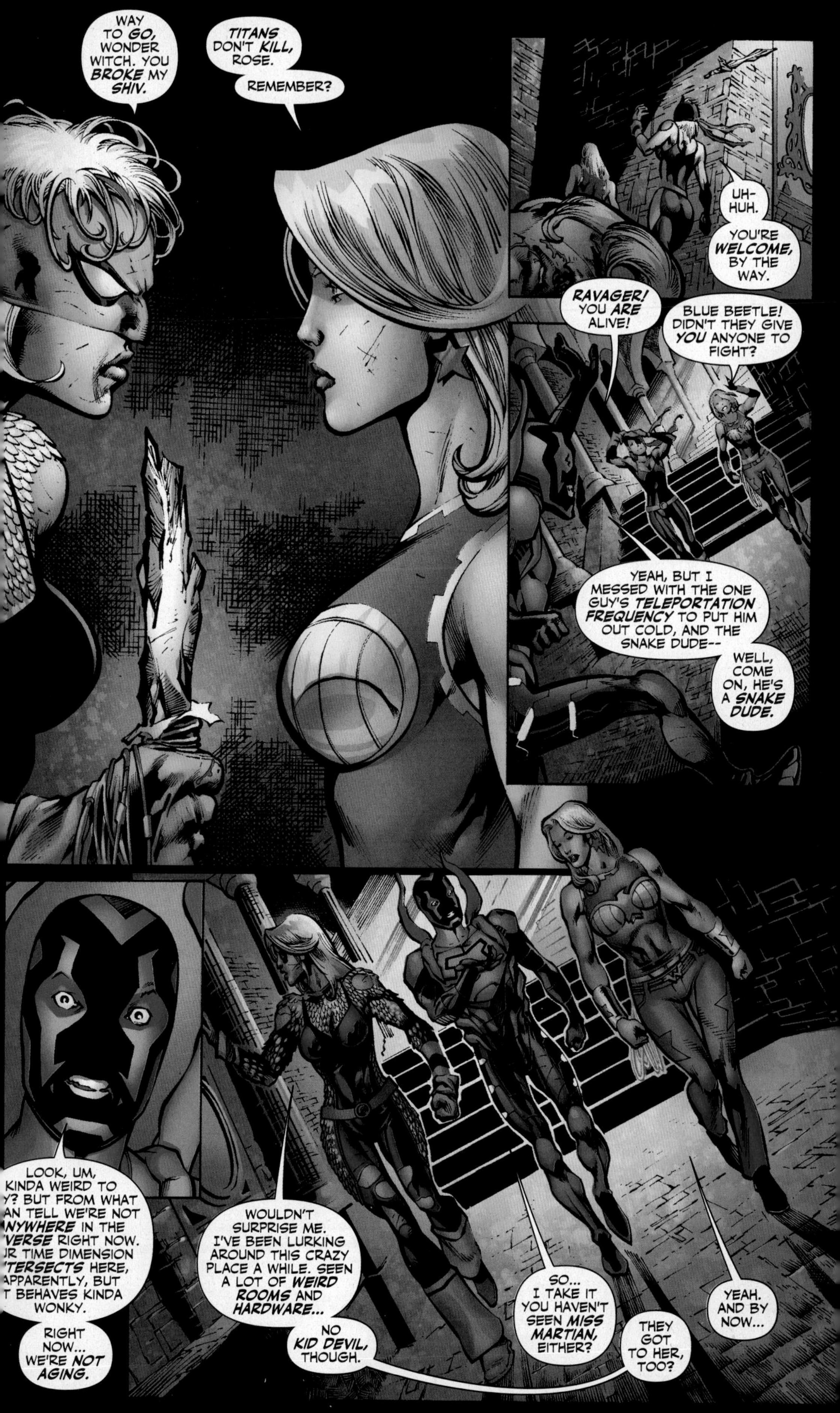
WAY TO GO, WONDER WITCH. YOU BROKE MY SHIV.
TITANS DON'T KILL, ROSE.
REMEMBER?
UH-HUH.
YOU'RE WELCOME, BY THE WAY.
RAVAGER! YOU ARE ALIVE!
BLUE BEETLE! DIDN'T THEY GIVE YOU ANYONE TO FIGHT?
YEAH, BUT I MESSED WITH THE ONE GUY'S TELEPORTATION FREQUENCY TO PUT HIM OUT COLD, AND THE SNAKE DUDE--
WELL, COME ON, HE'S A SNAKE DUDE.
LOOK, UM, KINDA WEIRD TO Y? BUT FROM WHAT AN TELL WE'RE NOT NYWHERE IN THE VERSE RIGHT NOW. UR TIME DIMENSION TERSECTS HERE, APPARENTLY, BUT T BEHAVES KINDA WONKY.
RIGHT NOW... WE'RE NOT AGING.
WOULDN'T SURPRISE ME. I'VE BEEN LURKING AROUND THIS CRAZY PLACE A WHILE. SEEN A LOT OF WEIRD ROOMS AND HARDWARE...
NO KID DEVIL, THOUGH.
SO... I TAKE IT YOU HAVEN'T SEEN MISS MARTIAN, EITHER?
THEY GOT TO HER, TOO?
YEAH. AND BY NOW...

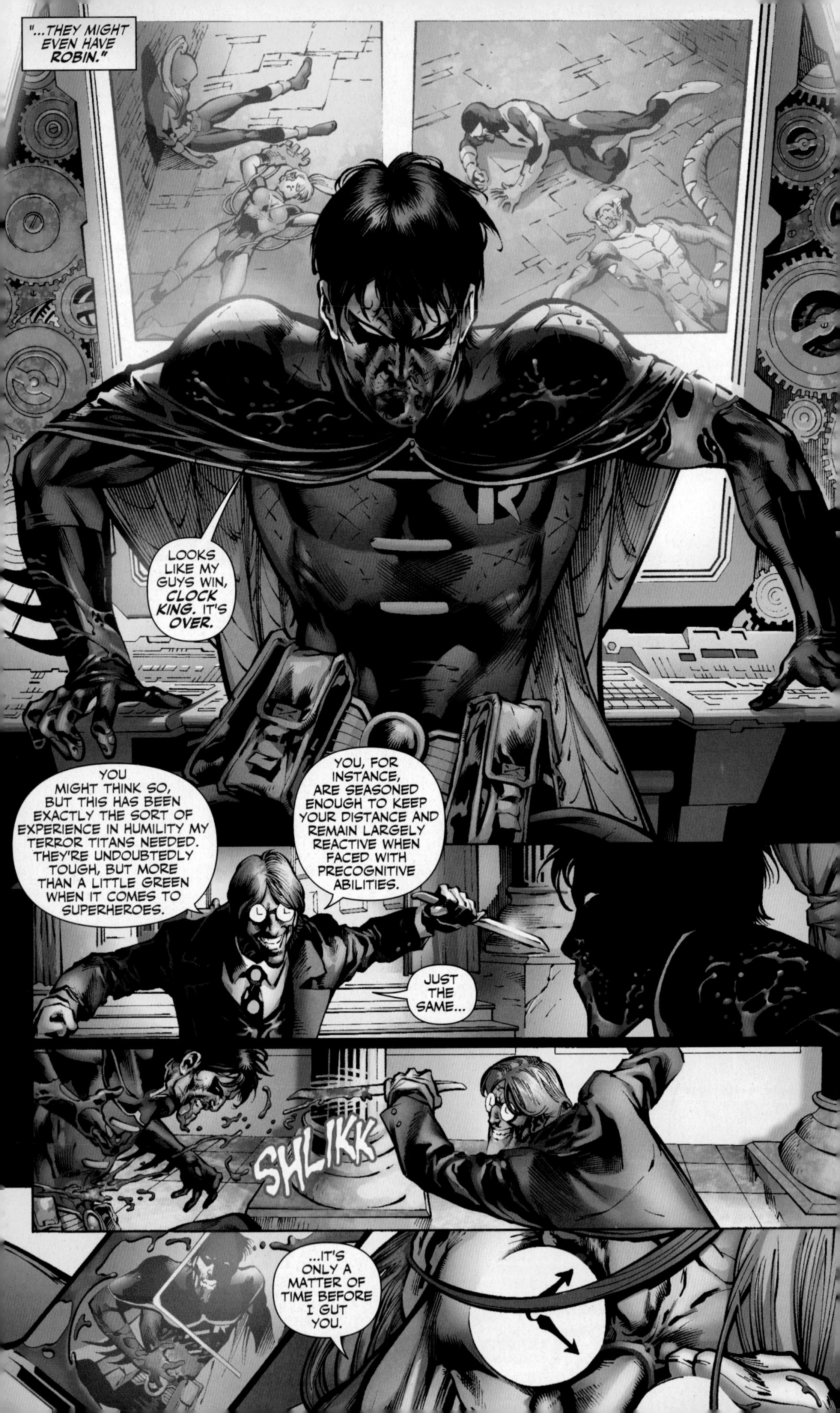
"...THEY MIGHT EVEN HAVE ROBIN."
LOOKS LIKE MY GUYS WIN, CLOCK KING. IT'S OVER.
YOU MIGHT THINK SO, BUT THIS HAS BEEN EXACTLY THE SORT OF EXPERIENCE IN HUMILITY MY TERROR TITANS NEEDED. THEY'RE UNDOUBTEDLY TOUGH, BUT MORE THAN A LITTLE GREEN WHEN IT COMES TO SUPERHEROES.
YOU, FOR INSTANCE, ARE SEASONED ENOUGH TO KEEP YOUR DISTANCE AND REMAIN LARGELY REACTIVE WHEN FACED WITH PRECOGNITIVE ABILITIES.
JUST THE SAME...
SHLIKK
...IT'S ONLY A MATTER OF TIME BEFORE I GUT YOU.

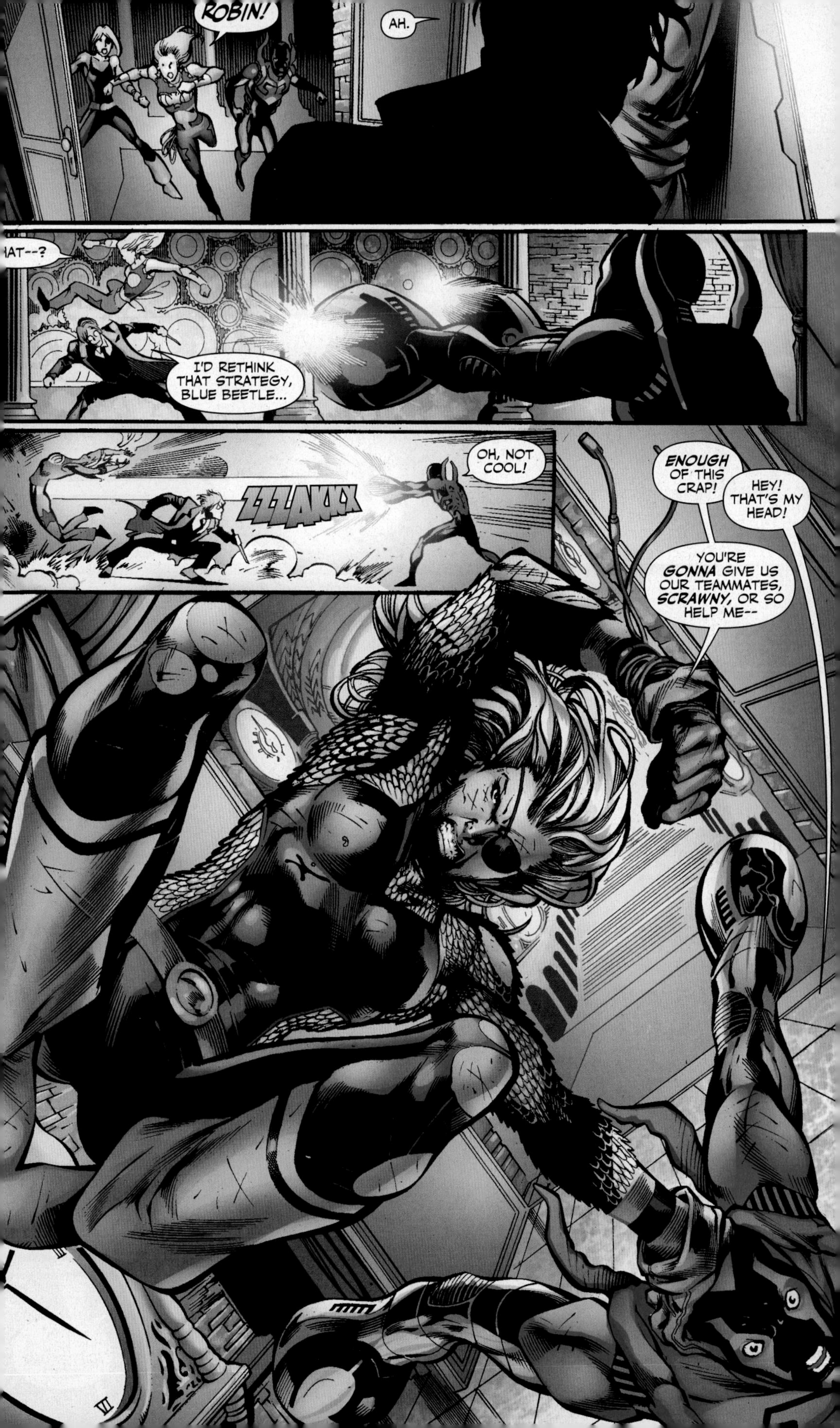
ROBIN!
AH.
HAT--?
I'D RETHINK THAT STRATEGY, BLUE BEETLE...
ZZZLAKKK
OH, NOT COOL!
ENOUGH OF THIS CRAP!
HEY! THAT'S MY HEAD!
YOU'RE GONNA GIVE US OUR TEAMMATES, SCRAWNY, OR SO HELP ME--

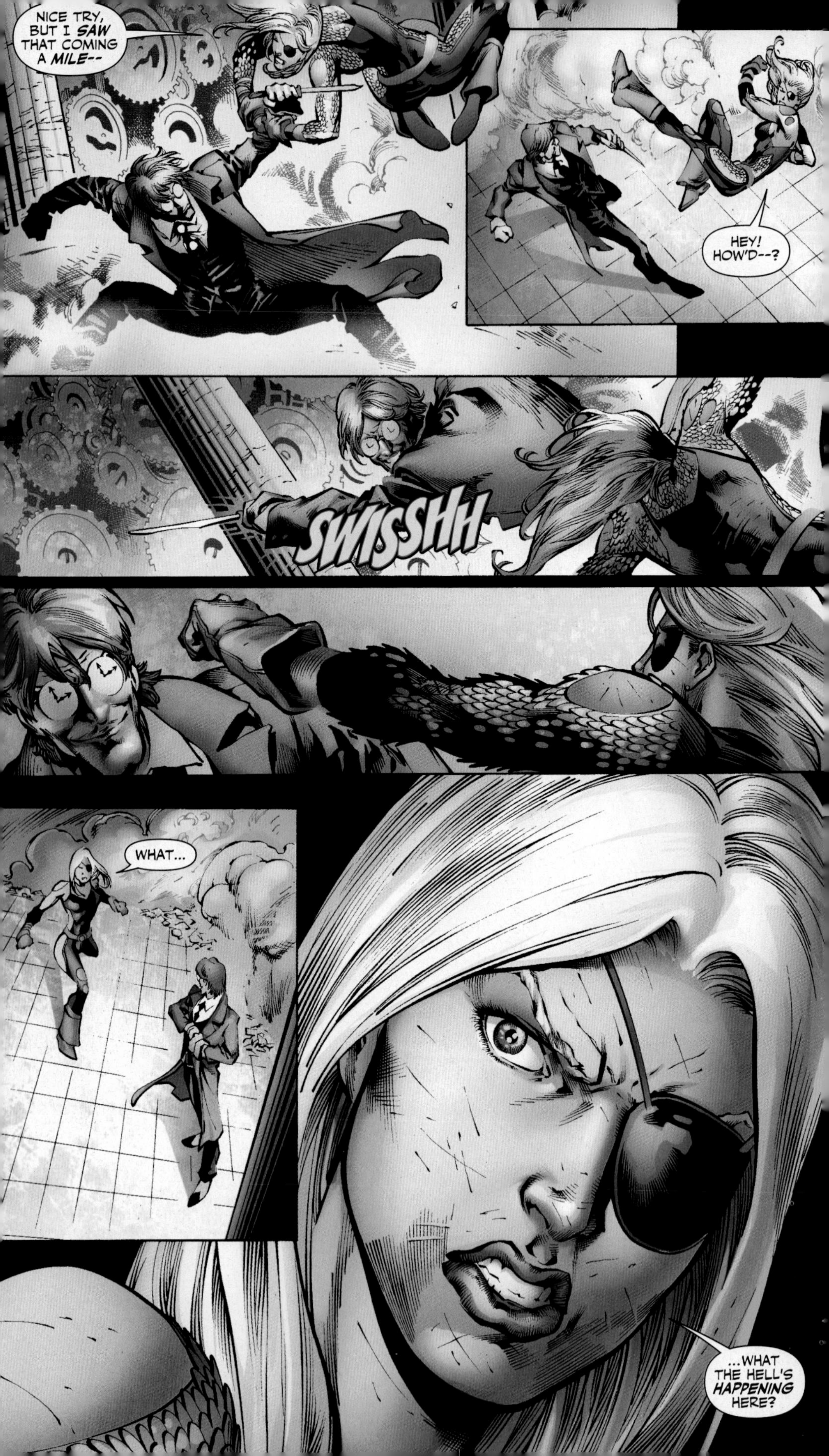

NICE TRY, BUT I *SAW* THAT COMING A *MILE*--
HEY! HOW'D--?
SWISSHH
WHAT...
...WHAT THE HELL'S *HAPPENING* HERE?

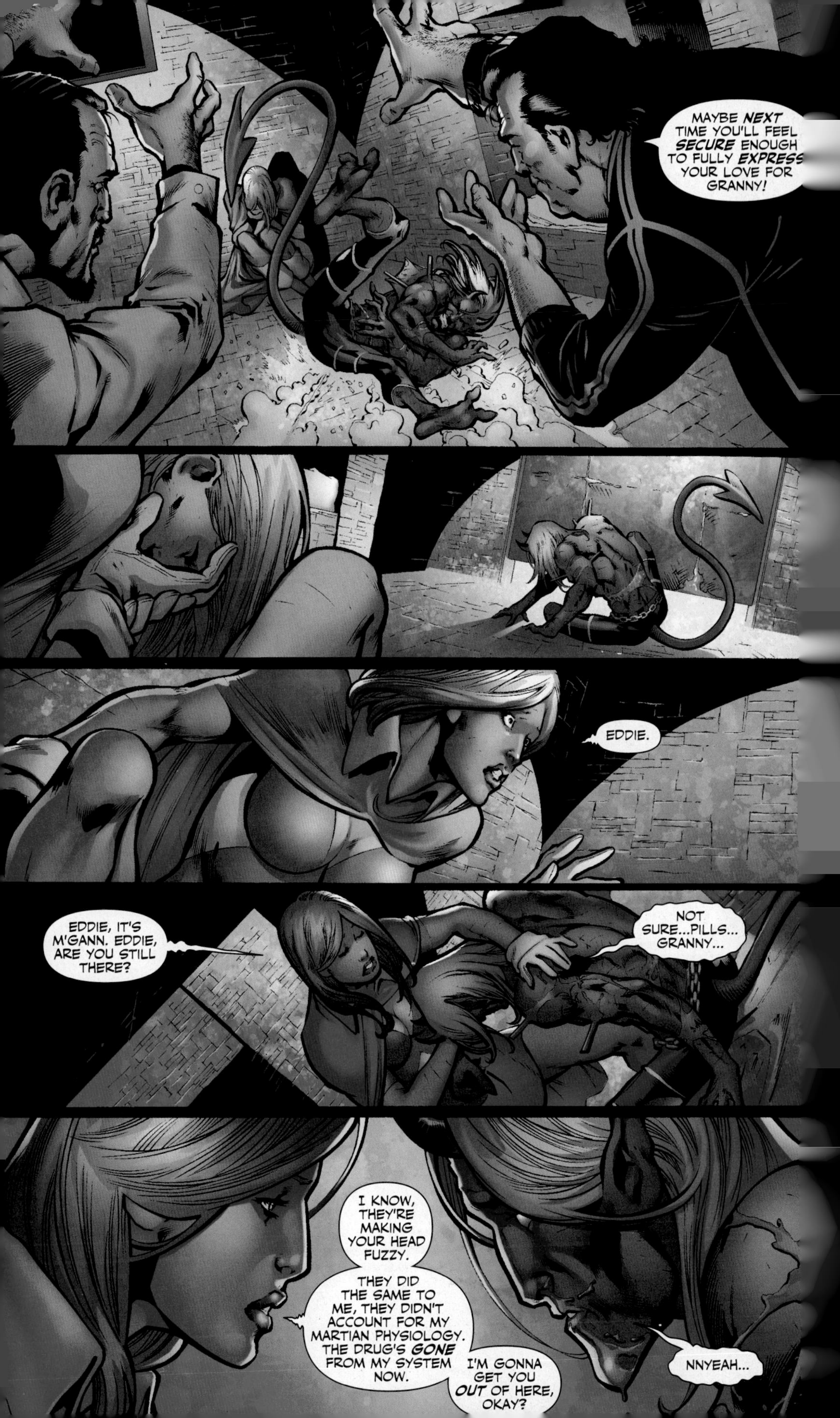
MAYBE *NEXT* TIME YOU'LL FEEL *SECURE* ENOUGH TO FULLY *EXPRESS* YOUR LOVE FOR GRANNY!
EDDIE.
EDDIE, IT'S M'GANN. EDDIE, ARE YOU STILL THERE?
NOT SURE...PILLS... GRANNY...
I KNOW, THEY'RE MAKING YOUR HEAD FUZZY.
THEY DID THE SAME TO ME, THEY DIDN'T ACCOUNT FOR MY MARTIAN PHYSIOLOGY. THE DRUG'S *GONE* FROM MY SYSTEM NOW.
I'M GONNA GET YOU *OUT* OF HERE, OKAY?
NNYEAH...

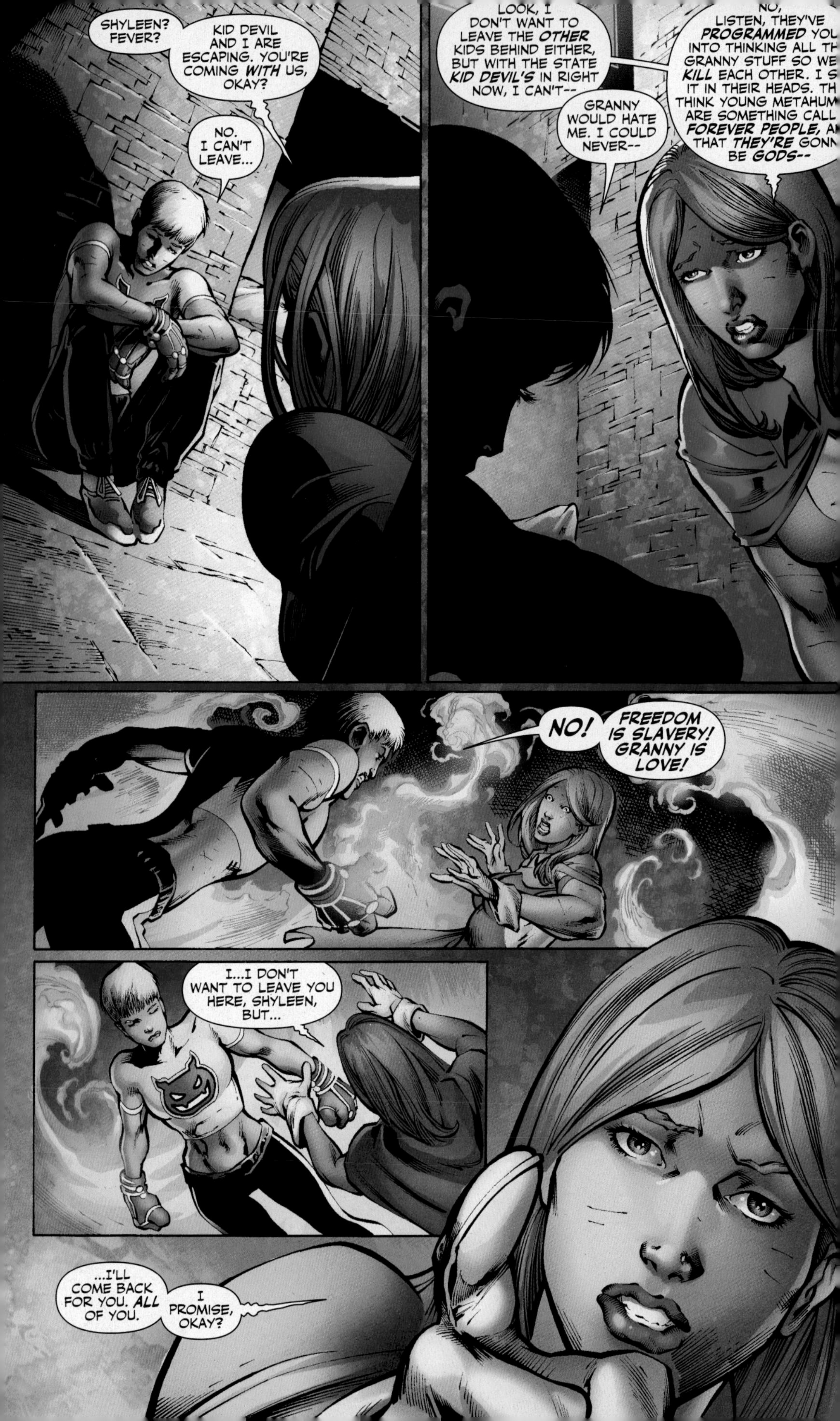

SHYLEEN? FEVER?
KID DEVIL AND I ARE ESCAPING. YOU'RE COMING WITH US, OKAY?
NO. I CAN'T LEAVE...
LOOK, I DON'T WANT TO LEAVE THE OTHER KIDS BEHIND EITHER, BUT WITH THE STATE KID DEVIL'S IN RIGHT NOW, I CAN'T--
GRANNY WOULD HATE ME. I COULD NEVER--
NO, LISTEN, THEY'VE PROGRAMMED YOU INTO THINKING ALL TH GRANNY STUFF SO WE KILL EACH OTHER. I S IT IN THEIR HEADS. TH THINK YOUNG METAHUM ARE SOMETHING CALL FOREVER PEOPLE, AN THAT THEY'RE GONN BE GODS--
NO!
FREEDOM IS SLAVERY! GRANNY IS LOVE!
I...I DON'T WANT TO LEAVE YOU HERE, SHYLEEN, BUT...
...I'LL COME BACK FOR YOU. ALL OF YOU.
I PROMISE, OKAY?

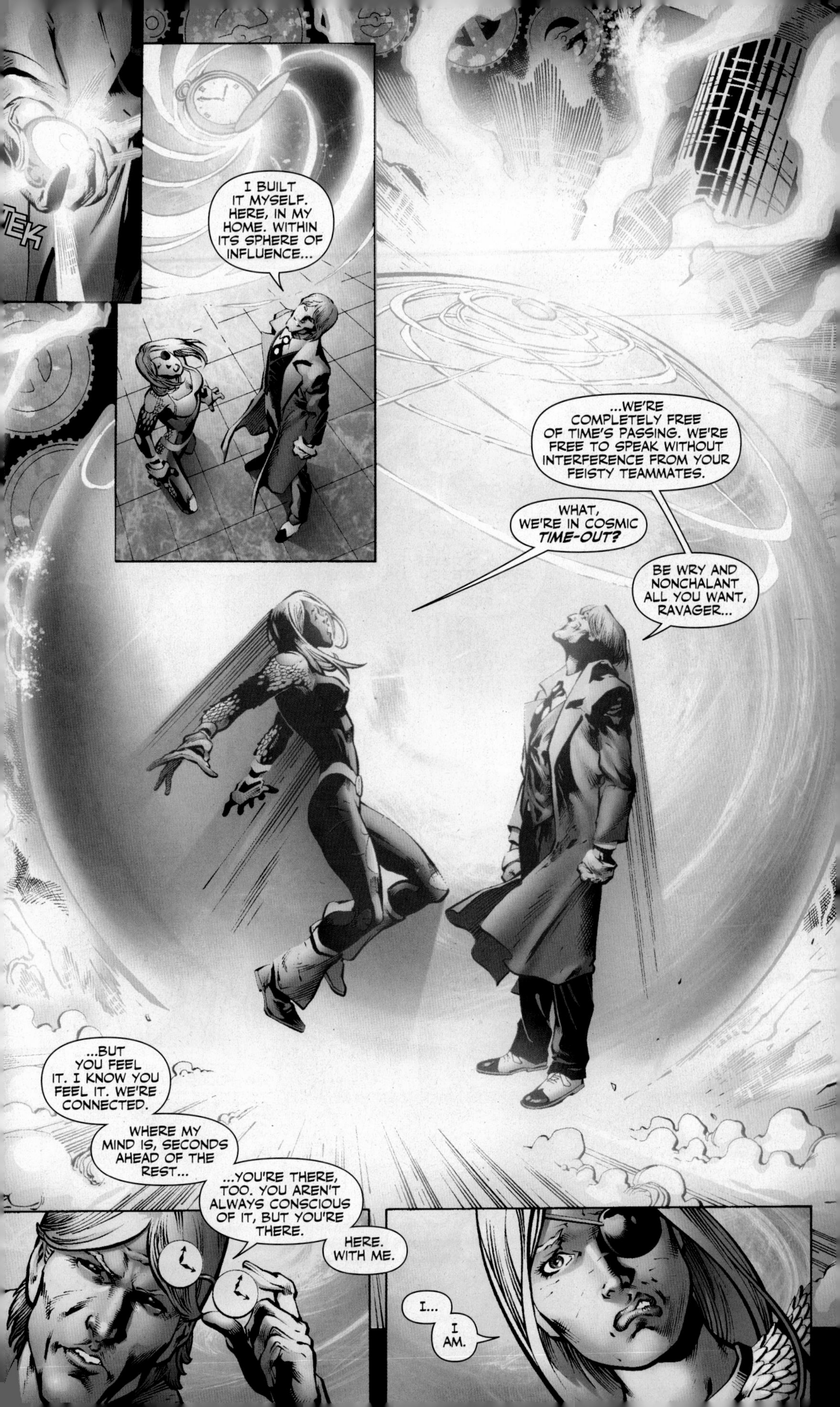

TEK
I BUILT IT MYSELF. HERE, IN MY HOME. WITHIN ITS SPHERE OF INFLUENCE...
...WE'RE COMPLETELY FREE OF TIME'S PASSING. WE'RE FREE TO SPEAK WITHOUT INTERFERENCE FROM YOUR FEISTY TEAMMATES.
WHAT, WE'RE IN COSMIC *TIME-OUT?*
BE WRY AND NONCHALANT ALL YOU WANT, RAVAGER...
...BUT YOU FEEL IT. I KNOW YOU FEEL IT. WE'RE CONNECTED.
WHERE MY MIND IS, SECONDS AHEAD OF THE REST...
...YOU'RE THERE, TOO. YOU AREN'T ALWAYS CONSCIOUS OF IT, BUT YOU'RE THERE.
HERE. WITH ME.
I... I AM.

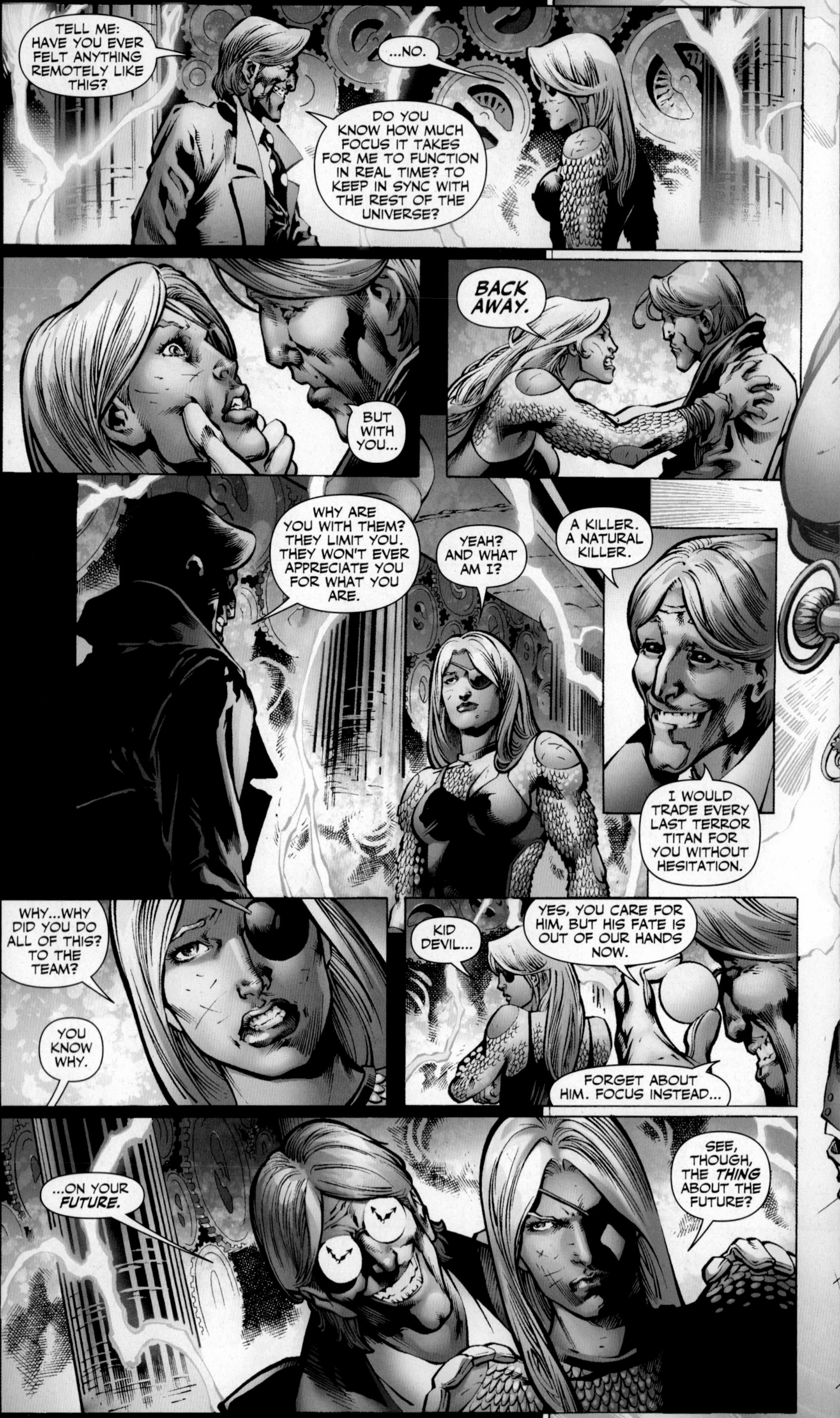
TELL ME: HAVE YOU EVER FELT ANYTHING REMOTELY LIKE THIS?
...NO.
DO YOU KNOW HOW MUCH FOCUS IT TAKES FOR ME TO FUNCTION IN REAL TIME? TO KEEP IN SYNC WITH THE REST OF THE UNIVERSE?
BUT WITH YOU...
BACK AWAY.
WHY ARE YOU WITH THEM? THEY LIMIT YOU. THEY WON'T EVER APPRECIATE YOU FOR WHAT YOU ARE.
YEAH? AND WHAT AM I?
A KILLER. A NATURAL KILLER.
I WOULD TRADE EVERY LAST TERROR TITAN FOR YOU WITHOUT HESITATION.
WHY...WHY DID YOU DO ALL OF THIS? TO THE TEAM?
YOU KNOW WHY.
KID DEVIL...
YES, YOU CARE FOR HIM, BUT HIS FATE IS OUT OF OUR HANDS NOW.
FORGET ABOUT HIM. FOCUS INSTEAD...
...ON YOUR FUTURE.
SEE, THOUGH, THE THING ABOUT THE FUTURE?

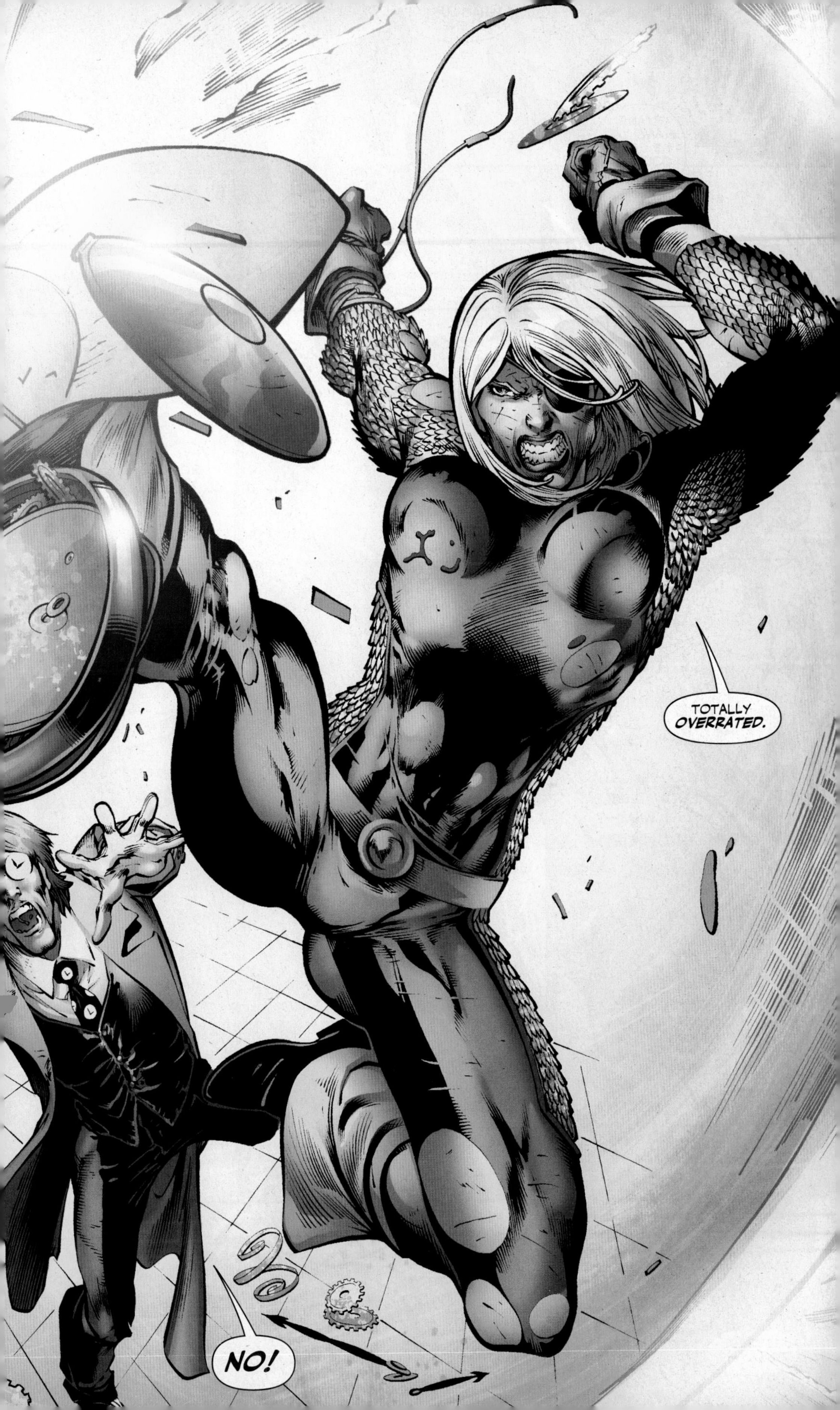
TOTALLY OVERRATED.
NO!

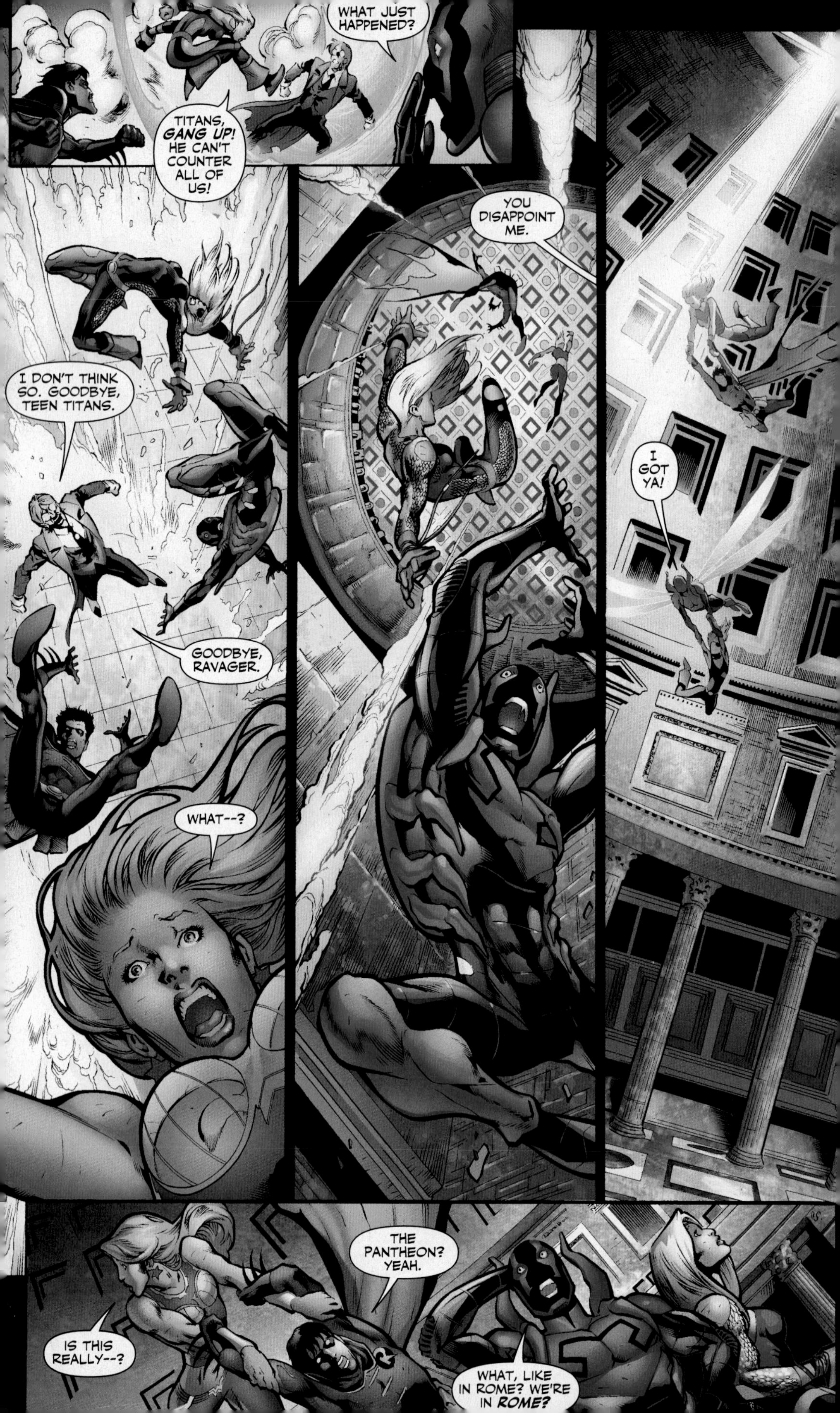
WHAT JUST HAPPENED?
TITANS, GANG UP! HE CAN'T COUNTER ALL OF US!
YOU DISAPPOINT ME.
I DON'T THINK SO. GOODBYE, TEEN TITANS.
I GOT YA!
GOODBYE, RAVAGER.
WHAT--?
IS THIS REALLY--?
THE PANTHEON? YEAH.
WHAT, LIKE IN ROME? WE'RE IN ROME?

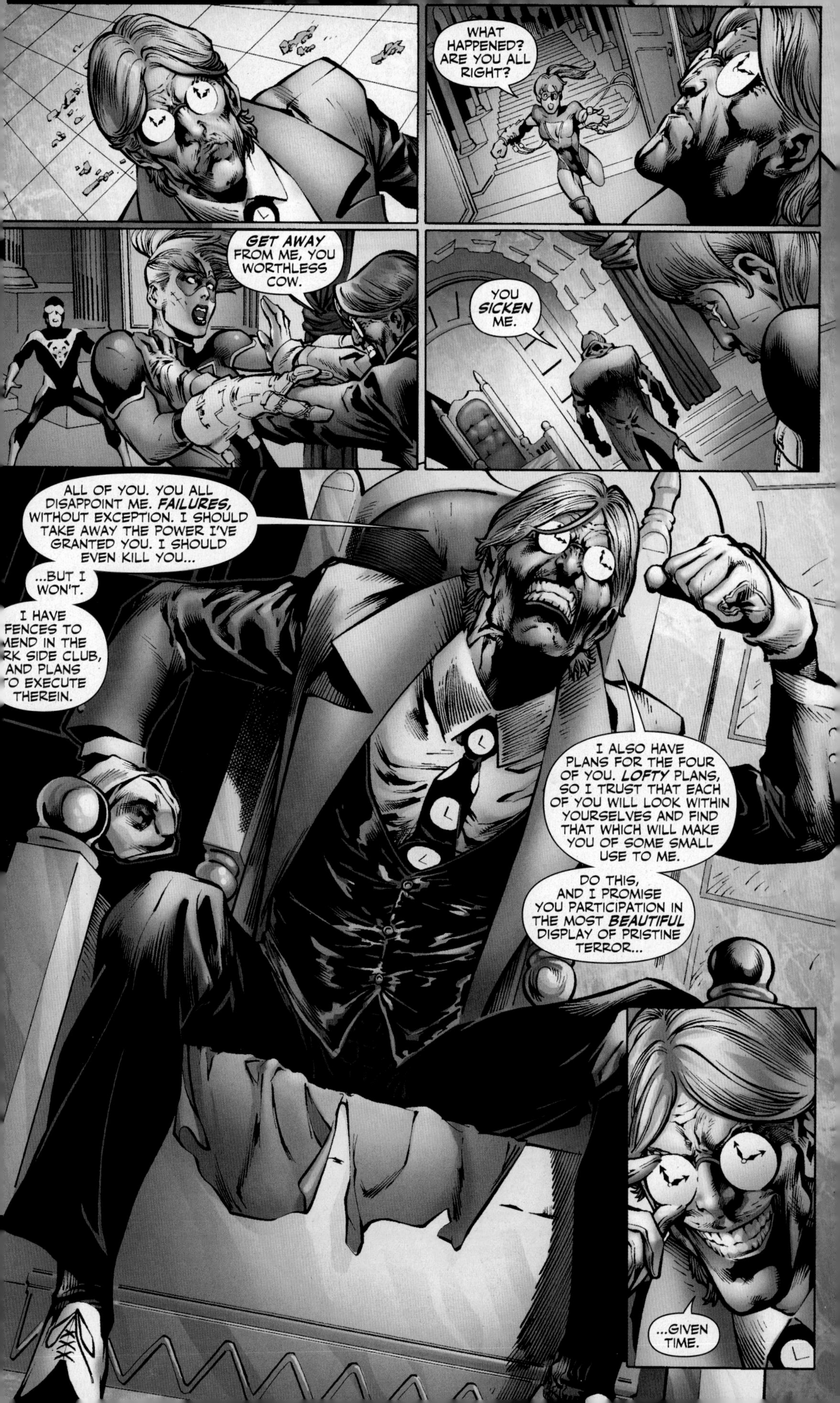

WHAT HAPPENED? ARE YOU ALL RIGHT?
GET AWAY FROM ME, YOU WORTHLESS COW.
YOU SICKEN ME.
ALL OF YOU. YOU ALL DISAPPOINT ME. FAILURES, WITHOUT EXCEPTION. I SHOULD TAKE AWAY THE POWER I'VE GRANTED YOU. I SHOULD EVEN KILL YOU...
...BUT I WON'T.
I HAVE FENCES TO MEND IN THE RK SIDE CLUB, AND PLANS TO EXECUTE THEREIN.
I ALSO HAVE PLANS FOR THE FOUR OF YOU. LOFTY PLANS, SO I TRUST THAT EACH OF YOU WILL LOOK WITHIN YOURSELVES AND FIND THAT WHICH WILL MAKE YOU OF SOME SMALL USE TO ME.
DO THIS, AND I PROMISE YOU PARTICIPATION IN THE MOST BEAUTIFUL DISPLAY OF PRISTINE TERROR...
...GIVEN TIME.

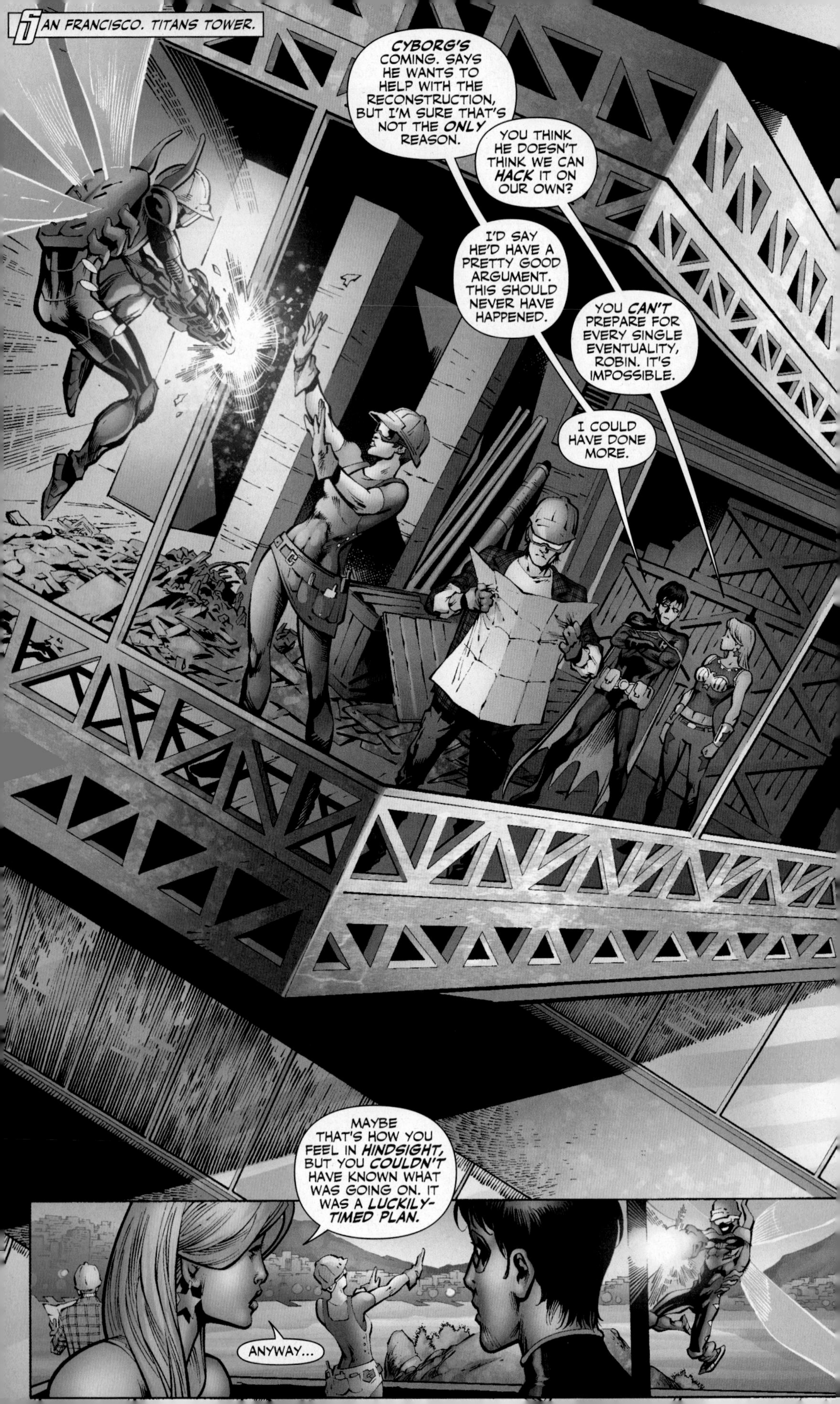
SAN FRANCISCO. TITANS TOWER.
CYBORG'S COMING. SAYS HE WANTS TO HELP WITH THE RECONSTRUCTION, BUT I'M SURE THAT'S NOT THE ONLY REASON.
YOU THINK HE DOESN'T THINK WE CAN HACK IT ON OUR OWN?
I'D SAY HE'D HAVE A PRETTY GOOD ARGUMENT. THIS SHOULD NEVER HAVE HAPPENED.
YOU CAN'T PREPARE FOR EVERY SINGLE EVENTUALITY, ROBIN. IT'S IMPOSSIBLE.
I COULD HAVE DONE MORE.
MAYBE THAT'S HOW YOU FEEL IN HINDSIGHT, BUT YOU COULDN'T HAVE KNOWN WHAT WAS GOING ON. IT WAS A LUCKILY-TIMED PLAN.
ANYWAY...

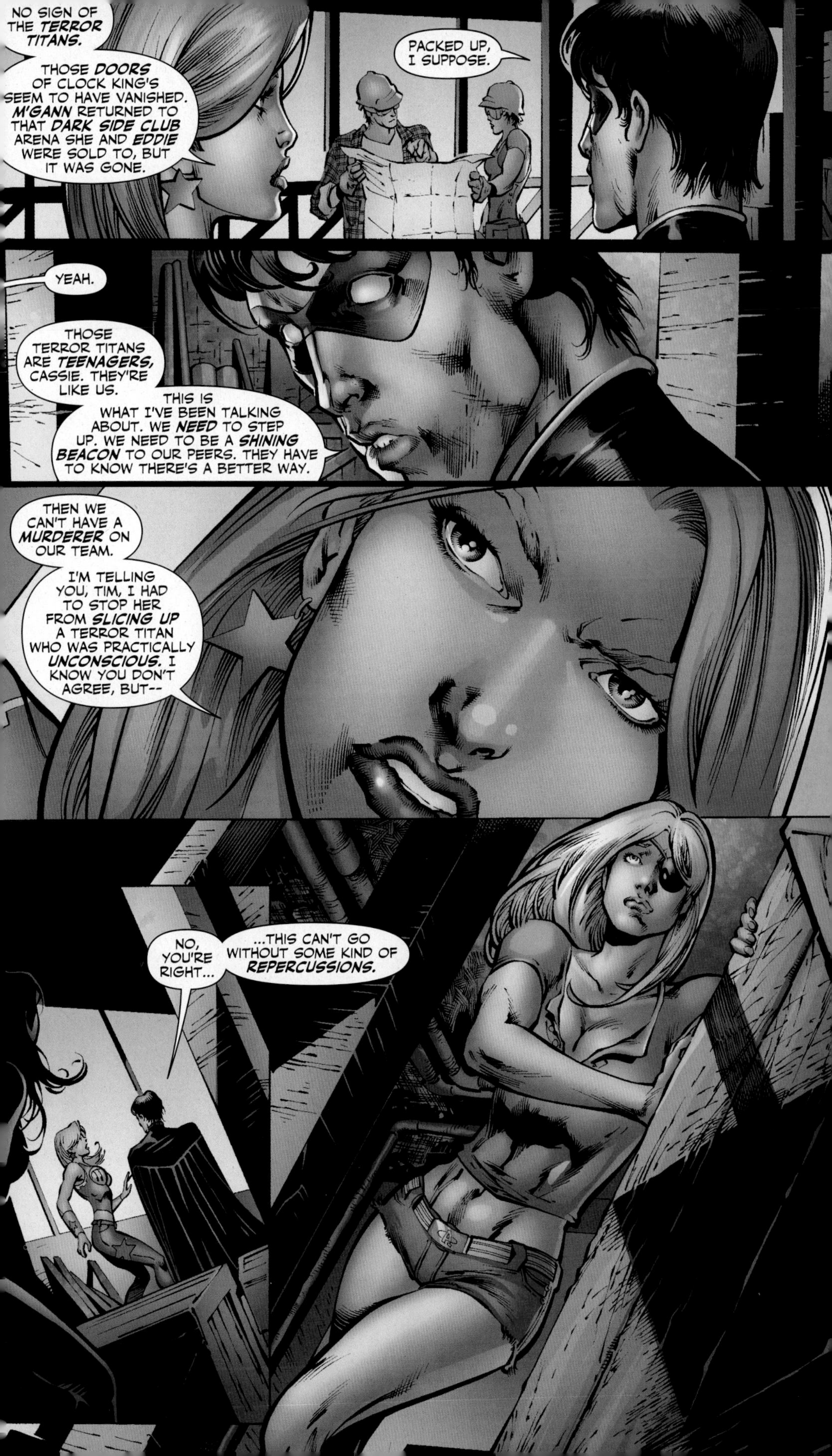
NO SIGN OF THE TERROR TITANS.
THOSE DOORS OF CLOCK KING'S SEEM TO HAVE VANISHED. M'GANN RETURNED TO THAT DARK SIDE CLUB ARENA SHE AND EDDIE WERE SOLD TO, BUT IT WAS GONE.
PACKED UP, I SUPPOSE.
YEAH.
THOSE TERROR TITANS ARE TEENAGERS, CASSIE. THEY'RE LIKE US.
THIS IS WHAT I'VE BEEN TALKING ABOUT. WE NEED TO STEP UP. WE NEED TO BE A SHINING BEACON TO OUR PEERS. THEY HAVE TO KNOW THERE'S A BETTER WAY.
THEN WE CAN'T HAVE A MURDERER ON OUR TEAM.
I'M TELLING YOU, TIM, I HAD TO STOP HER FROM SLICING UP A TERROR TITAN WHO WAS PRACTICALLY UNCONSCIOUS. I KNOW YOU DON'T AGREE, BUT--
NO, YOU'RE RIGHT...
...THIS CAN'T GO WITHOUT SOME KIND OF REPERCUSSIONS.

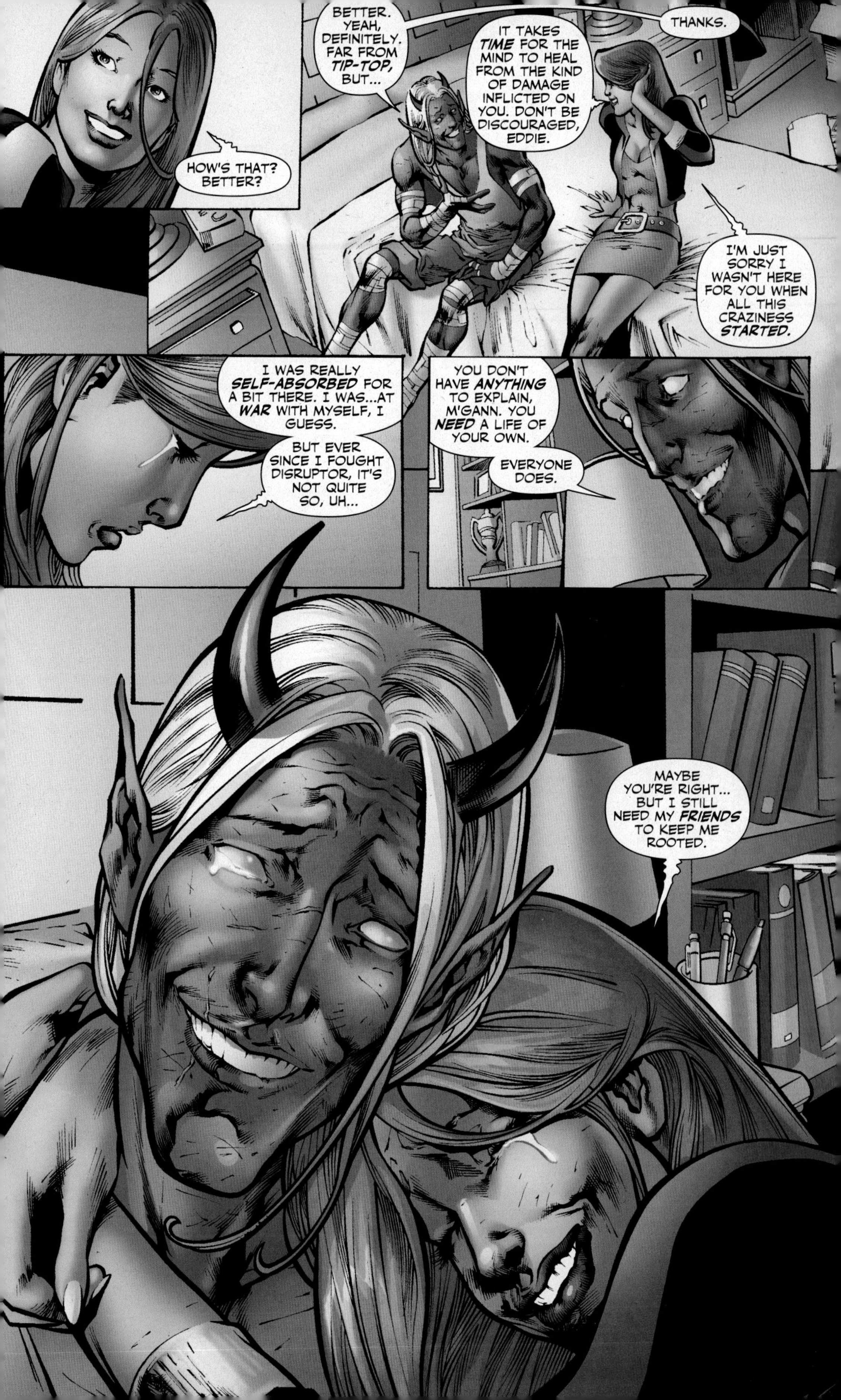
HOW'S THAT? BETTER?
BETTER. YEAH, DEFINITELY. FAR FROM TIP-TOP, BUT...
IT TAKES TIME FOR THE MIND TO HEAL FROM THE KIND OF DAMAGE INFLICTED ON YOU. DON'T BE DISCOURAGED, EDDIE.
THANKS.
I'M JUST SORRY I WASN'T HERE FOR YOU WHEN ALL THIS CRAZINESS STARTED.
I WAS REALLY SELF-ABSORBED FOR A BIT THERE. I WAS...AT WAR WITH MYSELF, I GUESS.
BUT EVER SINCE I FOUGHT DISRUPTOR, IT'S NOT QUITE SO, UH...
YOU DON'T HAVE ANYTHING TO EXPLAIN, M'GANN. YOU NEED A LIFE OF YOUR OWN.
EVERYONE DOES.
MAYBE YOU'RE RIGHT... BUT I STILL NEED MY FRIENDS TO KEEP ME ROOTED.

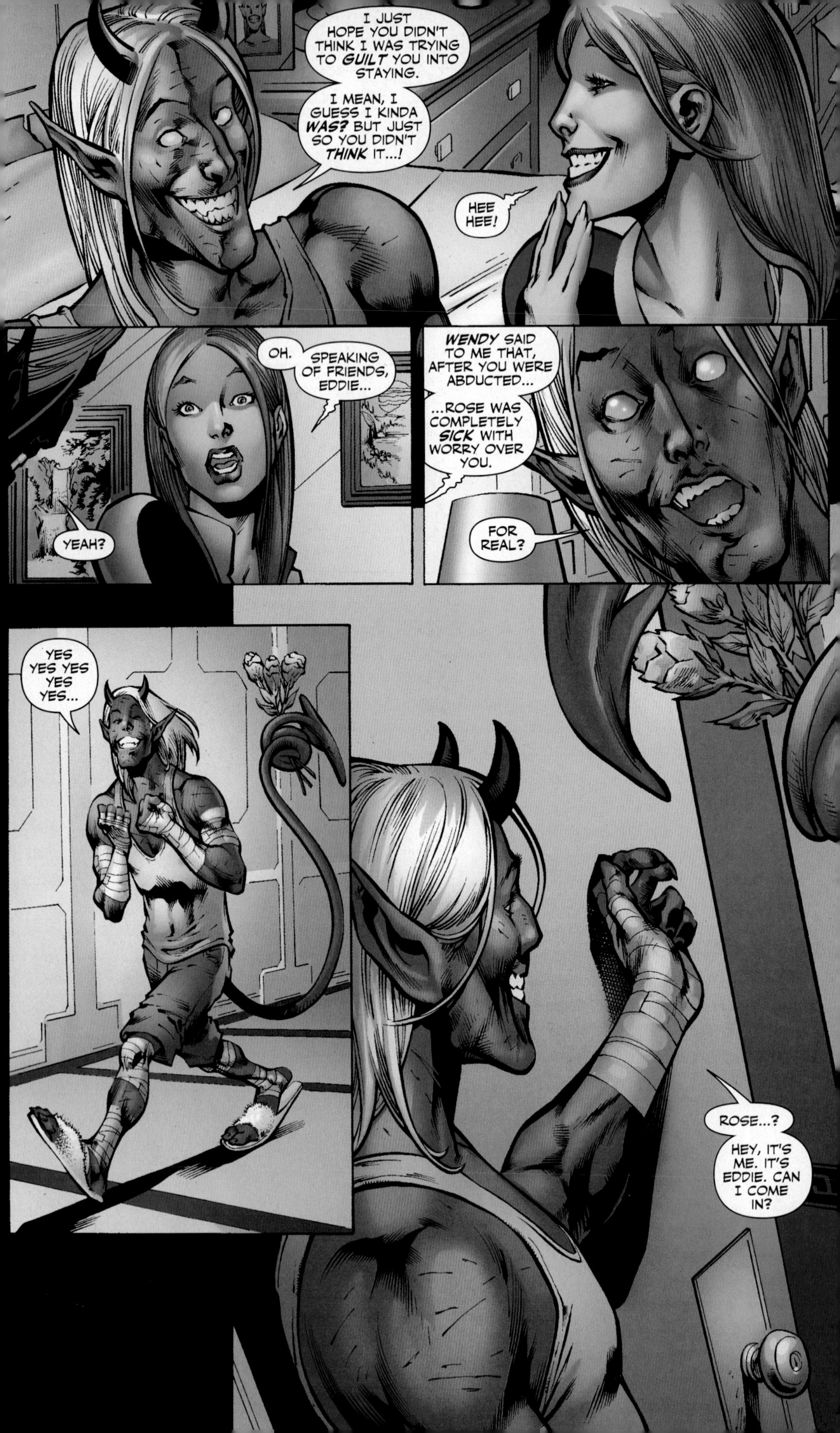

I JUST HOPE YOU DIDN'T THINK I WAS TRYING TO *GUILT* YOU INTO STAYING.
I MEAN, I GUESS I KINDA *WAS?* BUT JUST SO YOU DIDN'T *THINK* IT...!
HEE HEE!
OH.
SPEAKING OF FRIENDS, EDDIE...
YEAH?
WENDY SAID TO ME THAT, AFTER YOU WERE ABDUCTED...
...ROSE WAS COMPLETELY *SICK* WITH WORRY OVER YOU.
FOR REAL?
YES YES YES YES YES...
ROSE...?
HEY, IT'S ME. IT'S EDDIE. CAN I COME IN?

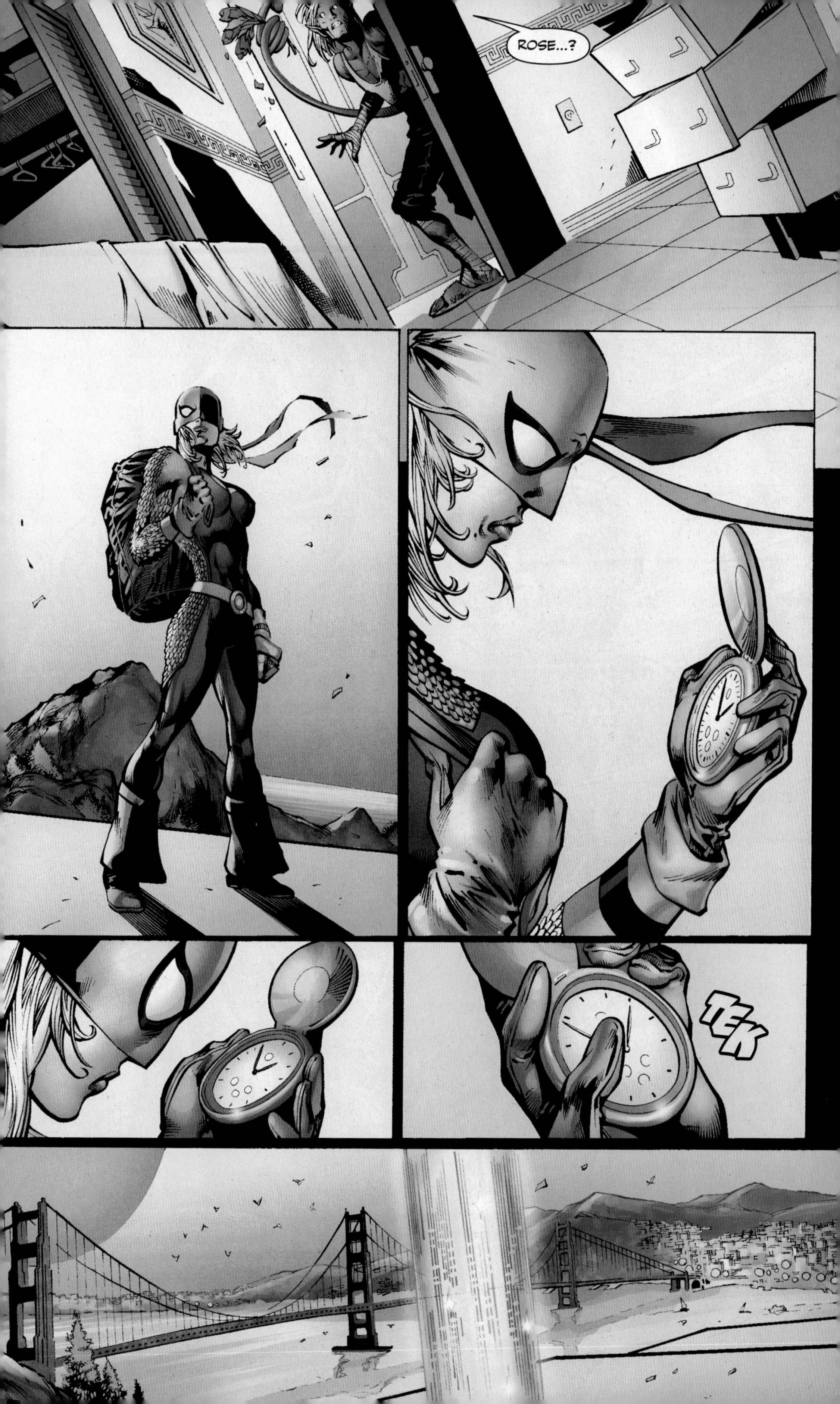
ROSE...?
TEK

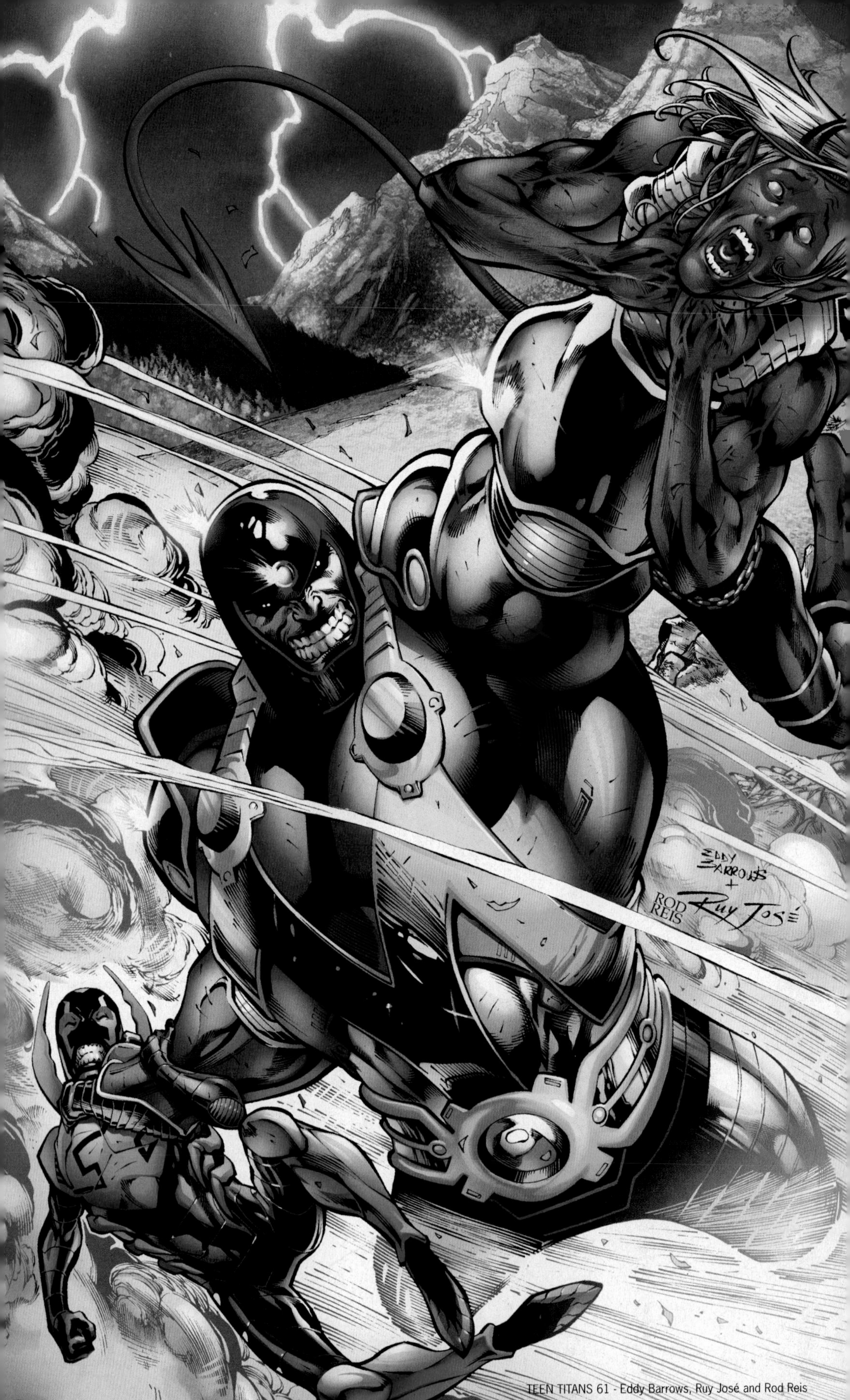
EDDY BARROWS
+
ROD REIS
Ruy José

TEEN TITANS 61 - Eddy Barrows, Ruy José and Rod Reis

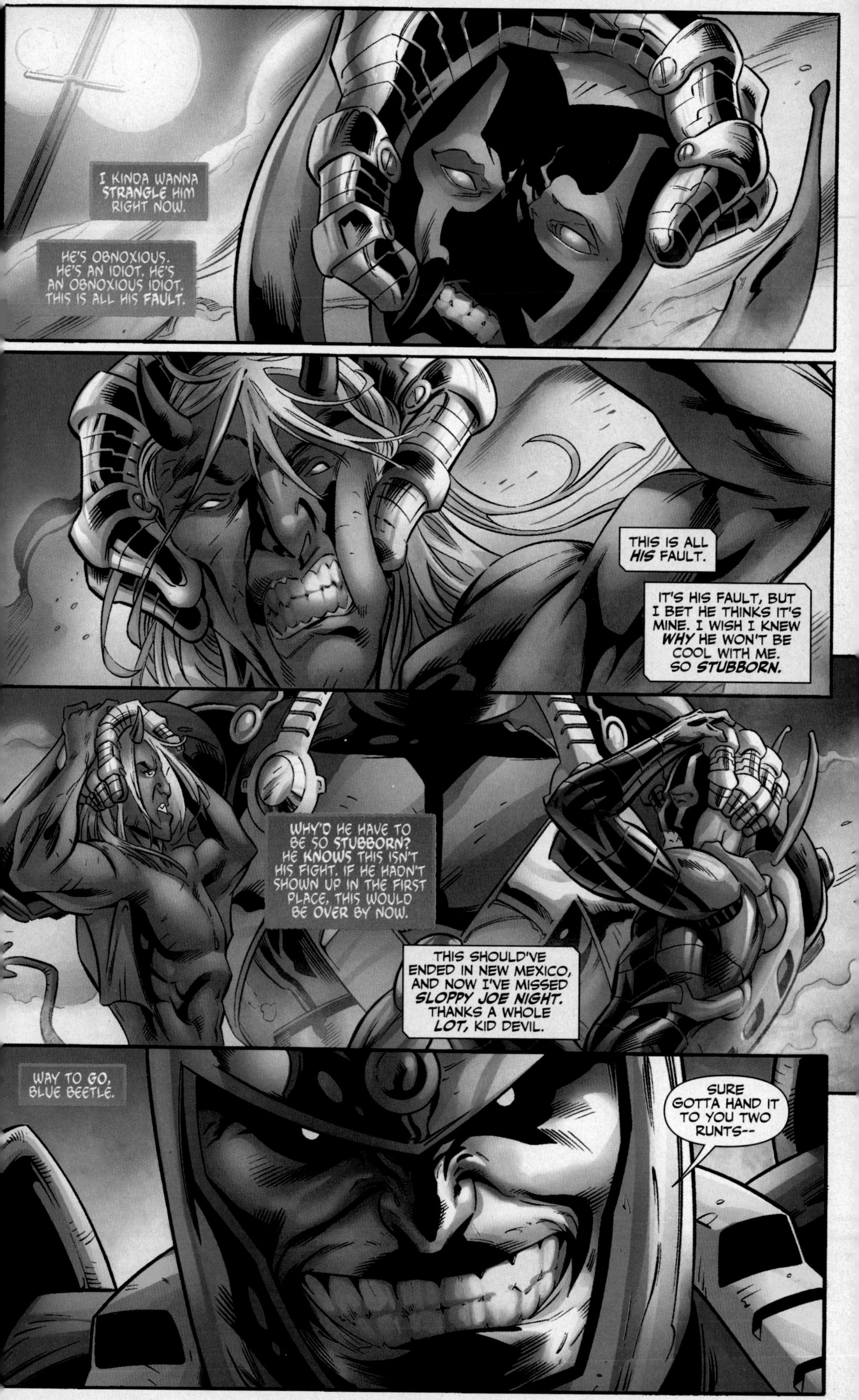
I KINDA WANNA STRANGLE HIM RIGHT NOW.
HE'S OBNOXIOUS. HE'S AN IDIOT. HE'S AN OBNOXIOUS IDIOT. THIS IS ALL HIS FAULT.
THIS IS ALL HIS FAULT.
IT'S HIS FAULT, BUT I BET HE THINKS IT'S MINE. I WISH I KNEW WHY HE WON'T BE COOL WITH ME. SO STUBBORN.
WHY'D HE HAVE TO BE SO STUBBORN? HE KNOWS THIS ISN'T HIS FIGHT. IF HE HADN'T SHOWN UP IN THE FIRST PLACE, THIS WOULD BE OVER BY NOW.
THIS SHOULD'VE ENDED IN NEW MEXICO, AND NOW I'VE MISSED SLOPPY JOE NIGHT. THANKS A WHOLE LOT, KID DEVIL.
WAY TO GO, BLUE BEETLE.
SURE GOTTA HAND IT TO YOU TWO RUNTS--

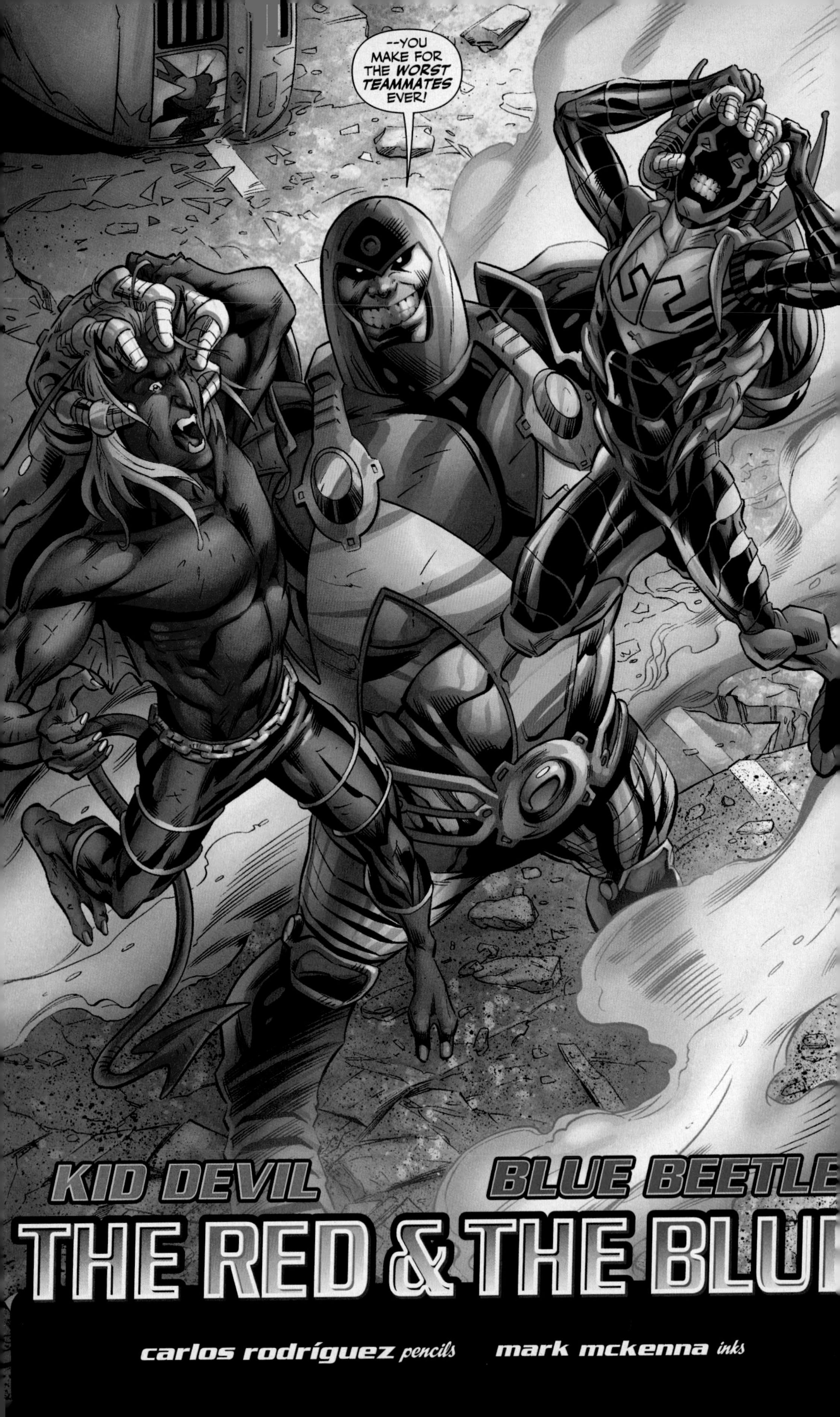
--YOU MAKE FOR THE WORST TEAMMATES EVER!
KID DEVIL
BLUE BEETLE
THE RED & THE BLU
carlos rodríguez pencils
mark mckenna inks

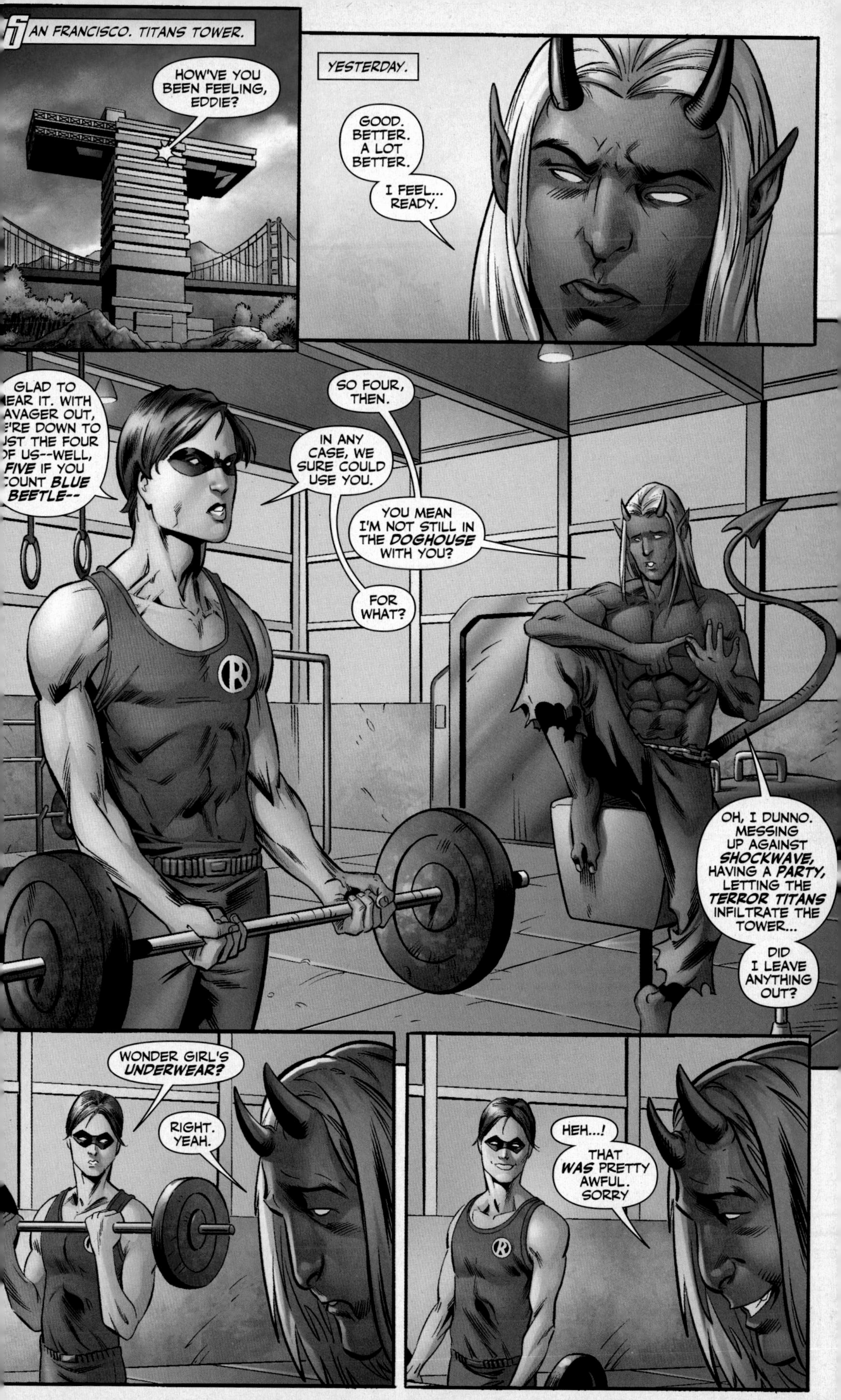
SAN FRANCISCO. TITANS TOWER.
HOW'VE YOU BEEN FEELING, EDDIE?
YESTERDAY.
GOOD. BETTER. A LOT BETTER.
I FEEL... READY.
GLAD TO HEAR IT. WITH SAVAGER OUT, WE'RE DOWN TO JUST THE FOUR OF US--WELL, FIVE IF YOU COUNT BLUE BEETLE--
SO FOUR, THEN.
IN ANY CASE, WE SURE COULD USE YOU.
YOU MEAN I'M NOT STILL IN THE DOGHOUSE WITH YOU?
FOR WHAT?
OH, I DUNNO. MESSING UP AGAINST SHOCKWAVE, HAVING A PARTY, LETTING THE TERROR TITANS INFILTRATE THE TOWER...
DID I LEAVE ANYTHING OUT?
WONDER GIRL'S UNDERWEAR?
RIGHT. YEAH.
HEH...!
THAT WAS PRETTY AWFUL. SORRY

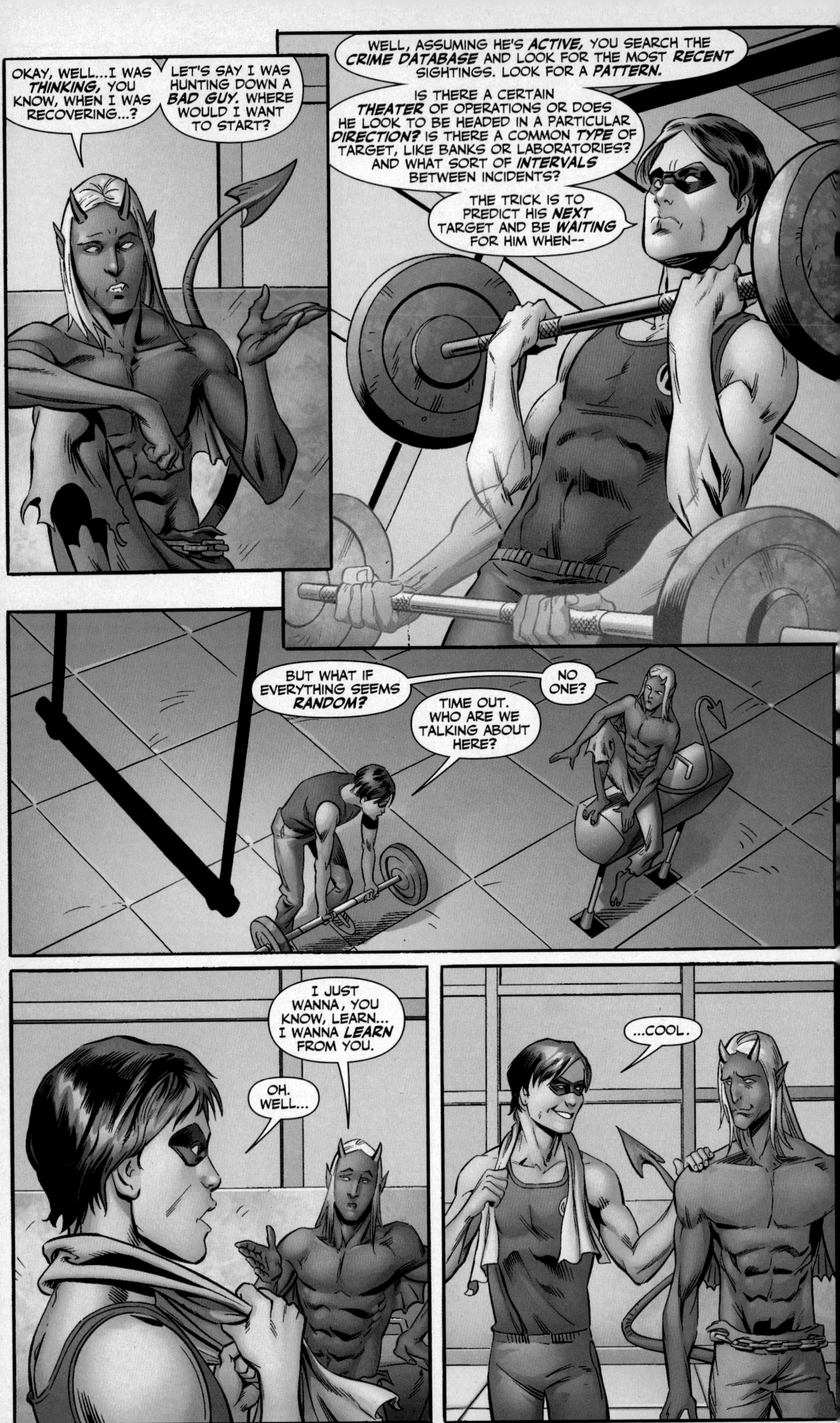
OKAY, WELL...I WAS *THINKING,* YOU KNOW, WHEN I WAS RECOVERING...?
LET'S SAY I WAS HUNTING DOWN A *BAD GUY.* WHERE WOULD I WANT TO START?
WELL, ASSUMING HE'S *ACTIVE,* YOU SEARCH THE *CRIME DATABASE* AND LOOK FOR THE MOST *RECENT* SIGHTINGS. LOOK FOR A *PATTERN.*
IS THERE A CERTAIN *THEATER* OF OPERATIONS OR DOES HE LOOK TO BE HEADED IN A PARTICULAR *DIRECTION?* IS THERE A COMMON *TYPE* OF TARGET, LIKE BANKS OR LABORATORIES? AND WHAT SORT OF *INTERVALS* BETWEEN INCIDENTS?
THE TRICK IS TO PREDICT HIS *NEXT* TARGET AND BE *WAITING* FOR HIM WHEN--
BUT WHAT IF EVERYTHING SEEMS *RANDOM?*
TIME OUT. WHO ARE WE TALKING ABOUT HERE?
NO ONE?
I JUST WANNA, YOU KNOW, LEARN... I WANNA *LEARN* FROM YOU.
OH. WELL...
...COOL.

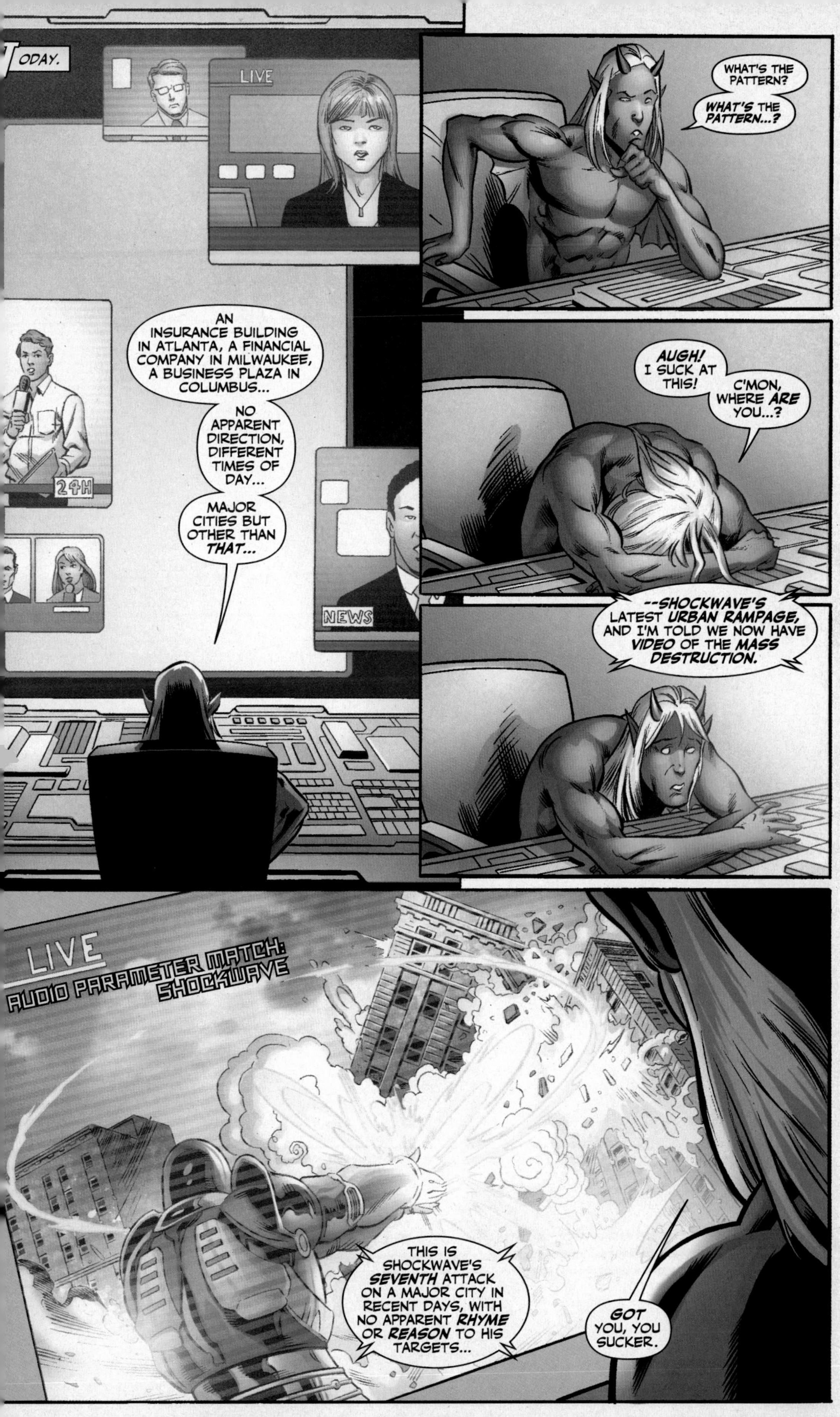
TODAY.
LIVE
WHAT'S THE PATTERN?
WHAT'S THE PATTERN...?
AN INSURANCE BUILDING IN ATLANTA, A FINANCIAL COMPANY IN MILWAUKEE, A BUSINESS PLAZA IN COLUMBUS...
NO APPARENT DIRECTION, DIFFERENT TIMES OF DAY...
MAJOR CITIES BUT OTHER THAN THAT...
24H
NEWS
AUGH! I SUCK AT THIS!
C'MON, WHERE ARE YOU...?
--SHOCKWAVE'S LATEST URBAN RAMPAGE, AND I'M TOLD WE NOW HAVE VIDEO OF THE MASS DESTRUCTION.
LIVE
AUDIO PARAMETER MATCH: SHOCKWAVE
THIS IS SHOCKWAVE'S SEVENTH ATTACK ON A MAJOR CITY IN RECENT DAYS, WITH NO APPARENT RHYME OR REASON TO HIS TARGETS...
GOT YOU, YOU SUCKER.

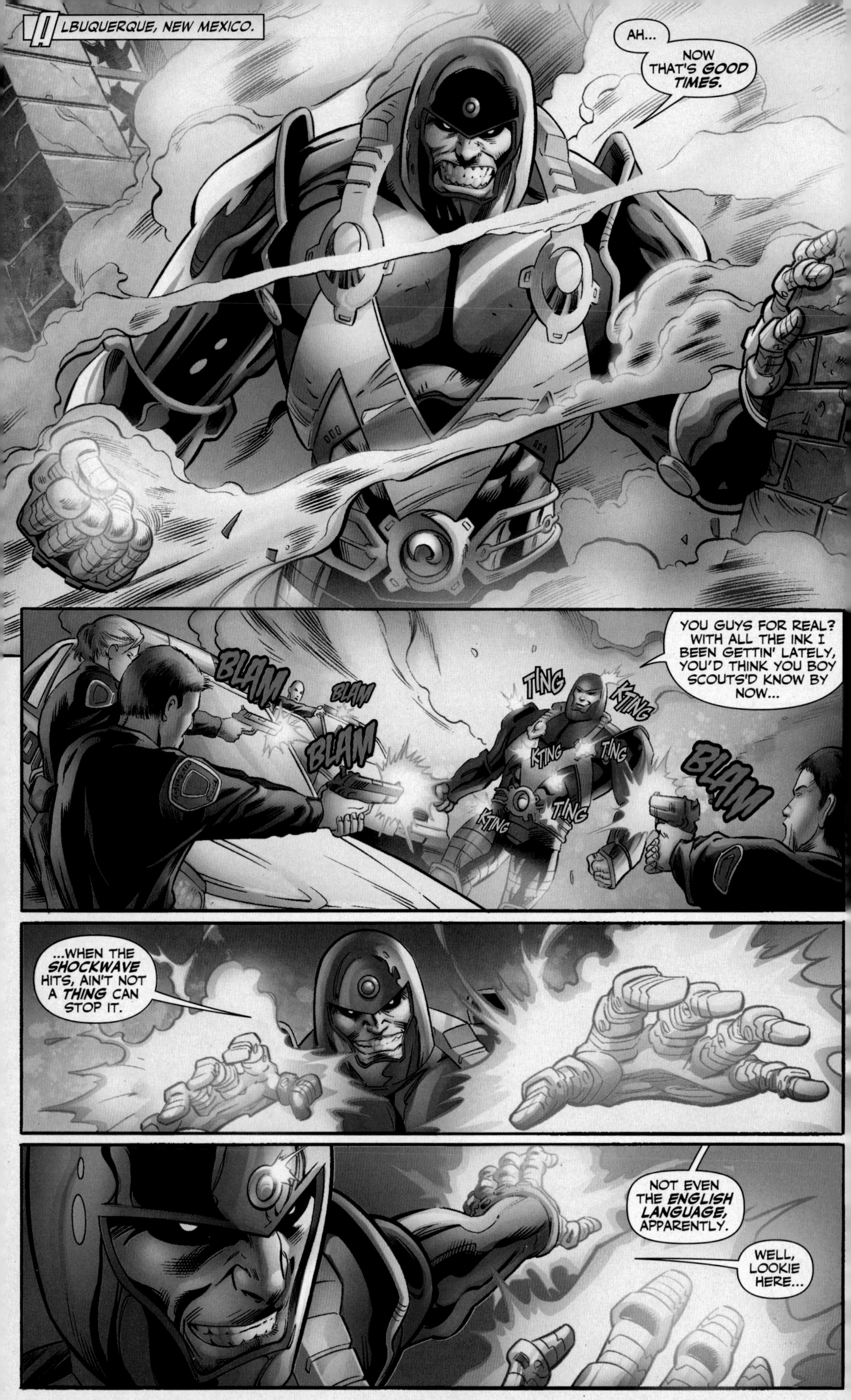
ALBUQUERQUE, NEW MEXICO.
AH... NOW THAT'S GOOD TIMES.
BLAM
BLAM
BLAM
TING
KTING
KTING
TING
TING
KTING
BLAM
YOU GUYS FOR REAL? WITH ALL THE INK I BEEN GETTIN' LATELY, YOU'D THINK YOU BOY SCOUTS'D KNOW BY NOW...
...WHEN THE SHOCKWAVE HITS, AIN'T NOT A THING CAN STOP IT.
NOT EVEN THE ENGLISH LANGUAGE, APPARENTLY.
WELL, LOOKIE HERE...

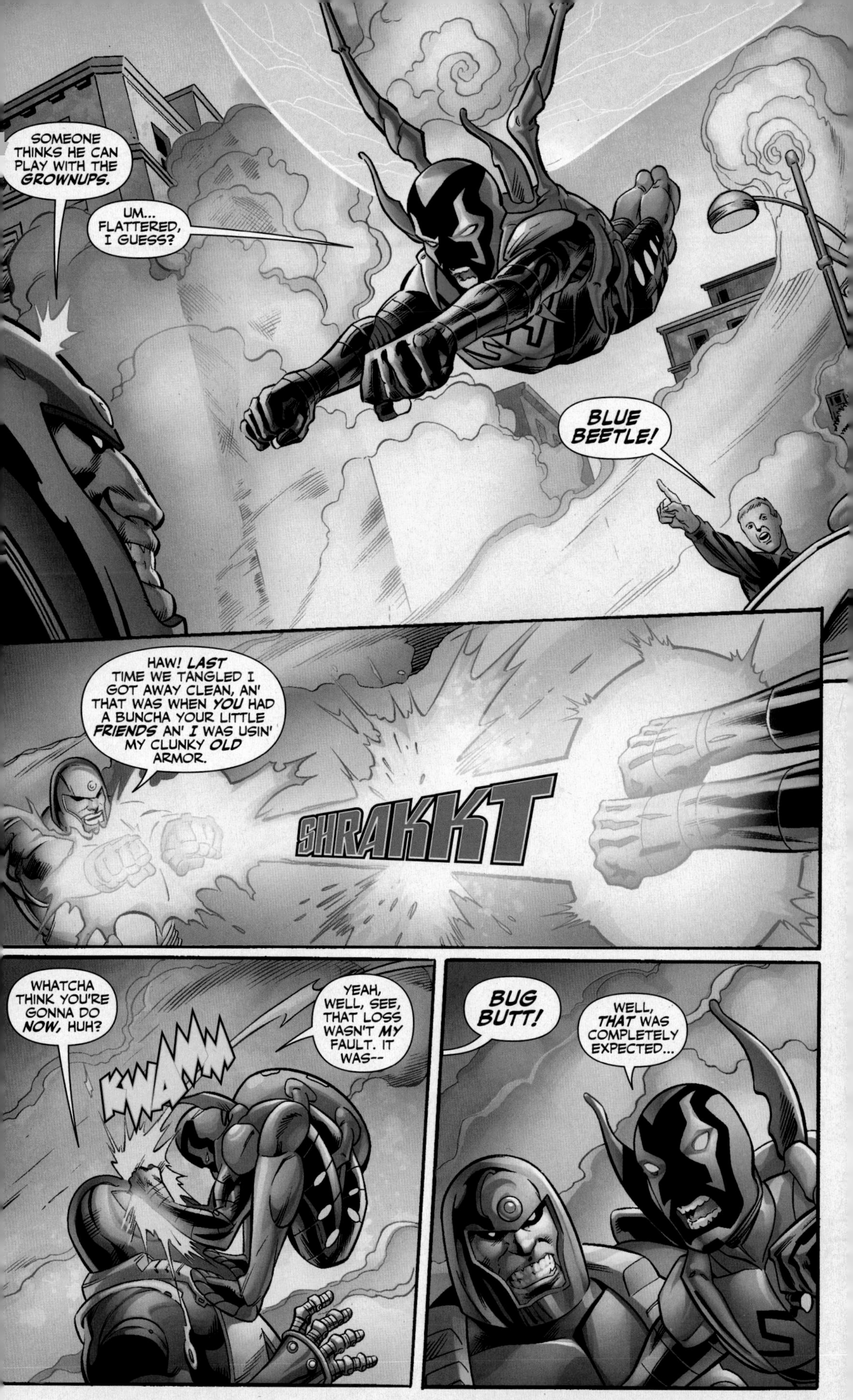
SOMEONE THINKS HE CAN PLAY WITH THE GROWNUPS.
UM... FLATTERED, I GUESS?
BLUE BEETLE!
HAW! LAST TIME WE TANGLED I GOT AWAY CLEAN, AN' THAT WAS WHEN YOU HAD A BUNCHA YOUR LITTLE FRIENDS AN' I WAS USIN' MY CLUNKY OLD ARMOR.
SHRAKKT
WHATCHA THINK YOU'RE GONNA DO NOW, HUH?
KWAMM
YEAH, WELL, SEE, THAT LOSS WASN'T MY FAULT. IT WAS--
BUG BUTT!
WELL, THAT WAS COMPLETELY EXPECTED...

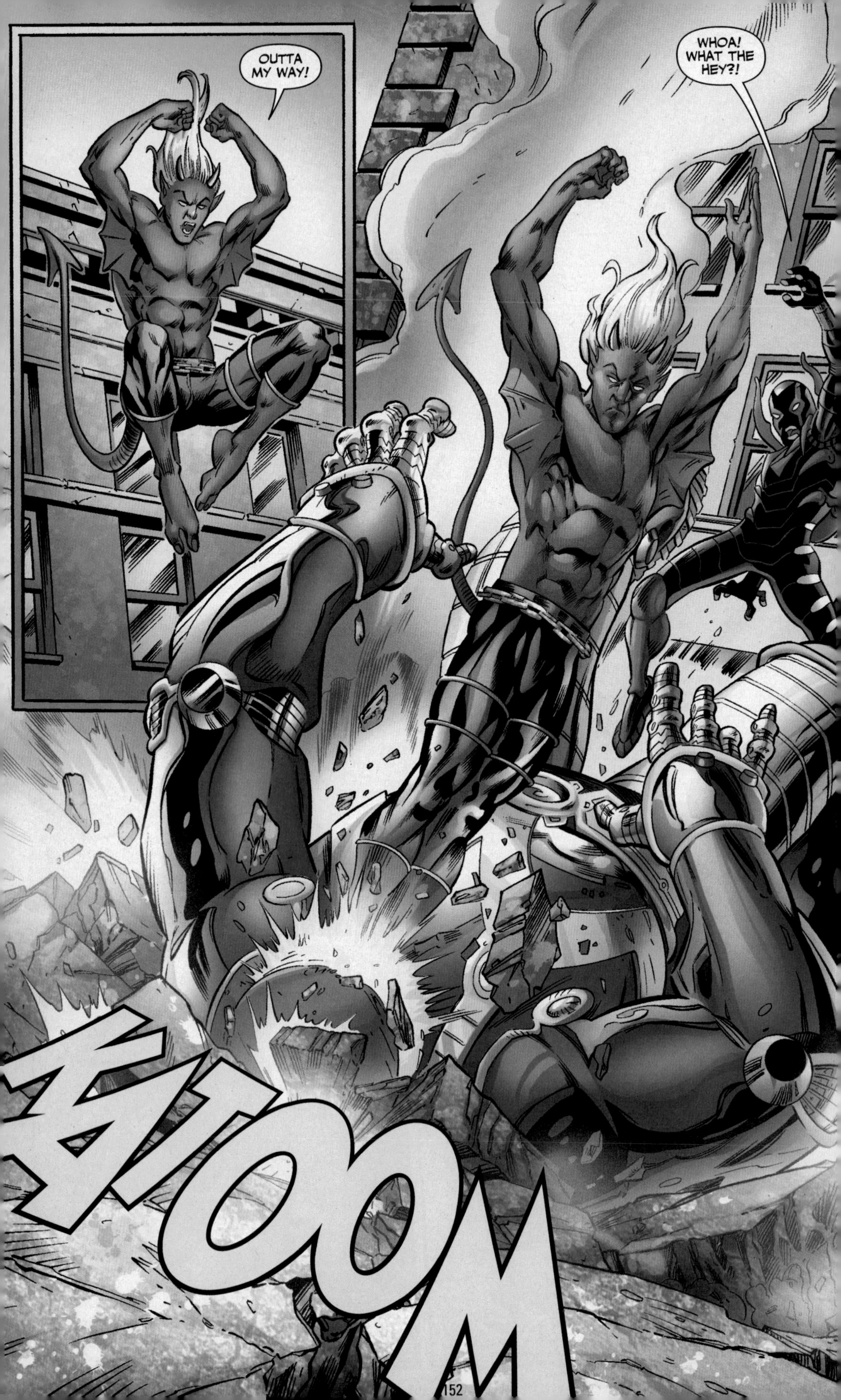

OUTTA MY WAY!
WHOA! WHAT THE HEY?!
KABOOM

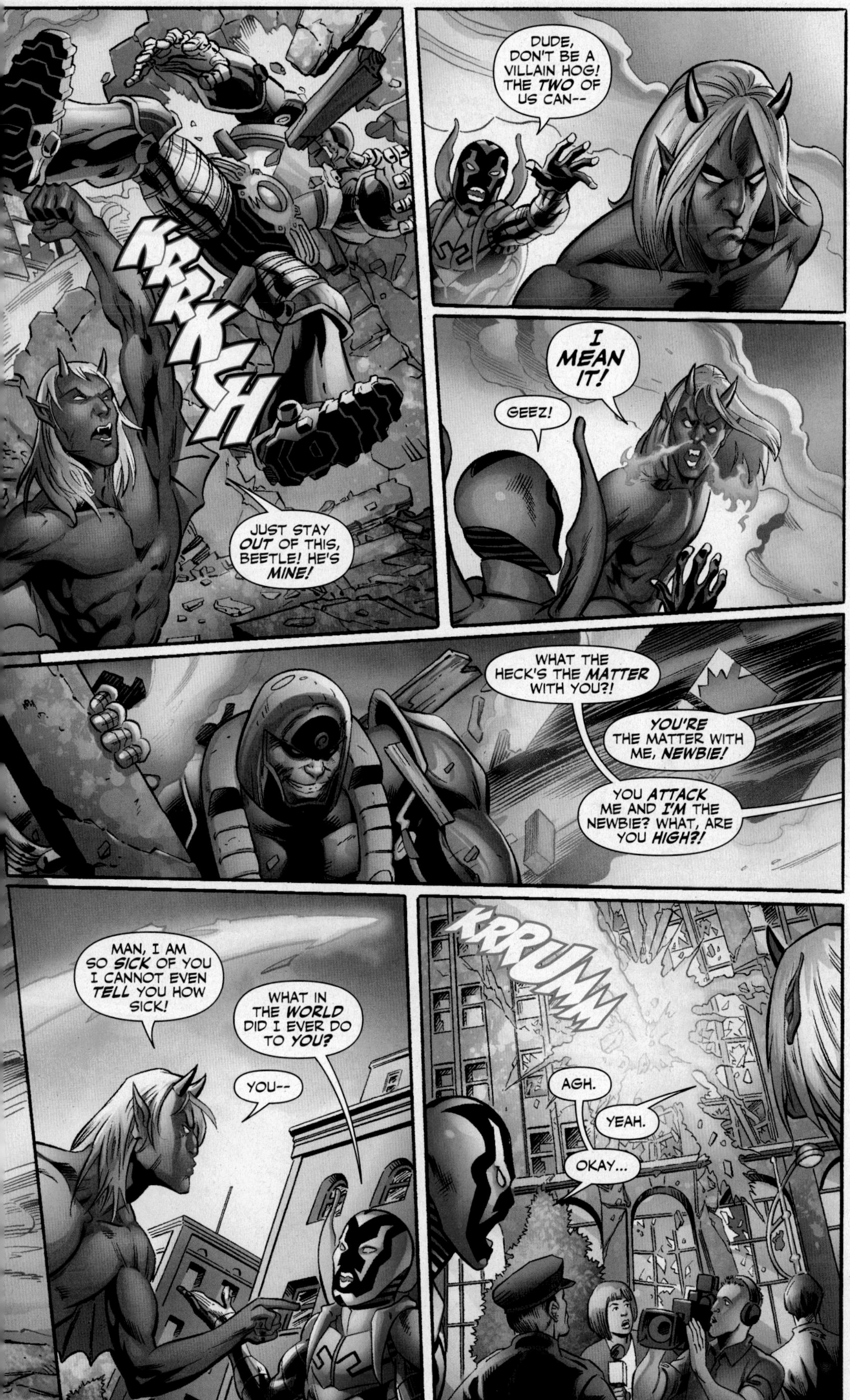
KRRKKH
JUST STAY OUT OF THIS, BEETLE! HE'S MINE!
DUDE, DON'T BE A VILLAIN HOG! THE TWO OF US CAN--
I MEAN IT!
GEEZ!
WHAT THE HECK'S THE MATTER WITH YOU?!
YOU'RE THE MATTER WITH ME, NEWBIE!
YOU ATTACK ME AND I'M THE NEWBIE? WHAT, ARE YOU HIGH?!
MAN, I AM SO SICK OF YOU I CANNOT EVEN TELL YOU HOW SICK!
WHAT IN THE WORLD DID I EVER DO TO YOU?
YOU--
KRRUMM
AGH.
YEAH.
OKAY...

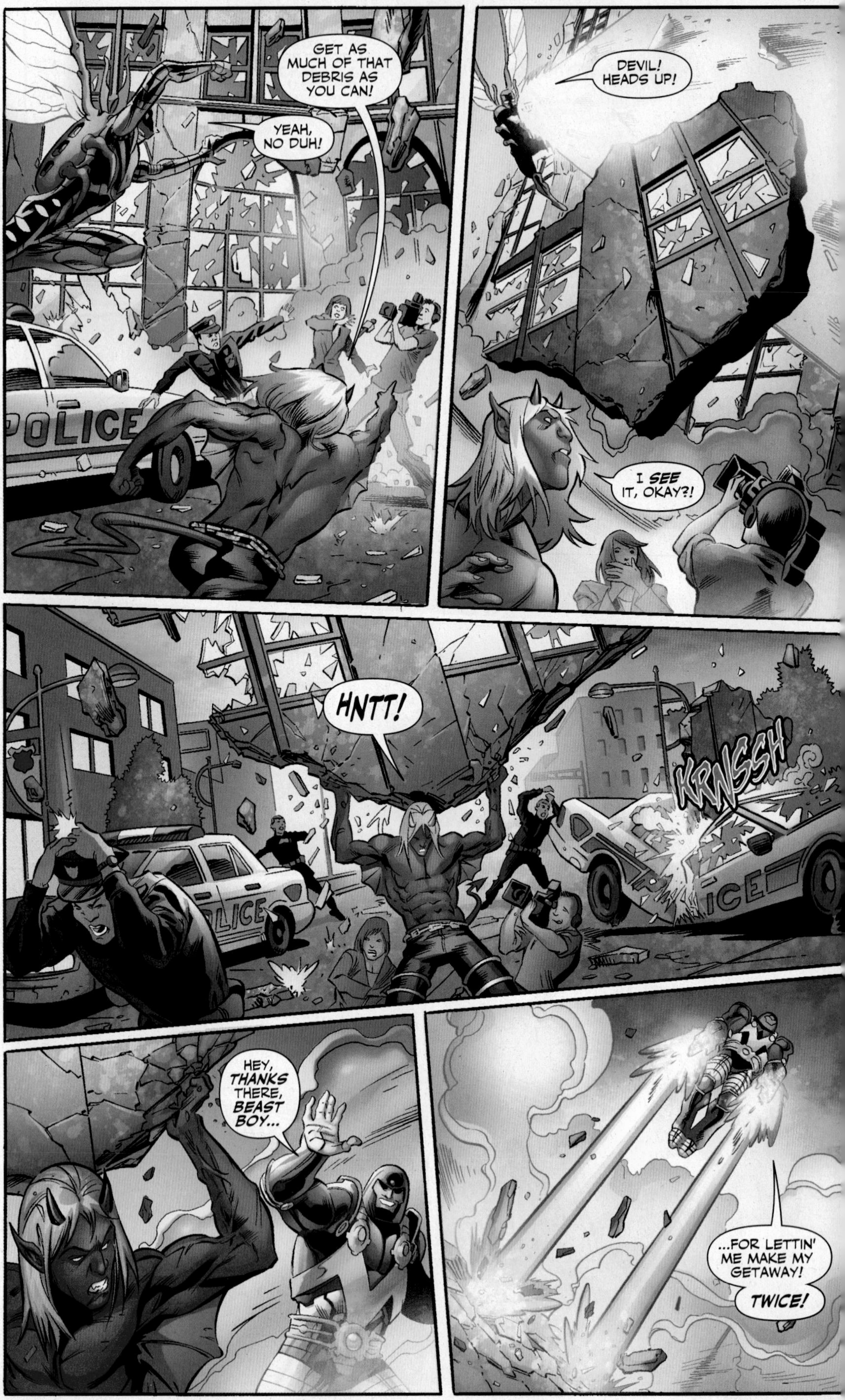
GET AS MUCH OF THAT DEBRIS AS YOU CAN!
YEAH, NO DUH!
DEVIL! HEADS UP!
I SEE IT, OKAY?!
HNTT!
KRNSSH
HEY, THANKS THERE, BEAST BOY...
...FOR LETTIN' ME MAKE MY GETAWAY!
TWICE!

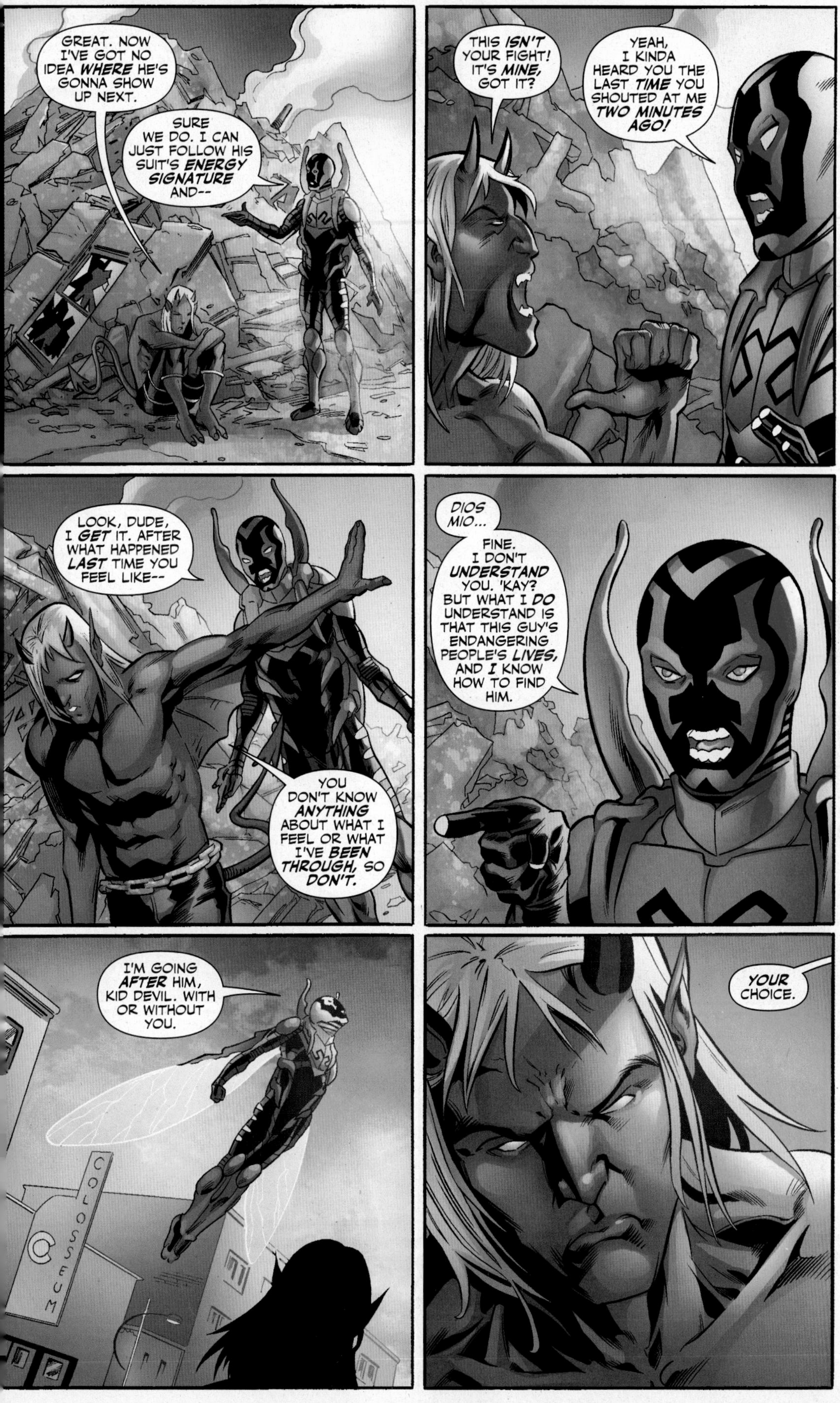
GREAT. NOW I'VE GOT NO IDEA WHERE HE'S GONNA SHOW UP NEXT.
SURE WE DO. I CAN JUST FOLLOW HIS SUIT'S ENERGY SIGNATURE AND--
THIS ISN'T YOUR FIGHT! IT'S MINE, GOT IT?
YEAH, I KINDA HEARD YOU THE LAST TIME YOU SHOUTED AT ME TWO MINUTES AGO!
LOOK, DUDE, I GET IT. AFTER WHAT HAPPENED LAST TIME YOU FEEL LIKE--
YOU DON'T KNOW ANYTHING ABOUT WHAT I FEEL OR WHAT I'VE BEEN THROUGH, SO DON'T.
DIOS MIO...
FINE. I DON'T UNDERSTAND YOU. 'KAY? BUT WHAT I DO UNDERSTAND IS THAT THIS GUY'S ENDANGERING PEOPLE'S LIVES, AND I KNOW HOW TO FIND HIM.
I'M GOING AFTER HIM, KID DEVIL. WITH OR WITHOUT YOU.
COLOSSEUM
YOUR CHOICE.

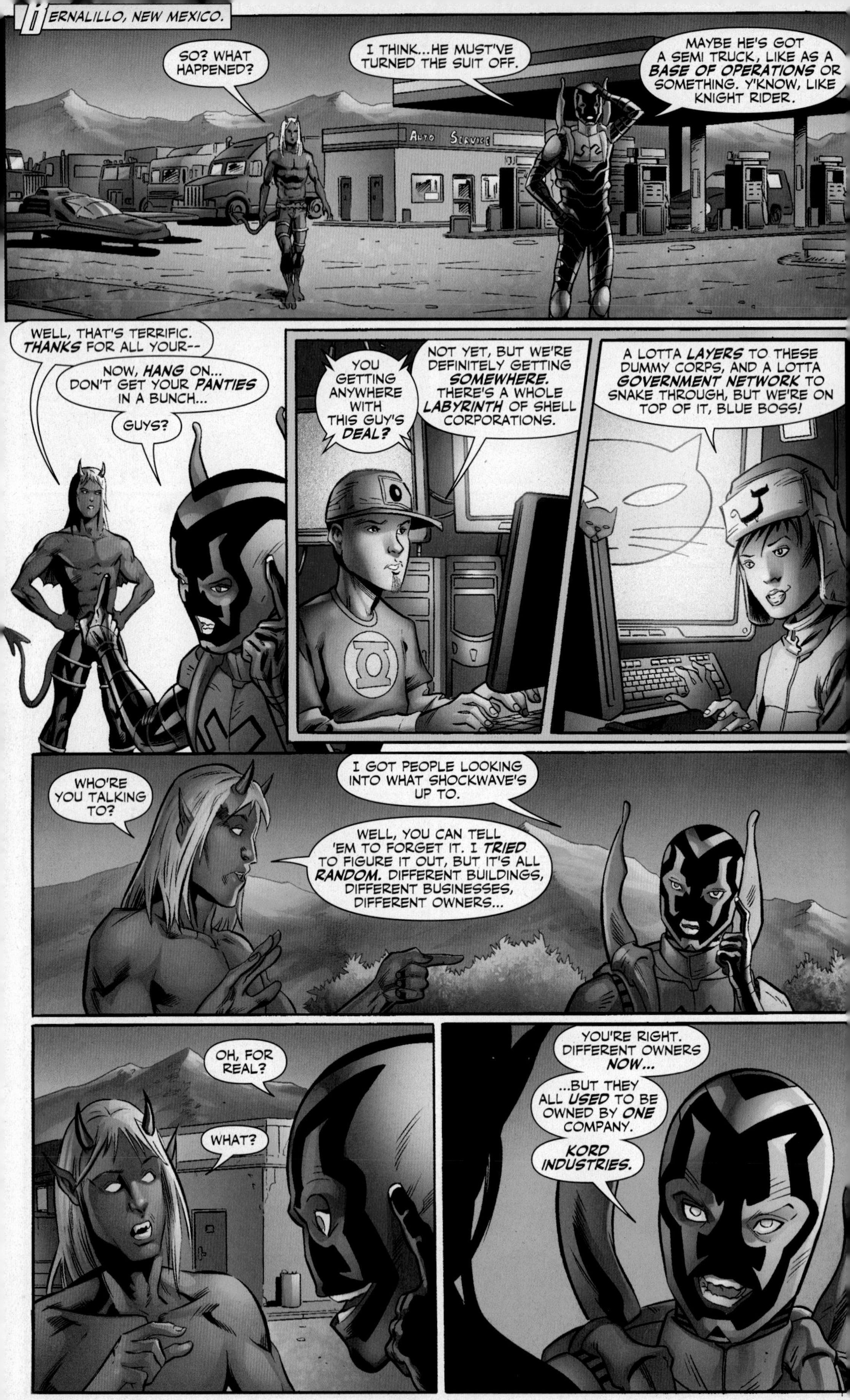
BERNALILLO, NEW MEXICO.
SO? WHAT HAPPENED?
I THINK...HE MUST'VE TURNED THE SUIT OFF.
MAYBE HE'S GOT A SEMI TRUCK, LIKE AS A BASE OF OPERATIONS OR SOMETHING. Y'KNOW, LIKE KNIGHT RIDER.
AUTO SERVICE
WELL, THAT'S TERRIFIC. THANKS FOR ALL YOUR--
NOW, HANG ON... DON'T GET YOUR PANTIES IN A BUNCH...
GUYS?
YOU GETTING ANYWHERE WITH THIS GUY'S DEAL?
NOT YET, BUT WE'RE DEFINITELY GETTING SOMEWHERE. THERE'S A WHOLE LABYRINTH OF SHELL CORPORATIONS.
A LOTTA LAYERS TO THESE DUMMY CORPS, AND A LOTTA GOVERNMENT NETWORK TO SNAKE THROUGH, BUT WE'RE ON TOP OF IT, BLUE BOSS!
WHO'RE YOU TALKING TO?
I GOT PEOPLE LOOKING INTO WHAT SHOCKWAVE'S UP TO.
WELL, YOU CAN TELL 'EM TO FORGET IT. I TRIED TO FIGURE IT OUT, BUT IT'S ALL RANDOM. DIFFERENT BUILDINGS, DIFFERENT BUSINESSES, DIFFERENT OWNERS...
OH, FOR REAL?
WHAT?
YOU'RE RIGHT. DIFFERENT OWNERS NOW...
...BUT THEY ALL USED TO BE OWNED BY ONE COMPANY.
KORD INDUSTRIES.

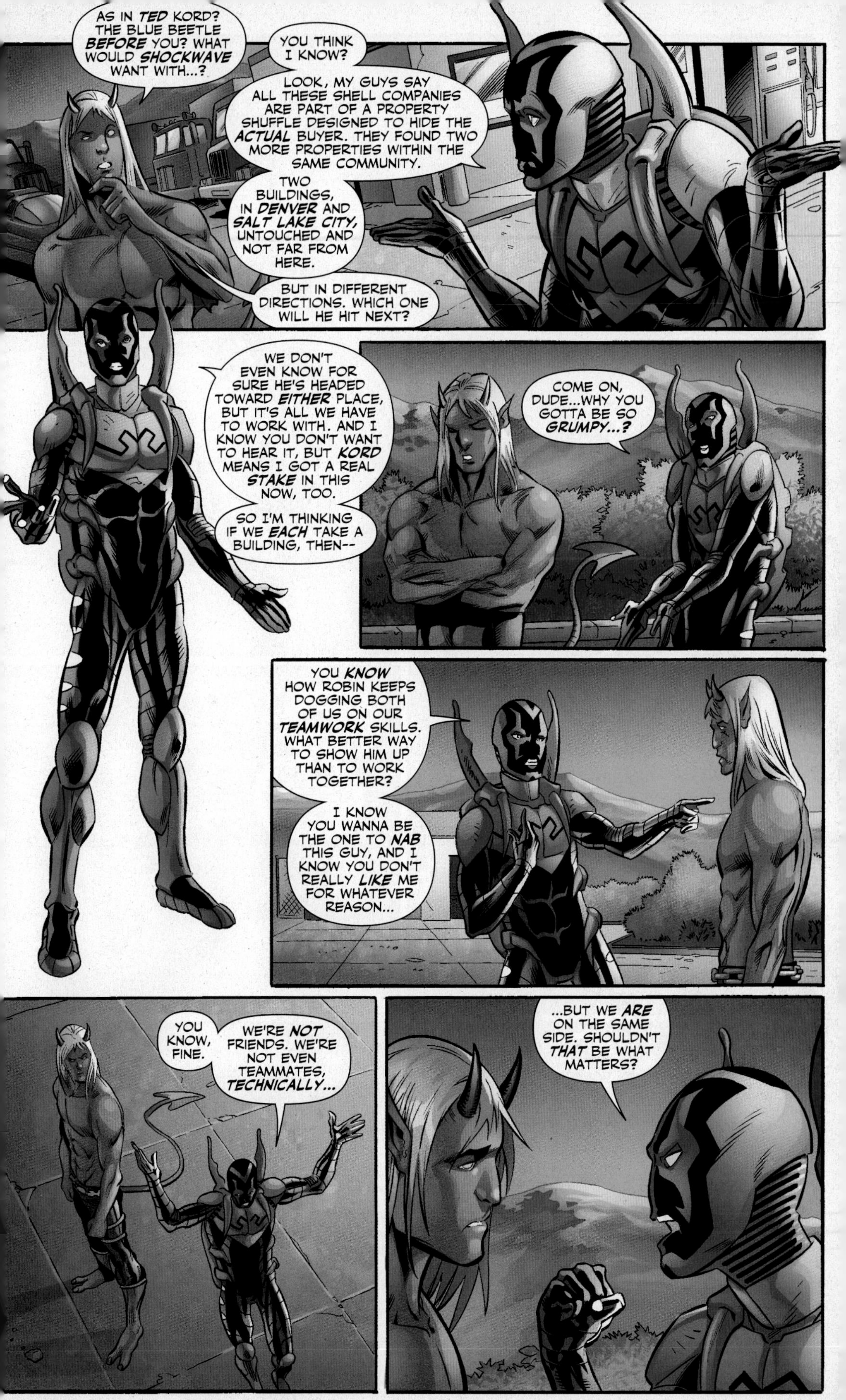
AS IN TED KORD? THE BLUE BEETLE BEFORE YOU? WHAT WOULD SHOCKWAVE WANT WITH...?
YOU THINK I KNOW?
LOOK, MY GUYS SAY ALL THESE SHELL COMPANIES ARE PART OF A PROPERTY SHUFFLE DESIGNED TO HIDE THE ACTUAL BUYER. THEY FOUND TWO MORE PROPERTIES WITHIN THE SAME COMMUNITY.
TWO BUILDINGS, IN DENVER AND SALT LAKE CITY, UNTOUCHED AND NOT FAR FROM HERE.
BUT IN DIFFERENT DIRECTIONS. WHICH ONE WILL HE HIT NEXT?
WE DON'T EVEN KNOW FOR SURE HE'S HEADED TOWARD EITHER PLACE, BUT IT'S ALL WE HAVE TO WORK WITH. AND I KNOW YOU DON'T WANT TO HEAR IT, BUT KORD MEANS I GOT A REAL STAKE IN THIS NOW, TOO.
SO I'M THINKING IF WE EACH TAKE A BUILDING, THEN--
COME ON, DUDE...WHY YOU GOTTA BE SO GRUMPY...?
YOU KNOW HOW ROBIN KEEPS DOGGING BOTH OF US ON OUR TEAMWORK SKILLS. WHAT BETTER WAY TO SHOW HIM UP THAN TO WORK TOGETHER?
I KNOW YOU WANNA BE THE ONE TO NAB THIS GUY, AND I KNOW YOU DON'T REALLY LIKE ME FOR WHATEVER REASON...
YOU KNOW, FINE.
WE'RE NOT FRIENDS. WE'RE NOT EVEN TEAMMATES, TECHNICALLY...
...BUT WE ARE ON THE SAME SIDE. SHOULDN'T THAT BE WHAT MATTERS?

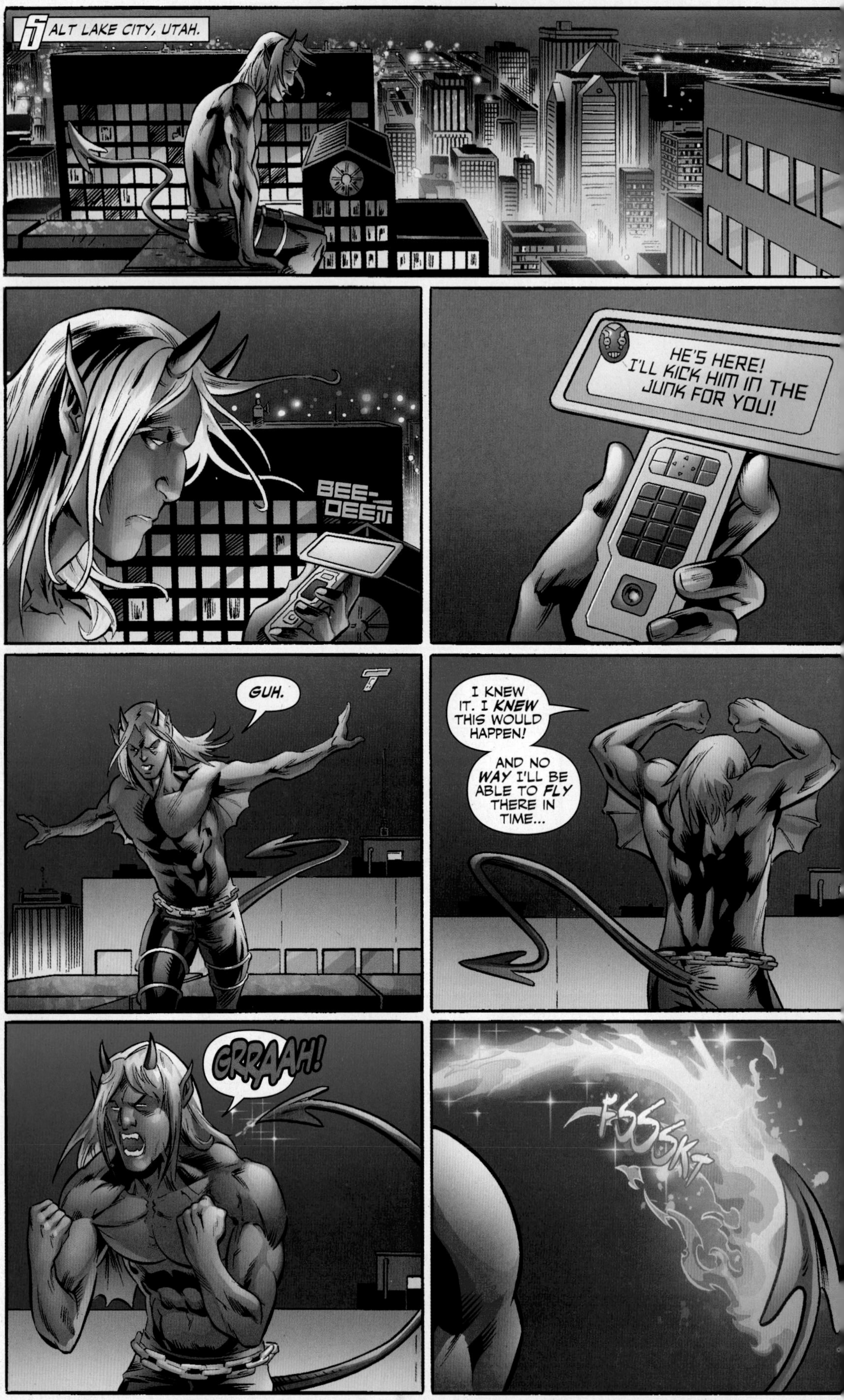
SALT LAKE CITY, UTAH.
BEE-DEET!
HE'S HERE! I'LL KICK HIM IN THE JUNK FOR YOU!
GUH.
I KNEW IT. I KNEW THIS WOULD HAPPEN!
AND NO WAY I'LL BE ABLE TO FLY THERE IN TIME...
GRRAAH!
FSSSKT

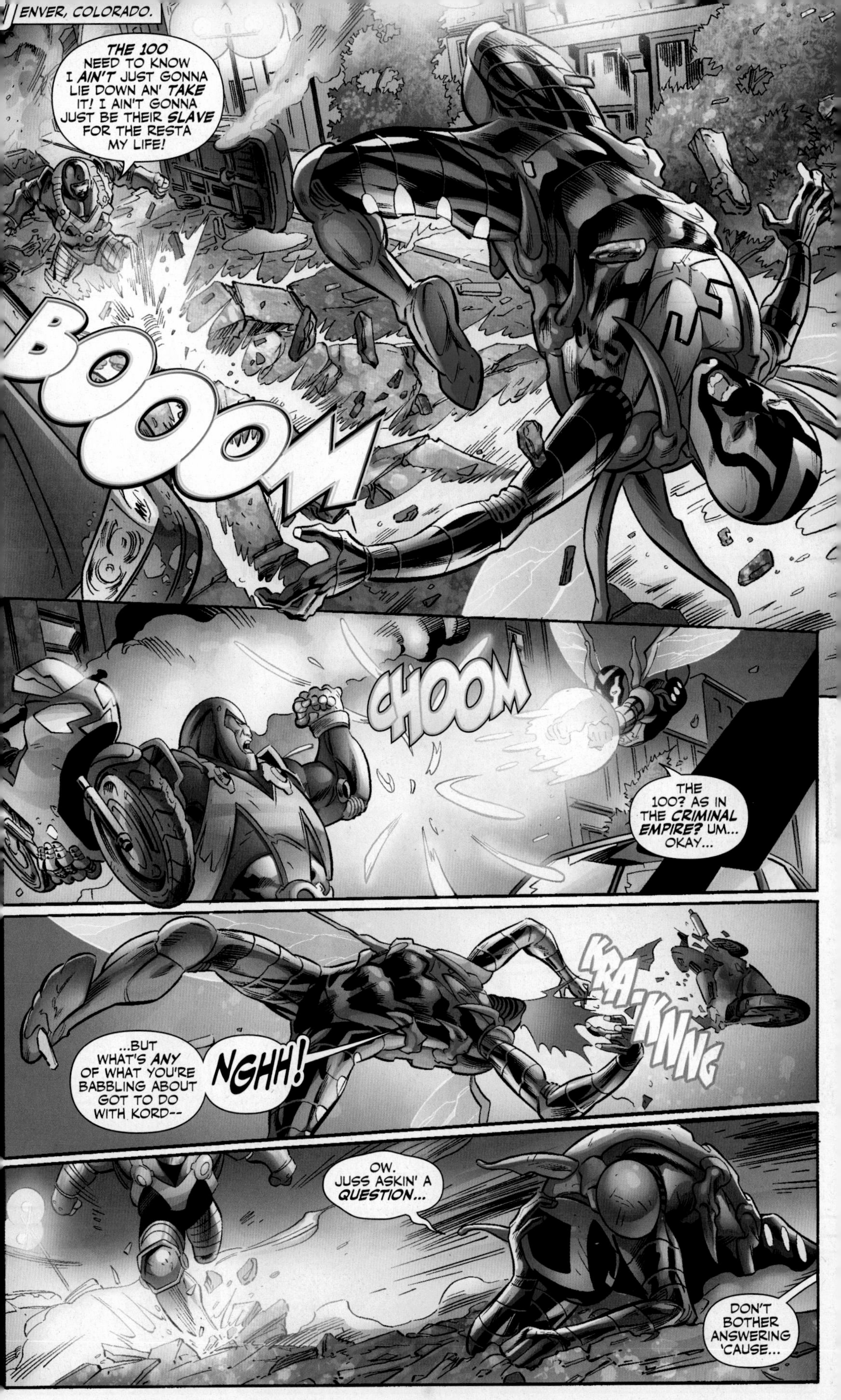
DENVER, COLORADO.
THE 100 NEED TO KNOW I AIN'T JUST GONNA LIE DOWN AN' TAKE IT! I AIN'T GONNA JUST BE THEIR SLAVE FOR THE RESTA MY LIFE!
BOOOOM
CHOOM
THE 100? AS IN THE CRIMINAL EMPIRE? UM... OKAY...
KRA-KNNG
...BUT WHAT'S ANY OF WHAT YOU'RE BABBLING ABOUT GOT TO DO WITH KORD--
NGHH!
OW. JUSS ASKIN' A QUESTION...
DON'T BOTHER ANSWERING 'CAUSE...

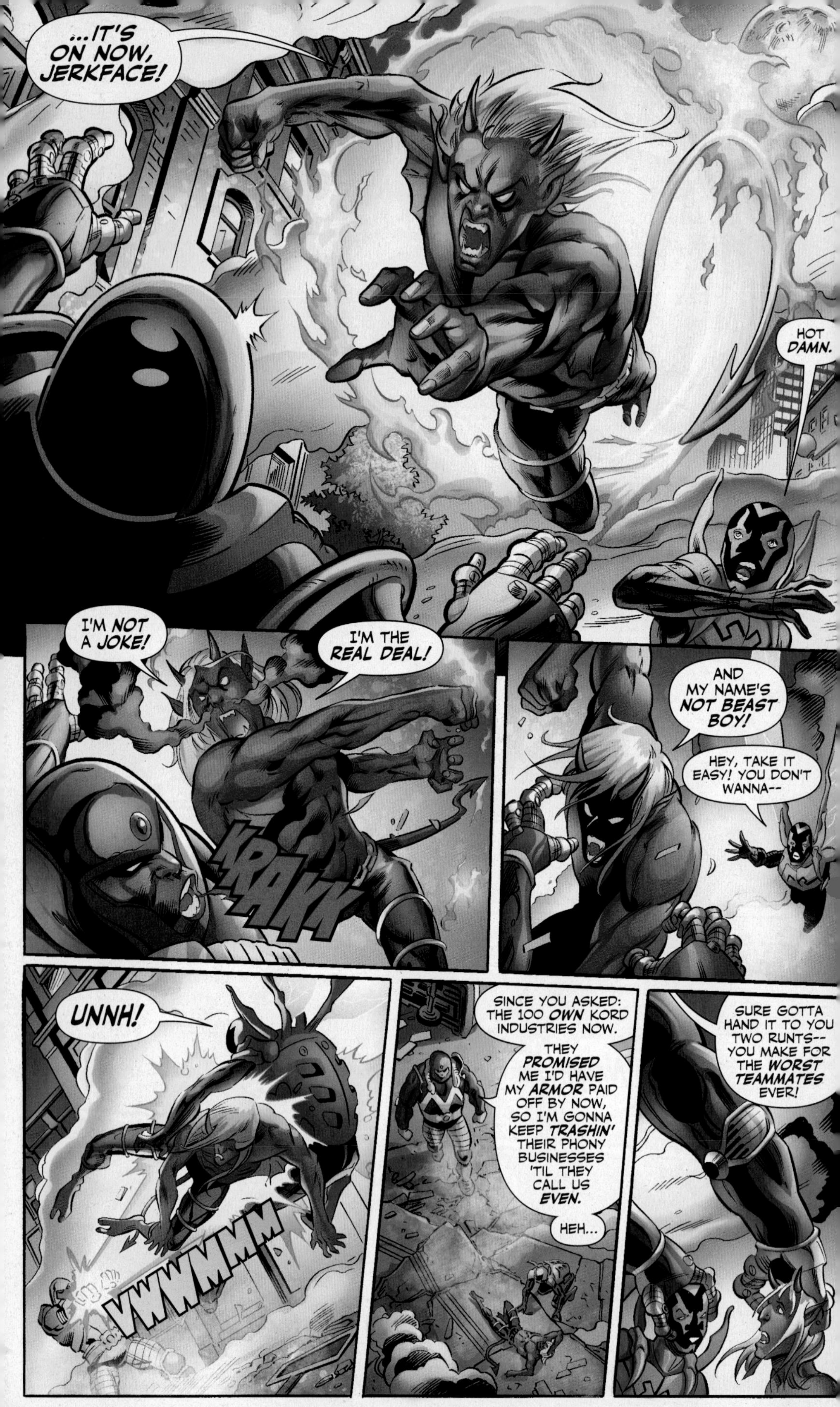
...IT'S ON NOW, JERKFACE!
HOT DAMN.
I'M NOT A JOKE!
I'M THE REAL DEAL!
KRAKK
AND MY NAME'S NOT BEAST BOY!
HEY, TAKE IT EASY! YOU DON'T WANNA--
UNNH!
VWWMMM
SINCE YOU ASKED: THE 100 OWN KORD INDUSTRIES NOW.
THEY PROMISED ME I'D HAVE MY ARMOR PAID OFF BY NOW, SO I'M GONNA KEEP TRASHIN' THEIR PHONY BUSINESSES 'TIL THEY CALL US EVEN.
HEH...
SURE GOTTA HAND IT TO YOU TWO RUNTS-- YOU MAKE FOR THE WORST TEAMMATES EVER!

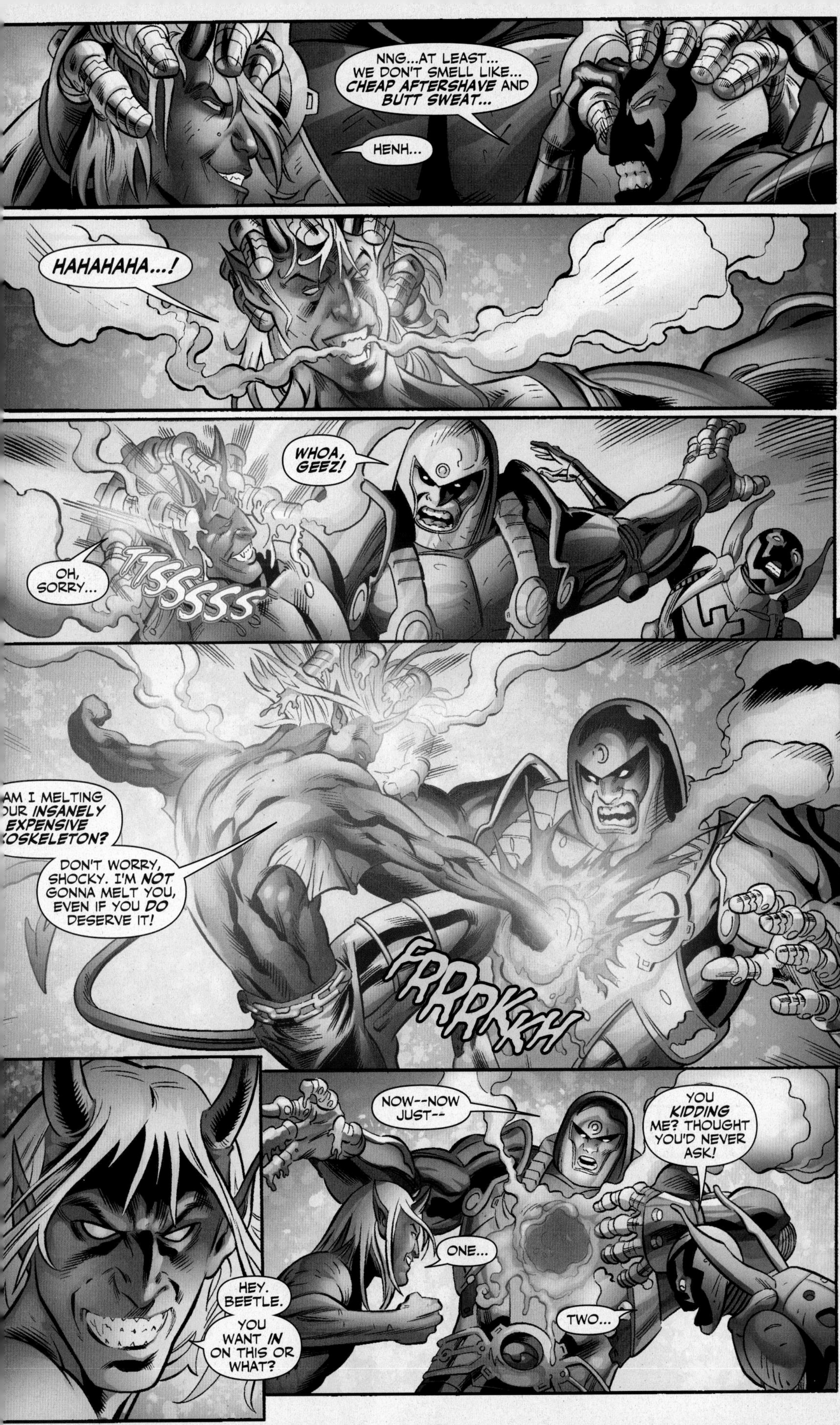

NNG...AT LEAST... WE DON'T SMELL LIKE... CHEAP AFTERSHAVE AND BUTT SWEAT...
HENH...
HAHAHAHA...!
WHOA, GEEZ!
OH, SORRY...
TTSSSSSS
AM I MELTING OUR INSANELY EXPENSIVE EXOSKELETON?
DON'T WORRY, SHOCKY. I'M NOT GONNA MELT YOU, EVEN IF YOU DO DESERVE IT!
FRRRKKH
NOW--NOW JUST--
YOU KIDDING ME? THOUGHT YOU'D NEVER ASK!
ONE...
HEY. BEETLE.
YOU WANT IN ON THIS OR WHAT?
TWO...

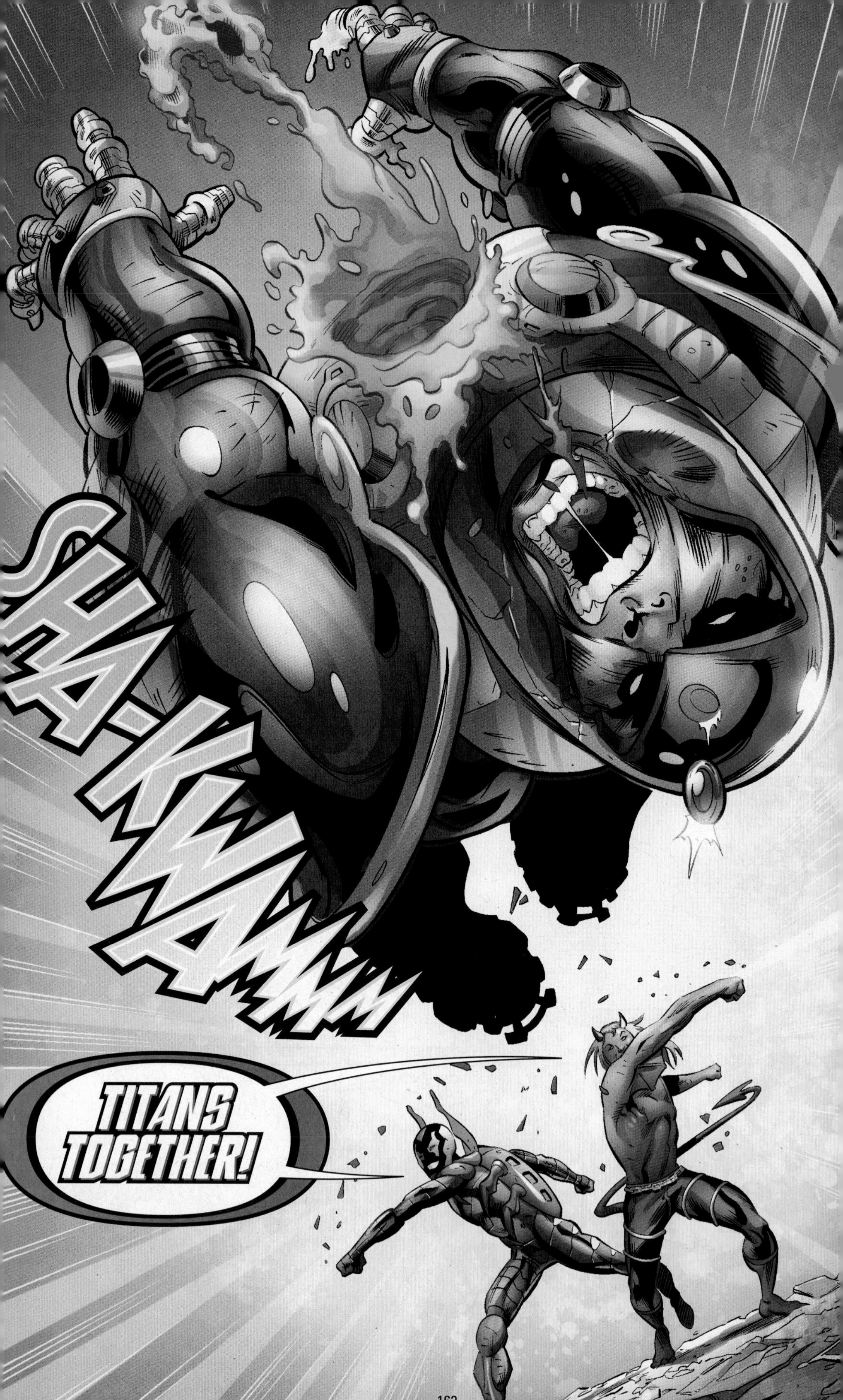
SHA-KWAMMM
TITANS TOGETHER!

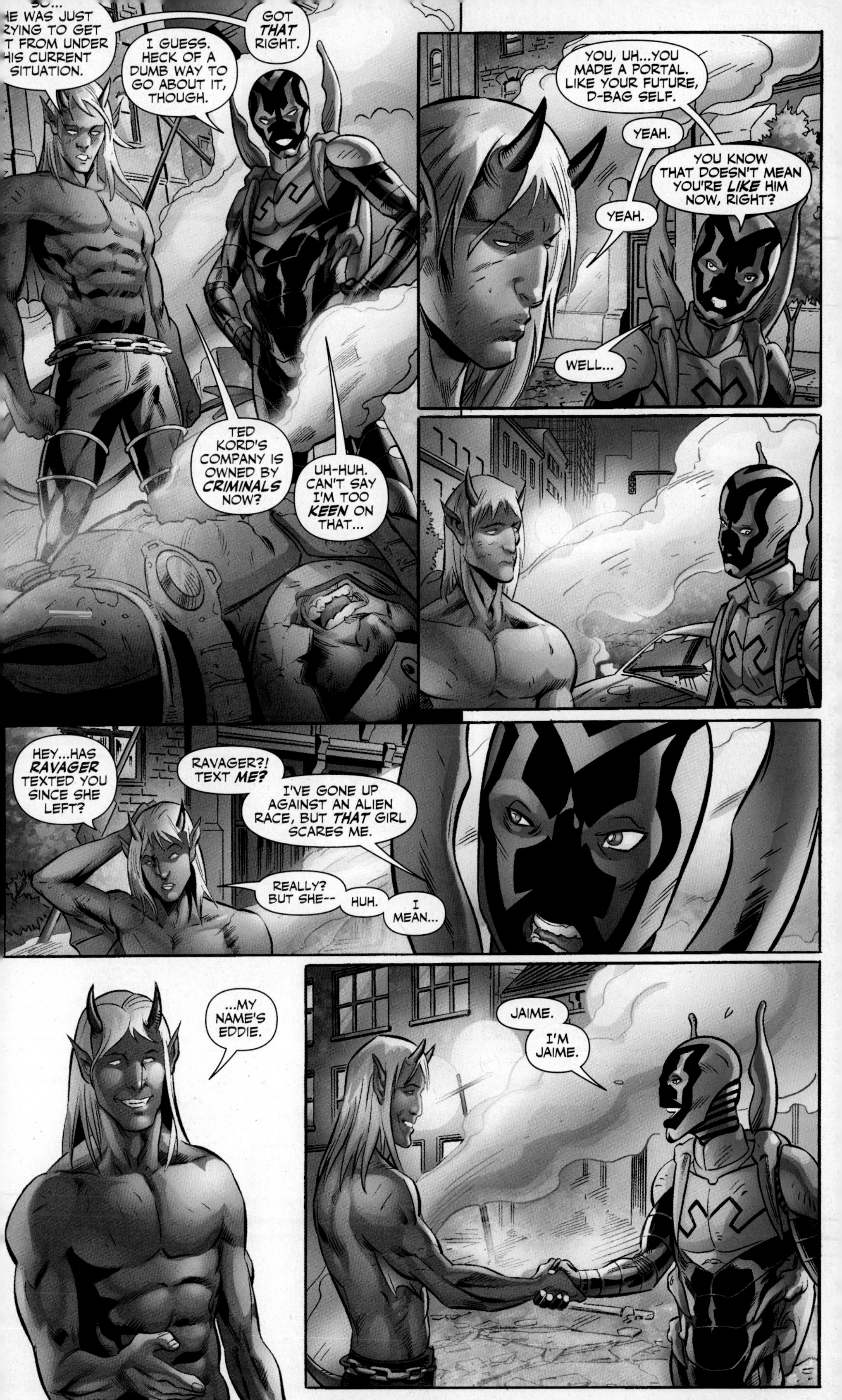
SO... HE WAS JUST TRYING TO GET OUT FROM UNDER HIS CURRENT SITUATION.
I GUESS. HECK OF A DUMB WAY TO GO ABOUT IT, THOUGH.
GOT THAT RIGHT.
TED KORD'S COMPANY IS OWNED BY CRIMINALS NOW?
UH-HUH. CAN'T SAY I'M TOO KEEN ON THAT...
YOU, UH...YOU MADE A PORTAL. LIKE YOUR FUTURE, D-BAG SELF.
YEAH.
YOU KNOW THAT DOESN'T MEAN YOU'RE LIKE HIM NOW, RIGHT?
YEAH.
WELL...
HEY...HAS RAVAGER TEXTED YOU SINCE SHE LEFT?
RAVAGER?! TEXT ME?
I'VE GONE UP AGAINST AN ALIEN RACE, BUT THAT GIRL SCARES ME.
REALLY? BUT SHE--
HUH.
I MEAN...
...MY NAME'S EDDIE.
JAIME.
I'M JAIME.

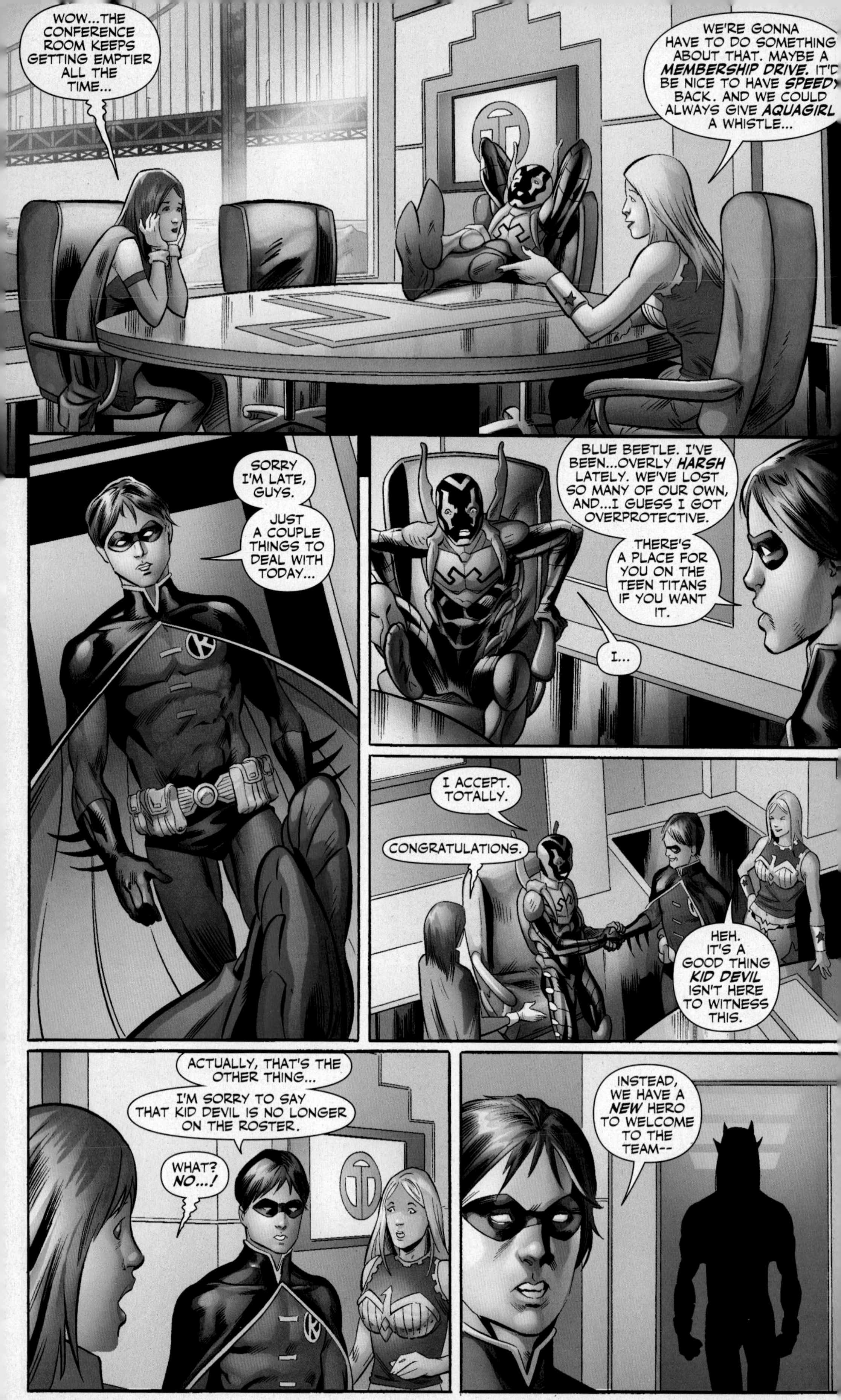
WOW...THE CONFERENCE ROOM KEEPS GETTING EMPTIER ALL THE TIME...
WE'RE GONNA HAVE TO DO SOMETHING ABOUT THAT. MAYBE A MEMBERSHIP DRIVE. IT'D BE NICE TO HAVE SPEEDY BACK. AND WE COULD ALWAYS GIVE AQUAGIRL A WHISTLE...
SORRY I'M LATE, GUYS.
JUST A COUPLE THINGS TO DEAL WITH TODAY...
BLUE BEETLE. I'VE BEEN...OVERLY HARSH LATELY. WE'VE LOST SO MANY OF OUR OWN, AND...I GUESS I GOT OVERPROTECTIVE.
THERE'S A PLACE FOR YOU ON THE TEEN TITANS IF YOU WANT IT.
I...
I ACCEPT. TOTALLY.
CONGRATULATIONS.
HEH. IT'S A GOOD THING KID DEVIL ISN'T HERE TO WITNESS THIS.
ACTUALLY, THAT'S THE OTHER THING...
I'M SORRY TO SAY THAT KID DEVIL IS NO LONGER ON THE ROSTER.
WHAT? NO...!
INSTEAD, WE HAVE A NEW HERO TO WELCOME TO THE TEAM--

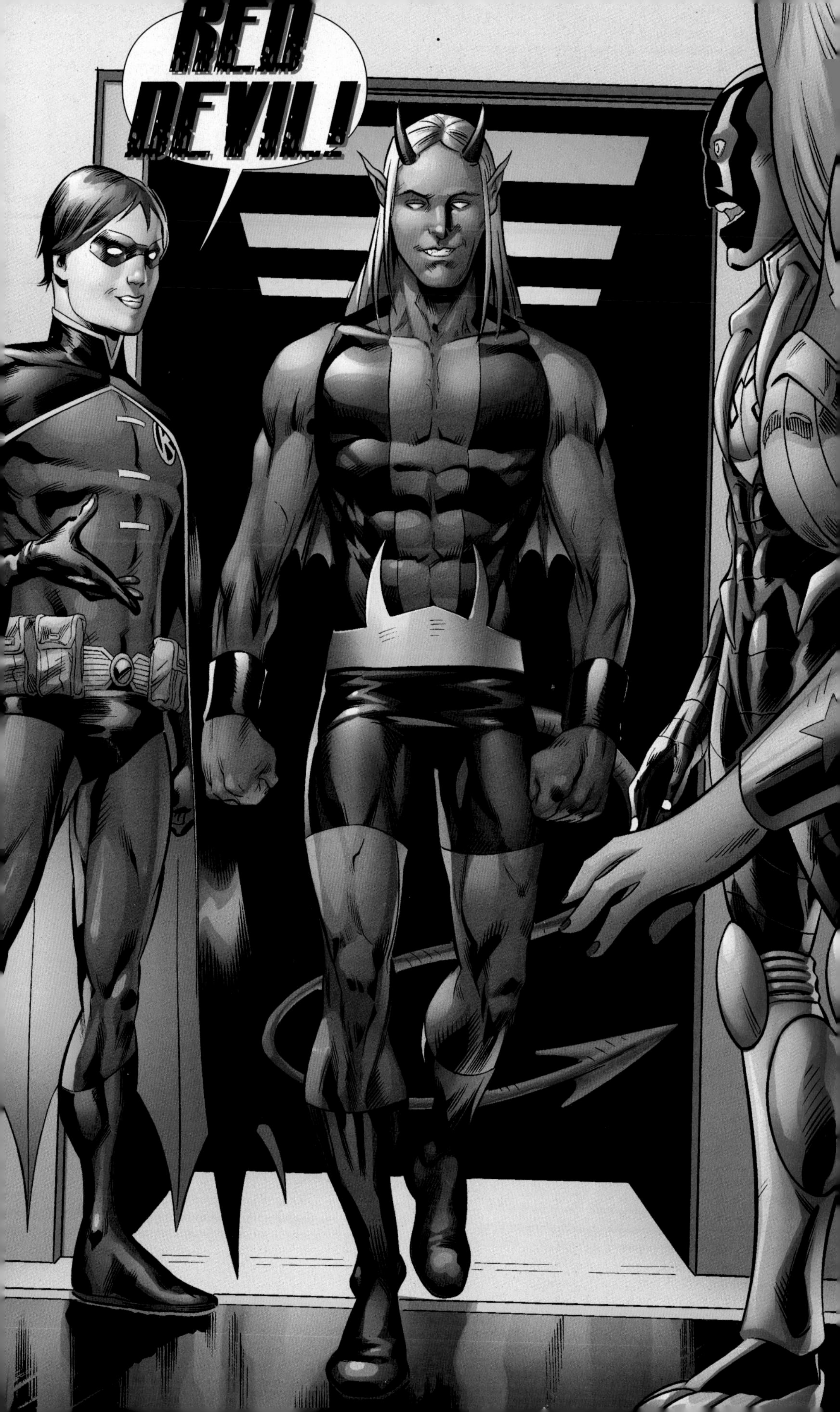
RED DEVIL!

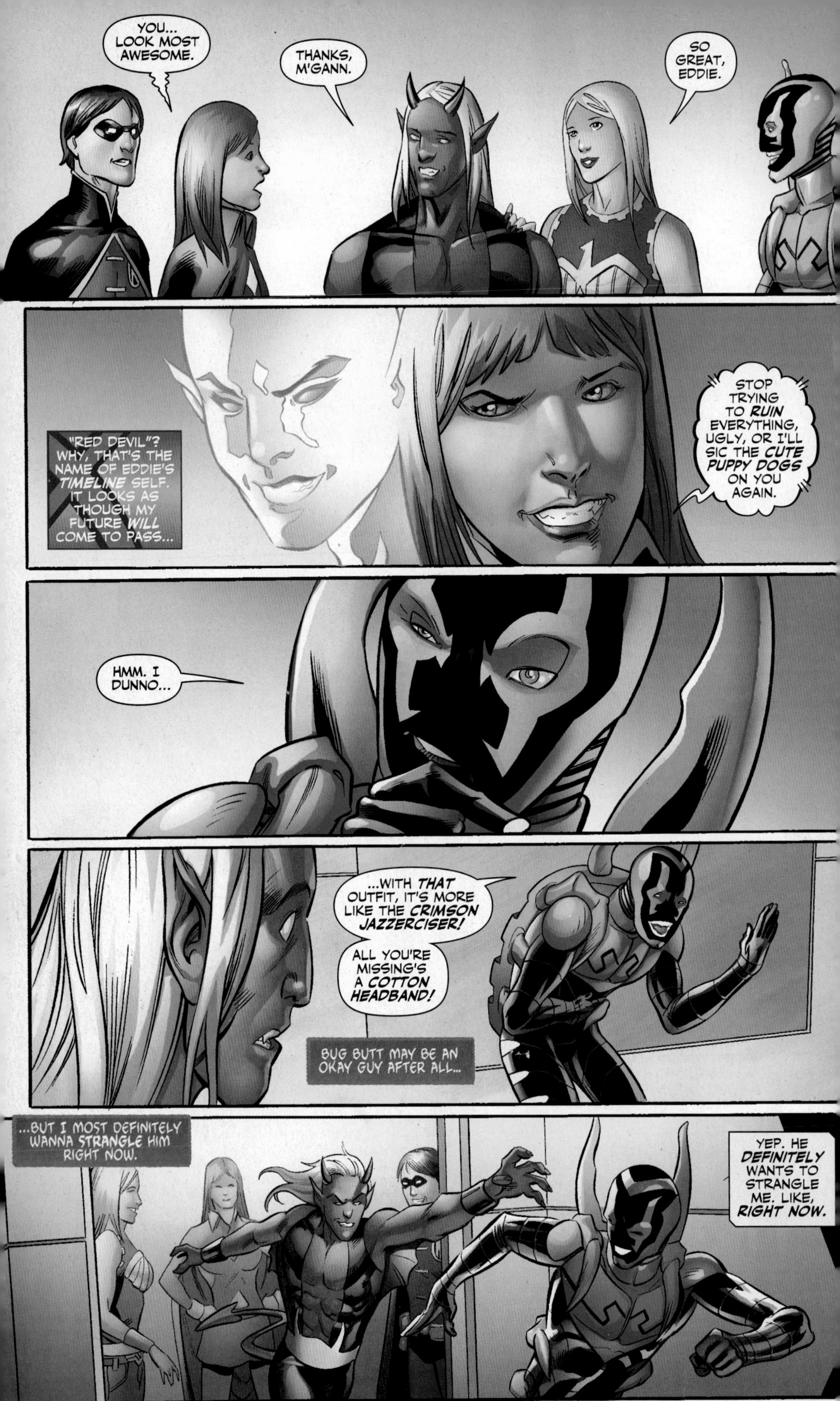

YOU... LOOK MOST AWESOME.
THANKS, M'GANN.
SO GREAT, EDDIE.
"RED DEVIL"? WHY, THAT'S THE NAME OF EDDIE'S *TIMELINE* SELF. IT LOOKS AS THOUGH MY FUTURE *WILL* COME TO PASS...
STOP TRYING TO *RUIN* EVERYTHING, UGLY, OR I'LL SIC THE *CUTE PUPPY DOGS* ON YOU AGAIN.
HMM. I DUNNO...
...WITH *THAT* OUTFIT, IT'S MORE LIKE THE *CRIMSON JAZZERCISER!*
ALL YOU'RE MISSING'S A *COTTON HEADBAND!*
BUG BUTT MAY BE AN OKAY GUY AFTER ALL...
...BUT I MOST DEFINITELY WANNA *STRANGLE* HIM RIGHT NOW.
YEP. HE *DEFINITELY* WANTS TO STRANGLE ME. LIKE, *RIGHT NOW.*

FROM THE WRITER OF
GREEN LANTERN *AND* JSA

GEOFF JOHNS

Witness the gathering of a new team of Teen Titans and their initial battle against an old, familiar foe: the most lethal mercenary on earth, Deathstroke!

with MIKE McKONE

VOL. 1: A KID'S GAME

VOL. 2: FAMILY LOST

VOL. 3: BEAST BOYS AND GIRLS

VOL. 4: THE FUTURE IS NOW

VOL. 5: LIFE AND DEATH

VOL. 6: TITANS AROUND THE WORLD

TEEN TITANS / OUTSIDERS: THE INSIDERS

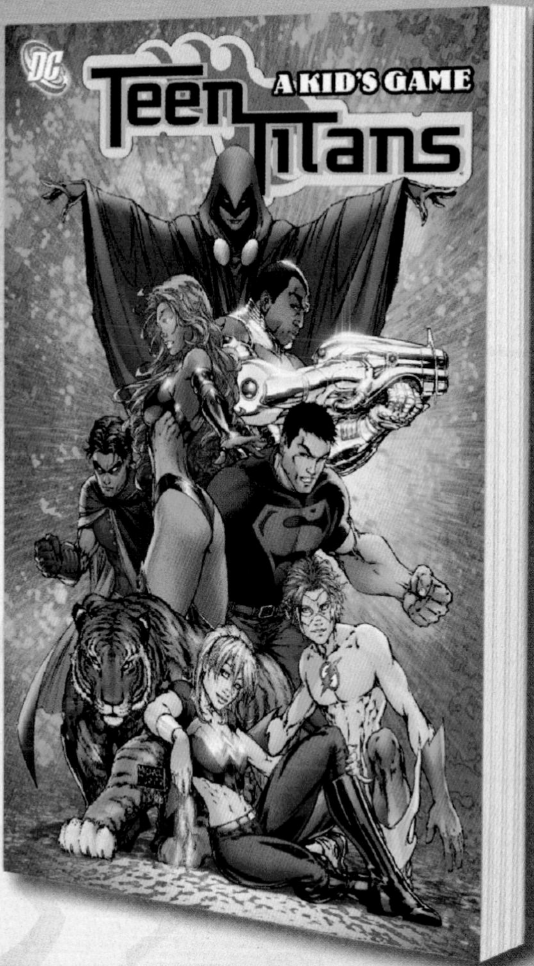
Teen Titans
A KID'S GAME

TEEN TITANS VOL. 2:
FAMILY LOST

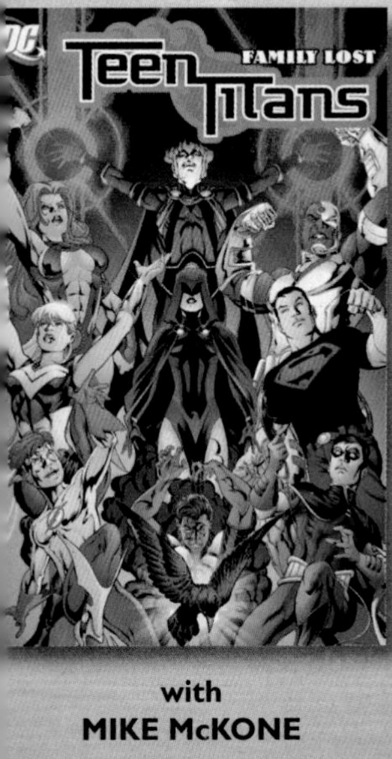
Teen Titans
FAMILY LOST

with
MIKE McKONE

TEEN TITANS VOL. 4:
THE FUTURE IS NOW

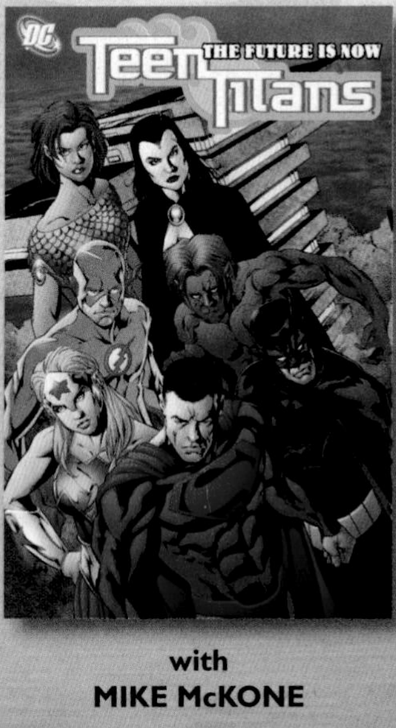
Teen Titans
THE FUTURE IS NOW

with
MIKE McKONE

TEEN TITANS VOL. 5
LIFE AND DEATH

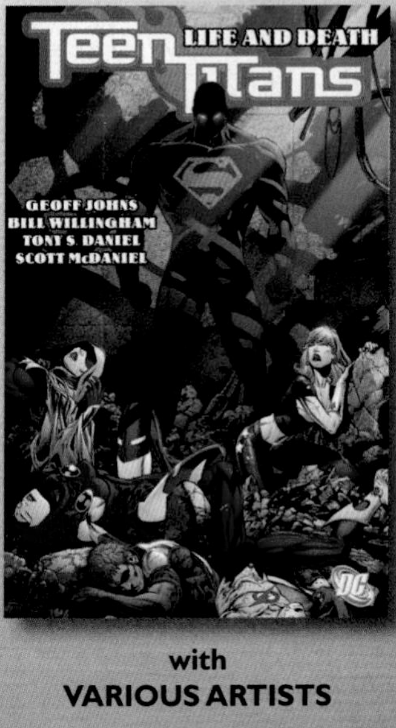
Teen Titans
LIFE AND DEATH
GEOFF JOHNS
BILL WILLINGHAM
TONY S. DANIEL
SCOTT McDANIEL

with
VARIOUS ARTISTS

SEARCH THE GRAPHIC NOVELS SECTION OF
DCCOMICS.COM
FOR ART AND INFORMATION ON ALL OF OUR BOOKS!

MORE CLASSIC TALES OF THE DARK KNIGHT

BATMAN: HUSH
VOLUME ONE

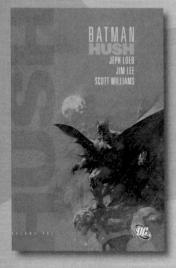

BATMAN
HUSH
JEPH LOEB
JIM LEE
SCOTT WILLIAMS

JEPH LOEB
JIM LEE

BATMAN: HUSH
VOLUME TWO

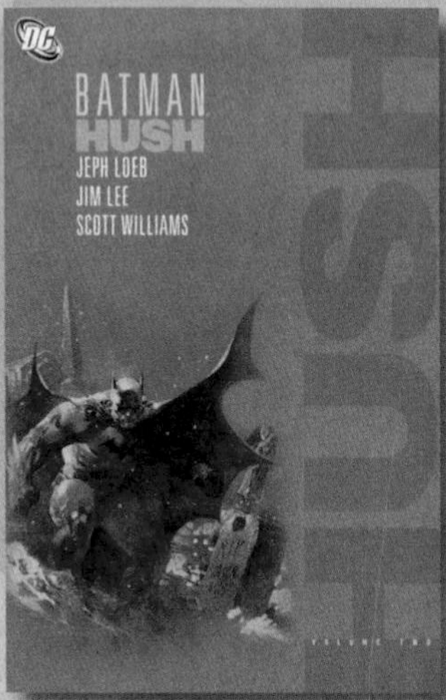

BATMAN
HUSH
JEPH LOEB
JIM LEE
SCOTT WILLIAMS

JEPH LOEB
JIM LEE

BATMAN:
THE LONG HALLOWEEN

JEPHLOEB TIMSALE
BATMAN
THE LONG HALLOWEEN

JEPH LOEB
TIM SALE

BATMAN:
DARK VICTORY

JEPHLOEB TIMSALE
BATMAN
Dark Victory

JEPH LOEB
TIM SALE

BATMAN:
HAUNTED KNIGHT

JEPHLOEB TIMSALE
BATMAN
HAUNTED KNIGHT

JEPH LOEB
TIM SALE

BATMAN:
YEAR 100

Batman
Year 100
by PAUL POPE
with JOSE VILLARRUBIA

PAUL POPE

SEARCH THE GRAPHIC NOVELS SECTION OF
DCCOMICS.COM
FOR ART AND INFORMATION ON ALL OF OUR BOOKS!

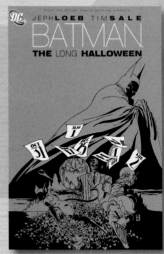

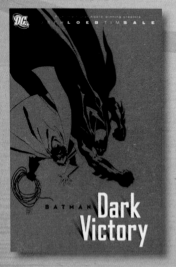

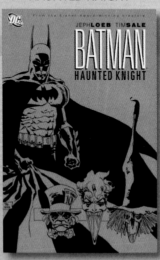

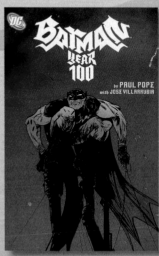